Master Data Transformation in Power BI with Power Query

Author: Noel Yarngo

Edition: 7, January 2024

PUBLISHED BY
RADACAD Systems Limited
24 Riverhaven Drive,
Wade Heads,
Whangaparaoa 0932
New Zealand
Copyright © 2019 by RADACAD
All rights reserved. No part of the contents of this book may be reproduced or transmitted in any form or by any means without the written permission of the publisher.
Cover: Virgin Silberhorn Ebnefluh, Pixabay

About the New Edition and New Structure

The Power BI from Rookie to Rock Star been such a popular book from the time that it published, and I added content to it every single week. After edition 3 which released July 2017, there have been many contents added. The edition 3 itself was more than 1100 pages, and If I wanted to continue the book as an all-in-one, it would have been more than 2000 pages now. So I decided to break the book into a book series. Each book in this series is a complete book and can be read individually. However, each book covers a specific area of the Power BI, and if you want to learn Power BI from ground zero to sky hero, you would need to read them all. Here is the new structure:

This book is the book three of the series. You will learn all about Power Query in this book. Through many demos and examples, you will learn all aspects of Power Query, from getting Data to different types of transformations. You will also learn about features such as Custom functions that can make your code more automated. You will learn about the scripting language of Power Query which is called M. at the end of the book, you will learn some use cases of using Power Query; for example, for creating a Date dimension. If you want to learn more about other parts of Power BI not just Power Query, your answer is within books 1 to 5.

About the book; Quick Intro from Author

In July 2015, after the first release of Power BI Desktop, I had been encouraged to publish a Power BI online book through a set of blog posts. The main reason to publish this book online was that with the fast pace of updates for Power BI Desktop, it is impossible to publish a paperback book because it will be outdated in a few months. From that time till now, I've been writing blog posts (or sections) of this book almost weekly in RADACAD blog. So far, I have more than 60 sections wrote for this book. The book covers all aspects of Power BI; from data preparation to modeling, and visualization. From novice to the professional level, that's why I called it Power BI from Rookie to Rock Star. You can start reading this book with no prerequisite. Each section can be read by itself; normally you don't need to follow a specific order. However, there are some sections, that need an example previously built in another section. These sections have a prerequisite section mentioning this requirement. After a year and half of writing online, I decided to release this book as a PDF version as well, for two reasons; First to help community members who are more comfortable with PDF books, or printed version of materials. Second; as a giveaway in my Power BI training courses. Feel free to print this book and keep it in your library, and enjoy. This book is FREE! This book will be updated with newer editions (hopefully every month), so you can download the latest version of it anytime from my blog post Because I've been writing these chapters and sections from mid-2015, there are some topics or images or sections outdated with new changes in Power BI. I will do my best to update any changes in the next few editions. However, to keep you informed; There is a date at the beginning of each section under the header that mentioned the publish date of that section.

About Author

Author is a Microsoft Regional Director, an Author, Trainer, Speaker and Consultant. He has a BSc in Computer engineering; he has more than 15 years' experience in data analysis, BI, databases, programming, and development mostly on Microsoft technologies. He is a Microsoft Data Platform MVP for eight continuous years (from 2011 till now) for his dedication in Microsoft BI. He's a active blogger and co- founder of RADACAD. Also co-founder and co-organizer of Difinity conference in New Zealand. His articles on different aspects of technologies, especially on MS BI, can be found on his blog: He wrote some books on MS SQL BI and also is writing some others, He was also an active member on online technical forums such as MSDN and Experts-Exchange, and was a moderator of MSDN SQL Server forums, and is an MCP, MCSE, and MCITP of BI. He is the leader of the New Zealand Business Intelligence users group. He is also the author of very popular book Power BI Playbook, which is free with more than 1100 pages of content. He is an International Speaker in Microsoft Ignite, Microsoft Business Applications Summit, Data Insight Summit, PASS Summit, SQL Saturday and SQL user groups. And He is a Microsoft Certified Trainer.

Who should read this book?

BI Developers and Consultants who want to know how to develop solutions with this technology. BI Architects and Decision Makers who want to make their decision about using or not using Power BI in their BI applications. Business Analysts who want to have a better tool for playing with the data and learn tricks of producing insights easier. The book titled "Power BI from Rookie to Rockstar" and that means it will cover a wide range of readers. I'll start by writing 100 level, and we will go deep into 400 level at some stage. So, if you don't know what Power BI is, or If you are familiar with Power BI but want to learn some deep technical topics about Power Query M language, then this book is for you.

Upcoming Training Courses

Reza runs Power BI training courses both online and in-person. RADACAD also runs Advanced Analytics with R, Power BI, Azure Machine Learning and SQL Server courses ran by Dr. Leila Etaati. Our courses run both online and in-person in major cities and countries around the world.

Check the schedule of upcoming courses here:

http://radacad.com/events

http://radacad.com/power-bi-training

Heading Table of Content

About the New Edition and New Structure 3
About the book; Quick Intro from Author 4
About Author 5
Who should read this book? 6
Upcoming Training Courses 7
Heading Table of Content 8
Detailed Table of Content 11

Part I: Getting Started with Power Query
What Is Power Query? Introduction to Data Mash-up Engine of Power BI 22
Get Started with Power Query: Movies Data Mash-Up 34
Data Preparation; First and Foremost Important Task in Power BI.................................... 61

Part II: Get Data 71
Power BI Get Data From Excel: Everything You Need to Know.. 88
.... 115

Part III: Transformations
Reference vs Duplicate in Power BI; Power Query Back to Basics 142
Append vs. Merge in Power BI and Power Query.. 157
Choose the Right Merge Join Type in Power BI 167
How to Change Joining Types in Power BI and Power Query
Find Mismatch Rows with Power Query in Power BI
Dates Between Merge Join in Power Query
Pivot and Unpivot with Power BI
Warning! Misleading Power Query Filtering

Grouping in Power Query; Getting The Last Item in Each Group
Fuzzy Matching in Power BI and Power Query; Match based on Similarity Threshold .. 231
Fetch Files and/or Folders with Filtering and Masking: Power Query 243

Part IV: Dealing with Errors
Exception Reporting in Power BI: Catch the Error Rows in Power Query

Flawless Date Conversion in Power Query .... 268 Make Your Numeric Division Faultless in Power Query 279

Part V: Power Query Formula Language: M

Power Query Formula Language: M 288
M or DAX? That is the Question! 301
Basics of M: Power Query Formula Language 309
Basics of Value Structures in M – Power Query Formula Language 321
Power Query Formula Language M : Table Functions Part 1 334
List.Accumulate Hidden Gem of Power Query List Functions in Power BI 345
Power Query; Convert Time Stamp to Date Time 357
Get List of Queries in Power BI 359
Power Query Library of Functions; Shared Keyword 368
Writing Custom Functions in Power Query M 380
Day Number of Year, Power Query Custom Function 389
Power Query Function that Returns Multiple Values 399
Custom Functions Made Easy in Power BI Desktop 405
Search for a Column in the Entire Database with Table.ColumnNames in Power Query and Power BI
Power BI Custom Connector: Connect to Any Data Sources. Hello World! 442
Watch Your Steps! Power Query Performance Caution for Power BI
Performance Tip for Power BI; Enable Load Sucks Memory Up 458

Part VI: Performance Tuning 473
Not Folding; the Black Hole of Power Query Performance 491

Part VII: Power Query Use Cases

Create a Date Dimension in Power BI in 4 Steps – Step 1: Calendar Columns 497
Create a Date Dimension in Power BI in 4 Steps – Step 2: Fiscal Columns 510

Create a Date Dimension in Power BI in 4 Steps – Step 3: Public Holidays 520
Power Query Not for BI: Event Date and Time Scheduler – Part 1 ....
Power Query Not for BI: Event Date and Time Scheduler – Part 2   531
Power Query Not for BI: Event Date and Time Scheduler – Part 3   ....
549
....

Part VIII: A Tool to Help; Power BI Helper
Exposing M Code and Query Metadata of Power BI (PBIX) File 567

Export the Entire M Power Query Script from a Power BI File, New Version of Power BI Helper, Search based on Field Description in the Model

Beautify M Script and Extract Row Level Security with Power BI Helper Version 4.0 584
Other modules of the book 593
Power BI Training... 594

Detailed Table of Content

About the New Edition and New Structure... 3
About the book; Quick Intro from Author.. 4
About Author.. 5
Who should read this book?... 6
Upcoming Training Courses.. 7
Heading Table of Content... 8
Detailed Table of Content... 11
.... 22
What Is Power Query?.. 23
How to Use Power Query?
What Can You Do With Power Query? 25
Get Data From Wide Range of Sources
Apply Transformation In a Development Editor
Load Data into Destination
What Are Features of Power Query Premium?
Get Started with Power Query: Movies Data Mash-Up
Let's Get Started 34
Query Editor 36
.... 40
Use a Query as a Reference... 44
Append Queries 45
Extract First Characters... 46
Remove Columns... 49
Split Column 50
Replace Values.. 53
Trim.. 55
Applied Steps
Final Merge
Summary

Data Preparation; First and Foremost Important Task in Power BI....................................... 61
Why Data Preparation? 61
How to Design a Star Schema? 64
Design Tips 67
More to Come 69
Power BI Get Data From Excel: Everything You Need to Know 71
Excel Data Source 71
Loading Excel Tables into Power Query 73
Loading Excel Sheets into Power Query 75
What Happens If Excel Contains Formatting? 76
What Happens to Power View Sheets in Excel? 76
Pivot Tables and Pivot Charts? 77
What If Your Excel Table Has Merged Cells? 78
Example Excel Data Source: Olympic Games 79
Summary 87
Power BI Get Data: From Azure SQL Database.. 88
Preparation 89
Get Data From Azure SQL Database... 98
Schedule Data Refresh 105
Direct Connection to Azure SQL Database from Power BI Website 109
Summary 113

Meetup Data Source for Power BI

Null Check 284
Function to Check All Anomalies.. 285
Summary 286

Power Query Formula Language M: Table Functions Part 1 334
List.Accumulate Hidden Gem of Power Query List Functions in Power BI 345
    List Transformations in Graphical Interface of Power Query.. 345
    List Functions in M; Power Query Formula Language... 346
    List.Accumulate Function.. 348
    Accumulate to Calculate Sum ....
    Accumulate to Calculate Max .   348
    Accumulate as Product or Divide,,351
    Accumulate as Count ....349.. 351
    Accumulate as Concatenate (with a delimiter or without)
    Accumulate as Count Token Exact Match
    Accumulate as Count Token Partial Match
    Accumulate as Conditions on Records
    Summary
Power Query; Convert Time Stamp to Date Time... 357
    What is Timestamp 357
    Power Query Convert Timestamp to Date Time 357
Get List of Queries in Power BI

Power Query Library of Functions; Shared Keyword.. 368
    #shared Keyword 369
    Use the Result set as a Table.. 373
    Documentation of Function 376
    Enumerators 378
    Summary 378
Writing Custom Functions in Power Query M 380
Day Number of Year, Power Query Custom Function
Power Query Function that Returns Multiple Values

Custom Functions Made Easy in Power BI Desktop 405
What is Custom Function? 405
Benefits of Custom Function 406
How to Create a Custom Function? 407
Using Generator 418
Consuming Function 420
Editing Function 423
Limitations 425
Example at the End 426
Summary 427

and Power BI

What is a Custom Connector?
Install Power Query SDK
Create the First Project
Coding Language: M
Structure of Query Files 447
Write a Sample Function 449
Testing the Result 450
Publishing Custom Connector 451
Using the Connector 452
Summary 455
Not Folding; the Black Hole of Power Query Performance 458
   Query Folding 459
   Is Query Folding Good or Bad? 461
   Can I see the Native Query? 462
   So Why Not Query Folding? 463

Merge Date Dimension with Public Holidays 526
Summary 530
Power Query Not for BI: Event Date and Time Scheduler – Part 1 531
Why? 532
What You Will Learn? 536
Get Data from Web 537
Apply Basic Transformations 540
Insert a Step 544
Append Queries 546
Next Steps 548

Power Query Not for BI: Event Date and Time Scheduler – Part 2

Power Query Not for BI: Event Date and Time Scheduler – Part 3

Call to Action 565
Exposing M Code and Query Metadata of Power BI (PBIX) File 567
Structure of a PBIX File 567
DataMashup File: Everything You Need 569
M Script File 570
Metadata Information in XML Format 572
Summary 575

Helper, Search based on Field Description in the Model

Beautify M Script and Extract Row Level Security with Power BI Helper Version 4.0 584

Download...			
...	585	Row-Level	Security
....		589	Summary
Other modules of the book..			592

Power BI Training

Part I: Getting Started with Power Query

Power BI from Rookie to Rock Star – Book 3: Power Query and Data Transformation in Power BI

What Is Power Query? Introduction to Data Mash-up Engine of Power BI

Published Date: August 15, 2015

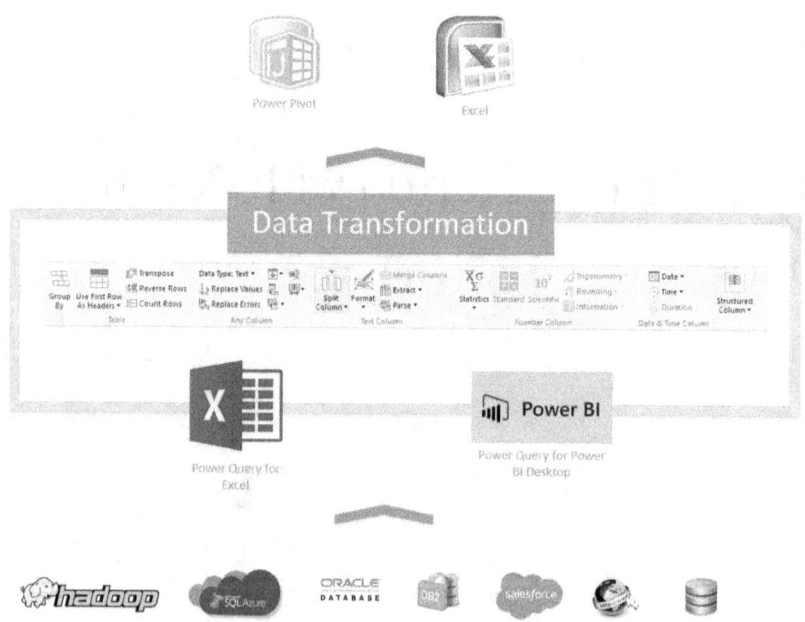

When you get data in Power BI, you use Power Query Component. In this chapter, you will learn about What Power Query is, and what are different types of sources that Power Query can connect. Power Query also has a great list of transformations that can be applied on the data set as well (which will be covered in next chapter), and the Power Query formula language M can be used for complex and powerful data transformation situations (will be covered in a chapter after).

In this section, you will read an introduction to Power Query. You will learn;

- What is Power Query?
- What types of works can be done with Power Query?
- What are requirements to run Power Query?

- What are features of Power Query Premium?

What Is Power Query?

Power Query previously named as Data Explorer. Data Explorer was released as a public preview for the first time in February 2013. Data Explorer then renamed to Power Query at July 2013, and from that time it had lots of enhancement on the product. Power Query is on a regular and frequent update plan by Microsoft team, and usually, you can see monthly updates on this, here is the latest update notes (released yesterday!) Power Query has been tested a lot during this period and nowadays used in many real-world data transformations and BI solutions.

Power Query is a data extraction and transformation engine. The engine comes with a formula language and a graphical tool. The graphical tool has two major setup versions; one embedded in Power BI Desktop tool and the other one as an Add-In for Excel. The graphical tool has a list of transformations that can be applied on a data set, and it also supports different data sources. However, the Power Query formula language is much more powerful than the GUI. There are some features in Power Query engine that not yet has been implemented through GUI, but they are available through M (formula language).

Power Query can connect to a set of data sources and read data from them. Set of data sources is variable from text files, to web URLs, from database systems to some applications. A wide range of data sources is supported. So to respond to one of the very first questions that usually appears when I introduce this product that Can Power Query connect to Oracle? Sure it does! Not only Oracle, but also MySQL, PostgreSQL, DB2, Sybase, and Teradata.

Power Query can apply many transformations to the data set. You can apply simple transformations such as trimming a text value and applying numeric calculations to complex transformations easily such as pivot and unpivot. Power Query uses a function library for applying transformations, and the function library contains heaps of transformations for every data type such as table, text, record, list, date, number and so on.

Power Query graphical interface is so easy to work with that even business analyst, or a power user can work with it, on the other hand, Power Query M language is so powerful that can be used for complex real-world challenges of data transformations. Power Query can load the result set into an Excel spreadsheet, or it can load it into Power Pivot for data modeling. The version of Power Query used in Power BI Desktop loads the result set into a Power Pivot model. I will go through details of Power Pivot in future

Power BI from Rookie to Rock Star – Book 3: Power Query and Data Transformation in Power BI

chapters, for now, it would be enough to know that Power Pivot is In-Memory tabular data model engine. Here is a screenshot or the Query Editor window

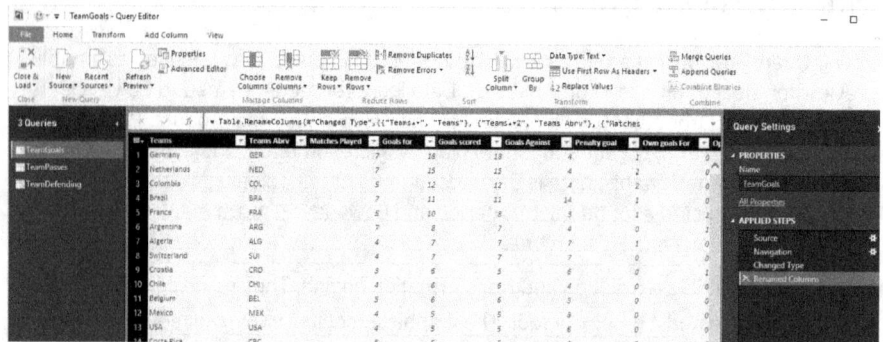

In below you can see a high-level diagram of Power Query conceptually:

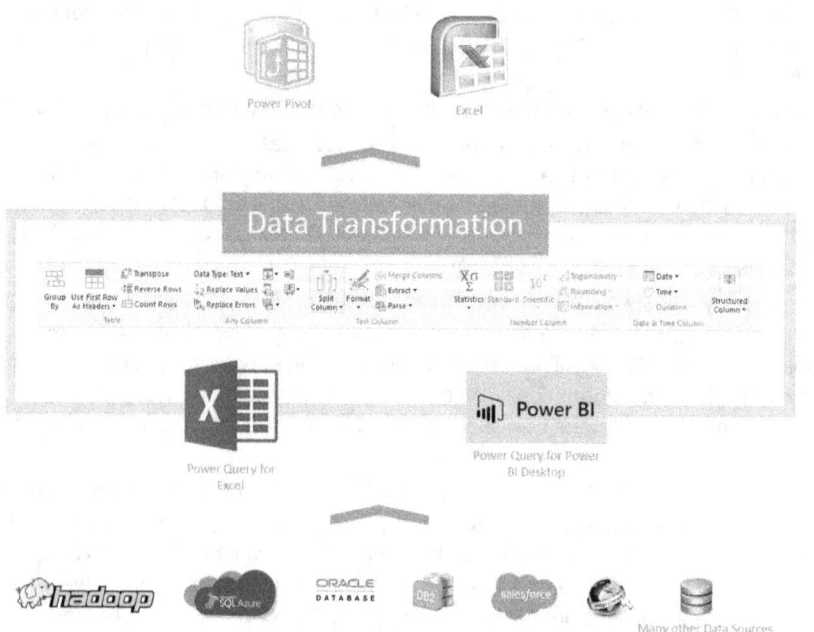

How to Use Power Query?

Power Query is available in three different setups:

1. As an Excel Add-In for Excel 2010 and 2013
2. Embedded in Excel 2016
3. Embedded in Power BI Desktop

So if you want to install then you have to install one of the options below:

Excel Add-In for Excel 2010 and 2013:

https://www.microsoft.com/en-us/download/details.aspx?id=39379

Please note that the link above might change because Power Query updates frequently and a new version will be available almost every month. So you can simply Google it as Power Query Excel add-in.

Excel 2016 download link:

https://products.office.com/en-us/office-2016-preview

At the time of writing this blog post, Excel 2016 is in the preview stage, so the link is likely to change.

Power BI Desktop:

https://powerbi.microsoft.com/desktop

What Can You Do With Power Query?

Get Data From Wide Range of Sources

With Power Query, you can connect to a wide range of data sources. SQL Server or DB2 or Oracle…. All of this database are supported as a source. You can even connect to an Analysis Services instance and fetch data from it. You can connect to file data structures such as text files, XML, CSV, and Excel. You can even read the list of files in a folder! You can connect to a range of applications such as Facebook, Salesforce, CRM Online, etc. and get data from them. You can get data from Azure services such as Azure SQL database, Azure HD Insight, Azure Blob storage, etc. There are many data sources supported for Power Query (and obviously for Power BI). Also, more data sources will be available in every update of Power Query or Power BI.

Here is an example set of data sources supported in Power Query (Excel version):

File Data Sources

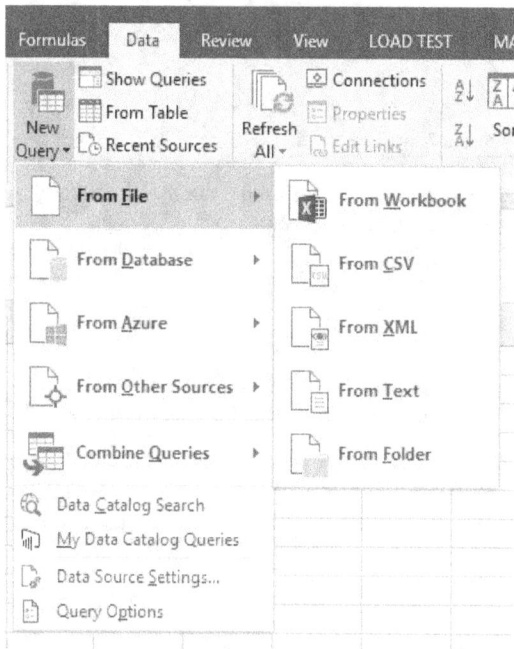

Databases

Azure

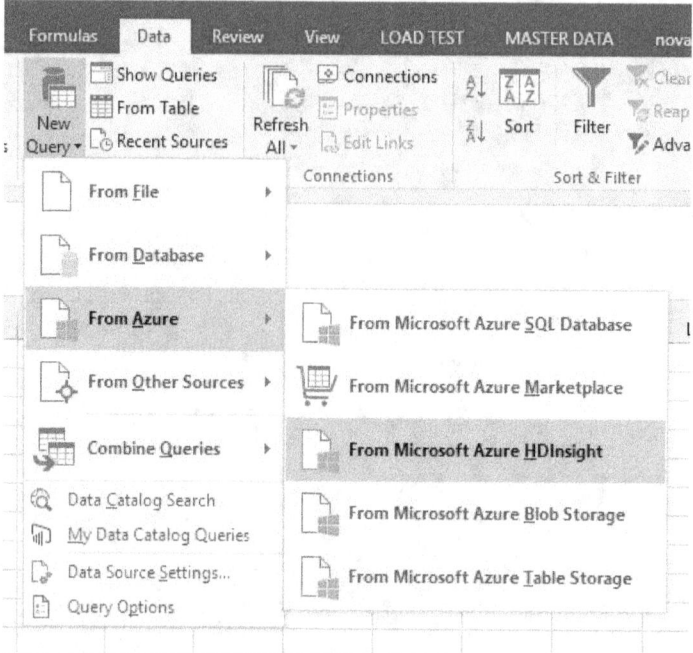

Other Sources

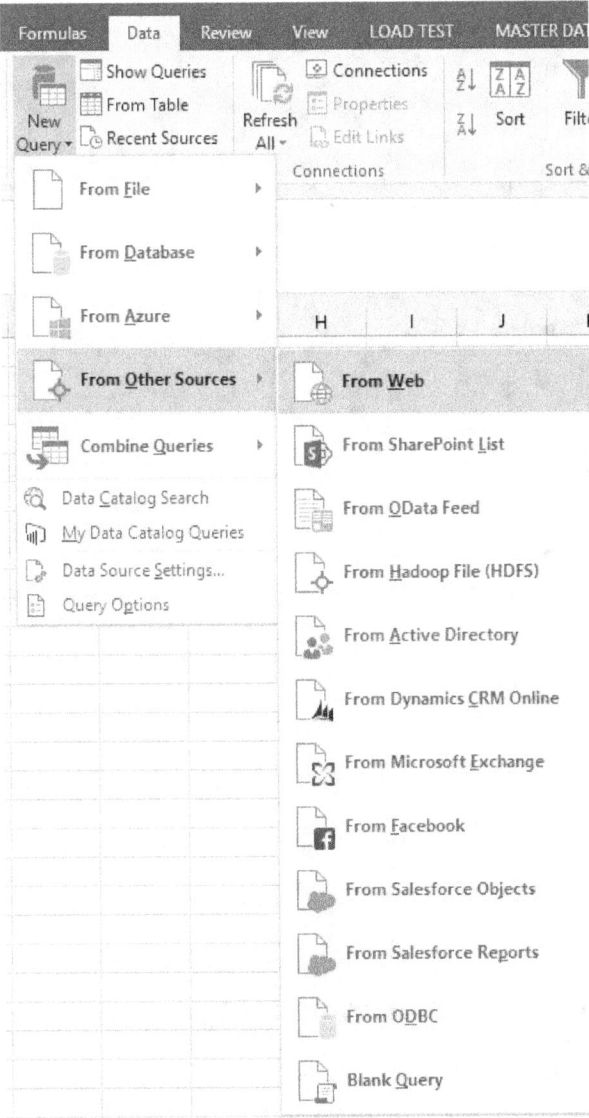

The Power Query version in Power BI Desktop supports some new applications that still is not implemented as Power Query for Excel; you see some of them below:

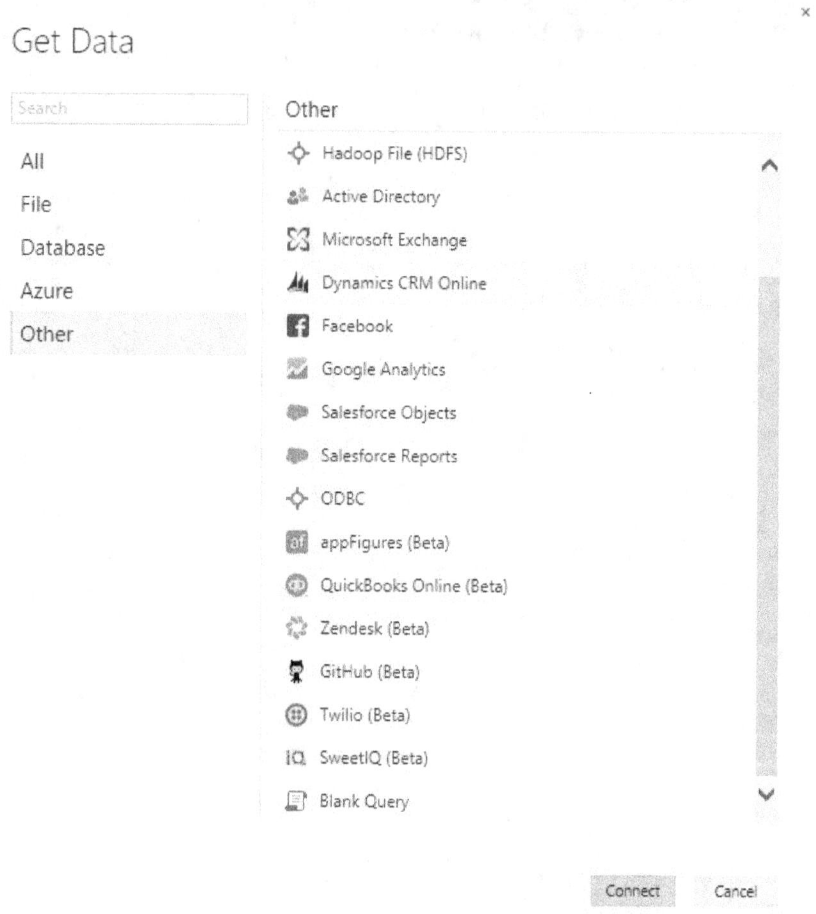

Apply Transformation In a Development Editor

Power Query looks at the data values with data types such as Table, Record, List, DateTime, Text, Number, Boolean, etc. There are many data transformation functions for any of these data types. You can apply Merge (similar to join) or Append (similar to UNION) to two tables. You can apply text functions such as getting part of a string, trimming it or length of the string. You can apply mathematical functions. You can apply

DateTime functions such as functions for the year, Month, day and week. There are two way to apply these transformations;

1. From Query Editor: Graphical User Interface
2. From M query language: scripting language

Query Editor will give you a great experience of most common transformations through the very easy user interface. You can apply most of the transformation with the matter of a few clicks. The Query Editor in Power BI Desktop or Power Query Add-In for Excel has many common transformations listed. You can see some of them in below screenshots:

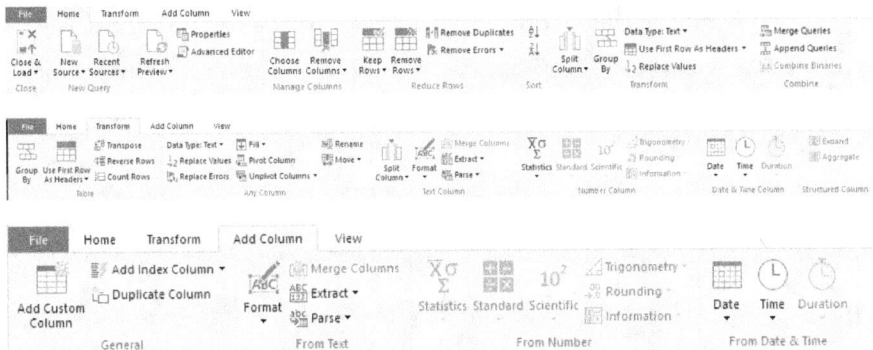

M is the formula language behind the scenes of Power Query. Everything you do in the Query Editor will be translated to an M script. M contains a full list of functions that you can use. So the powerful side of Power Query is M. I will go deep into details of M in this book because you would need it for solving complex challenges. M is a functional language, and it has a simple structure. The screenshot below shows an M Code. The details of information about M scripting will be covered in the next sections.

```
let
    Source = Folder.Contents("C:\Users\Reza\Dropbox\Speaking"),
    TypeAdded=Table.AddColumn(Source,"Type",each Value.Is([Content],type table)),
    Folders=Table.SelectRows(TypeAdded, each [Type]=true),
    Sorted=Table.Sort(Folders,{"Date created", Order.Descending})
in
    Sorted
```

Load Data into Destination

You can use Power Pivot as the destination for Power Query to load result set into a data model, or you can use a simple Excel spreadsheet for loading data. If you use Power BI Desktop the result set of Power Query automatically will be loaded into a model.

What Are Features of Power Query Premium?

This question might sound weird at first glance, but makes sense when you think about it that all features I mentioned above are available for free! You don't have to pay anything for it. Getting data from different sources, applying all kind of transformations to it, and loading it into a data model is all free. So now the question makes sense; What are features of Power Query Premium?

Using Data Catalog

Data Catalog is a metadata definition service that you can define data sources from your organizational data stores or from public data stores that you trust. You can define descriptors for the data structure so Power Query can search through the Data Catalog and fetch information based on it.

Sharing Queries

You can share your Power Query scripts and queries within your organization

Management using of Shared Queries

You can check the usage of queries that you've shared

As you see in above most of the features for Power Query Premium is related to Office 365 usage for sharing or Power BI and Azure for data catalog and structure. Most of the features in Power Query (Essential features I have to say) is available for free!

In summary in this section you've learned about What is Power Query and what are components of it, you've learned features of Power Query, and now you are probably thinking about the usage of it in scenarios and challenges that you might have right now! Good start, in next sections I will go through the experience of getting data with Power Query and Power BI Desktop.

Power BI from Rookie to Rock Star – Book 3: Power Query and Data Transformation in Power BI

Get Started with Power Query: Movies Data Mash-Up

Published Date: September 1, 2015

As another section of the Power BI online book: from Rookie to Rockstar, I would like to get started working with Power Query. From my point of view learning through an example is the best way to learn new technology. For this post, I have decided to use the movie's data to be mashed up. I used this example because the movie's data is a fun example at the early sections of the book, you all watch movies, and you will see many familiar titles here. If you want to learn about Power Query or you need a Power Query introduction before this example, read the previous post: What Is Power Query? Introduction to Data Mashup Engine of Power BI.

You can use either Power Query for Excel or Power Query as part of the Power BI Desktop for running this example. I use two data sets for this example:

1. Worldwide gross sales information of movies

This information is available on http://www.boxofficemojo.com website, as below:

1. Top 250 movies ranked by people in IMDB website

IMDB is the movie database on the internet that users can rate movies. List of top 250 movies rated by users listed here in the website as below:

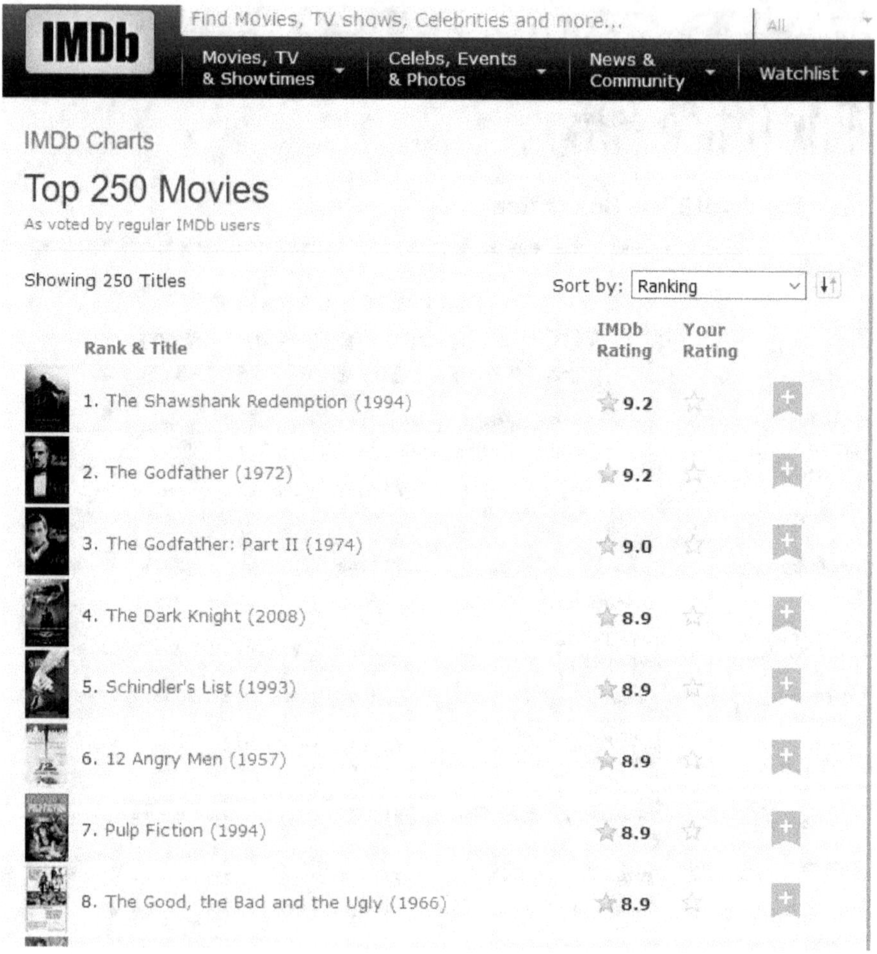

Let's Get Started

Start by getting gross sales data; Open Excel, then Power Query Tab, and then from Web;

Or Open Power BI Desktop and Get Data from Web

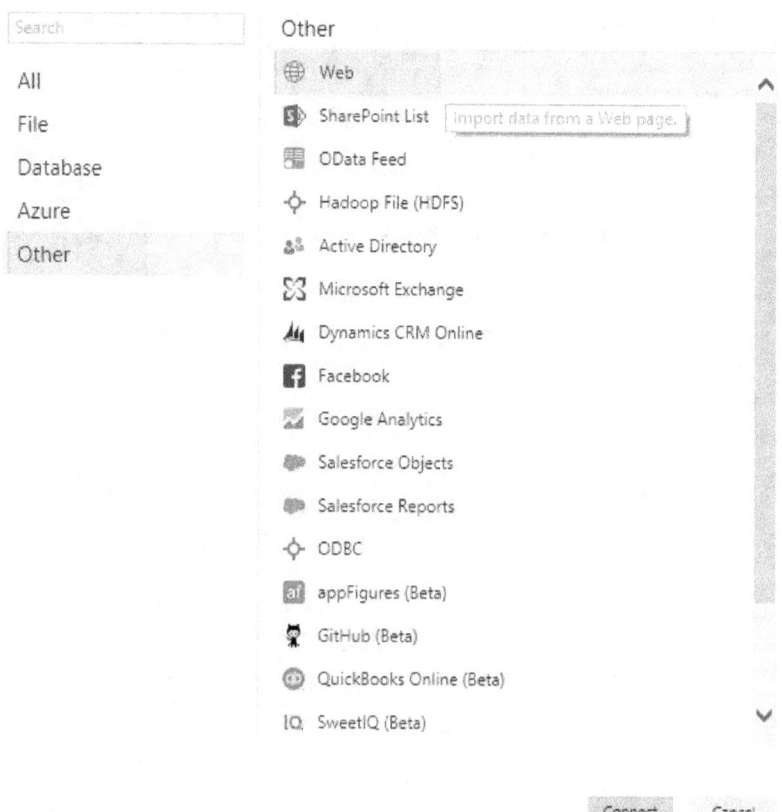

Then Enter the web page URL for the top 100 sold movies all the time from this link:
http://www.boxofficemojo.com/alltime/world/

From Web

Enter a Web page URL.

URL

http://www.boxofficemojo.com/alltime/world/?pagenum=1&p=.htm

OK   Cancel

Click OK, after quick processing; you will see a Navigator window. Power Query will check for any tables in the HTML web page and will come back with a list of tables on the left side under the URL address;

Click on Table 0. You will see a preview of data in the table in the main pane. Now tick the checkbox for Table 0 and click on Edit button in Navigator

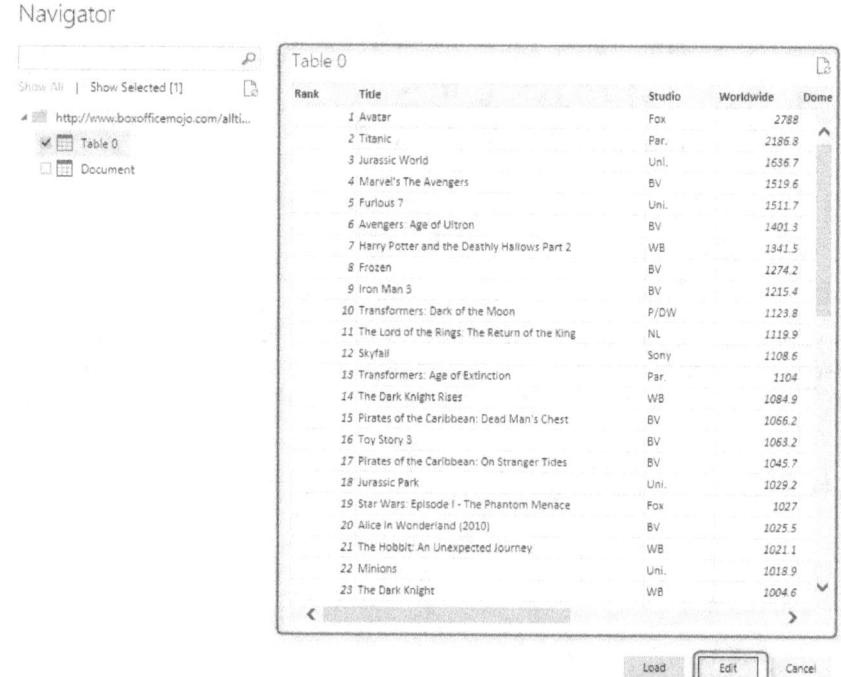

Query Editor

After clicking on Edit, you will see the Query Editor window opened. This is an editor that you will spend most of your time on data mash-up here.

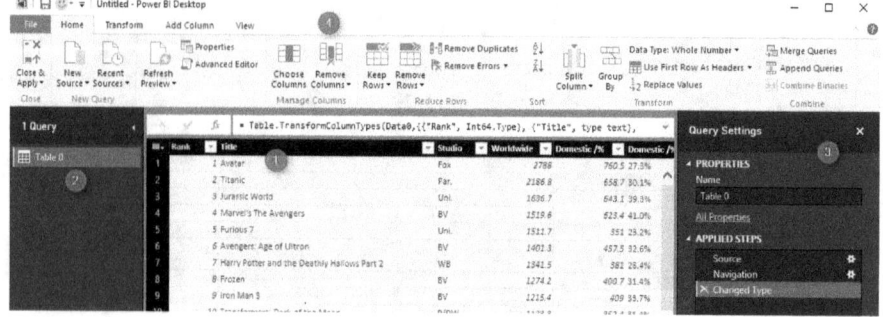

Query Editor has four main sections (numbers matched to screenshot above);

1. Main dataset pane; This is the central area that the result set will be displayed as a preview with a limited number of rows
2. List of Queries; Left-hand side pane will show a list of all queries in this solution or file
3. Query Settings pane; Properties such as Name of the query can be set here. Also, a list of all applied steps to the current query is visible in this pane.
4. Transformations Menu; Power Query has many transformations options in GUI that are available through the menu in the top section

Rename the existing query to Top Sales 100

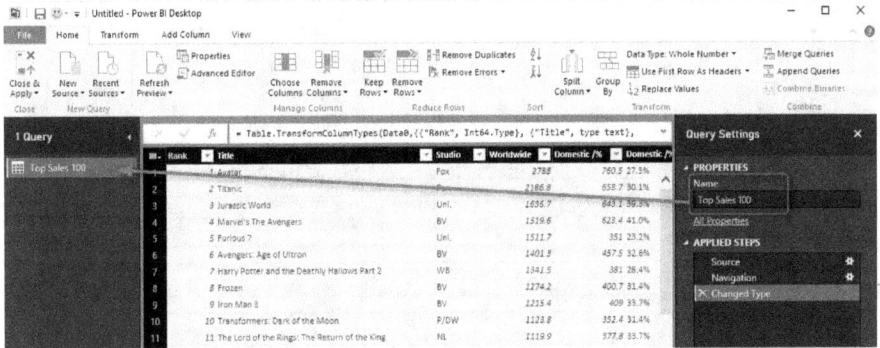

Our goal in this example is to join the data set of global gross sales with the IMDB user rating, and then analyze to see what are best sellers in movie titles among the best-rated movies or not? So the more data in gross sales we get would give us better analysis. The above URL only gives us top 100 sold movies. But the option to go to pages for rest of the result set is available;

So Let's add the list of movies from 101 to 200 in best sellers;

In the existing Query Editor window go to New Source, and then choose From Web. Enter the URL as http://www.boxofficemojo.com/alltime/world/?pagenum=2&p=.htm

Power BI from Rookie to Rock Star – Book 3: Power Query and Data Transformation in Power BI

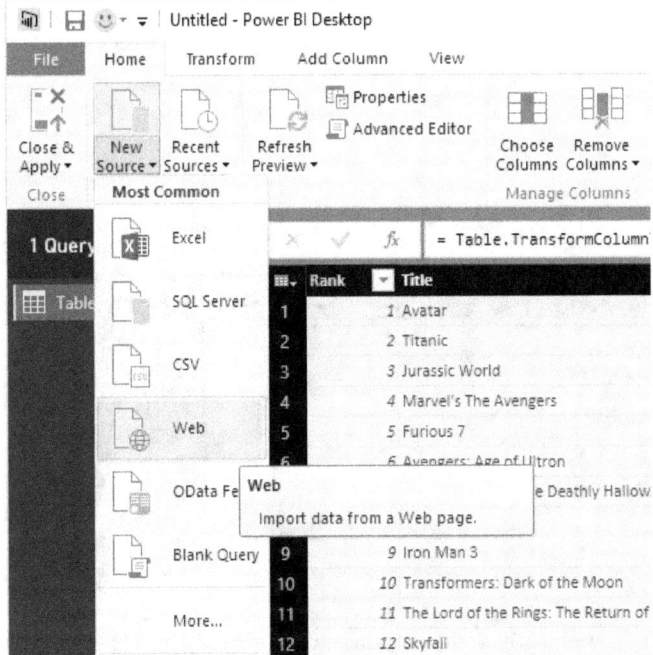

This will lead you to the top second 100 movies sold. Click on Table 0 in navigator window and then OK. in the Query Editor rename this query as Top Sales 200

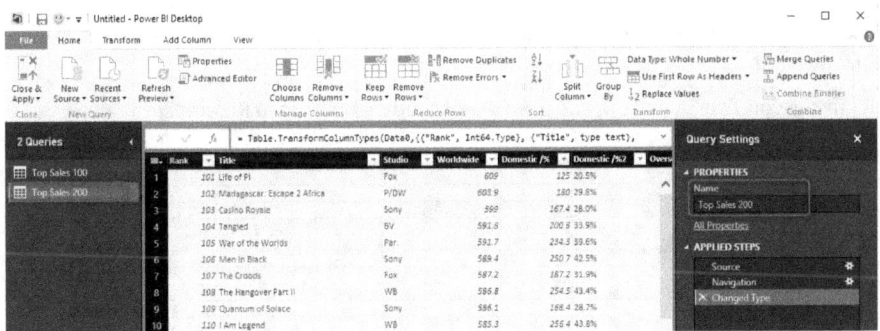

Follow this process for links below;

http://www.boxofficemojo.com/alltime/world/?pagenum=3&p=.htm

http://www.boxofficemojo.com/alltime/world/?pagenum=4&p=.htm

...

Bring data for all top 615 movies in Power Query

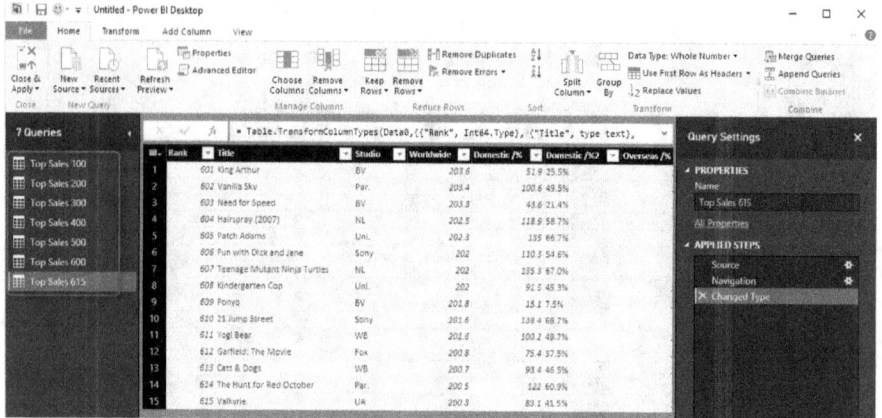

As you see in query editor, all of these queries are separate from each other. Let's combine them all. In database and SQL world that can be done with UNION. Here in Power Query we can do Append Queries;

Use a Query as a Reference

First Create a reference from Top Sales 100 (because for this example I want to keep that query as is);

Right click on Top Sales 100, and from the pop-up menu choose Reference

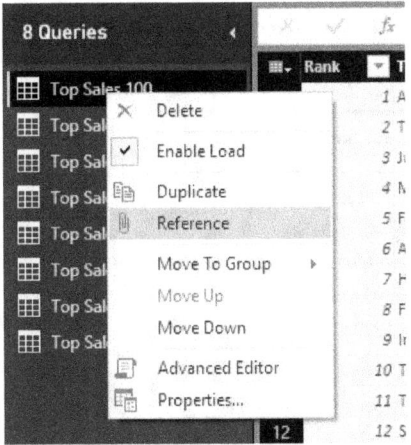

This will create a new query that users Top Sales 100 as the source (or reference). Rename this new query to be just "Top Sales."

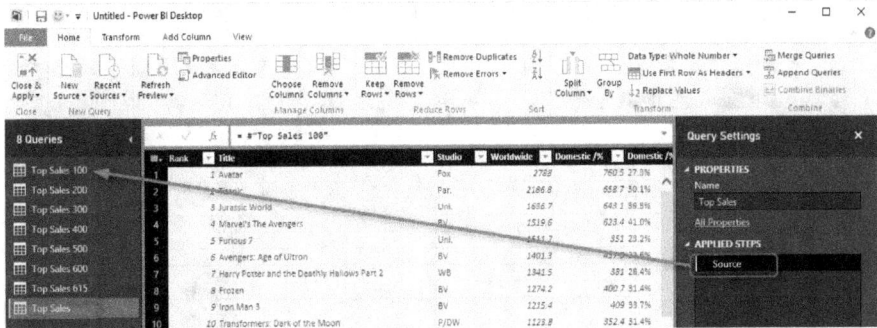

Append Queries

Now let's combine queries into this new query;

Click on Top Sales and then from the menu (Home) click on Append Queries

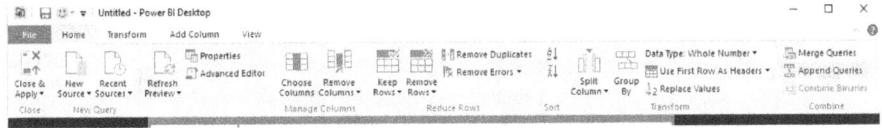

For append to work you need two queries; the first query is the query that you are on it (Top Sales), the second query name should be entered in the Append dialog box;

as you see in the screenshot above you can choose other queries. For append to works, best queries have to be in the same structure (number of columns, the order of columns, the data type of columns….). Choose Top Sales 200 in this window and click OK. This will create another step in the query setting named Appended Query. And the result set in the main pane (if you scroll down) will show you first top 200 movies sold.

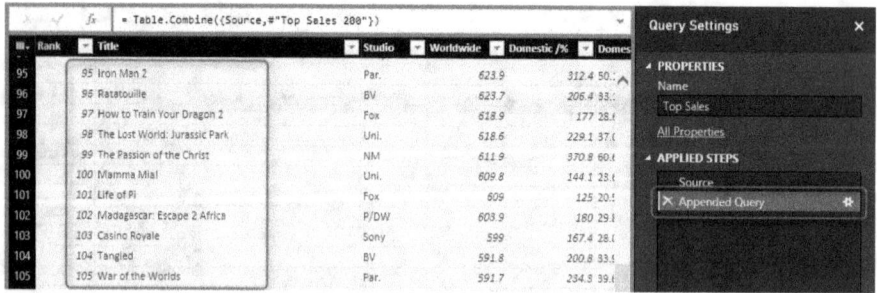

Continue this process to add all 615 top movies into Top Sales query.

Extract First Characters

After doing this change Let's clean the Year column data; Year column has a special character in some values as below;

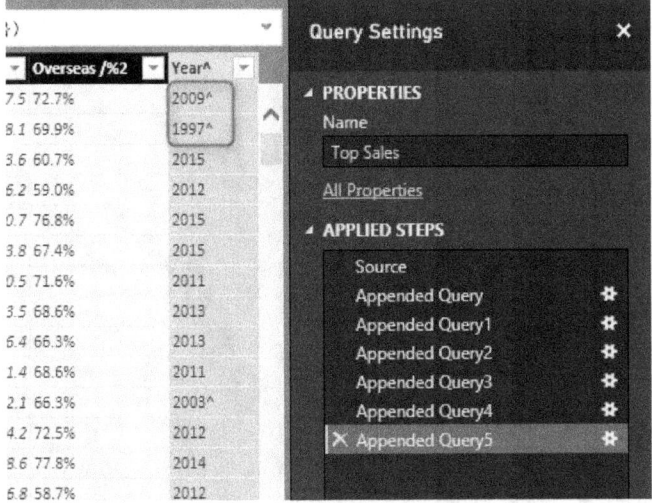

Click on Year Column, and then from Transform menu under Text Column click on Extract, and then choose First Characters

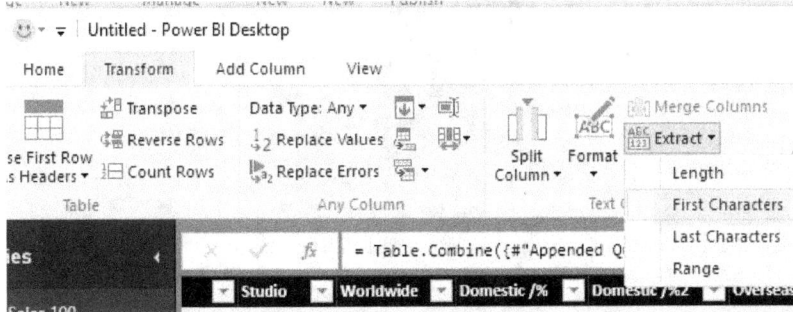

Enter 4 in the Extract First Characters dialog box (because the year isn't more than four characters). Then click on OK.

Extract First Characters

Enter how many starting characters to keep.

Count

4

OK   Cancel

You will see that year column is clean now without any extra characters. That was easy data transform. This option in the transformation menu (Extract First Characters) has been added recently in Power BI Desktop.

You can even now change the data type of this column to the whole number. Right click on Year column and then under Change Type choose the Whole Number.

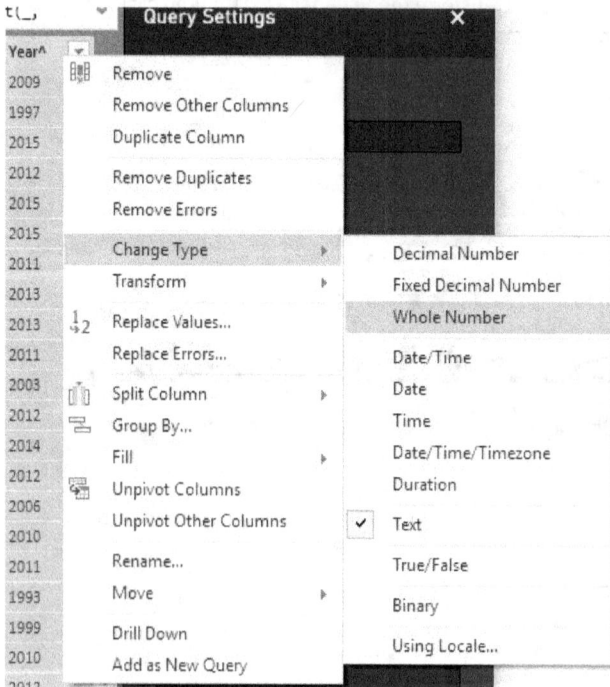

Great We've done enough with the first data set. Let's work on the second data set (IMDB user rating);
Go to Home Tab in Query Editor again, and Get data from the New Source and Web.
Enter the URL as http://www.imdb.com/chart/top
In the Navigator window, Table 0 contains the data that we want, so load it with clicking on OK. the data loads into the Query Editor as the screenshot below illustrates

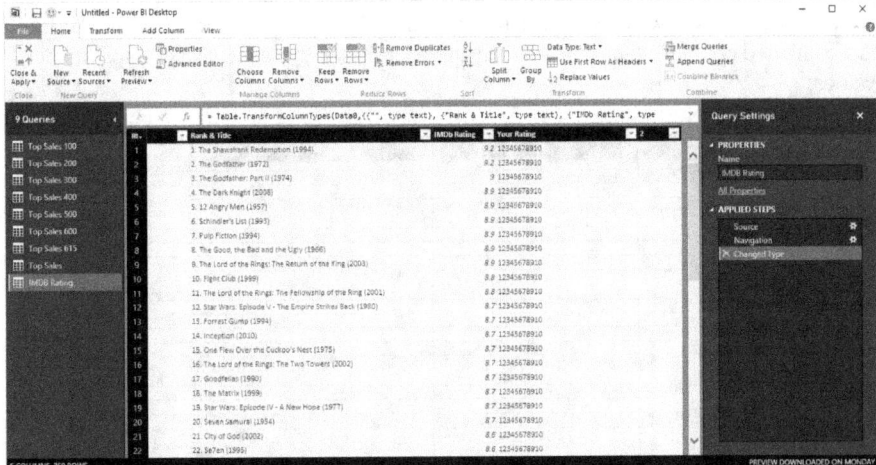

Rename the query to IMDB Rating.

Remove Columns

You can see that there are three useless columns in the data set; the first column, and the last two columns. Remove these columns simply by clicking on them and then right click and Remove.

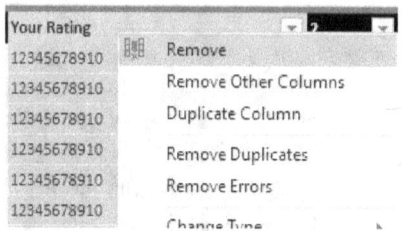

Split Column

Now in the result set, we have two columns; Rank & Title, and IMDB Rating. Rank & Title is a combined column which contains rank, title, and year of the movie. Let's split these values;

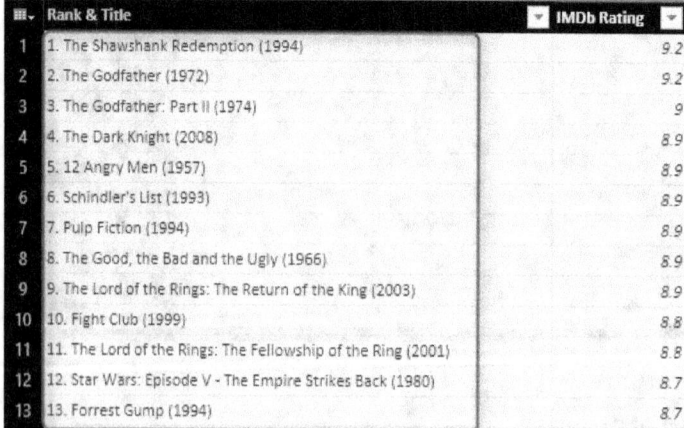

A single dot separates rank (.). So we can use Split Column transformation to split it easily; Right click on Rank & Title column first. then Choose Split Column, and then By Delimiter

```
= Table.RemoveColumns(#"Changed Type",{"Your Rating", "2", ""})
```

	Rank & Title			IMDb Rating
1	1. The Shawshank Redemption (1994)		Remove	9.2
2	2. The Godfather (1972)		Remove Other Columns	9.2
3	3. The Godfather: Part II (1974)		Duplicate Column	9
4	4. The Dark Knight (2008)		Remove Duplicates	8.9
5	5. 12 Angry Men (1957)		Remove Errors	8.9
6	6. Schindler's List (1993)		Change Type ▶	8.9
7	7. Pulp Fiction (1994)		Transform ▶	8.9
8	8. The Good, the Bad and the Ugly (1966)			8.9
9	9. The Lord of the Rings: The Return of the		Replace Values...	8.9
10	10. Fight Club (1999)		Replace Errors...	8.8
11	11. The Lord of the Rings: The Fellowship		Split Column ▶	By Delimiter...
12	12. Star Wars: Episode V - The Empire Stri		Group By...	By Number of Characters...
13	13. Forrest Gump (1994)		Fill ▶	8.7
14	14. Inception (2010)		Unpivot Columns	8.7
15	15. One Flew Over the Cuckoo's Nest (197			8.7

In the Split Column by the Delimiter dialog box, you can choose one of the common delimiters such as comma or color ... or you can use a custom delimiter. Set it to Custom, and enter a single dot (.) in the box underneath. You can also specify how the split works. The default option is At each occurrence of the delimiter. This default option might not be best for our case, because sometimes there might be a dot in the movie's title. So select the split method as At the left-most delimiter. This option will scan text from the left, and will stop splitting after finding the first delimiter.

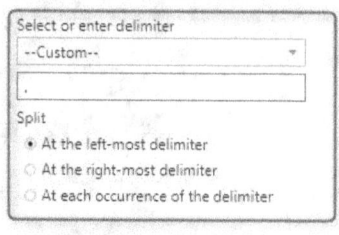

after the split the result set would look like below;

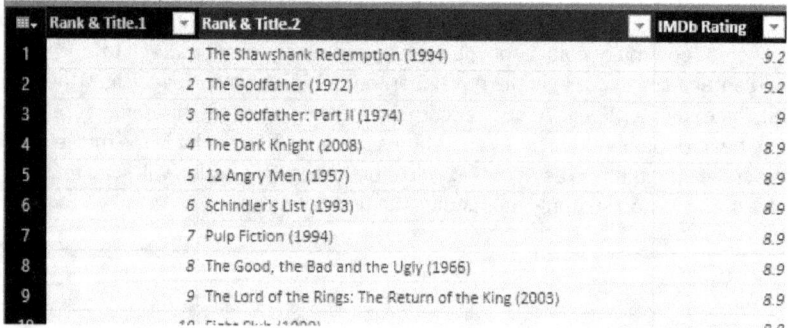

Rename the Rank & Title.1 column to Rank.

Now Let's split title and year. Year value is surrounded between brackets, so we can use the same split column method, this time using open bracket as below;

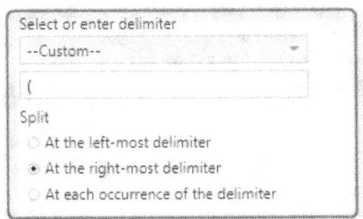

The result set looks like below screenshot;

Replace Values

Rank & Title.2.2 column has the year value with an extra close bracket. Click on this column and then from Transform menu under Any Column click on Replace Values

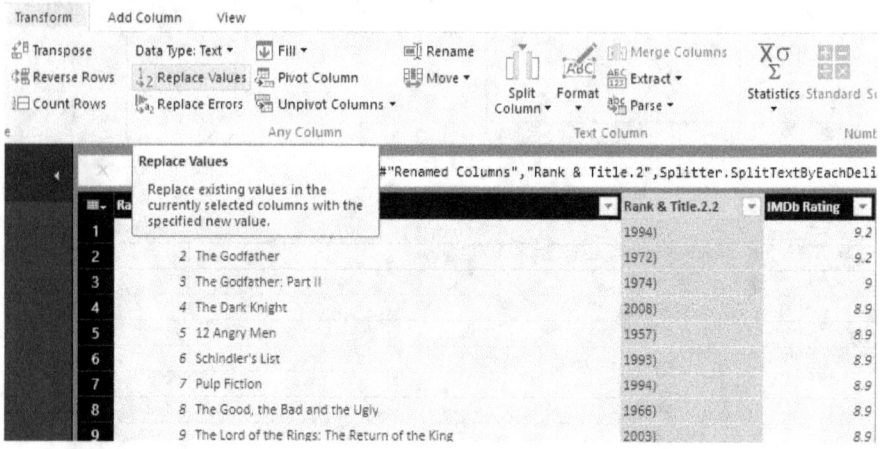

Replace close bracket with an empty string as below;

Replace Values

Replace one value with another in the selected columns.

Value To Find
)

Replace With

☐ Match entire cell contents

OK   Cancel

Result set would have the close bracket removed. rename the column to Year, and change its data type to Whole number (change data type with right click on the column)

Trim

Also, rename the Rank & Title.2.1 column to Title. Because this column might have extra spaces at the beginning and end of values (as the result of split column steps), let's remove extra spaces;

Right click on this column and then under transform choose Trim. This will remove all heading and trailing spaces from values in this column.

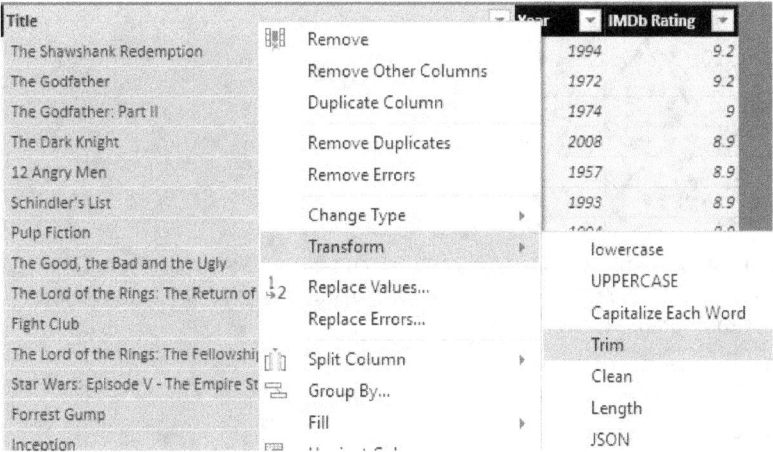

Awesome, our work with this data set has been finished as well.

Applied Steps

One of the most useful sections of the Query Editor window is Applied Steps in the Query Settings Pane. This section of the Query Editor window is very useful for debugging and tracking steps and changes. You can see all the steps that you've applied on the current data set in this pane. And this is not all of it! You can click on a step, and the main pane will show you the data at that step! Such an awesome way of keeping track of steps.

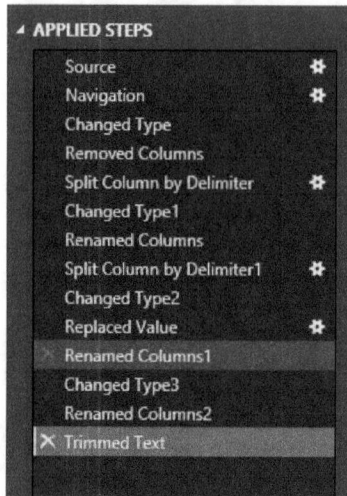

You can even remove a step, or you can change settings of a step with clicking on remove icon (on the left side of step) or setting icon (on the right side of the step, but only for steps that settings apply to them).

Final Merge

We've prepared both data sets for a final merge together to see how best-selling movies are among top user rated films. So we are one step away from this result. We have to merge these two data sets or Join them in another word.

Click on Top Sales query and create a reference of it, name the new query as Merge Result. Now click on Merge Result, and then from Home tab, under Combine choose Merge Queries

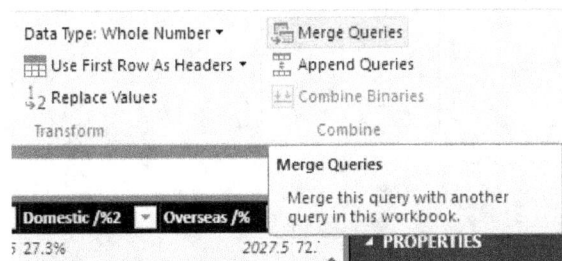

Merge Queries is equivalent to Join in SQL or database terminology.

Merging queries requires two queries; the first query is the query that you are currently on it (Merge Result), and you can choose the second query in the Merge dialog box. Choose the second query as IMDB Rating. Now select joining keys as Title (you can also choose multiple joining columns with pressing ctrl keyboard key). Set also join kindly to Left outer join (this will only select all records from the first query with matched rows of that from the second query)

Merge

Select a table and matching columns to create a merged table.

Rank	Title	Studio	Worldwide	Domestic /%	Domestic /%2	Overseas /%	Overseas /%
1	Avatar	Fox	2788	760.5	27.3%	2027.5	72.7%
2	Titanic	Par.	2186.8	658.7	30.1%	1528.1	69.9%
3	Jurassic World	Uni.	1636.7	643.1	39.3%	993.6	60.7%
4	Marvel's The Avengers	BV	1519.6	623.4	41.0%	896.2	59.0%
5	Furious 7	Uni.	1511.7	351	23.2%	1160.7	76.8%

IMDB Rating

Rank	Title	Year	IMDb Rating
1	The Shawshank Redemption	1994	9.2
2	The Godfather	1972	9.2
3	The Godfather: Part II	1974	9
4	The Dark Knight	2008	8.9
5	12 Angry Men	1957	8.9

Join Kind

Inner (only matching rows)

ⓘ The selection has matched 58 out of the first 615 rows.

OK   Cancel

Notice in the screenshot above that merge dialog mentioned only 58 records out of 615 movies matched! It means only 58 of best seller movies are among top user rated list! Such a pity. The screenshot showed only Inner Join result, but you choose Left Outer and then click on OK to look at the data;

Joining experience in Power Query is a bit different from database tables. As a result of the join, you will get the first table with a new column for the new table. This new column holds table values which need to be expanded. If you click on the column header icon, you can choose which columns of the nested table you want to expand.

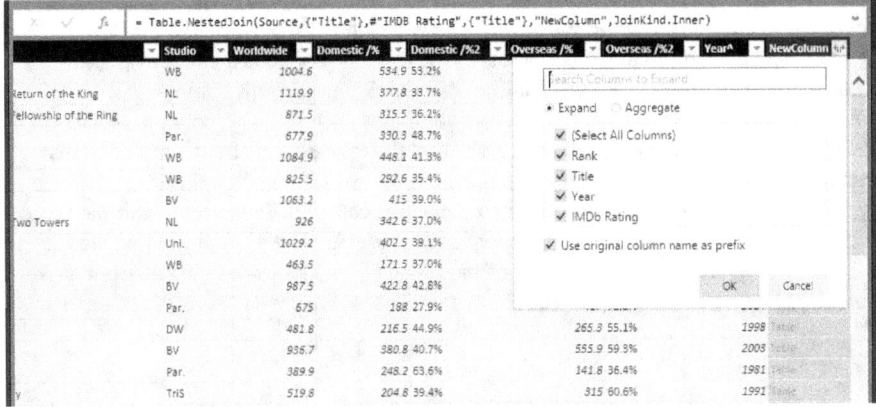

Let's keep all columns and click OK. You can now see some movies that are among best sellers but not in top 250 users rated list of IMDB; There are movies name such as Iron Man 3, Skyfall, Furious 7 and list goes on. Play with that yourself to see what you explore!

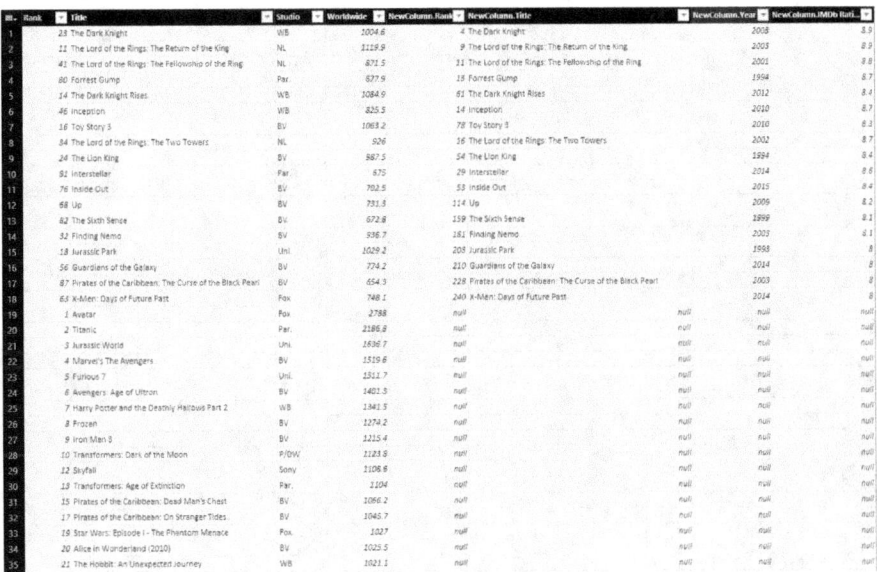

Summary

In this section, you've learned the basics of Power Query through an example. You've seen how Power Query can analyze tables in a web page and load it into query editor. You've experienced Query Editor, and you've learned how to apply some transformations. You've learned that transformations such as a split column, replace values, change the data type, and extract part of the text are easy transformations that can be simply done through Power Query editor. In next sections, I will explain different types of data sources that Power Query or Power BI can work with through the Get Data Experience. You will see that Power Query and Power BI can get data from text files such as CSV, Text as well as database connections such as MySQL, Oracle, and SQL Server, it can also bring data from on-premises data stores as well as cloud Azure-based services.

Data Preparation; First and Foremost Important Task in Power BI

Posted by Reza Rad on Dec 21, 2016

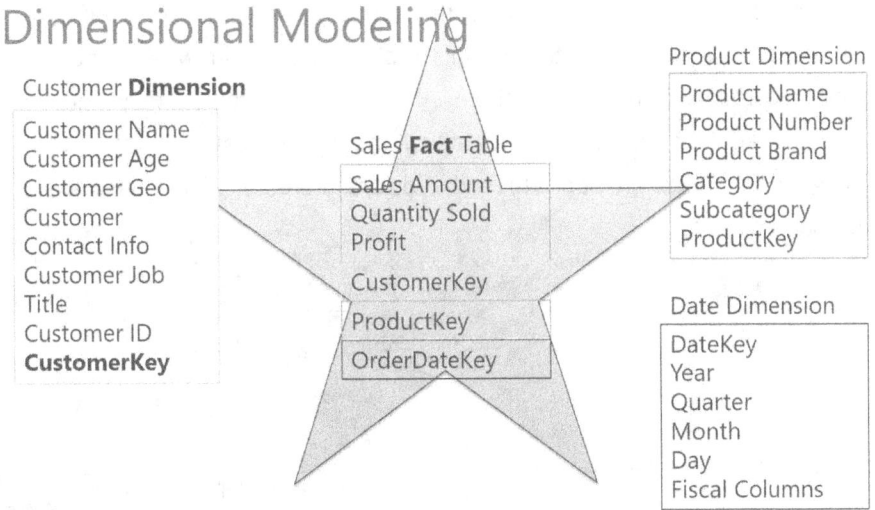

I've talked about Data Preparation many times in conferences such as PASS Summit, BA Conference, and many other conferences. Every time I talk about this I realize how much more I need to explain this. Data Preparation tips are basic but very important. In my opinion as someone who worked with BI systems for more than 15 years, this is the most important task in building in BI system. In this post, I'll explain why data preparation is necessary and what are five basic steps you need to be aware of when building a data model with Power BI (or any other BI tools). This post is conceptual, and you can apply these rules to any tools.

Why Data Preparation?

All of us have seen many data models like the screenshot below. Transactional databases have the nature of many tables and the relationship between tables.

Transactional databases are built for CRUD operations (Create, Retrieve, Update, Delete rows). Because of this single purpose, transactional databases are build in Normalized way, to reduce redundancy and increase the consistency of the data. For example, there should be one table for Product Category with a Key related to a Product Table, because then whenever a product category name changes there is only one record to update and all products related to that will be updated automatically because they are just using the key. There are books to read if you are interested in how database normalization works.

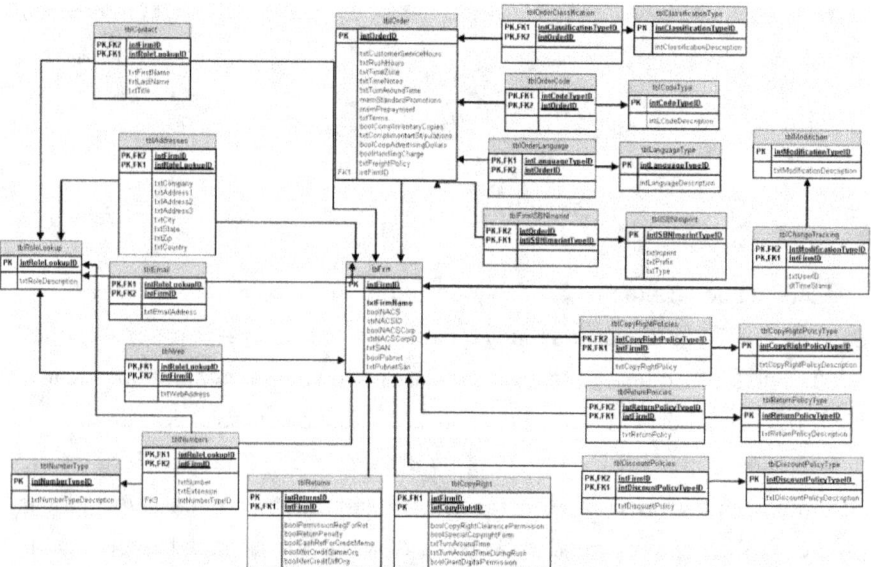

I'm not going to talk about how to build these databases. In fact for building a data model for a BI system you need to avoid this type of modeling! This model works perfectly for the transactional database (when there are systems and operators do data entry and modifications). However, this model is not good for a BI system. There are several reasons for that, here are the two most important reasons;

1. The model is hard to understand for a Report User
2. Too many tables and many relationships between tables makes a reporting query (that might use 20 of these tables at once) very slow and not efficient.

You never want to wait for hours for a report to respond. The response time of reports should be fast. You also never want your report users (of self-service report users) to understand the schema above. It is sometimes even hard for a database developer to understand how this works in the first few hours! You need to make your model simpler, with a few tables and relationships. Your first and the most important job as a BI developer should be transforming above schema to something like below;

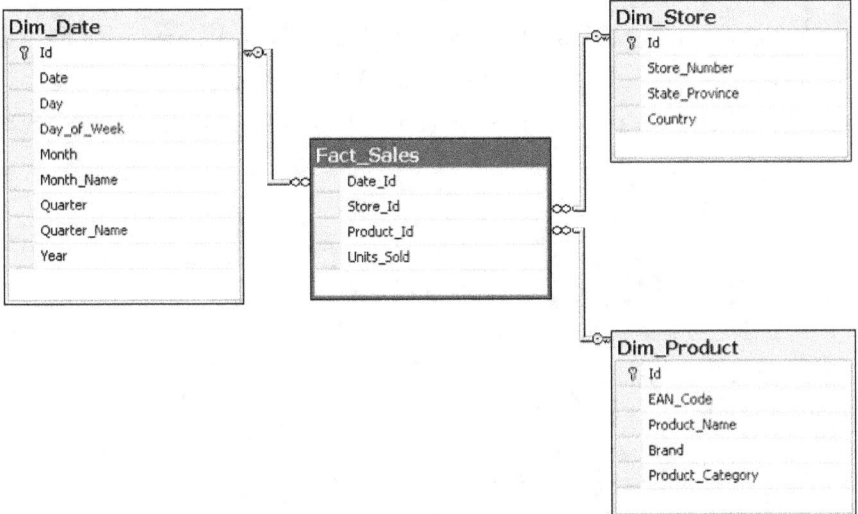

This model is far simpler and faster. There is one table that keeps sales information (Fact_Sales), and a few other tables which keep descriptions (such as Product description, name, brand, and category). There is one relationship that connects the table in the middle (Fact) to tables around (Dimensions). This is the best model to work within a BI system. This model is called **Star**

Schema. Building a star schema or dimensional modeling is your most important task as a BI developer.

How to Design a Star Schema?

To build a star schema for your data model, I strongly suggest you take one step at a time. What I mean by that is choosing one or few use cases and start building the model for that. For example; instead of building a data model for the whole Dynamics AX or CRM which might have more than thousands of tables, choose Sales side of it, or Purchasing, or GL. After choosing one subject area (for example Sales), then start building the model for it considering what is required for the analysis.

Fact Table

Fact tables are tables that are holding numeric and additive data normally. For example, quantity sold, or sales amount, or discount, or cost, or things like that. These values are numeric and can be aggregated. Here is an example of a fact table for sales;

Sales **Fact** Table

Sales Amount
Quantity Sold
Profit

Dimension Table

Any descriptive information will be kept in Dimension tables. For example; customer name, customer age, customer geoinformation, customer contact information, customer job, customer id, and any other customer related information will be kept in a table named Customer Dimension.

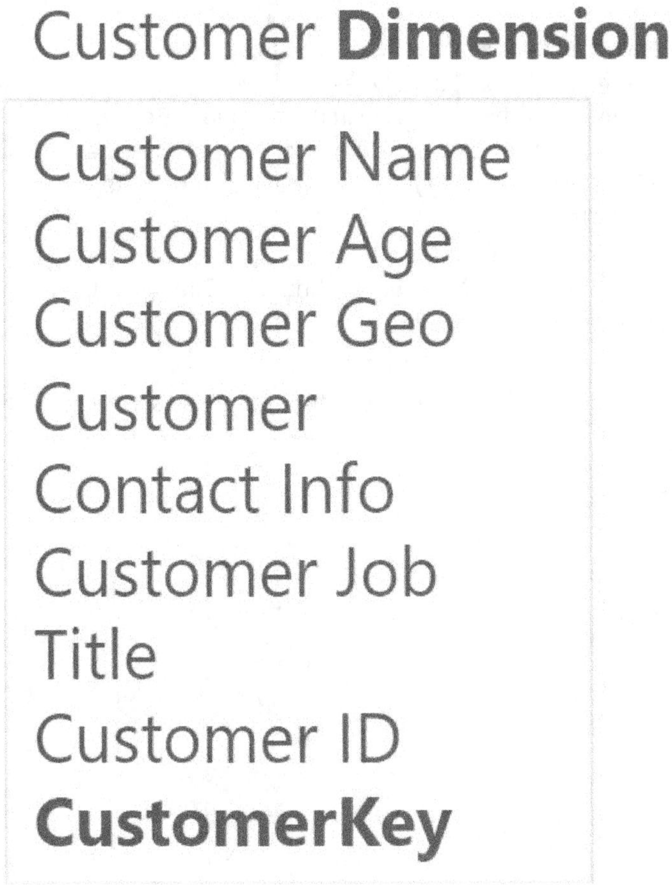

Customer **Dimension**

Customer Name
Customer Age
Customer Geo
Customer Contact Info
Customer Job Title
Customer ID
CustomerKey

each dimension table should contain a key column. This column should be numeric (integer or big integer depends on the size of dimension) which is auto increment (Identity in SQL Server terminology). This column should be unique per each row in the dimension table. This column will be the primary key of this table and will be used in fact table as a relationship. This column

SHOULDN'T be the ID of the source system. There are several reasons for why. This column is called **Surrogate Key**. Here are a few reasons why you need to have the surrogate key:

- Codes (or IDs) in source system might be Text, not Integer.
- Short Int, Int, or Big Int are the best data types for the surrogate key because these are values which will be used in the fact table. Because fact table is the largest table in the dataset, it is important to keep it in the smallest size possible (using Int data types for dimension foreign keys is one of the main ways of doing that).
- Codes (or IDs) might be recycled.
- You might want to keep track of changes (Slowly Changing Dimension), so one ID or Code might be used for multiple rows.
- ...

Surrogate key of the dimension should be used in the fact table as a foreign key. Here is an example;

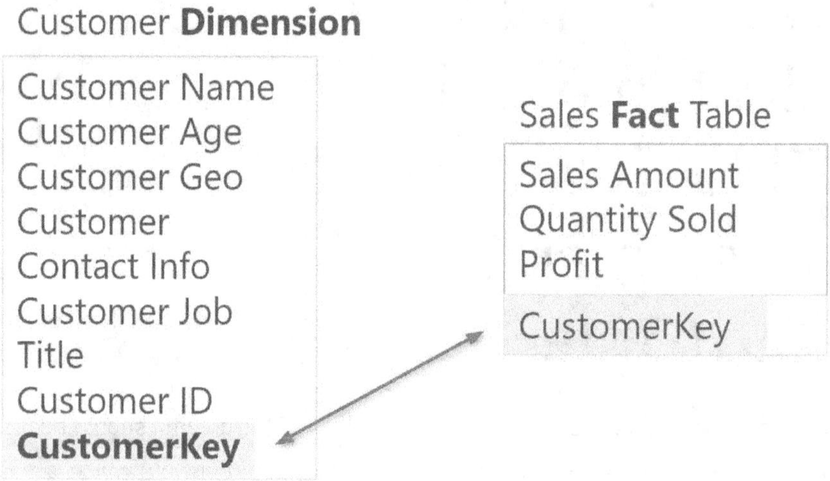

Customer **Dimension**

Customer Name
Customer Age
Customer Geo
Customer
Contact Info
Customer Job Title
Customer ID
CustomerKey

Sales **Fact** Table

Sales Amount
Quantity Sold
Profit

CustomerKey

Other dimensions should also be added in the same way. In the example below a Date Dimension and Product, Dimension is also created. You can easily see in the screenshot below that why it is called star schema; Fact table is in the middle, and all other dimensions are around with one relationship from fact table to other dimensions.

Dimensional Modeling

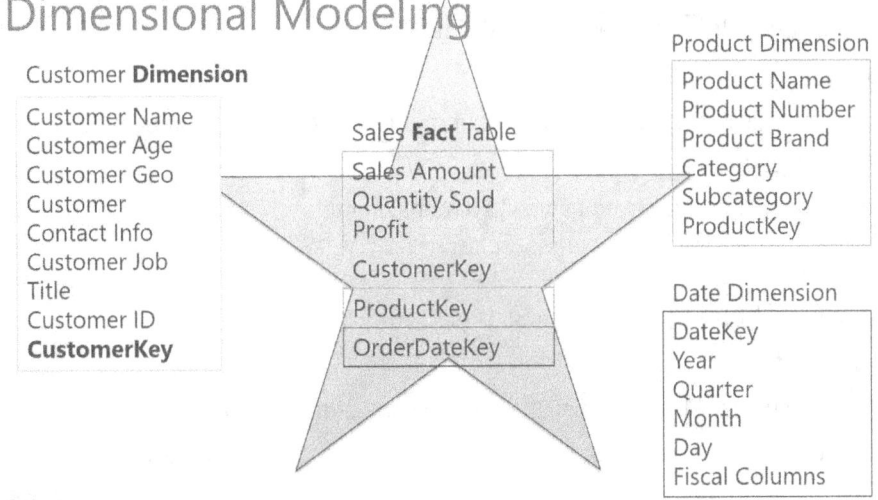

Design Tips

Building star schema or dimensional modeling is something that you have to read books about it to get it right. I will write some more blog posts and explain these principles more in details. However it would be great to leave some tips here for you to get things started towards better modeling. These tips are simple but easy to overlook. A number of BI solutions that I have seen suffer from not obeying these rules are countless. These are rules that if you do not follow, you will be soon far away from proper data modeling, and you have to spend ten times more to build your model proper from the beginning. Here are tips:

Tip 1: DO NOT add tables/files as is

Why?
Tables can be joined together to create more flatten and simpler structure.

Solution: DO create a flatten structure for tables (especially dimensions)

Tip 2: DO NOT flatten your FACT table
Why?
Fact table is the largest entities in your model. Flattening them will make them even larger!
Solution: DO create relationships to dimension tables

Tip 3: DO NOT leave naming as is
Why?
Names such as std_id, or dimStudent are confusing for users.
Solution: DO set naming of your tables and columns for the end user

Tip 4: DO NOT leave data types as is
Why?
Some data types are spending memory (and CPU) like decimals. Appropriate data types are also helpful for engines such as Q&A in Power BI which is working based on the data model.
Solution: DO set proper data types based on the data in each field

Tip 5: DO NOT load the whole data if you don't require it
Why?
Filtering part of the data before loading it into memory is cost and performance effective.
Solution: DO Filter part of the data that is not required.

More to Come

This was just a very quick introduction to data preparation with some tips. This is the beginning of blog post series I will write in the future about principles of dimensional modeling and how to use them in Power BI or any other BI tools. You can build a BI solution without using these concepts and principles, but your BI system will slow down, and users will suffer from using it after few months, I'll give you my word on it. Stay tuned for future posts on this subject.

Part II: Get Data

Power BI Get Data From Excel: Everything You Need to Know

Posted by Reza Rad on Sep 2, 2015

In the Previous section, you learned about Power Query through an example of data mash-up of movies. Also prior than that you've learned about Power BI and its components in Power BI online book from rookie to rockstar. In this section, I would like to start an exploration of different data sources in Power BI, and I want to start that with an Excel source. Excel source seems to be an easy one, but on the other hand, it is one of the most common sources of the data. In this section, I want to share some tips about Excel data source, and then I show an example of working with Olympic data source in an Excel file.

Excel Data Source

Power Query or Power BI can connect to many data sources, one of the supported data sources in Excel. Power Query for Excel get data from Excel in this way:

Power BI from Rookie to Rock Star – Book 3: Power Query and Data Transformation in Power BI

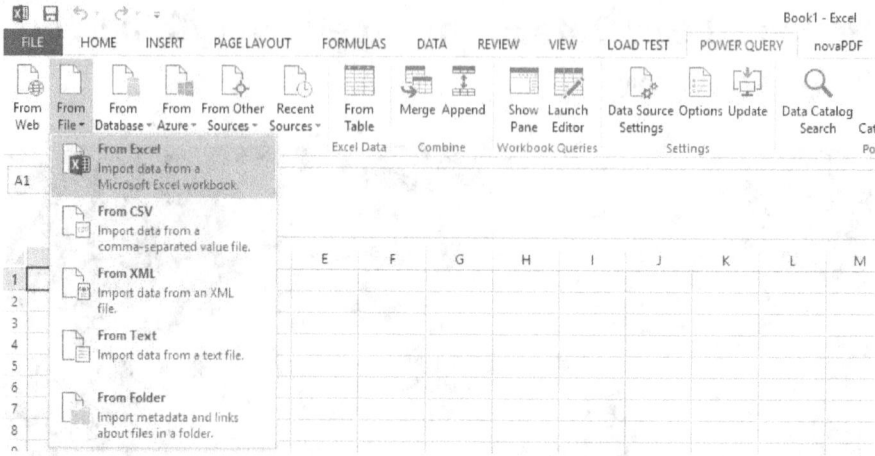

Power BI Desktop connects to Excel through getting Data experience

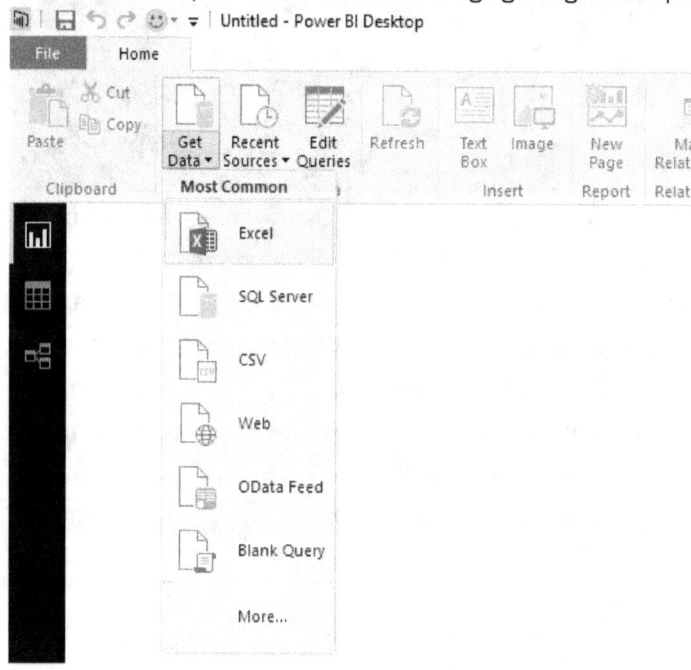

For getting data from excel you need to specify the path of the file. After specifying the file, Power Query will analyze contents of the file and distinguish all sheets and tables in the file and list them in the Navigator dialog box as a preview;

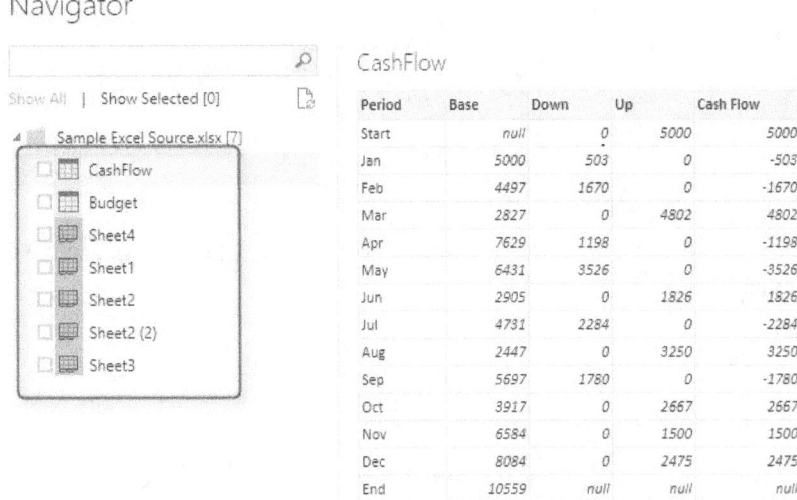

As you see in the Navigator dialog box screenshot above, Power Query will distinguish Tables and Sheets and show the appropriate icon for any of these types (note to the highlighted section in the screenshot above).

Loading Excel Tables into Power Query

If you have data in an Excel Table then it can be easily detected and picked by Power Query as you see in the screenshot above, CashFlow is a table in Excel. The screenshot below shows the Excel table for CashFlow;

Power BI from Rookie to Rock Star – Book 3: Power Query and Data Transformation in Power BI

	A	B	C	D	E
1	Period	Base	Down	Up	Cash Flow
2	Start		$0	$5,000	$5,000
3	Jan	$5,000	$503	$0	-$503
4	Feb	$4,497	$1,670	$0	-$1,670
5	Mar	$2,827	$0	$4,802	$4,802
6	Apr	$7,629	$1,198	$0	-$1,198
7	May	$6,431	$3,526	$0	-$3,526
8	Jun	$2,905	$0	$1,826	$1,826
9	Jul	$4,731	$2,284	$0	-$2,284
10	Aug	$2,447	$0	$3,250	$3,250
11	Sep	$5,697	$1,780	$0	-$1,780
12	Oct	$3,917	$0	$2,667	$2,667
13	Nov	$6,584	$0	$1,500	$1,500
14	Dec	$8,084	$0	$2,475	$2,475
15	End	$10,559			

As you can see in the screenshot below Power Query (or Power BI) fetched the table fully

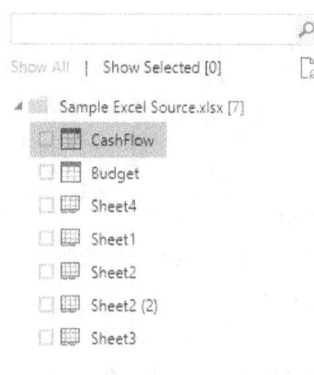

Period	Base	Down	Up	Cash Flow
Start	null	0	5000	5000
Jan	5000	503	0	-503
Feb	4497	1670	0	-1670
Mar	2827	0	4802	4802
Apr	7629	1198	0	-1198
May	6431	3526	0	-3526
Jun	2905	0	1826	1826
Jul	4731	2284	0	-2284
Aug	2447	0	3250	3250
Sep	5697	1780	0	-1780
Oct	3917	0	2667	2667
Nov	6584	0	1500	1500
Dec	8084	0	2475	2475
End	10559	null	null	null

Loading Excel Sheets into Power Query

You can get data directly from Excel sheets as well, No matter if you have tables or not. Power Query will always read the data from Excel sheets from all cells that contain data. If you have even two data sets in one Excel sheet Power Query still read that and load it correctly. Here is an example of an Excel sheet with two data sets;

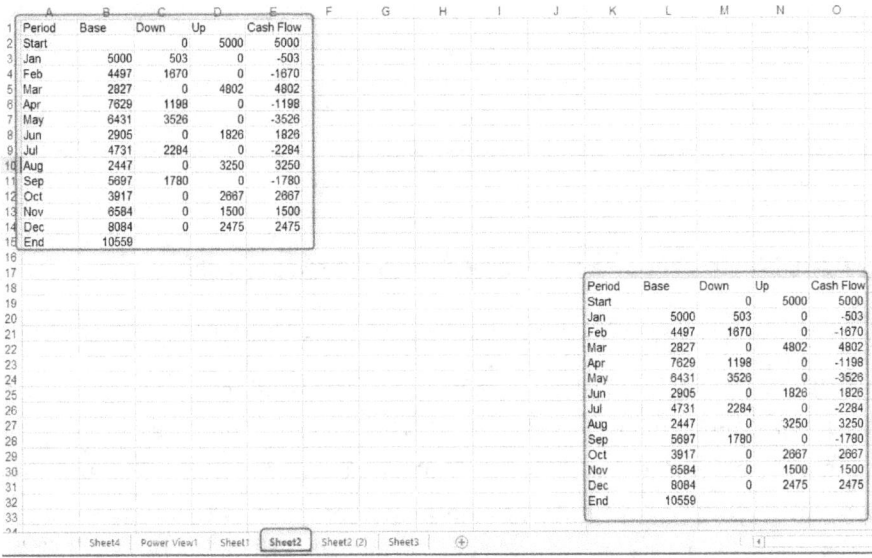

When you load this sheet in Power Query only data range of data cells up to the last cell's column and row will be fetched;

What Happens If Excel Contains Formatting?

Any formatting such as color, font, and the data type of cells would be ignored when it loads into Power Query. The reason is that Power Query is a data mash-up tools not modeling or visualization tools. You can apply these formatting later in the model (Power Pivot) or the report (Power View). As an example; if your data values contain decimal points such as 12.94 and in Excel, you've formatted cell to have zero decimal points (Excel will show cell value like 13 in this case). Power Query still fetches the original value which is 12.94.

What Happens to Power View Sheets in Excel?

You can have Power View sheets in Excel, and your Power View sheets can contain Data values, such as a table. However, Power Query won't load anything from a Power View Sheet at this stage. Because usually, Power View sheet uses a data source you can use that source directly in Power Query. Power View data source might be sources such as Pivot Table or SSAS Tabular connection that can be both used in Power Query directly.

Pivot Tables and Pivot Charts?

You cannot fetch data from Pivot Charts! Why? Because the chart is a visualization element, so the same principle that I said for Power View in above paragraph works here, connect to Pivot Chart's source directly. You can get data from PivotTables however. PivotTables data can be fetched exactly as they shaped in Excel file with the same structure of columns and rows. For example, if you have a Pivot Table like below screenshot:

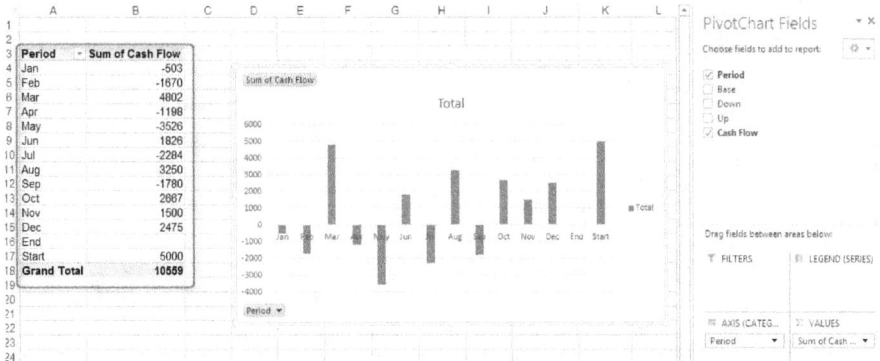

After loading that in Power Query, you will see the Pivot Table the same (without formatting);

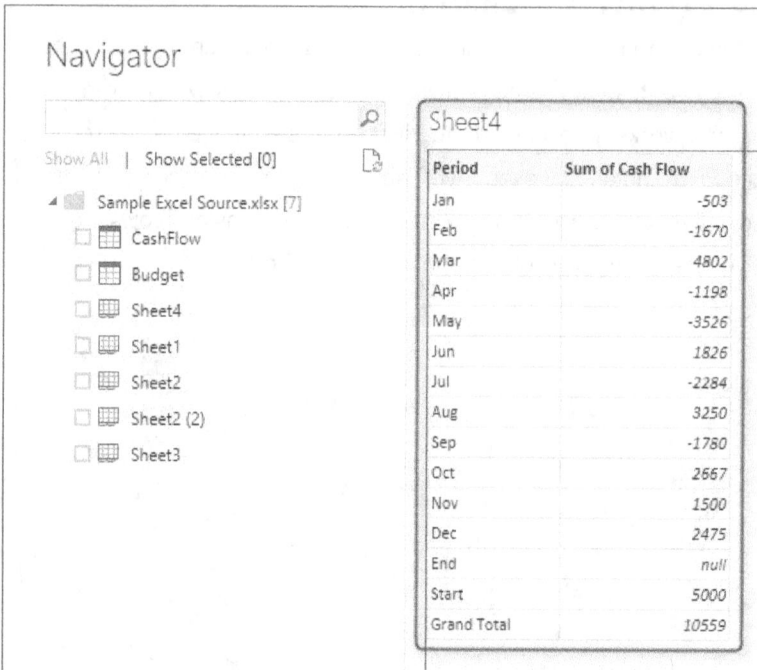

What If Your Excel Table Has Merged Cells?

Merged Cells in Excel are commonly used. You can have tables with cells merged vertically or horizontally or even both. Here is an example of a table with merged cells;

Period	Service Center	Budget	Total Budget
1/1	IT	100000	600000
	Finance	500000	
2/1	IT	150000	600000
	Finance	450000	
3/1	IT	170000	570000
	Finance	400000	
4/1	IT	200000	600000
	Finance	400000	

Power Query still reads cells in their original detailed format. It means merged cells won't be merged in Power Query; they will be seen as separate cells.

You can use transformations such as Fill Down to fill null values in the remaining cells of merged cells later on. Also, note in the above screenshot that the green highlighted column is a calculated column. This calculated value will be fetched in Power Query as static values.

Example Excel Data Source: Olympic Games

I've found a list of all medalists in Olympic games from the very first game (1896) till 2008 (unfortunately 2012 London games are not included in this data set). This is, fortunately, a public list made available by The Guardian, that you can download here. The list is well structured with the main sheet for all medalists as below;

As you see in the above sheet, all medalists with their main sports category and discipline and detailed event are available. Name of Athletes and their gender and Medals as well as the Olympic game (year) all are listed. Countries information listed as three character code. These three-character codes are available as a reference in another sheet of the file named IOC Country Codes as below;

Country	Int Olympic	ISO code	Country
Afghanistan	AFG	AF	Afghanistan
Albania	ALB	AL	Albania
Algeria	ALG	DZ	Algeria
American Samoa*	ASA	AS	American Samoa*
Andorra	AND	AD	Andorra
Angola	ANG	AO	Angola
Antigua and Barbuda	ANT	AG	Antigua and Barbuda
Argentina	ARG	AR	Argentina
Armenia	ARM	AM	Armenia
Aruba*	ARU	AW	Aruba*
Australia	AUS	AU	Australia
Austria	AUT	AT	Austria
Azerbaijan	AZE	AZ	Azerbaijan
Bahamas	BAH	BS	Bahamas
Bahrain	BRN	BH	Bahrain
Bangladesh	BAN	BD	Bangladesh
Barbados	BAR	BB	Barbados

Data is well structured and loading it into Power BI would be just matter of seconds! Start getting this information by getting Data From Excel and then address the downloaded Excel file. In Navigator dialog box choose All Medalists and IOC Country Codes sheets both to be checked. Also, note that All Medalists sheet's data shows in non-merged cell style (as you've learned earlier in this section; merged cells will be un-merged in Power Query). After selecting these two sheets click on Edit.

There are just a few changes that we need to make;

Remove Rows

All Medalists query contains four heading rows which we don't need them (it is just title and disclaimer) so better to remove those;

Go to All Medalists query and then click on Remove Rows in the Home menu.
From the "Remove Rows" popup menu, choose Remove Top Rows

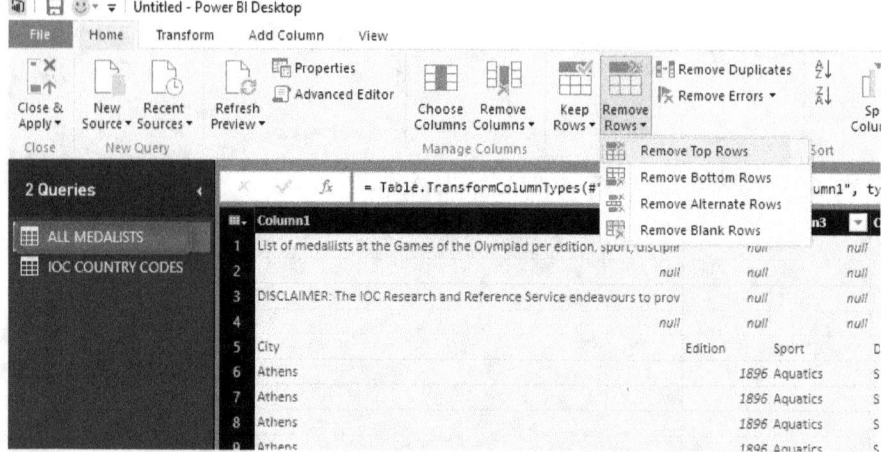

Remove Top 4 Rows in the dialog box by entering 4. and the result will look like below;

Use First Row As Headers

Headers of the query as you see in the screenshot above are Column1, Column2…. Fortunately, in the data set, the first row contains column headers. We can simply set that to be used for column headers in Power Query. in the Home tab click on Use First Row As Headers.

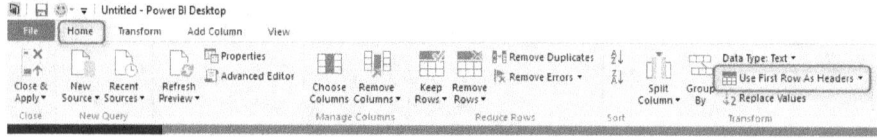

Dataset will look like the screenshot below after above change

City	Edition	Sport	Discipline	Athlete	NOC	Gender	Event	Event_gender	Medal
Athens	1896	Aquatics	Swimming	HAJOS, Alfred	HUN	Men	100m freestyle	M	Gold
Athens	1896	Aquatics	Swimming	HERSCHMANN, Otto	AUT	Men	100m freestyle	M	Silver
Athens	1896	Aquatics	Swimming	DRIVAS, Dimitrios	GRE	Men	100m freestyle for sailors	M	Bronze
Athens	1896	Aquatics	Swimming	MALOKINIS, Ioannis	GRE	Men	100m freestyle for sailors	M	Gold
Athens	1896	Aquatics	Swimming	CHASAPIS, Spiridon	GRE	Men	100m freestyle for sailors	M	Silver
Athens	1896	Aquatics	Swimming	CHOROPHAS, Efstathios	GRE	Men	1200m freestyle	M	Bronze
Athens	1896	Aquatics	Swimming	HAJOS, Alfred	HUN	Men	1200m freestyle	M	Gold
Athens	1896	Aquatics	Swimming	ANDREOU, Ioannis	GRE	Men	1200m freestyle	M	Silver
Athens	1896	Aquatics	Swimming	CHOROPHAS, Efstathios	GRE	Men	400m freestyle	M	Bronze
Athens	1896	Aquatics	Swimming	NEUMANN, Paul	AUT	Men	400m freestyle	M	Gold
Athens	1896	Aquatics	Swimming	PEPANOS, Antonios	GRE	Men	400m freestyle	M	Silver
Athens	1896	Athletics	Athletics	LANE, Francis	USA	Men	100m	M	Bronze
Athens	1896	Athletics	Athletics	SZOKOLYI, Alajos	HUN	Men	100m	M	Bronze
Athens	1896	Athletics	Athletics	BURKE, Thomas	USA	Men	100m	M	Gold
Athens	1896	Athletics	Athletics	HOFMANN, Fritz	GER	Men	100m	M	Silver
Athens	1896	Athletics	Athletics	CURTIS, Thomas	USA	Men	110m hurdles	M	Gold

For IOC Country Codes query just set the first row as headers. No more changes are required

Close and Load

After above changes, we can now load the result set into the Power BI model to build report for it. You can simply click on Close and Apply menu button in Home Tab

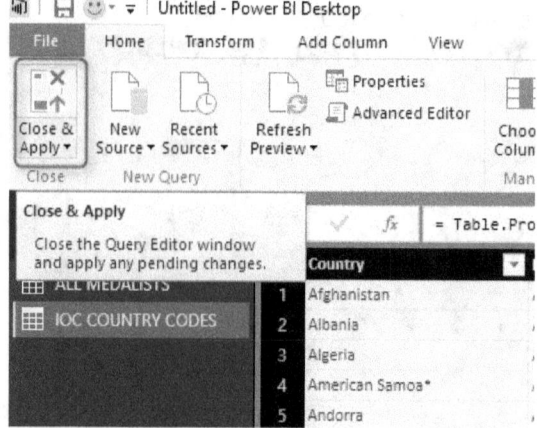

Power BI will load result sets into memory for further modeling and reporting.

A bit of Modeling

This section is not about data modeling. However, I want you to be able to play with this data set and build some nice reports with it (if you can't wait till modeling and visualization chapters of this book). So Let's create the relationship between All medalists and IOC Country Code. For doing this go to Relationship tab in Power BI Desktop and then click on Manage Relationship. Then create a new relationship as below;

Create Relationship

Select tables and columns that relate to one another.

ALL MEDALISTS

City	Edition	Sport	Discipline	Athlete	NOC	Gender	Event	Event_gender
London	1908	Athletics	Athletics	CARTMELL, John Nathaniel	USA	Men	4x400m relay	M
London	1908	Athletics	Athletics	HAMILTON, William Frank	USA	Men	4x400m relay	M
London	1908	Athletics	Athletics	SHEPPARD, Melvin	USA	Men	4x400m relay	M
London	1908	Athletics	Athletics	TAYLOR, John Baxter	USA	Men	4x400m relay	M
Stockholm	1912	Athletics	Athletics	LINDBERG, Edward F.	USA	Men	4x400m relay	M

IOC COUNTRY CODES

Country	Int Olympic Committee code	ISO code	Country_1
Afghanistan	AFG	AF	Afghanistan
Albania	ALB	AL	Albania
Algeria	ALG	DZ	Algeria
American Samoa*	ASA	AS	American Samoa*
Andorra	AND	AD	Andorra

▲ Advanced options

Cardinality
Many to One (*:1)

Cross filter direction
Single

✓ Make this relationship active

OK   Cancel

After the relationship has been created, you will see it in the relationship diagram

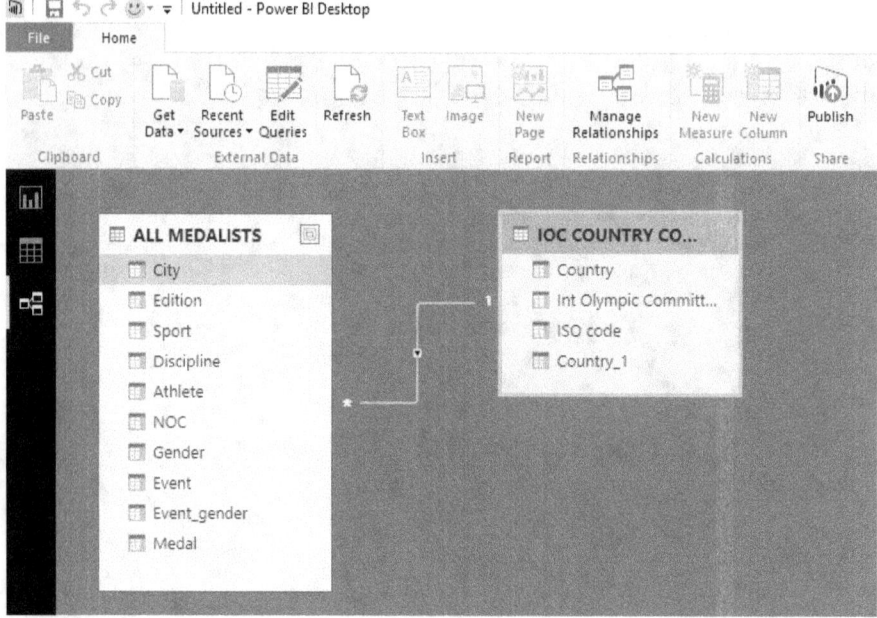

Play Time!

Now it's your turn to play with this data set and make some nice reports and visualization items. Here is what I've built with this data set:

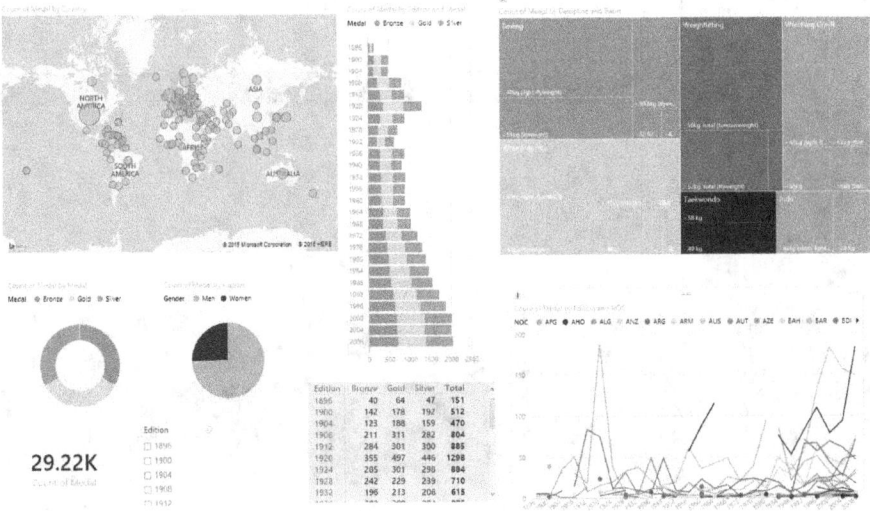

Don't be panic if you can't build report above. I will go through step by step process of building this report later in the Reporting Chapters.

Summary

In this section, you've learned some tips of working with Excel Data source from Power Query or Power BI Desktop. You've learned that merged cells would be loaded into Power Query Un-merged. Formatting won't be considered at the time of loading data into Power Query, and Power Query can load data from Pivot Tables, Excel Tables, and Sheets. You've also learned a real-world example of fetching Olympic medalists data from Excel file into Power BI Desktop. In next sections, I will get you through the journey of Getting data from some other data sources.

Power BI Get Data: From Azure SQL Database

Posted by Reza Rad on Sep 12, 2015

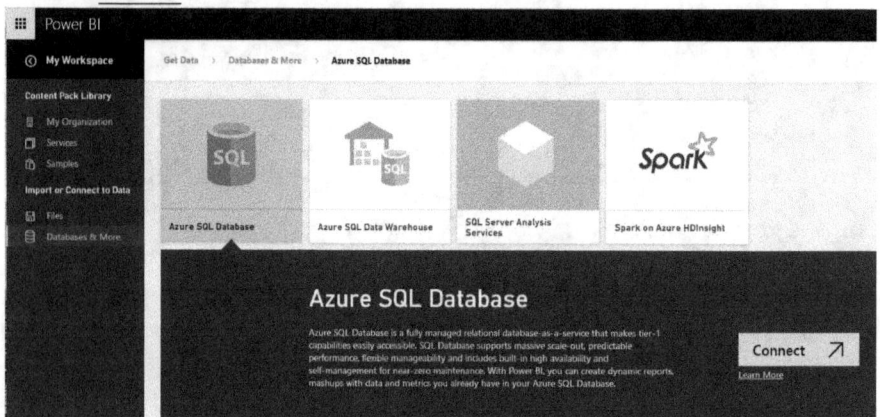

Power BI and Power Query can connect to files such as Excel, CSV, text files and on-premises databases such as SQL Server, Oracle, MySQL. Power BI can connect to many data sources on the cloud such as Azure SQL Database, Azure SQL Data Warehouse, etc. In this part, you will learn how to connect from Power BI Desktop to Azure SQL Database. There is also a way of connecting to Azure SQL Database with a direct connection from the Power BI website which will be explored in this section as well. You will also learn how you can schedule your report to refresh data loaded from Azure SQL DB. So, In general, you should expect to learn everything related to Power BI relation to Azure SQL Database in this section.

In this section you will learn;

- How to connect from Power BI Desktop to Azure SQL Database
- Schedule Power BI for refreshing data from Azure SQL Database
- Direct Connection to Azure SQL Database from Power BI Website

Preparation

For this section, you need an Azure SQL Database. I use AdveutureWorksLT example; this is the sample database in Azure SQL Database templates that you can easily install and configure. If you have this database set up on Azure, then you can skip this step. For creating an Azure SQL Database for AdventureWorksLT database follow below steps; **Do you need an Azure subscription to run this experiment?** Yes, but don't worry if you don't have it. You can have an Azure subscription free for 25 days with 200$ free credit for you to use, use the trial version. You can start the trial version by following this URL:

https://azure.microsoft.com/en-us/pricing/free-trial/

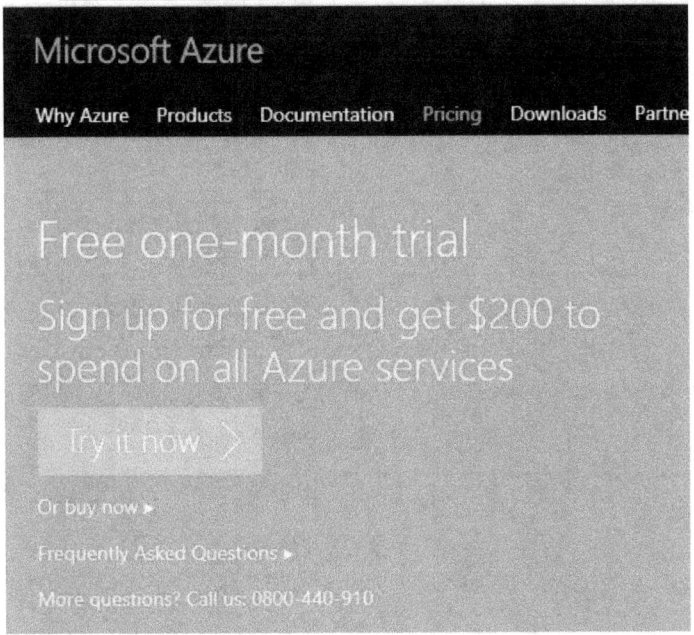

After setting up your Azure Account, go to Azure Portal. I have to mention here that there are two versions of the management portal for Azure. The new

Azure portal which is tablet friendly, with a newer and better look and feels, and the old management portal. Screenshots and steps described in this example all have been done in the new Azure Portal. You can go to the Azure portal by using this URL: https://portal.azure.com

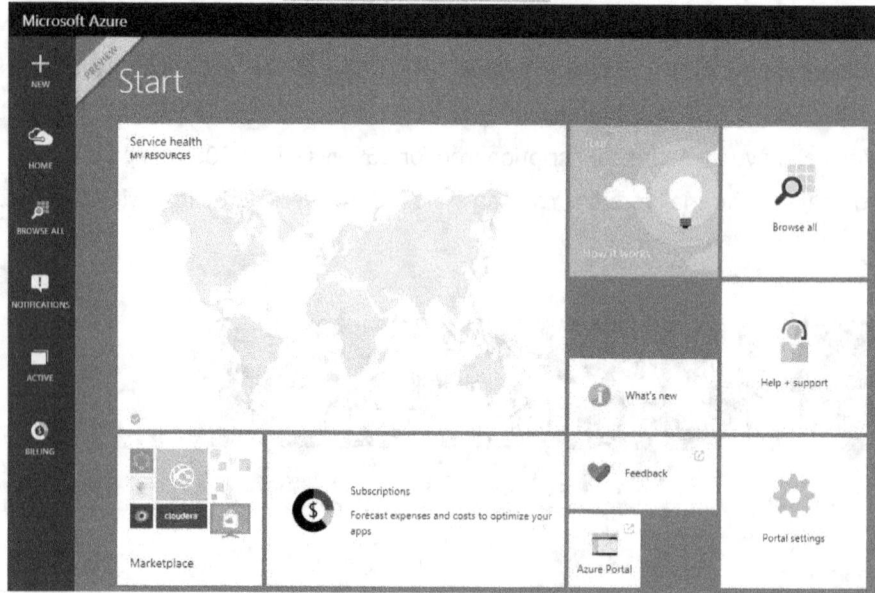

You can manage your Azure services in the management portal by creating new services, editing existing services. Talking about Azure services is out of scope for this example, and you need to read books on that topic. However, for this example let's smoothly continue steps to create an Azure SQL Database. Click on New on the top left side and then under Data + Storage choose SQL Database

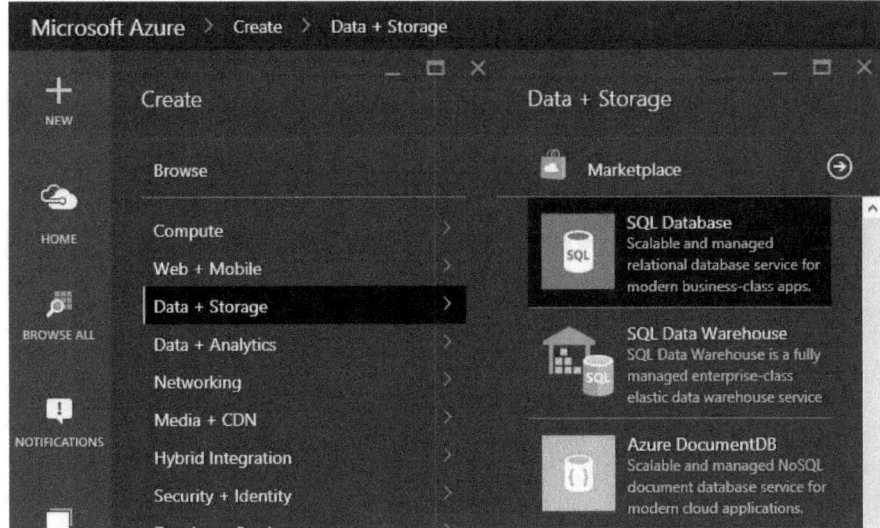

In the SQL Database Create pane, name the database as AdventureWorks LT. You have to choose the server also. The server is like a SQL Server instance that this database will be hosted on that. You can choose from an existing server, or you can create a new Server.

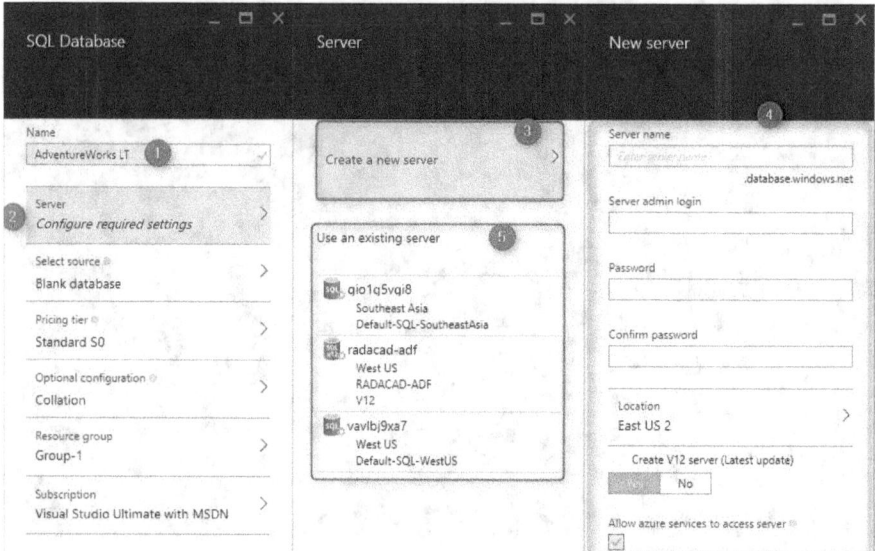

As you can see in the screenshot above, after going to Configure required Settings for the Server, you can choose to create a new server (numbered 3), which will redirect you to a new pane for setting up the server (numbered 4). or you can choose an existing server (numbered 5).

After setting up the server, you have to select the source for the database. For this example choose Sample. After choosing sample, you will see the Select Sample option below appears.

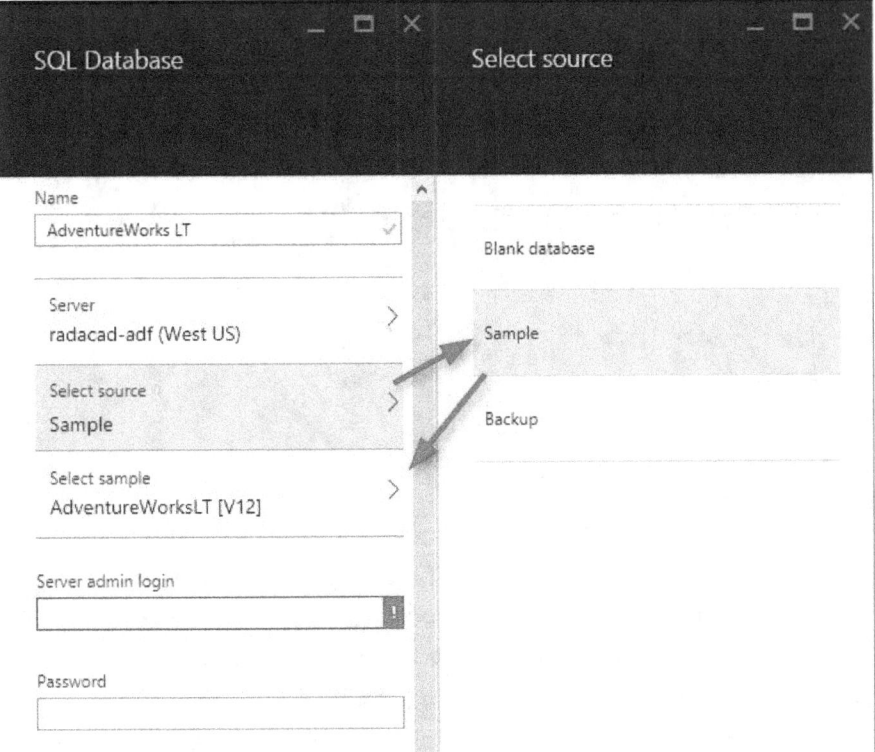

Choose the sample as AdventureWorksLT [V12], and then type in the server admin login and password (you have defined that when you set up the Server)

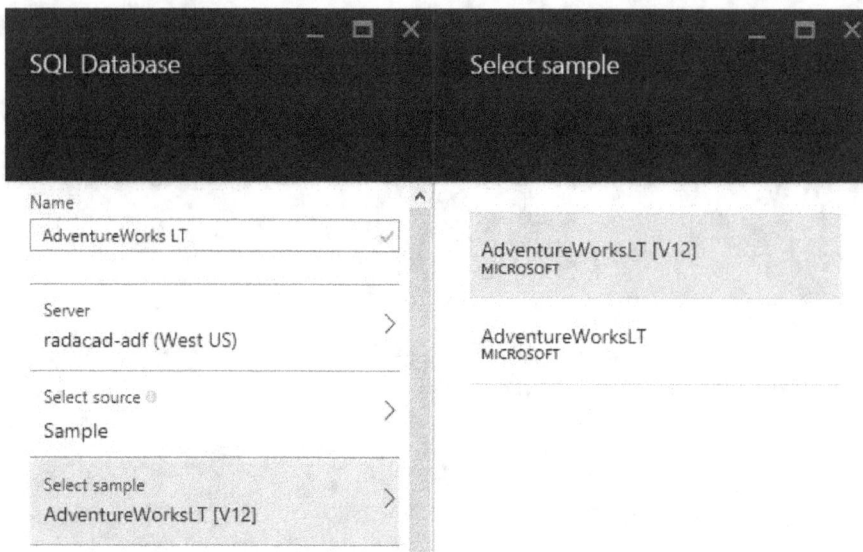

You have also to choose a pricing tier, and resource group. For pricing tier use one of the tiers (you can better choose yourself), and then for the resource group you can choose an existing one or create a new. A resource group is a grouping for Azure services; you can have a resource group and add all related azure services under that. For example, you can have a resource group for Power BI Online Book and create all examples of this book under that. Please note that the resource group name should not have spaces in the name, but it can have dashes.

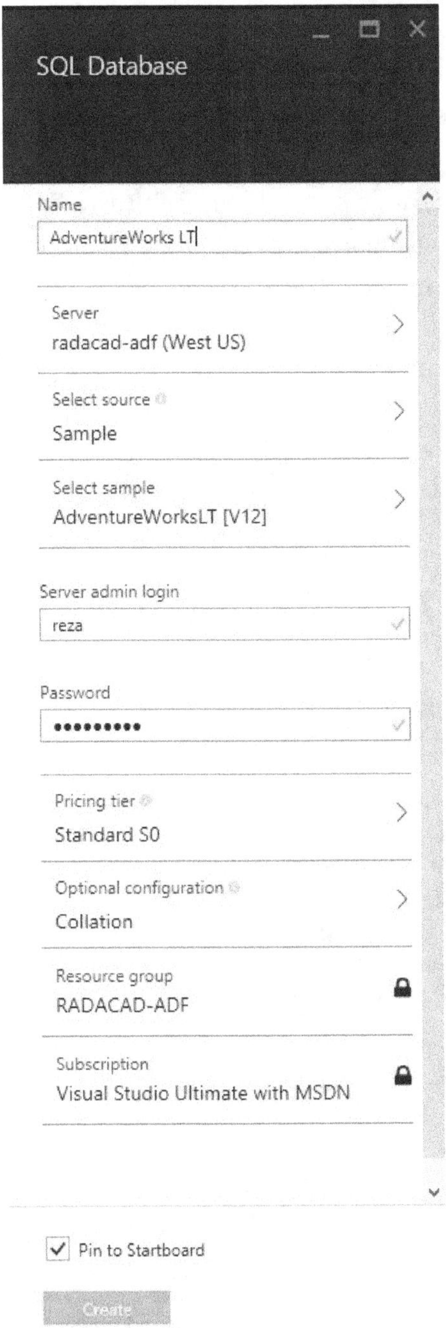

SQL Database

Name
AdventureWorks LT

Server
radacad-adf (West US)

Select source
Sample

Select sample
AdventureWorksLT [V12]

Server admin login
reza

Password
•••••••••

Pricing tier
Standard S0

Optional configuration
Collation

Resource group
RADACAD-ADF

Subscription
Visual Studio Ultimate with MSDN

☑ Pin to Startboard

Create

After all the configuration click on Create, so the SQL DB creates. The tick on the checkbox for the pin to Startboard will bring the SQL DB on the first welcome page (start board) of the Azure Portal. It may take a bit time for the database to be created. After completion of creating database process, you will be redirected to database page in the azure portal (if you didn't, then click on the AdventureWorks LT database on start board to go to its pane). the screenshot below is showing the database created

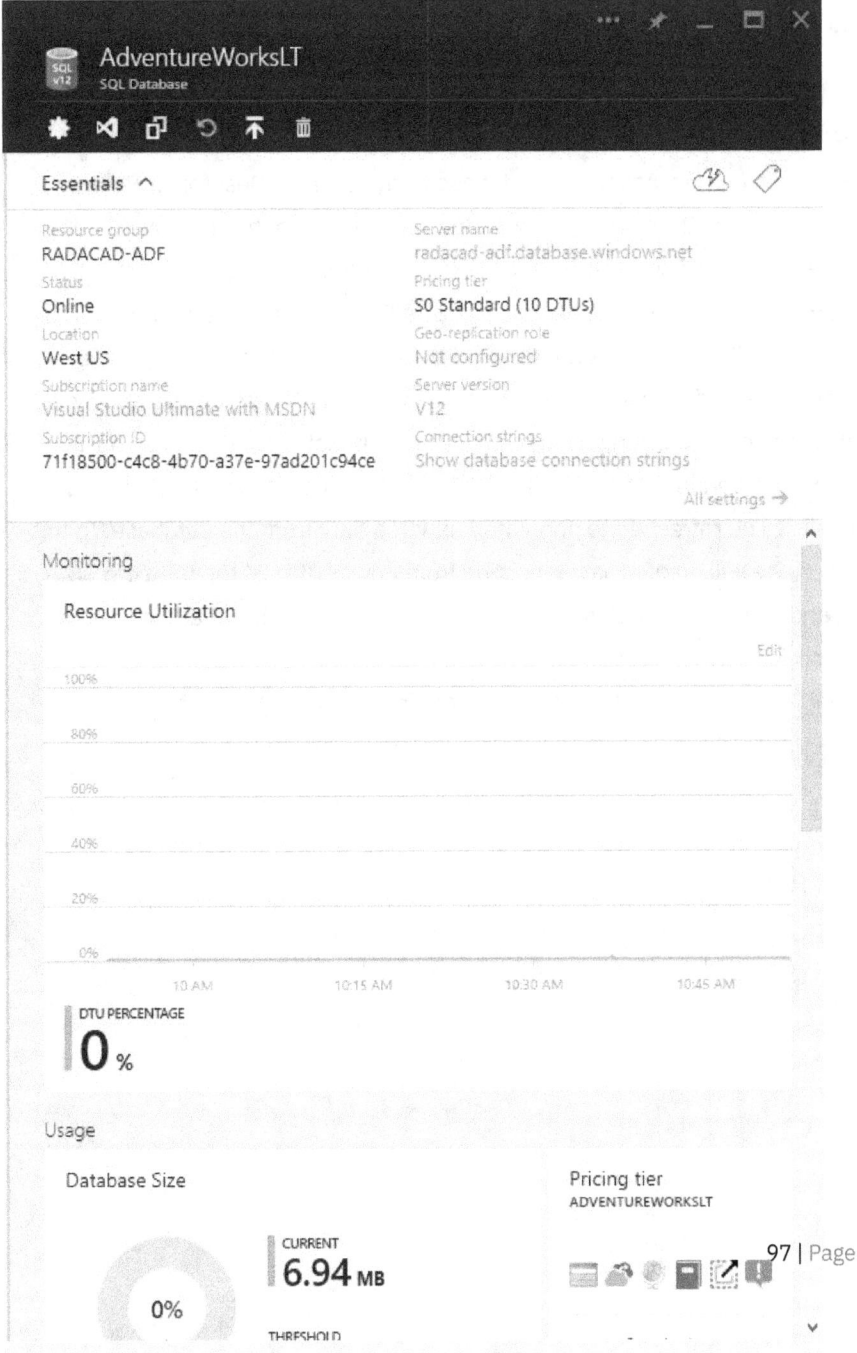

Now you are all set, example database is ready to be used in Power BI.

Get Data From Azure SQL Database

You can connect to Azure SQL Database from Power BI Desktop or Power Query for Excel. Both methods work the same. Let's go through the connection from Power BI Desktop. Before starting steps, I have to mention that Power BI Desktop connection to Azure SQL Database is an off-line connection. The off-line connection here means the data from Azure SQL Database will be loaded into the Power BI model and then reports will use the data in the model, this disconnected way of connection is what I call off-line. The off-line connection to Azure SQL DB can be scheduled in the Power BI website to be refreshed to populated updated data from the database. In this section, we will create the connection from Power BI Desktop to Azure SQL DB, and in the next section following you will learn how to schedule the data refresh.

Open the Power BI Desktop and Get Data from Azure SQL Database

In Power Query for Excel, you can also follow the path mentioned in the screenshot below

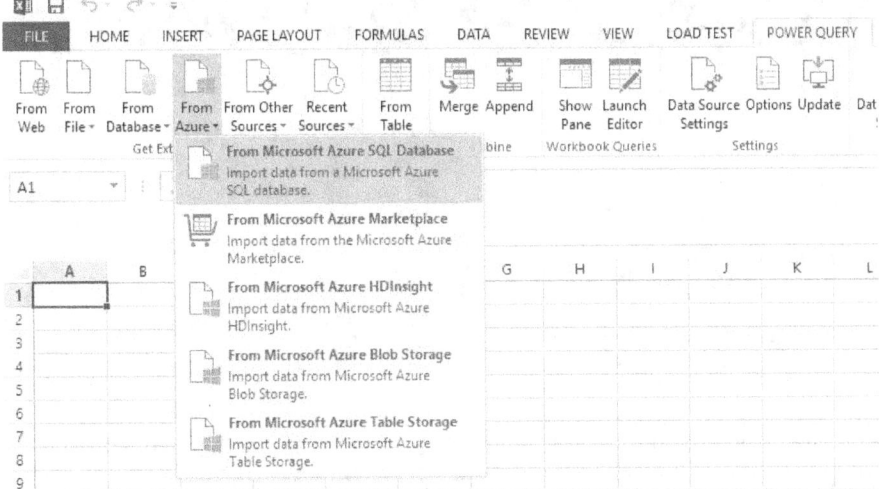

You need to enter the server name in SQL Server Database dialog box. Remember that you've set up the server when you created Azure SQL DB. If you don't know what the server for your database is, simply find it through Azure portal under the Azure SQL DB pane;

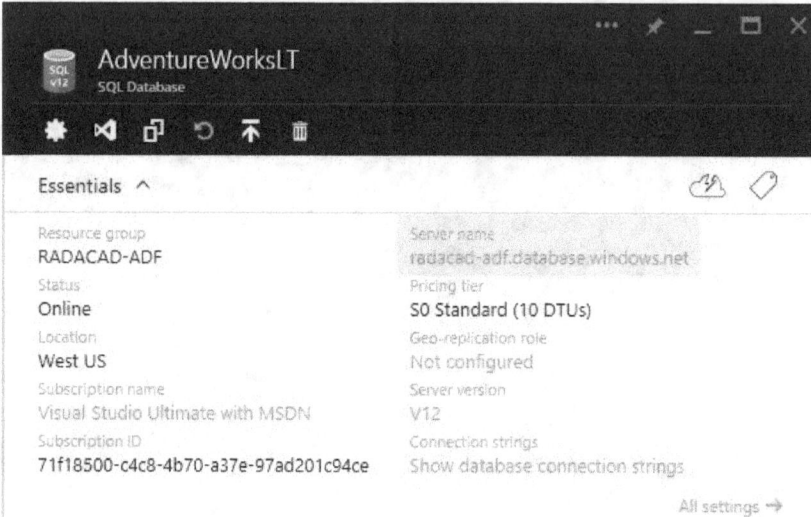

Type in the server name in SQL Server Database dialog box in Power BI Desktop. And type in the database as AdventureWorks LT. Leave the SQL statement as is. then press OK

It is very likely that you get to the window that says Unable to Connect. This window is saying that Power BI Desktop cannot connect to Azure SQL DB and the reason is that the Azure SQL Server didn't allow your IP address to pass through its firewall. I have to mention that Azure SQL Server by default doesn't allow external IP addresses to connect to it. If you want to connect to any databases on Azure SQL Server, you have to allow the IP of that machine to pass through. This is not your internal network IP; this is the IP that your internet connection has. You can find the IP easily. It is mentioned in Unable to Connect error message below!

We encountered an error while trying to connect to "…..". Details: Microsoft SQL: Cannot open server'…' Requested by the login. A client with IP address'210.246.15.145' is not allowed to access the server. To enable access, use the Windows Azure Management Portal or run sp_set_firewall_rule on the master database to create a firewall rule for this IP address or address range. It may take up to five minutes for this change to take effect."

So Let's add the IP in firewall pass list. Go to Azure Portal again. if you closed it, open it again, go to Browse All, then Choose SQL Databases, then choose AdventureWorksLT database in the list, and then click on the server name of it to open the Azure SQL Server administration pane

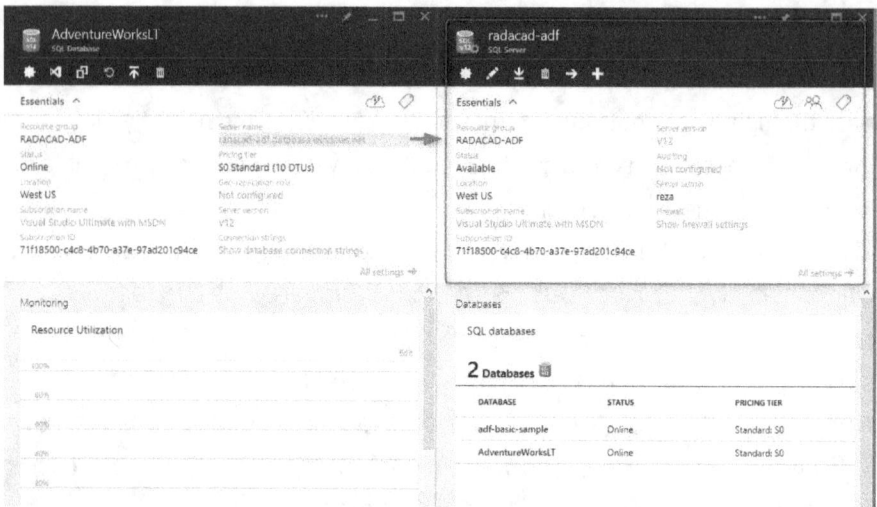

Click on Show firewall settings. In the Firewall Settings pane, enter the new IP as a rule, and then save it.

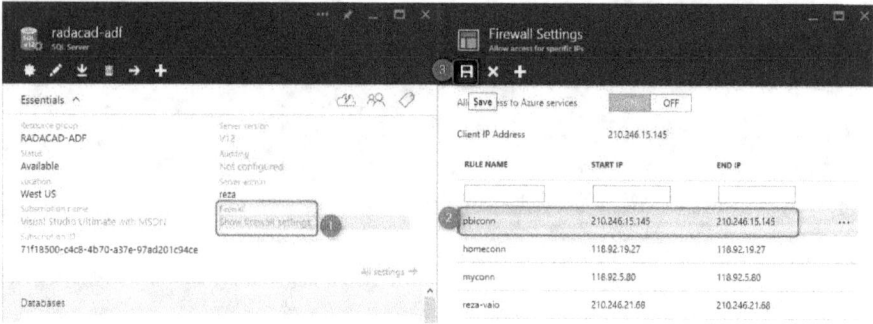

Now you can try again to connect from Power BI Desktop (if you get that error again, wait for few minutes and try again. Sometimes it takes few minutes for changes to take effect). After a successful connection, you should be able to see Navigator dialog box with the structure of AdventureWorksLT database

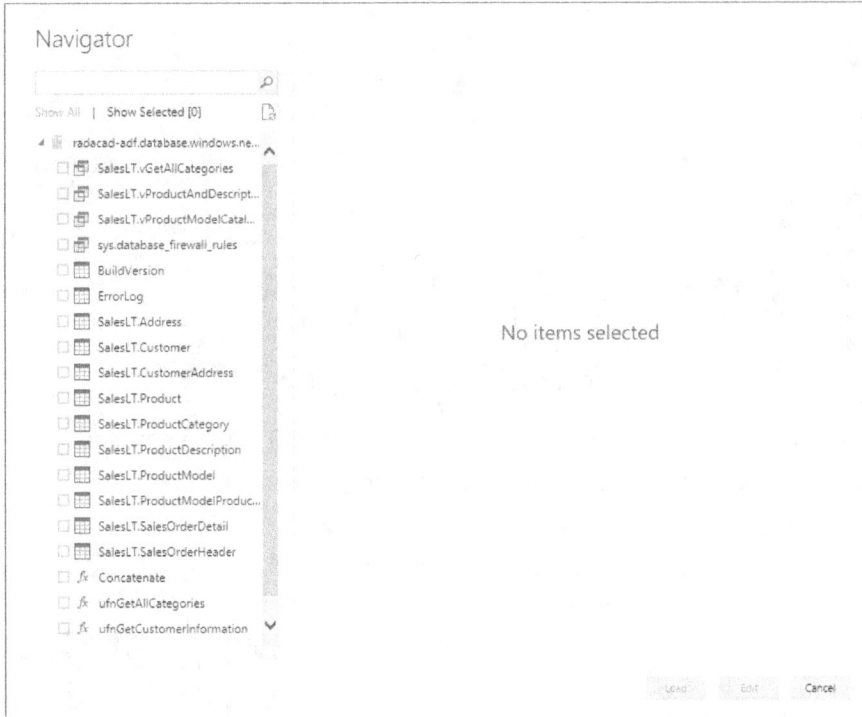

As you can see in the navigator all views, tables and functions will be listed. You can choose multiple objects and then continue editing them in the Edit Queries or Power Query Editor window. For this example, I've chosen these tables: Customer, Product, ProductCategory, ProductModel, SalesOrderDetail, and SalesOrderHeader.

You can then choose these tables with their fields to be used for building a report without any modification in Power Query or Data tab. You can even see that Power BI and Power Query understand the relationship in Azure SQL Database and load the same relationship in the Power BI model.

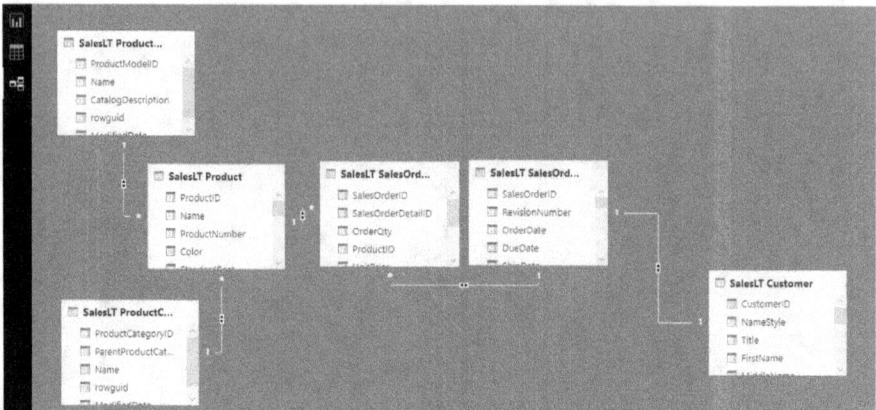

This section is still one of the early chapters of Power BI online book, and I don't want to discuss visualization and modeling. However for this example, I've built a simple chart, the chart is a clustered column chart with Color (from Product table) as Axis, and SalesPerson (from Customer) as Legend, and OrderQty (from SalesOderDetail) as Value.

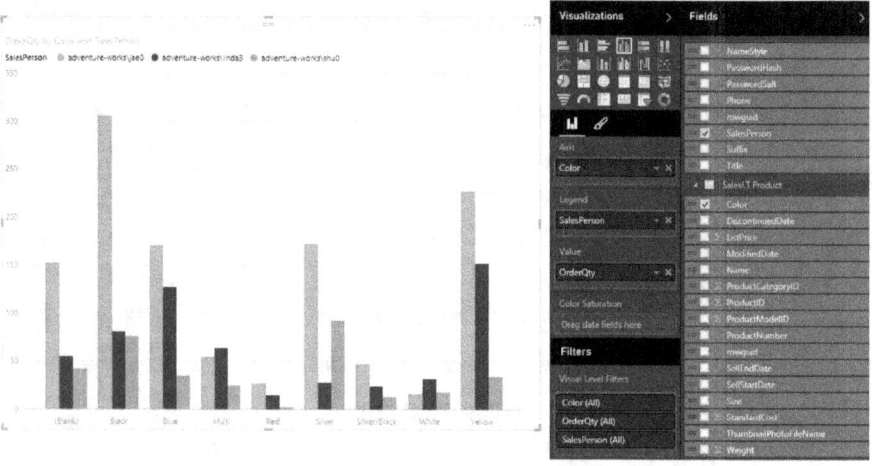

The chart is simple, but still revealing something interesting. Jae0 made the most sales, however color wise each sales person did the best in a specific color. shu0 was best at Yellow. lina3 at Silver, and Jae0 at Black. Now you can publish your report into Power BI website with the Publish menu option. After publishing the report, you would be able to see that under your Power BI account in the website.

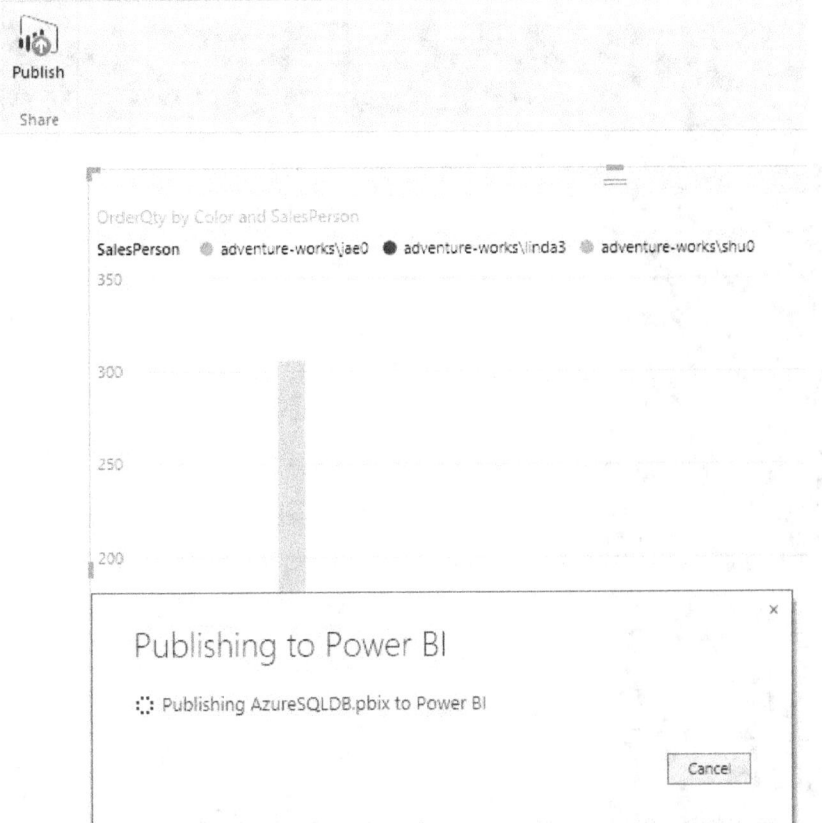

Schedule Data Refresh

In Power BI website you can set up scheduled data refresh for data sets, but not all datasets support this feature. Fortunately, Azure SQL Database supports it. To find out the list of all data sets that support data refresh read this link. To schedule, a refresh in Power BI website, under Datasets click on ellipsis besides the data source that you want. And then choose Schedule Refresh.

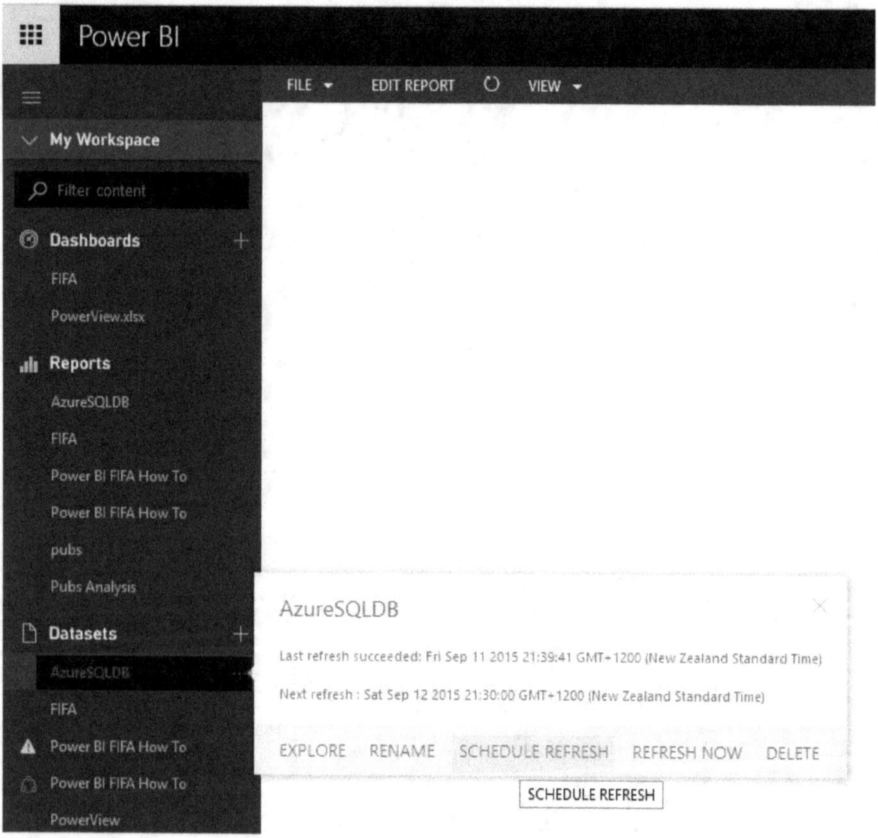

Set the Data Source Credentials for Azure SQL Database

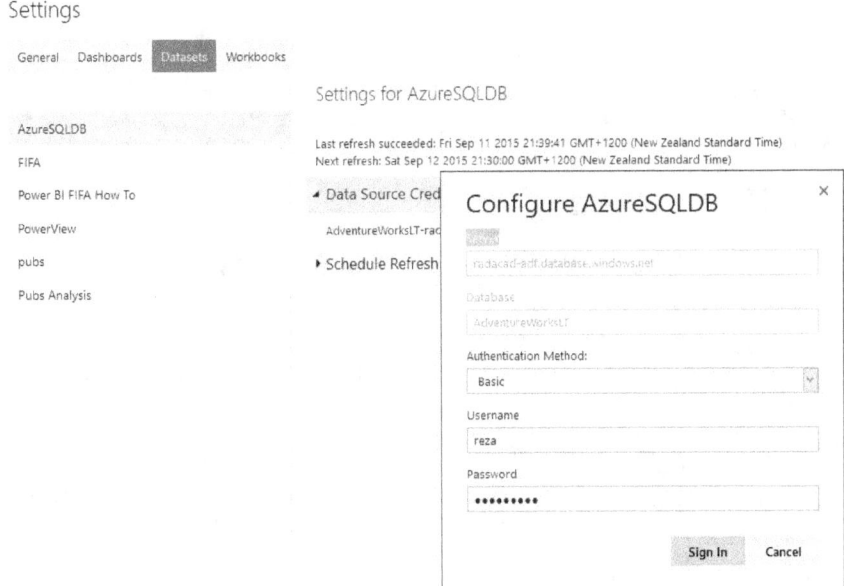

And then you can schedule refresh. You can choose the frequency to be daily or weekly. And you can add multiple times on the day under that.

Settings for AzureSQLDB

Last refresh succeeded: Fri Sep 11 2015 21:39:41 GMT+1200 (New Zealand Standard Time)
Next refresh: Sat Sep 12 2015 21:30:00 GMT+1200 (New Zealand Standard Time)

▲ Data Source Credentials

AdventureWorksLT-radacad-adf.database.windows.net   Edit credentials

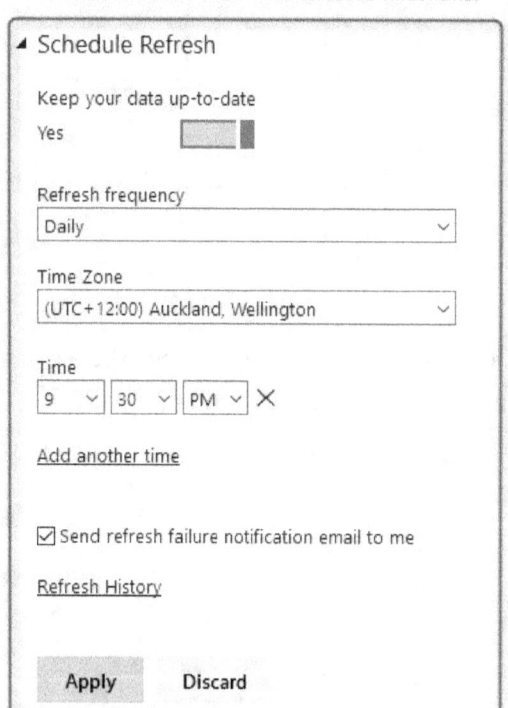

If you have a scheduled refresh set up for a while, then you can see the history of a refresh as well

Refresh History

Details	Type	Start	End	Status	Fail Message
	Scheduled	9/11/2015, 9:39:01 PM	9/11/2015, 9:39:41 PM	Completed	
	Scheduled	9/10/2015, 9:40:00 PM	9/10/2015, 9:40:32 PM	Completed	
	Scheduled	9/9/2015, 9:42:03 PM	9/9/2015, 9:42:28 PM	Completed	
	Scheduled	9/8/2015, 9:43:01 PM	9/8/2015, 9:43:28 PM	Completed	
	Scheduled	9/7/2015, 9:44:00 PM	9/7/2015, 9:44:29 PM	Completed	
	Scheduled	9/6/2015, 9:35:05 PM	9/6/2015, 9:35:46 PM	Completed	
	Scheduled	9/5/2015, 9:35:02 PM	9/5/2015, 9:35:30 PM	Completed	
	Scheduled	9/4/2015, 9:45:02 PM	9/4/2015, 9:45:33 PM	Completed	
	Scheduled	9/3/2015, 9:45:04 PM	9/3/2015, 9:45:57 PM	Completed	
	Scheduled	9/2/2015, 9:31:00 PM	9/2/2015, 9:31:34 PM	Completed	

After setting up the schedule refresh, you can see the latest refresh and the next refresh information easily with ellipsis button on the dataset

Direct Connection to Azure SQL Database from Power BI Website

So far you've learned how to connect from Power BI Desktop or Power Query to Azure SQL database. However, the connection in that way is off-line, and you need to set up a scheduled refresh to keep data up-to-date. Fortunately, there is another way of connection which is Direct Connection. The direct connection won't load data into Power BI model, it directly brings data into the report, and you won't need to schedule refresh anymore, because data is always up-to-date. There will be however a lag for loading the report depends on the data and volume required loaded in the report.

You can set Direct connection only from Power BI website at the moment. And this is one of Power BI Pro features, so you need to buy the pro plan (which costs 9.99$ per user per month at the moment). To set a direct connection, click on Get Data in Power BI website. you will be redirected to Get Data Page

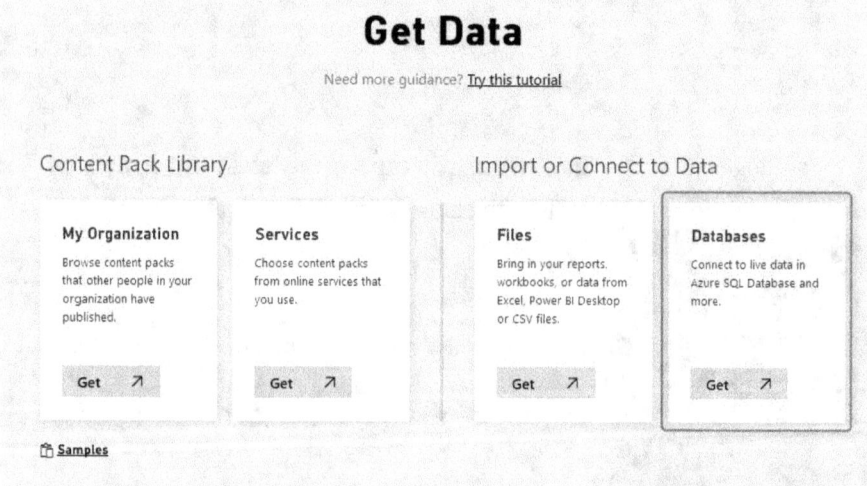

Click on the Get option from Databases. You can see that some databases are supported through this type of connection; Azure SQL Database, Azure SQL Data Warehouse, SQL Server Analysis Services, and Spark on Azure HDInsight. Click on Azure SQL Database and then Connect.

Set the connection information such as the server, database name, and user and password

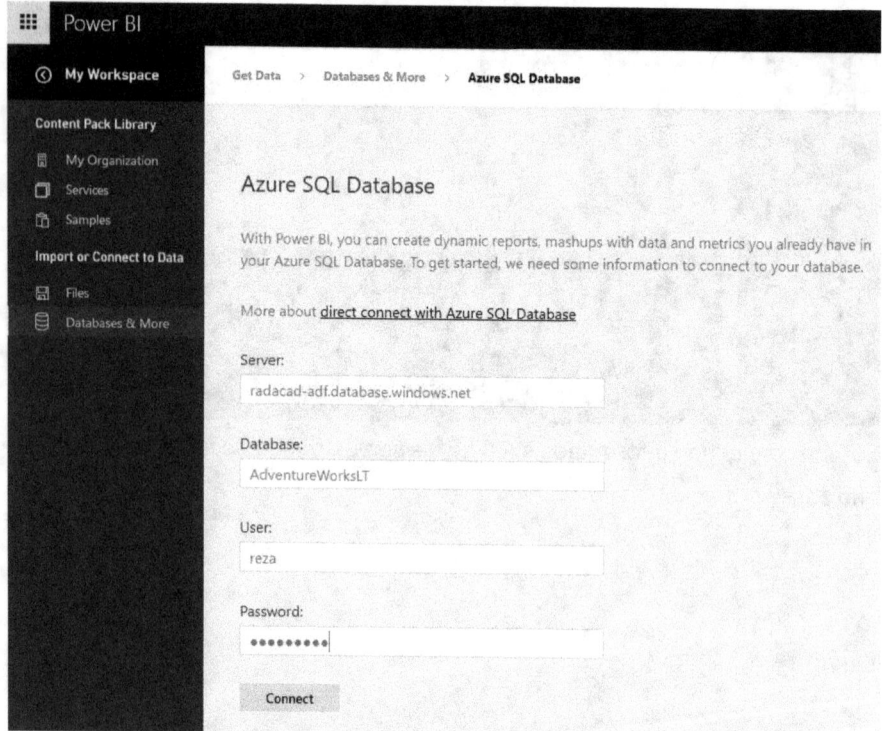

After creating the connection, you will see Azure SQL Database in your dashboard and also the dataset in the list of datasets.

by click on any of these items, you will be redirected to online Power BI report designer. You can see that all tables and views now are listed in the Fields pane, and ready for you to build reports from them.

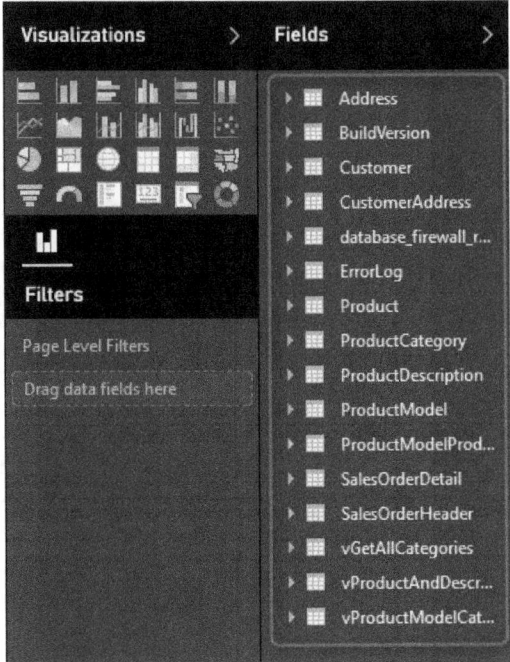

Summary

In this lesson, you've learned how to the connection from Power BI Desktop or Power Query in Excel to Azure SQL Database. You've also learned some basics about Azure SQL Database settings in Azure Portal. Then you've learned that you need to set firewall in Azure Portal for the server to pass your IP for connections. You then learned how you could set scheduled refresh for the data in Power BI website. At the last section, you've learned that you can create a direct connection from Power BI website to Azure SQL Database that doesn't load data into a model and works online with the data. In the next sections of this chapter, you will learn about other data sources that you can connect from Power BI.

Meetup Data Source for Power BI

Posted by Reza Rad on Jun 2, 2016

There are many SaaS (Software as a Service) data sources for Power BI, such as MailChimp, SalesForce, etc. However I haven't found anything for Meetup. Meetup, on the other hand, is a data source that event organizers such as myself use mostly. In this post, I will be using Meetup API to connect from Power BI Desktop and read the JSON output of Meetup API to build some nice visualizations in Power BI. You can read more about Power Query in Power BI online book from Rookie to Rock Star.

About Meetup

If you haven't heard about Meetup so far; it is a platform for scheduling in-person events. As an organizer, I announce meetings for my Meetup group (such as New Zealand BI user group), and Meetup helps with the registration for the event. As an audience, I can join to groups in my area of interest and be informed about their upcoming meetings and RSVP those to attend or not attend. Meetup website itself gives some useful information to organizers, however, as a Power BI geek, I would love to dig into its data with a better tool.

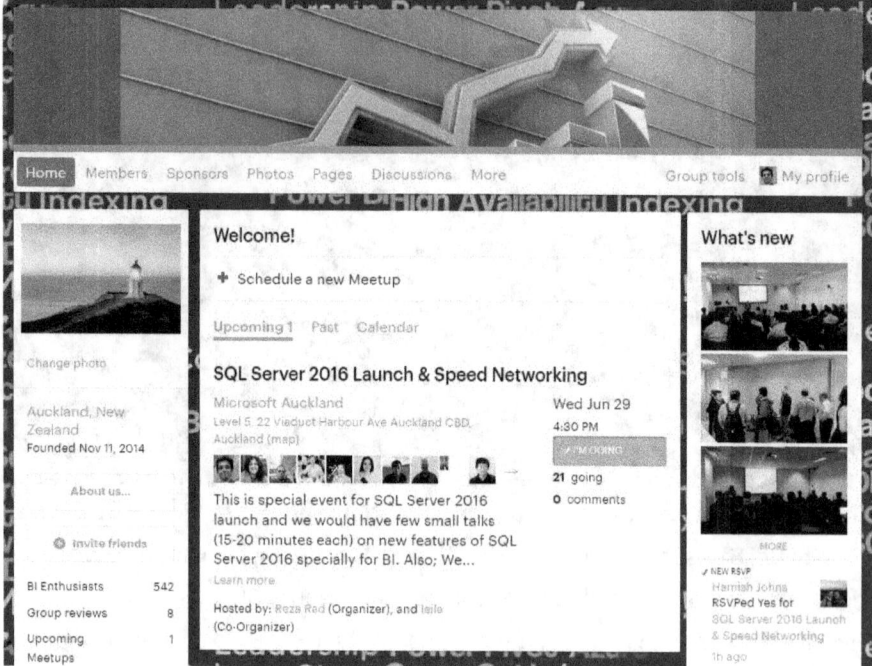

Fortunately, Meetup has a set of API restful services which returns output as JSON format.

Restful service means there are some URLs that I can browse, and it gives me a response in JSON format. First of all, I need to use my API key. API key would be different for anyone, and sorry I cannot share my API key with you, that's why it is blurred in the screenshot below. You can access your API key from here.

Getting an API Key

Hello, Reza Rad, click the lock below to reveal your API key

You'll need to provide this key with every request you make to t[he] you need to reset your key for any reason, you can do that belo[w] with the old key to fail.

Now I can call each service with this key. Fortunately, there is good documentation on each service, input parameters, and output result set here. As an example, if I want to get a list of all meetup events in the past for my group, I can use V2 Events service with input parameters such as URL name of the group, and status to be "past" (means only fetch past meetings);

1 *https://api.meetup.com/2/events?status=past&group_urlname=New-Zealand-Business-Intelligence-User-Group&key=XYZ*

Note that group_urlname of my Meetup group can be easily found on my group web URL:

as per the screenshot above my group URL name is: New-Zealand-Business-Intelligence-User-Group

and you have to use your own API Key instead of XYZ in URL above.

Power BI from Rookie to Rock Star – Book 3: Power Query and Data Transformation in Power BI

So if I browse URL above it gives me a JSON result. JSON is a format for data which usually doesn't have enter or space between fields, so as a result, I would see a big text result like this:

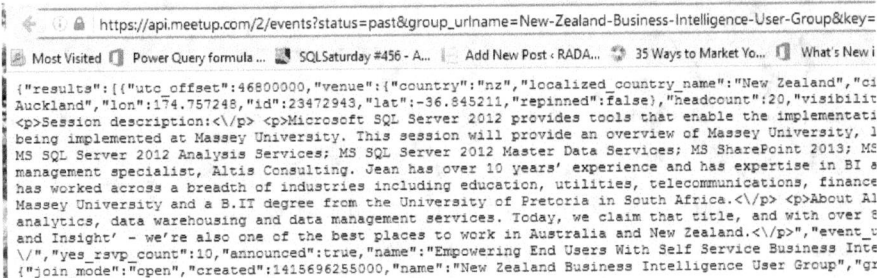

Get Data with Power BI

Now let's browse URL above in Power BI and Power Query to see what can I do with it. I open a Power BI Desktop file and Get Data from the Web. And I enter URL above there (with my API key obviously);

The result of this will show me a record in Power Query editor window with results and meta columns. You can also see in the screenshot below that Power Query uses *JSON.Document* and *Web.Contents* to get JSON result from a web URL.

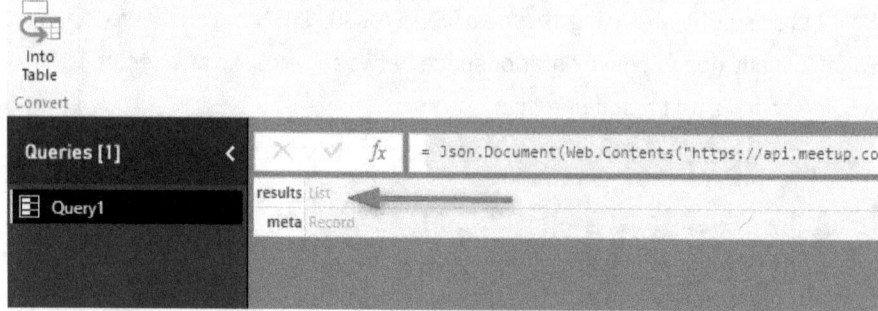

Now click on the results section List to expand that. This will drill down into the list, and you will see a list with multiple items in the next step. This list is a result set in our JSON data. The result set of the URL we run returns a list of events. That means this list is a list of events, and each row in this list is an event. As you can see I have a record in each row. I can convert the main list to the table with first highlighting the whole column, and then click on To Table option from the Transform menu in Power Query.

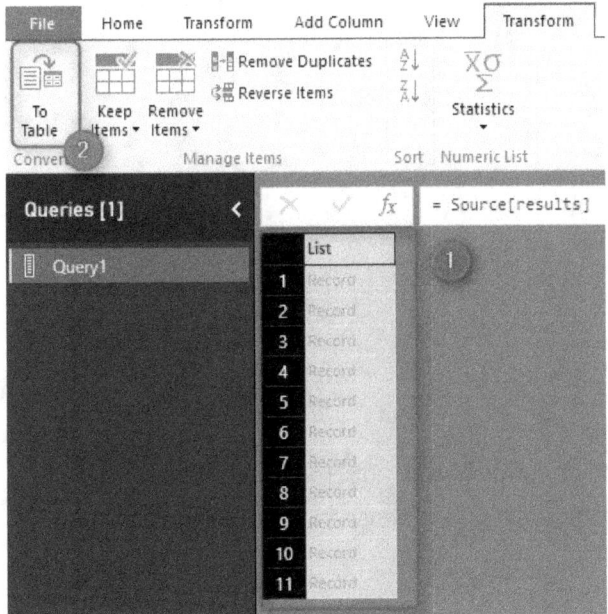

When I click on To Table, I will see To Table dialog box that asks for two configuration options, first one for the delimiter, and a second one for handling extra columns.

I don't do any changes and click on OK with default values. The result now would be a table with a single column, which has a record in each row. I can see the Expand button on my column1 header.

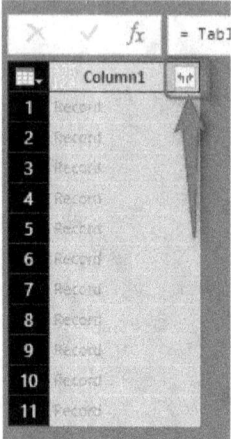

Click on the expand button as mentioned in the screenshot above, and it will list all columns in records and asks me to choose those I want.

Power BI from Rookie to Rock Star – Book 3: Power Query and Data Transformation in Power BI

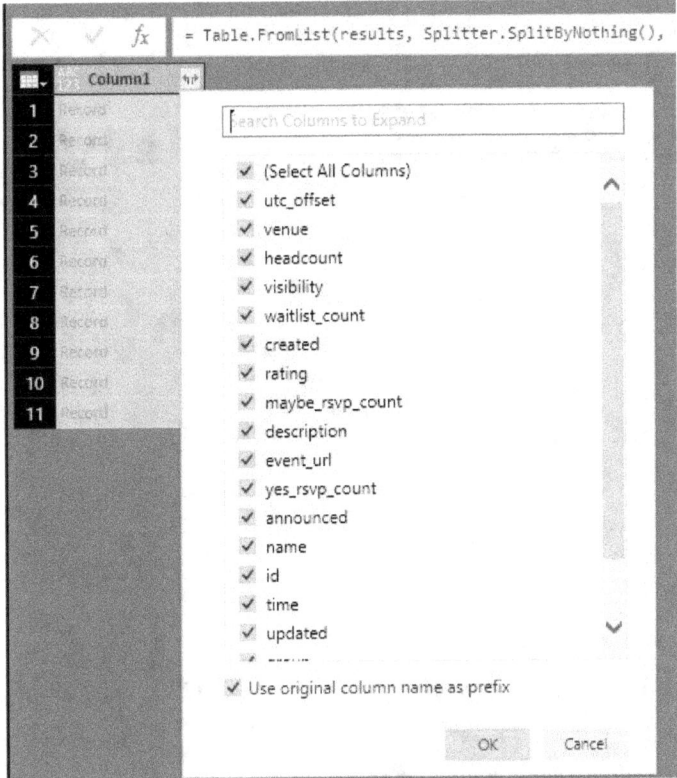

Well let's bring them all to see what we have, so I leave it with select all and click on OK. Here is my result set loaded in Power Query now:

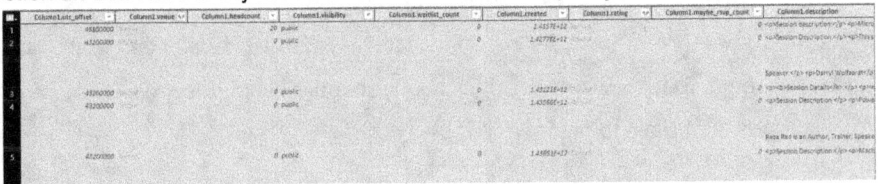

Now I have event information such as Name, Description, venue and other fields. Some values are a record by themselves, such as Venue and Rating. I can expand them if I want to. Let's leave it as is for now. I've loaded my first service result into Power Query. Now one important thing before any other step is to check time value. Because I want to do date/time analysis for my events, so it is important to see if I have my time value fetched. In the screenshot below it shows my Time column as a numeric value.

Column1.name	Column1.id	Column1.time	Column1.updated
Empowering End Users With Self Service Business Intelligence	218612715	1.41698E+12	1.46412E+12
BIML is the shizzle!!	221511579	1.42968E+12	1.42969E+12
Show Me Potential Customers: Data Mining Approach	222422339	1.4327E+12	1.43286E+12
Top 5 Functionalities of Power Query that You Don't Know	223599114	1.43815E+12	1.43816E+12
Be Smarter with Azure Machine Learning	224346643	1.44057E+12	1.44221E+12
SQL Saturday Auckland	224997769	1.44382E+12	1.44391E+12

TimeStamp to Date Time

In the documentation of this service in Meetup mentioned that Time column is:

time = UTC start time of the event, in milliseconds since the epoch

That means it is timestamp formatted. The timestamp value is a number of seconds from epoch which is 1970-01-01 00:00:00. I have previously written about how to change timestamp value to date time, and it is fairly easy with adding seconds to it. However for this case, our value is not seconds, it is milliseconds, so I have to first divide it by 1000.

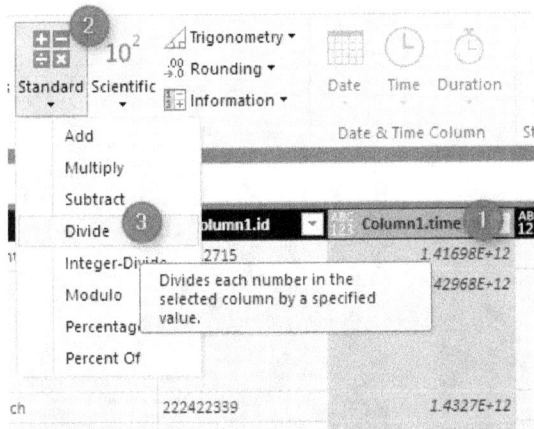

This makes my number smaller now, and I can now feed it into adding a custom column as Event Time as below;

1 #datetime(1970,1,1,0,0,0)+#duration(0,0,0,[Column1.time])

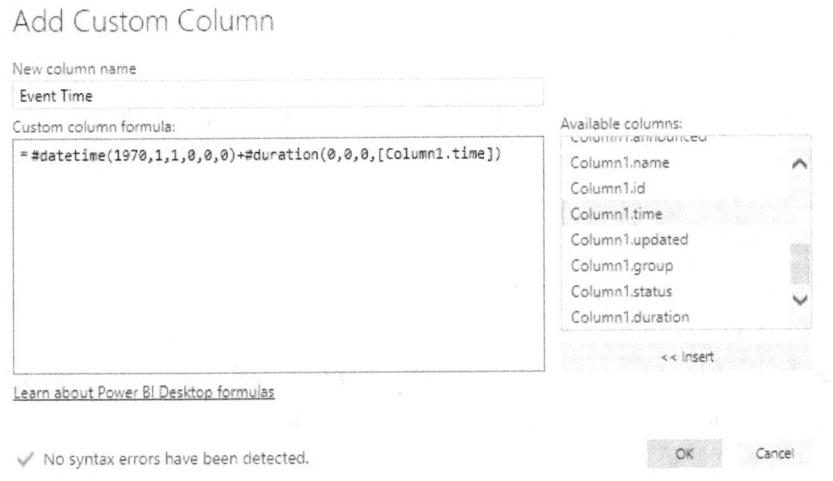

If you want more information about this conversion read my blog post here.
Now this will give me a date-time value as below:

Please note that times are UTC times, We never have meetings 4 AM! I won't be changing UTC time for now, because I want more Month analysis and this is fine for that analysis.

Visualization

Let's visualize what we've got so far. The first step I have to make sure the data type of my column in Power BI model loaded as Date Time. I can go to Data Tab, click on my Event Time column and under Modeling tab check the data type, and if it is text or anything else, change it to Date/Time

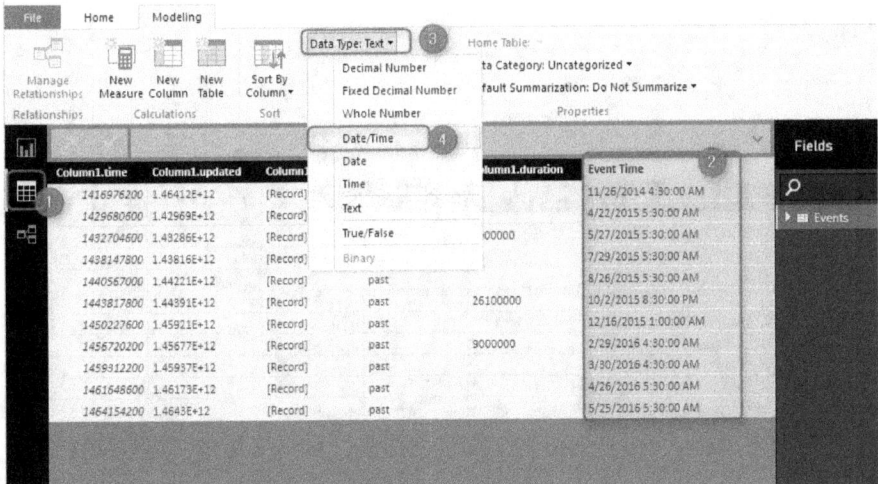

a warning message will be displayed for reports that are already using this field, as I don't have any report elements yet, I'll confirm and continue. I also have to make sure that yes_rsvp_count column (which is showing a number of audience for each session) set as data type whole number. If it is not the case, then I change it to be the whole number as below.

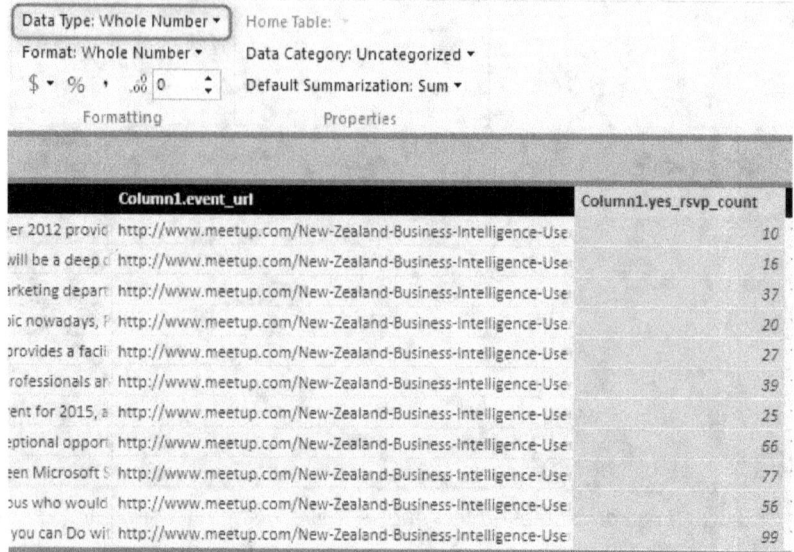

Let's build charts now. I start by an Area Chart to show the Event Time as an Axis (without hierarchy), and yes_rsvp_count as value.

I also apply some formatting and build a chart like this:

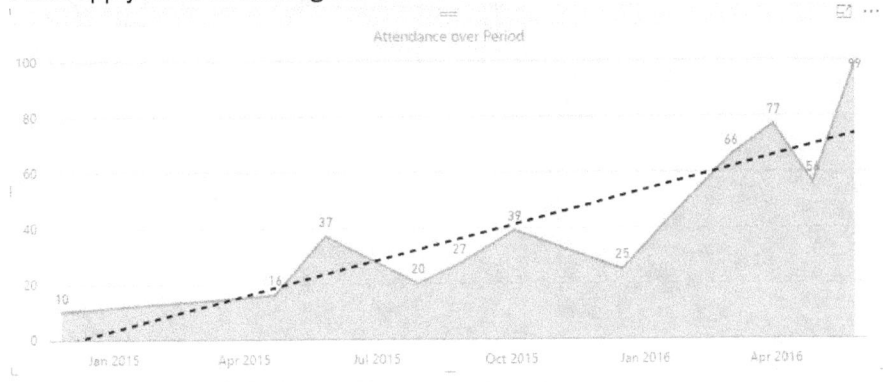

Well, it shows our group is performing well, the number of the audience raised from 10 to 99! and trend line shows that we are progressing better and better. I can build some other visualizations such as bar chart with the name of events and number of RSVP yes as below;

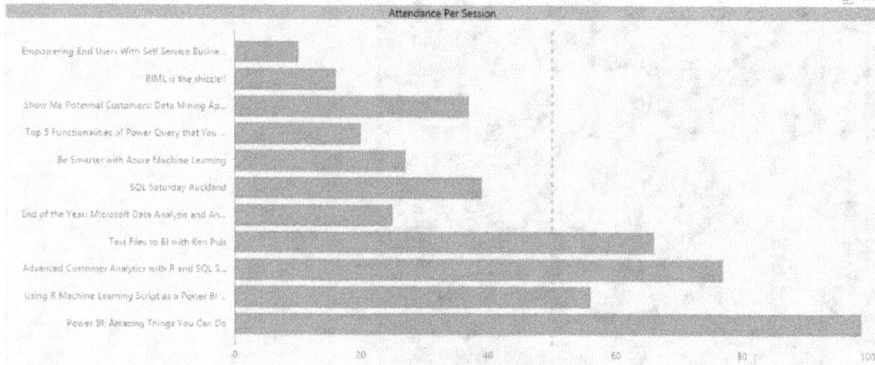

I can see the very first event that had more than 50 audiences was the event that my friend Ken Puls Excel MVP from Canada came here to speak in our user group, which was a start into our popular events afterward.

Adding More Data

I can add more data to build more meaningful insight out of it. For example, I can fetch Members information to show their locations (city and country) on the map. For this I use Members API service which I can call as below;

1 https://api.meetup.com/members?group_urlname=New-Zealand-Business-Intelligence-User-Group&key=XYZ

Power BI from Rookie to Rock Star – Book 3: Power Query and Data Transformation in Power BI

	Column1.zip	Column1.country	Column1.city	Column1.joined	Column1.topics
1	meetup1	nz	Auckland	Thu Nov 26 17:29:49 EST 2015	
2	meetup1	nz	Auckland	Wed Apr 08 06:49:50 EDT 2015	
3	meetup1	nz	Auckland	Thu Dec 17 02:29:11 EST 2015	
4	meetup1	nz	Auckland	Sun May 24 23:49:20 EDT 2015	
5	meetup1	nz	Auckland	Mon May 02 21:29:32 EDT 2016	
6	meetup1	nz	Auckland	Tue Jan 19 06:24:15 EST 2016	
7	1150	nz	Auckland	Thu Jan 28 12:06:41 EST 2016	
8	meetup1	nz	Auckland	Thu Jun 25 20:22:03 EDT 2015	
9	meetup1	nz	Auckland	Sat Apr 16 18:11:17 EDT 2016	
10	meetup1	nz	Auckland	Thu Nov 12 04:05:07 EST 2015	
11	meetup1	nz	Auckland	Wed Sep 09 22:32:28 EDT 2015	

This time I haven't explained step by step, but the process is similar to what we've done for Events, so I skip this part. Now I want to create a custom column concatenated of city and country as below;

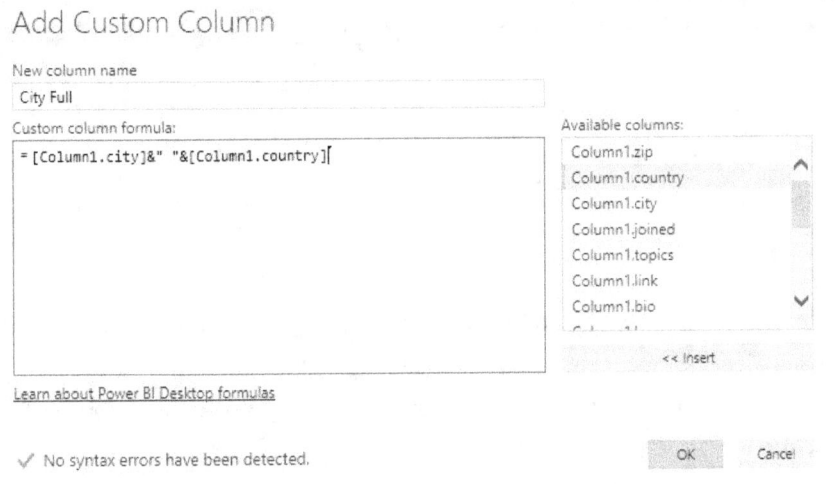

I then will be using this new City Full column because it gives me a more reliable map location than the city itself (because a city with the same name might be part of two different countries).

RSVP Data

RSVP data for each event is really useful for me because I can understand who attend in most events, and then contact them and thanks them for their commitment to the group. RSVP data can be fetched for each event. So I have to check it for each event ID that what is the RSVP for it. Here is RSVP service URL:

1 https://api.meetup.com/2/rsvps?event_id=230678189&key=XYZ

Note that you have to use your event_id for the URL above.

I start by fetching result of above URL into Power Query, and here is what I get after expanding the JSON list and records;

Note that I've also expanded Members column to get Member ID, this is what I would use later to join to Members query. I also have a column for the response which says if this member responded yes to the RSVP or not. I name this query as RSVP.

Add a Parameter and Create Function

The query above is only for one event, but I am looking for data for every event. So I have to create a function for getting RSVP result and apply that on every row in Events query. I create a duplicate version of Events, and remove everything and keep the only column1.id (which is event id).

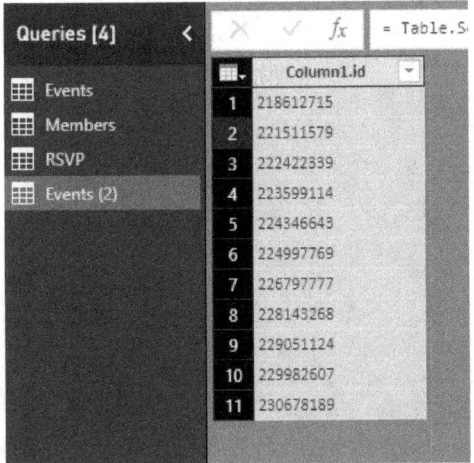

Now I create a parameter to make my RSVP query parametric. Click on Manage Parameters, and choose New Parameter.

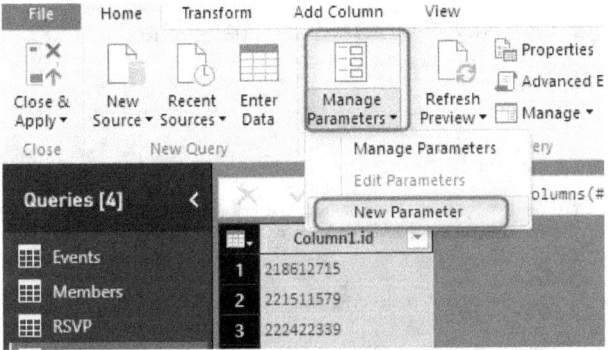

I create a parameter with name EventID and default value as one of my event IDs;

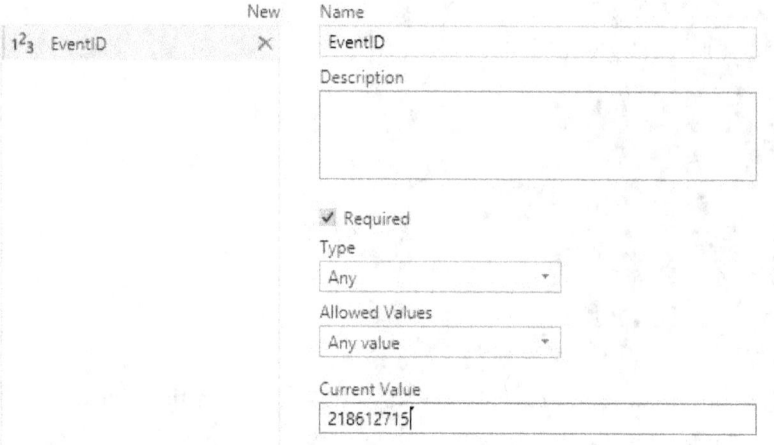

Now I go to advanced editor tab of my RSVP query, and change the script to use EventID variable as below;

```
let
    event=EventID,
    Source =
1 Json.Document(Web.Contents("https://api.meetup.com/2/rsvps?event_id="&Text.From(event)&"&key=XYZ")),
2   results = Source[results],
3   #"Converted to Table" = Table.FromList(results, Splitter.SplitByNothing(), null, null, ExtraValues.Error),
4   #"Expanded Column1" = Table.ExpandRecordColumn(#"Converted to Table", "Column1", {"venue", "created",
5 "member_photo", "answers", "rsvp_id", "mtime", "response", "tallies", "guests", "member", "event", "group"},
6 {"Column1.venue", "Column1.created", "Column1.member_photo", "Column1.answers", "Column1.rsvp_id",
7 "Column1.mtime", "Column1.response", "Column1.tallies", "Column1.guests", "Column1.member",
8 "Column1.event", "Column1.group"}),
9   #"Expanded Column1.member" = Table.ExpandRecordColumn(#"Expanded Column1", "Column1.member",
    {"member_id"}, {"Column1.member.member_id"})
in
    #"Expanded Column1.member"
```

Now that my query works with a parameter, I can right click on it, and Create Function.

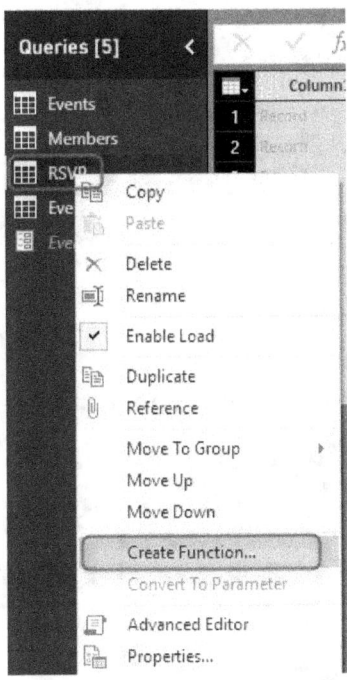

I name the function as GetRSVP, and it gets EventID as an input parameter

Create Function

Enter names for the new function and its parameters.

Function name
GetRSVP

Parameter name (EventID)
EventID

Now I can go to my copy of Events query which named Events(2) and adds a custom function that calls GetRSVP as below

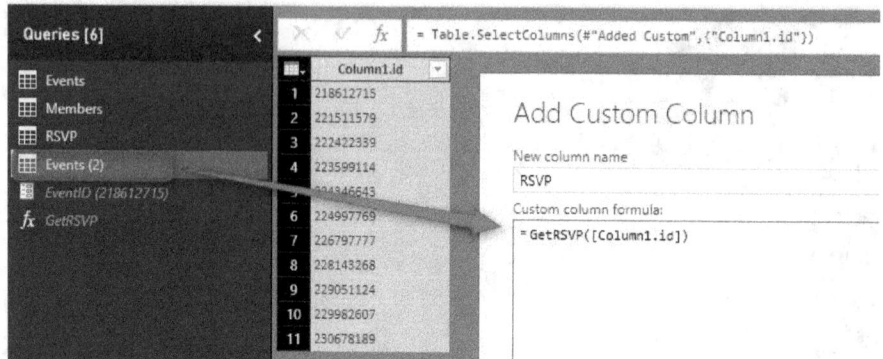

Result set would be a column with tables in each row, which I can expand to get RSVP columns there

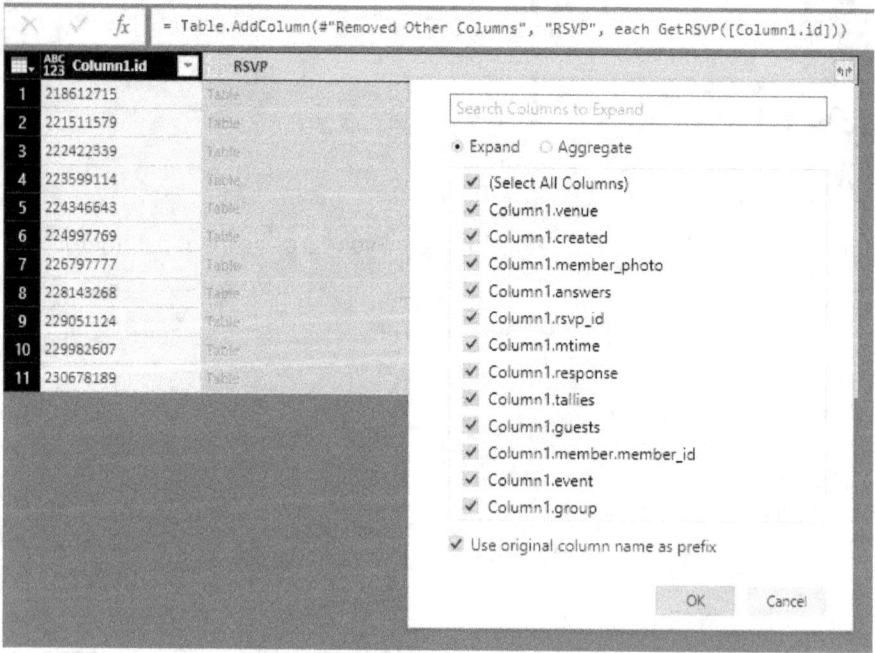

Note that you may hit the privacy configuration warning and errors at this step; because this is just for test. I went to Files -> Options and Settings ->

Option, and change privacy setting to ignore. This is not best practice, you have to set it up appropriate for a production environment, but here is just a demo and test, so let's have fun.

I rename this query as RSVPs and Close and Load data into Power BI. I'll create a relationship as below;

Events and RSVPs= column1.id from Events, Custom.Column1.event.id from RSVPs

RSVPs and Members= Custom.Column1.member.member_id from RSVPs, Column1.id from Members

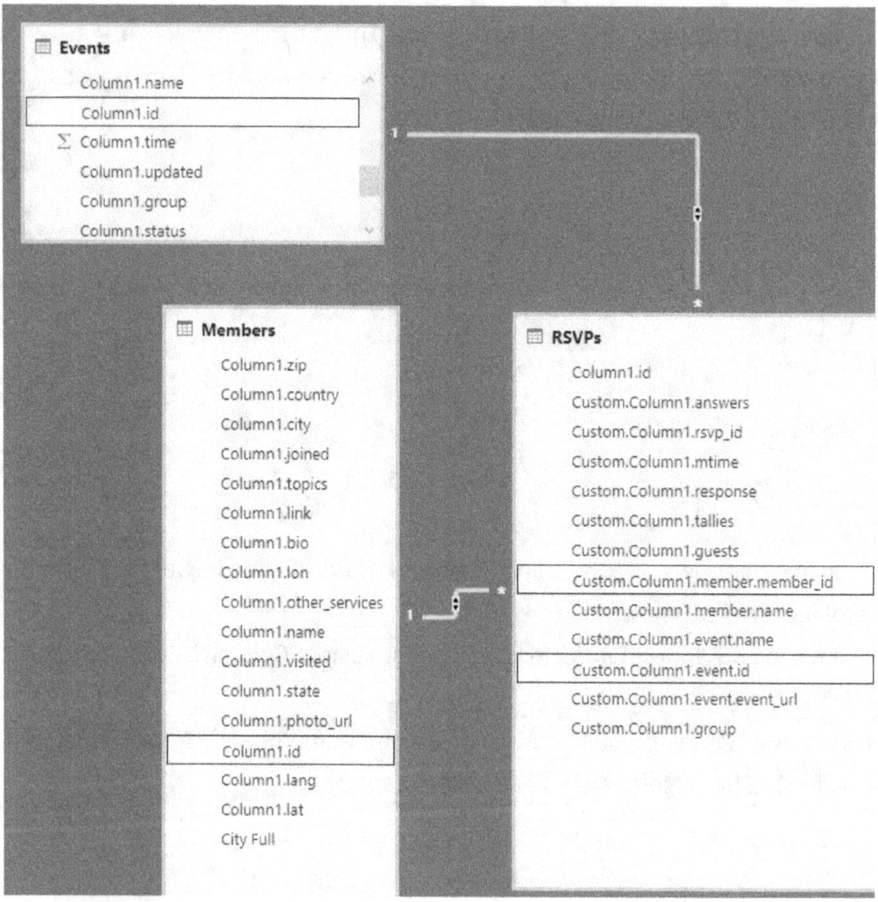

I can now visualize members by their geolocation city information in a map

It is interesting that we have some members in our user group in other continents However the majority are in Auckland, New Zealand as expected. I can also build another bar chart for members who RSVPed yes mostly. Here is my final visualization with some formatting:

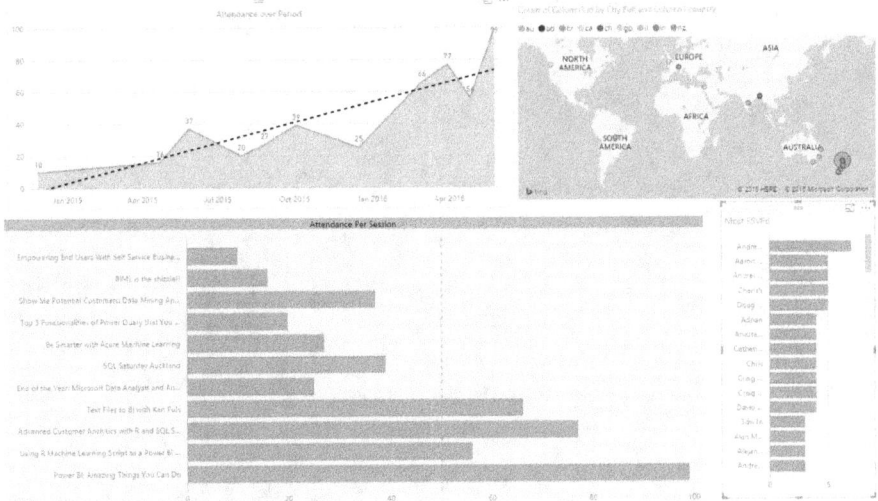

I can still dig into more details with adding more data into my Power BI model and visualization, but I leave it to you now from here to see how far you can go with it. Have fun with Power BI and Meetup API.

Part III: Transformations

Reference vs Duplicate in Power BI; Power Query Back to Basics

Posted by Reza Rad on Sep 25, 2018

When you work with tables and queries in Power Query and Power BI, you get the option to copy them through these actions: Duplicate, or Reference. It has always been a question in my sessions and courses that what is the actual difference between these two actions. The explanation is simple but very important to understand. Because when you know the difference, you will use it properly. In this short blog post, I'll explain what the Reference, and the difference of that with Duplicate is. To learn more about Power BI; read Power BI from Rookie to Rock Star book.

Duplicate

If you are looking to copy an entire query with all of its steps, then Duplicate is your friend. Let's see this in action. As an example, Let's assume that we got the data from a web page that shows us the best seller's movies information. If you have done the movies example of my book previously, the website is BoxOfficeMojo. Here is the link to the page:

https://www.boxofficemojo.com/alltime/world/?pagenum=1&p=.htm

In Power Query, we got data From Web, and selected this source;

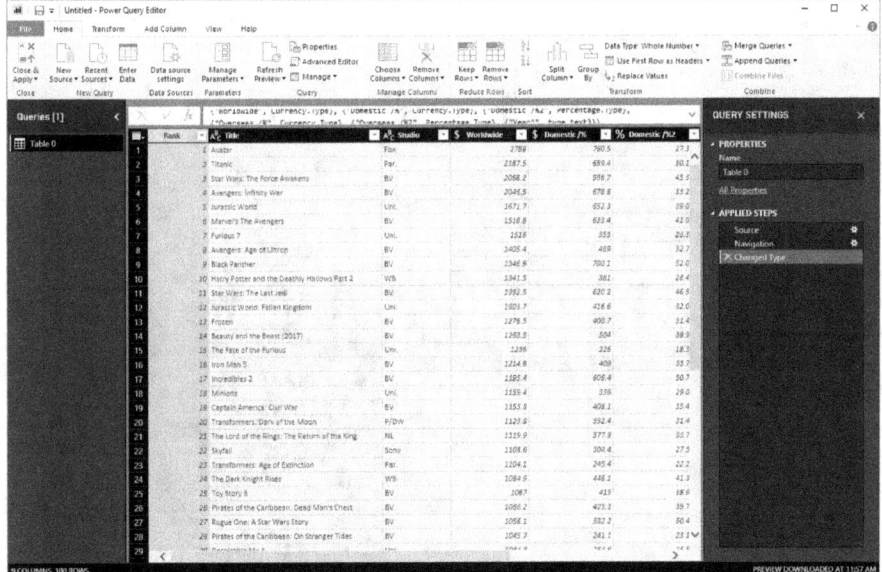

Let's say for this table; we do some transformations. For example; removing extra "^" character from the last column (Year column);

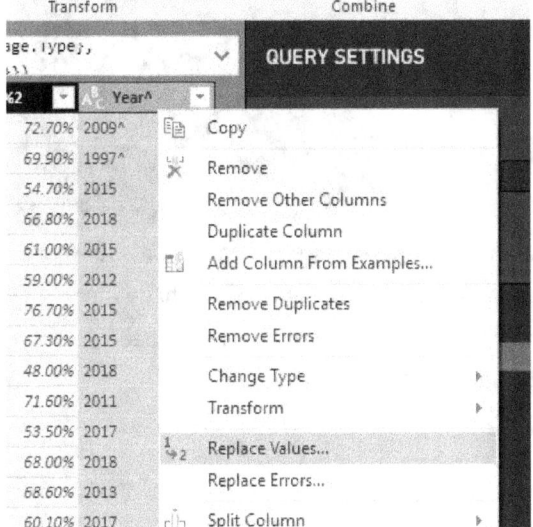

and then some other transformations, so we end up with some steps for this query.

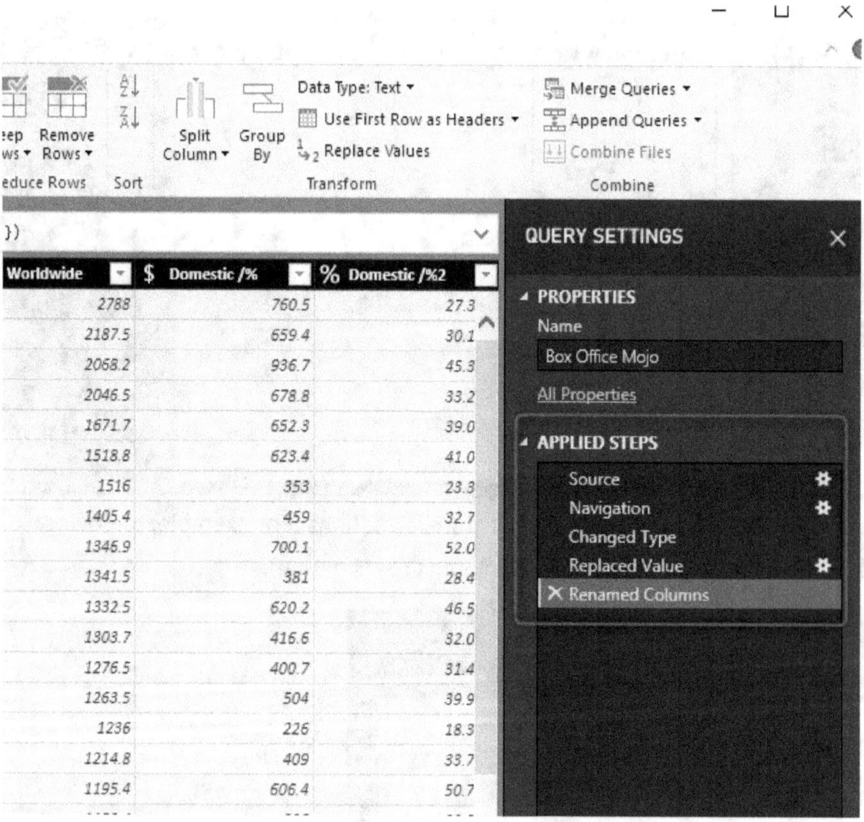

After doing all these transformations, you realize that this data is only for the first hundred best seller movies because that web page doesn't have the remaining movies. To get the remaining, you need to navigate to page 2, which has a different URL, but the same data structure.

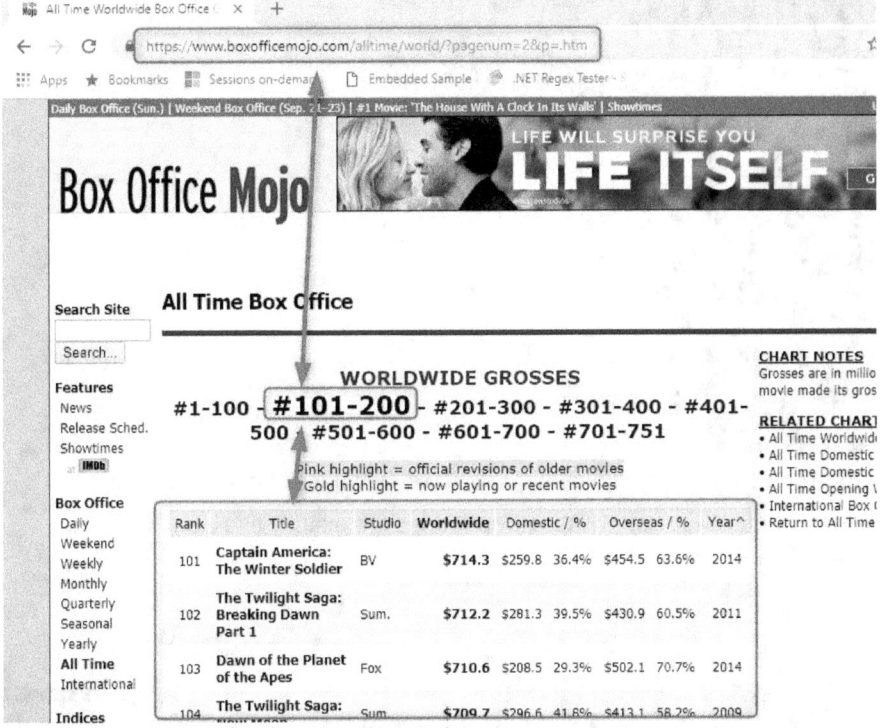

Well, what you need to do? You have to do all those steps on page 2 as well. Let's keep this example static and basic, (Because in complex scenarios when you have many pages, you may use functions and parameters to loop through all pages and combine them all. If you are interested in learning about that, read my post here). Let's say you want to do all those steps that you have done for page one, now for page two. To do that; you can leverage Duplicate. Create a duplicate of Box Office Mojo (I called it; Box Office Mojo Page 1)

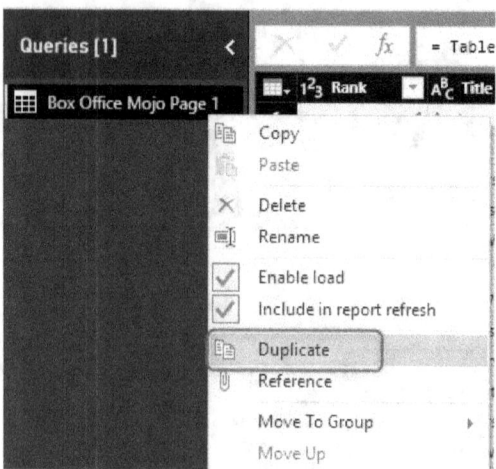

When you create the Duplicate query, it will be an exact copy of the first query, with all steps of it. These two queries are exactly like each other. No difference!

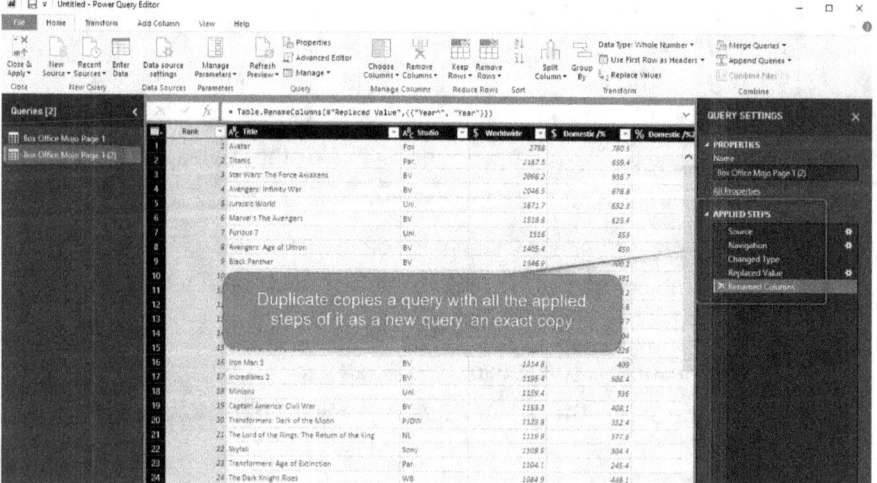

Duplicate copies a query with all the applied steps of it as a new query; an exact copy.

After creating the copy, then you can go to the source step to change the URL:

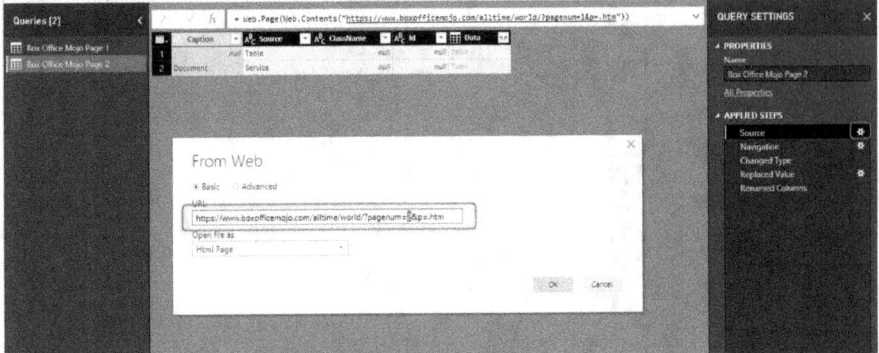

Using Duplicate, you managed to copy a query with all steps in it, and then make changes in your new query. Your original query is intact.
Duplicate is the option to choose when you want to copy a query, but do a different configuration in steps.

Reference

Reference is another way of copying a query. However, the big difference is that; When you reference a query, the new query will have only one step: sourcing from the original query. A referenced query, will not have the applied steps of the original query. Let's see this option in action. Continuing the example above; let's say we want to create a new query that is the result of combining the page 1 and page 2 result. However, we do NOT want to change any of the existing queries, because we want to use those as the source for other operations.

With a right click on Box Office Mojo Page 1, I can create a Reference.

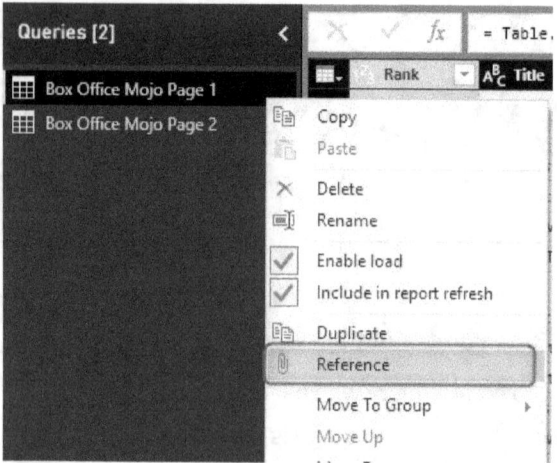

Reference will create a new query which is a copy of the Box Office Mojo Page 1, but only contains one single step:

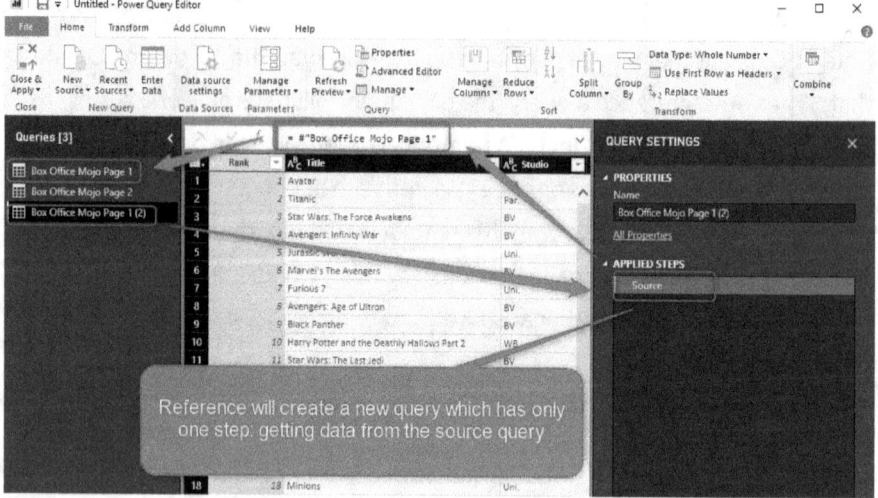

The only step in the new query is sourcing the data from the original query. What does it mean? It means if you make changes in the original query, then this new query will be impacted.

Reference will create a new query which has only one step: Getting data from the original query.

Now we can use this query, to append to the Box Office Mojo Page 2;

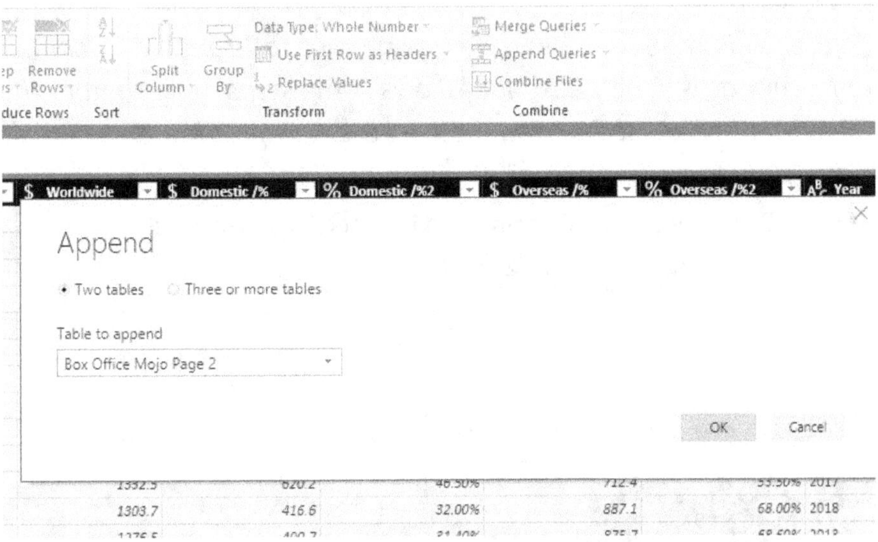

The result would be a query that contains both pages;

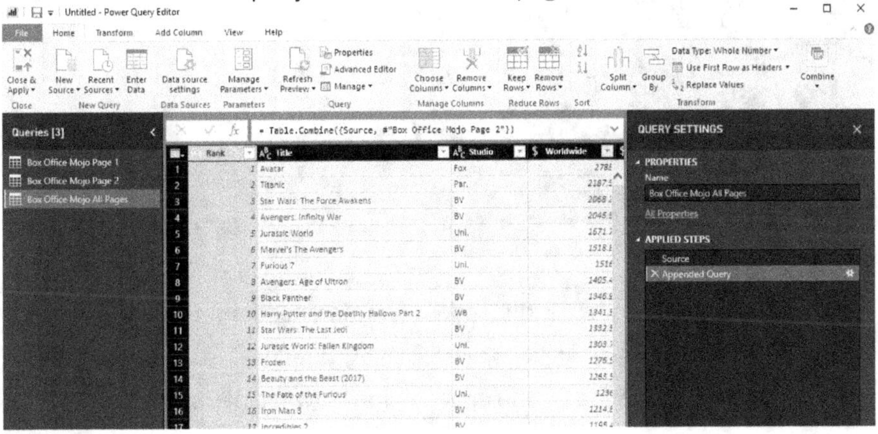

To learn more about append and the difference of that with Merge, read my blog post here. In this example; we used Reference option to create a copy of the original query, and then continue some extra steps. There are many other usages for the Reference.

Reference is a good choice when you want to branch a query into different paths. One path that follows some steps, and another that follows different steps, and both are sharing some steps in the original query.

After doing the append in this example, it is a good idea to uncheck the enable load on Page 1 and Page 2 queries to save some memory in Power BI.

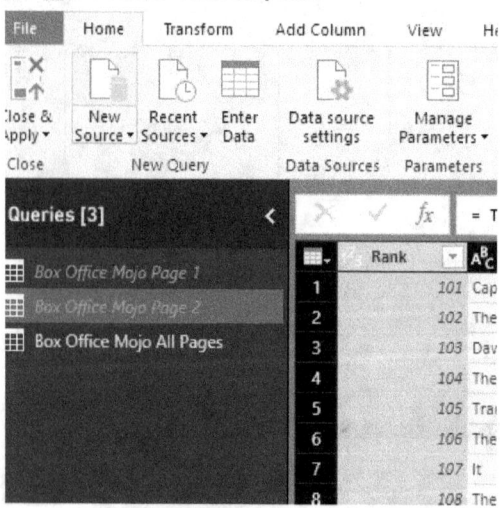

Query Dependency

Finding out that which query is dependent (or referenced from) which query can be a bit challenging when you have too many queries. That is why we have the Query Dependency menu option in the View tab of Power Query;

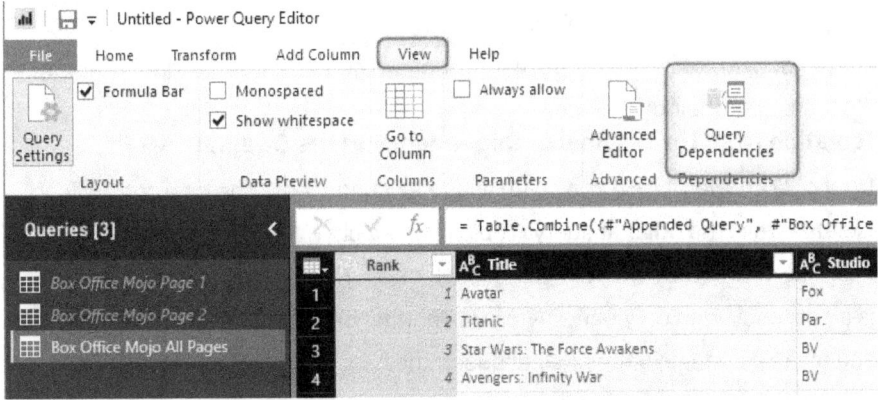

For our example above, this is the query dependency diagram;

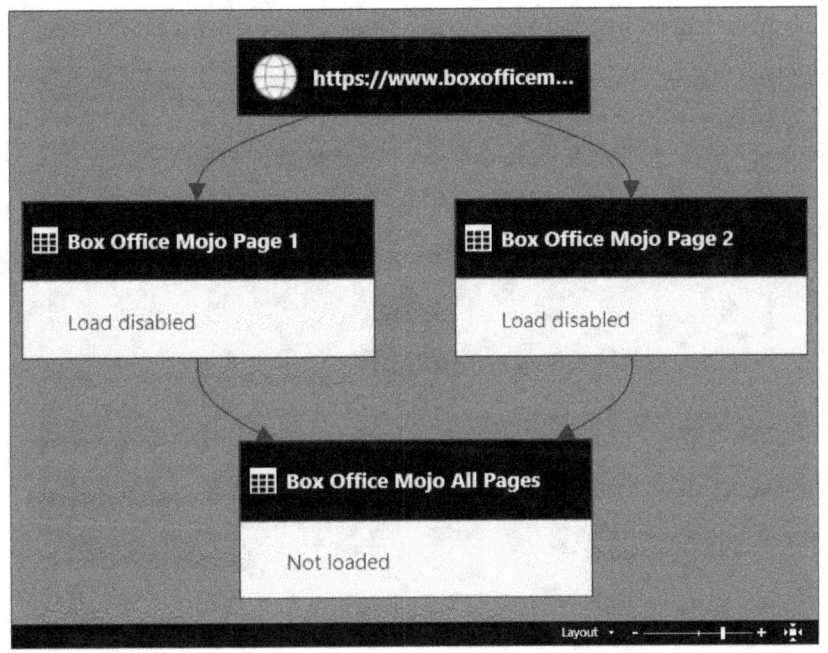

Duplicate vs. Reference

Now that you know there are two options when you copy a query let's have a closer look at their difference.

Isolation from the Original or Dependency to the Original

Duplicate creates a new copy with all the existing steps. The new copy will be isolated from the original query. You can make changes in the original or the new query, and they will NOT affect each other. Reference, on the other hand, is a new copy with only one single step: getting data from the original query. If you make a change in the original query, the new query will be impacted. For example; If you remove a column from the original query, the new query will not have it if it used the Reference method for copying.

Limitation of the Reference

You can not use referenced queries in all situations. As an example; If you have a Query 1, and then you created a reference from that as Query 2. You cannot use the result from Query 2 in Query 1! It will create a circular reference. You are combining a query with reference to the query itself, It is impossible!

Query Dependencies

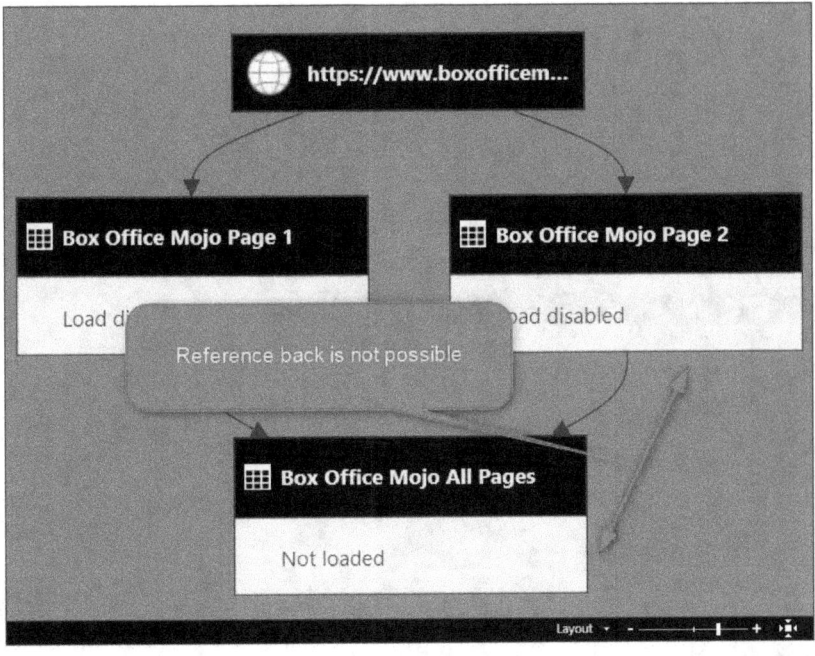

Some actions that invoke Reference or Duplicate

There are some actions in the Power Query that trigger Reference or Duplicate, let's check those options:

Append Queries as New / or Merge Queries as New is a Reference action

These two actions are creating a reference from the original query, and then they do Append or Merge with other queries.

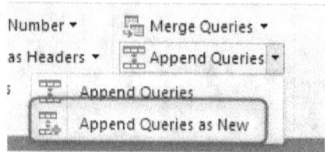

Add as New Query is a Duplicate action

Believe it or not, when you right click on a column or cell and select "Add as New Query" you are creating a duplicate of the original query.

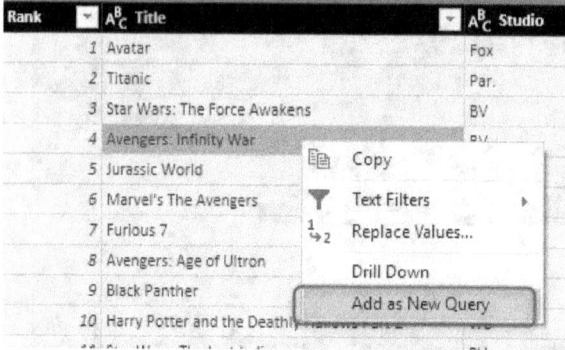

This can be misleading sometimes, because you may expect the new query to source from the original, and with the change of original, this query also to change. However, the truth is that this is a duplicate action, and after this action, your original query and the new copy will be isolated from each other.

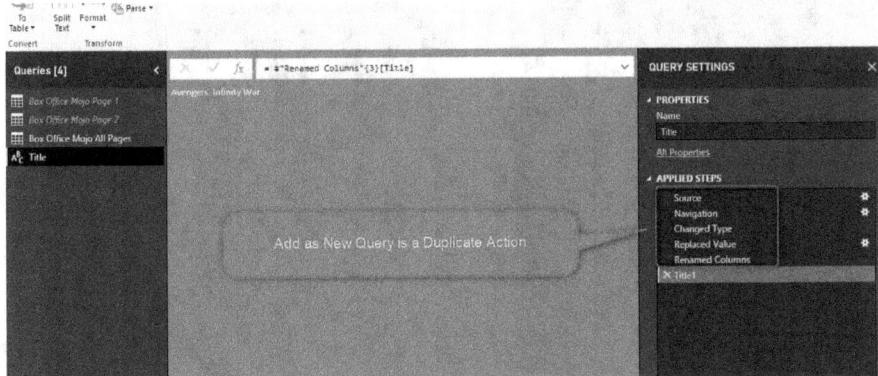

Copy and Paste is Neither Duplicate Nor Reference!

This is another misconception that Copy and Paste are similar to Duplicate. It is not, and it is not Reference either. When you do this action on a simple query (I mean a query that is not sourced from any other queries), then you get a result similar to Duplicate.

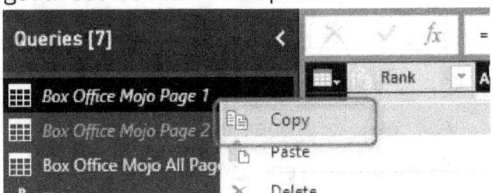

But when you do the Copy and Paste on a query that is sourced from other queries; the result is a copy of all original queries. Here is the result of Copy and Paste on Box Office Mojo All Pages (which is sourced from Page 1 and Page 2);

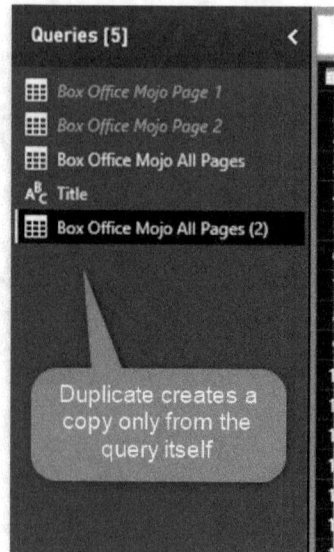
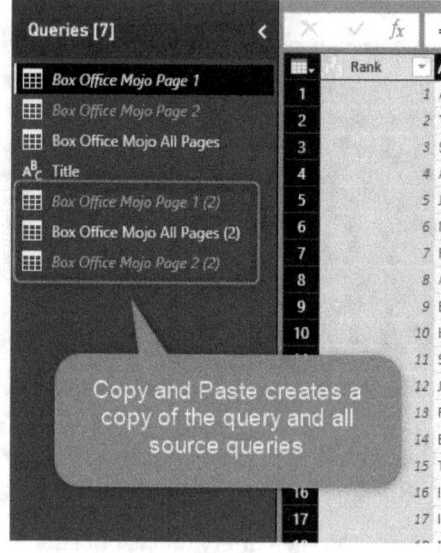

Summary

Duplicate and Reference are two different actions, and they are also different from Copy and Paste of a query. Duplicate will give you an exact copy of the query with all steps, and Reference will create a reference to the original query instead as a new query. Duplicate is a good option to choose when you want the two copies to be isolated from each other; Reference is a good option when you create different branches from one original query. There are some actions in Power Query that trigger Duplicate or Reference as listed in this blog post. Hope this was a good post for you to understand the difference between these two actions clearly, and use them wisely from now on.

Append vs. Merge in Power BI and Power Query

Posted by Reza Rad on Jan 5, 2017

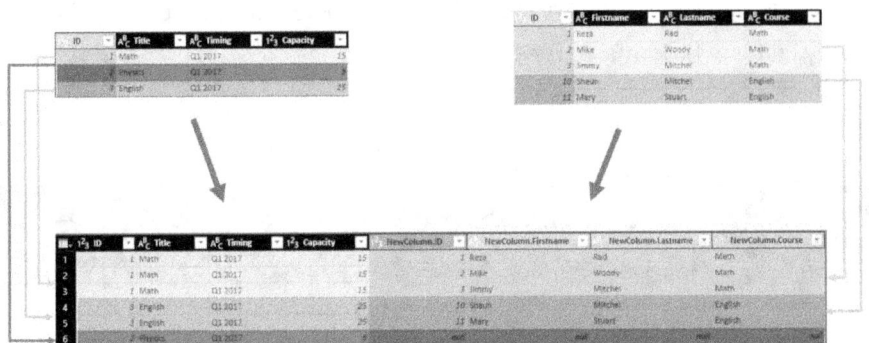

Combining two queries in Power Query or Power BI is one of the most basic and also essential tasks that you would need to do in most data preparation scenarios. There are two types of combining queries; Merge, and Append. Database developers easily understand the difference, but the majority of Power BI users are not developers. In this post, I'll explain the difference between Merge and Append, and situations that you should use each. If you want to learn more about Power BI, read Power BI online book, from Rookie to Rock Star.

Why Combine Queries?

This might be the first question comes into your mind; Why should I combine queries? The answer is that; You can do most of the things you want in a single query. However, it will be very complicated with hundreds of steps very quickly. On the other hand, your queries might be used in different places. For example one of them might be used as a table in Power BI model, and also playing the part of data preparation for another query. Combining queries is a big help in writing better and simpler queries. I'll show you some examples of combining queries.

The result of a combine operation on one or more queries will be only one query. You can find Append or Merge in the Combine Queries section of the Query Editor in Power BI or Excel.

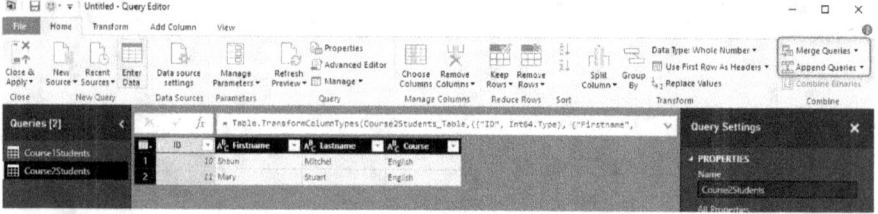

Append

Append means results of two (or more) queries (which are tables themselves) will be combined into one query in this way:
- Rows will be appended after each other. (for example, appending a query with 50 rows with another query with 100 rows, will return a result set of 150 rows)
- Columns will be the same number of columns for each query*. (for example, col1, col2,..., col10 in the first query, after appending with same columns in the second query will result into one query with a single set of col1,col2, ..., col10)

There is an exception for the number of columns which I'll talk about it later.

Let's first look at what Append looks like in action;

Consider two sample data sets; one for students of each course, Students of course 1:

ID	Firstname	Lastname	Course
1	Reza	Rad	Math
2	Mike	Woody	Math
3	Jimmy	Mitchel	Math

and Students of course 2:

ID	Firstname	Lastname	Course
10	Shaun	Mitchel	English
11	Mary	Stuart	English

To append these queries, Click on one of them and select Append Queries from the Combine section of Home tab in Query Editor

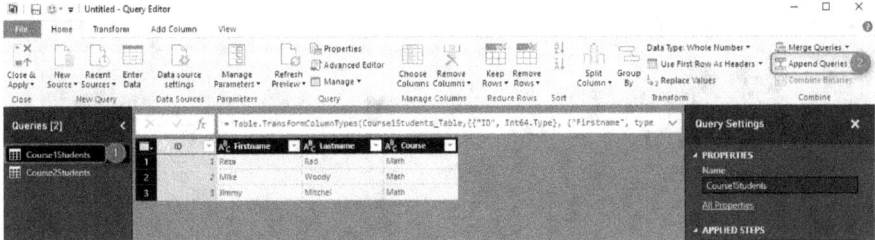

If you want to keep the existing query result as it is and create a new query with the appended result choose Append Queries as New, otherwise select Append Queries. In this example, I'll do Append Queries as New, because I want to keep existing queries intact.

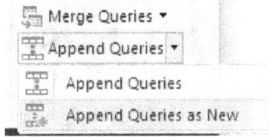

You can choose what is the primary table (normally this is the query that you have selected before clicking on Append Queries), and the table to append.

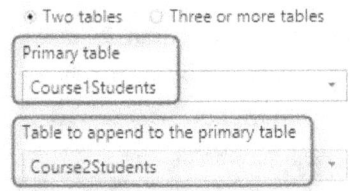

You can also choose to append Three or more tables and add tables to the list as you wish. For this example I have only two tables, so I'll continue with the above configuration. Append Queries append rows after each other, and because column names are exactly similar in both queries, the result set will have the same columns.

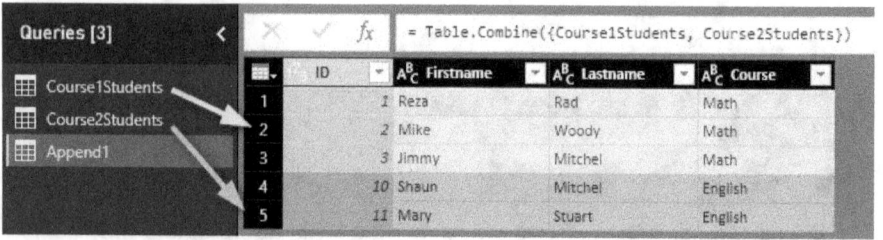

The result of Append as simple as that

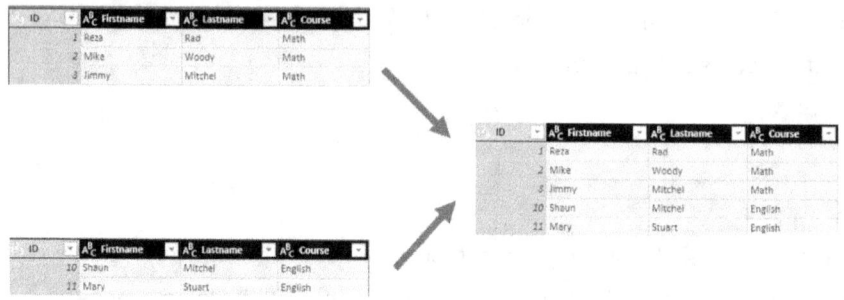

Append is similar to UNION ALL in T-SQL.
What about Duplicates?
Append Queries will NOT remove duplicates. You have to use Group By or Remove Duplicate Rows to get rid of duplicates.
What if columns in source queries are not exactly matched?
Append requires columns to be exactly similar to work in the best condition. If columns in source queries are different, append still works, but will create one

column in the output per each new column, if one of the sources doesn't have that column the cell value of that column for those rows will be null.

Merge

Merge is another type of combining queries which are based on matching rows, rather than columns. The output of Merge will be a single query with;
• There should be joining or matching criteria between two queries. (for example StudentID column of both queries to be matched with each other)
• Number of rows will be dependent on matching criteria between queries
• Number of Columns will be dependent on what columns selected in the result set. (Merge will create a structured column as a result).

Understanding how Merge works might look a bit more complicated, but it will be very easy with an example, let's have a look at that in action;

In addition to tables in the first example, consider that there is another table for Course's details as below:

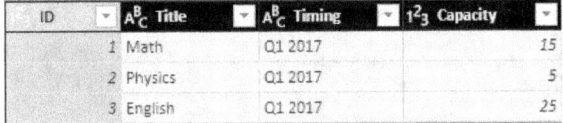

Now if I want to combine Course query with the Appended result of courseXstudents to see which students are part of which course with all details in each row, I need to use Merge Queries. Here is the appended result again;

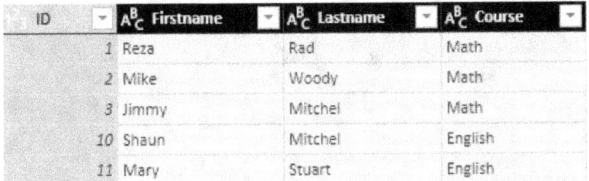

Select Course Query first, and then Select Merge Queries (as New)

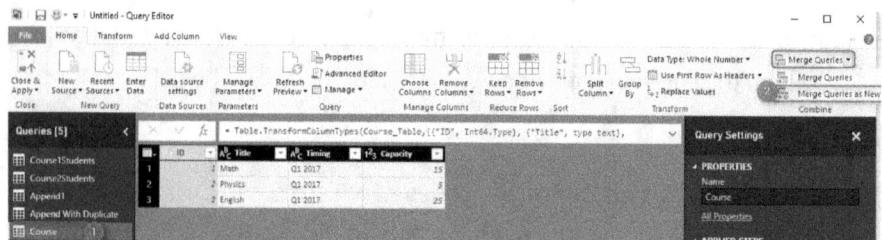

Merging Queries require joining criteria. Joining criteria is field(s) in each source query that should be matched with each other to build the resulting query. In this example, I want to Merge Course query with Append1, based on Title of the course.

Merge

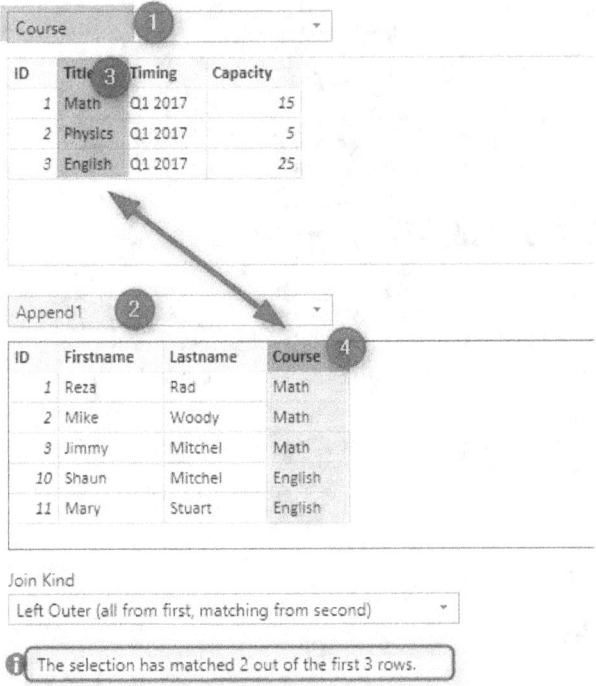

I'll talk about types of join later. For now, continue the selection, and you will see these two queries match with each other based on the Course title, result query will be same as the first query (Course in this example), plus one additional column named as NewColumn with a table in each cell. This is a structured column which can be expanded into underlying tables. If you click on an empty area of the cell containing one of these tables, you will see the sub table underneath.

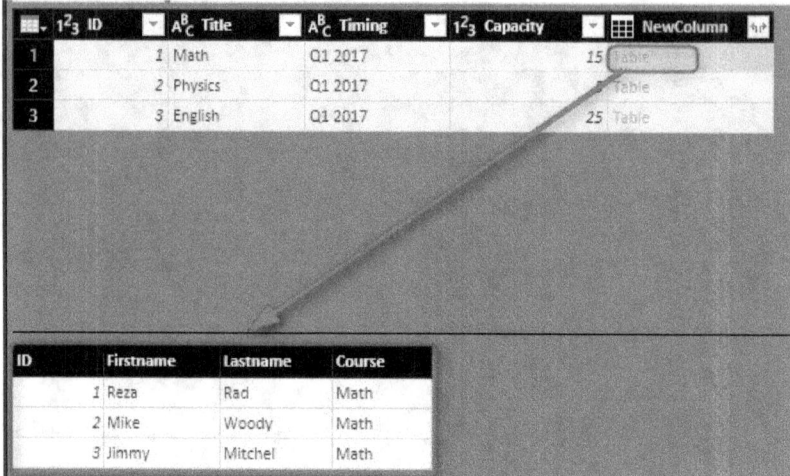

Now click on Expand column icon, and expand the New Column to all underneath table structure.

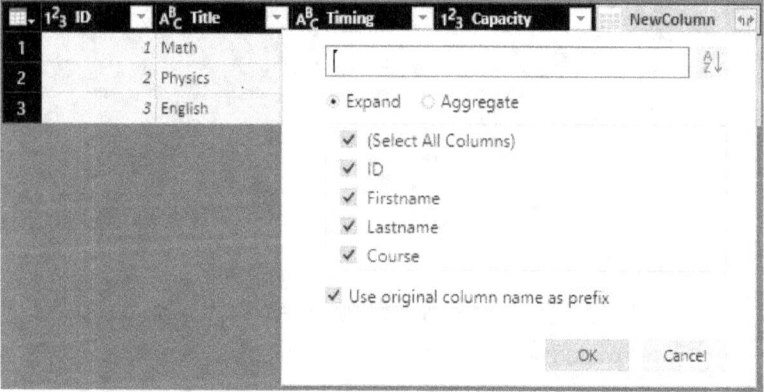

The result will be a table including columns from both tables, and rows matching with each other.

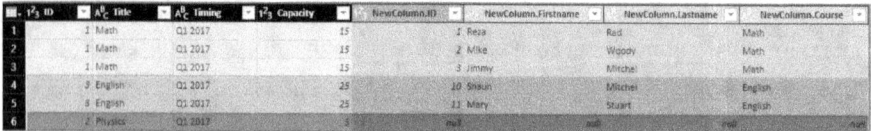

Columns in the left-hand side are coming from Course table, columns in the right-hand side are coming from Students table. Values in the rows only appear in matching criteria. First three rows are students of Math course, then two students for the English course, and because there is no student for Physics course you will see null values for students columns.

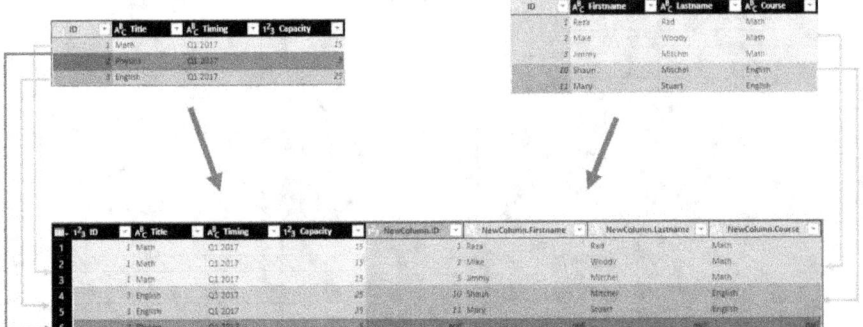

Merge is similar to JOIN in T-SQL

Join Types

There are six types of joins supported in Power BI as below, depends on the effect on the result set based on matching rows, each of these types works differently.

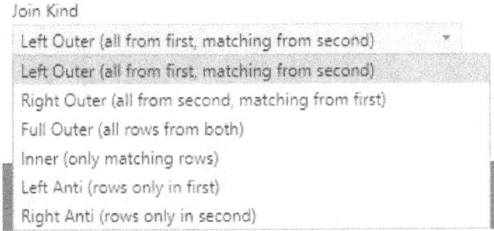

Explaining what each join type will do is a different post which I wrote about it here. For now, this picture explains it very well:

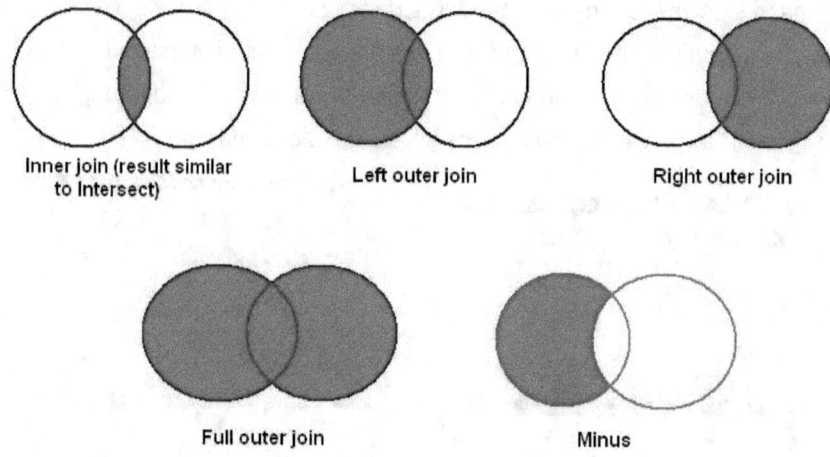

JOINS AND SET OPERATIONS IN RELATIONAL DATABASES

Inner join (result similar to Intersect)   Left outer join   Right outer join

Full outer join   Minus

Picture referenced from http://www.udel.edu/evelyn/SQL-Class2/SQLclass2_Join.html

Choose the Right Merge Join Type in Power BI

Posted by Reza Rad on Jul 26, 2017

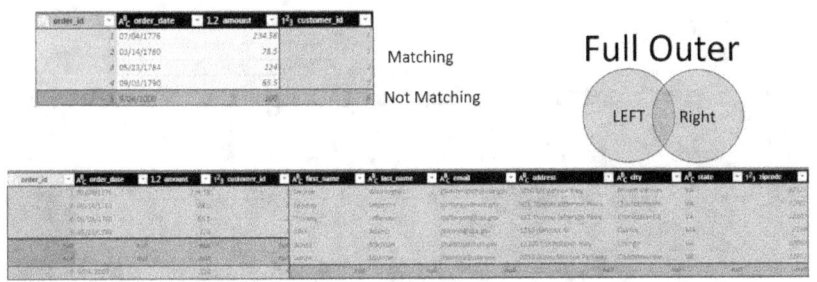

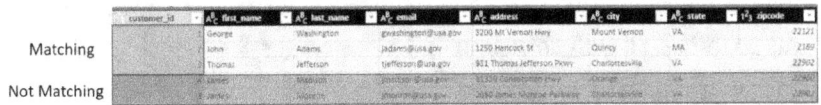

Previously I have written a blog post explaining two ways of combining data sets; Append vs. Merge. In this post, I want to explain in details what is the difference between all types of Merge Type and explaining how to choose the right merge (or Join) type. These Merge types are very similar to join types in relational databases. Because many of people who work with Power BI might not have experience working with relational databases, so I think this post is a good explanation in details what are these types and when to use them. If you want to learn more about Power BI; read Power BI book from Rookie to Rock Star.

What is Merge?

Combining two data sets can be done in multiple ways. One of the ways of combining data sets is Merging datasets. Merge is similar to Join in relational databases. Merging two data sets requires some joining fields, and the result will be combined set of columns from both data sets.

Power BI from Rookie to Rock Star – Book 3: Power Query and Data Transformation in Power BI

Merge

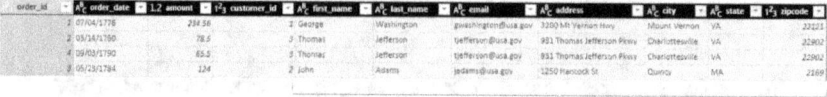

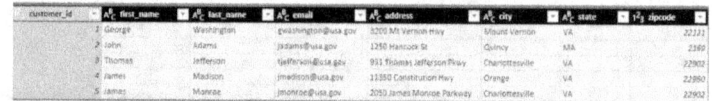

Let's go through it with an example;

Consider two data tables as below

*Data tables are sourced from this web page. Download it from the link at the top of this post.

Customers Table:

customer_id	first_name	last_name	email	address	city	state	zipcode
1	George	Washington	gwashington@usa.gov	3200 Mt Vernon Hwy	Mount Vernon	VA	22121
2	John	Adams	jadams@usa.gov	1250 Hancock St	Quincy	MA	2169
3	Thomas	Jefferson	tjefferson@usa.gov	931 Thomas Jefferson Pkwy	Charlottesville	VA	22902
4	James	Madison	jmadison@usa.gov	11350 Constitution Hwy	Orange	VA	22960
5	James	Monroe	jmonroe@usa.gov	2050 James Monroe Parkway	Charlottesville	VA	22902

Orders Table:

order_id	order_date	amount	customer_id
1	07/04/1776	$234.56	1
2	03/14/1760	$78.50	3
3	05/23/1784	$124.00	2
4	09/03/1790	$65.50	3

Merging these two tables, gives you a dataset with the combined set of columns like below;

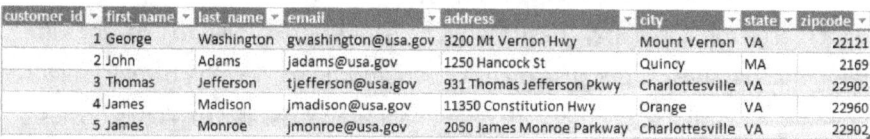

168 | Page

For merging data sets, you need to have some joining fields. In this example the joining field is customer_id. To get a data set that includes all columns from both tables based on customer_id relationship, this is how you can join tables to each other:

How to Merge Queries

Select the first query (for this example: Orders), and then from the home tab, Merge queries. There are two options here:

- Merge Queries: This will amend the existing query (orders), to be the result of Merging.
- Merge Queries as New: This will not change the existing query. It will create a reference from it, and the result of merging would be another query.

Select Merge Queries as New.

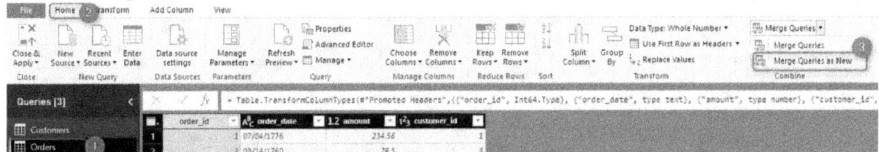

In the Merge configuration window, select the second table (Customers), then select the joining the field in each table (Customer_id). You will also see a number of matching rows as extra information there.

Merge

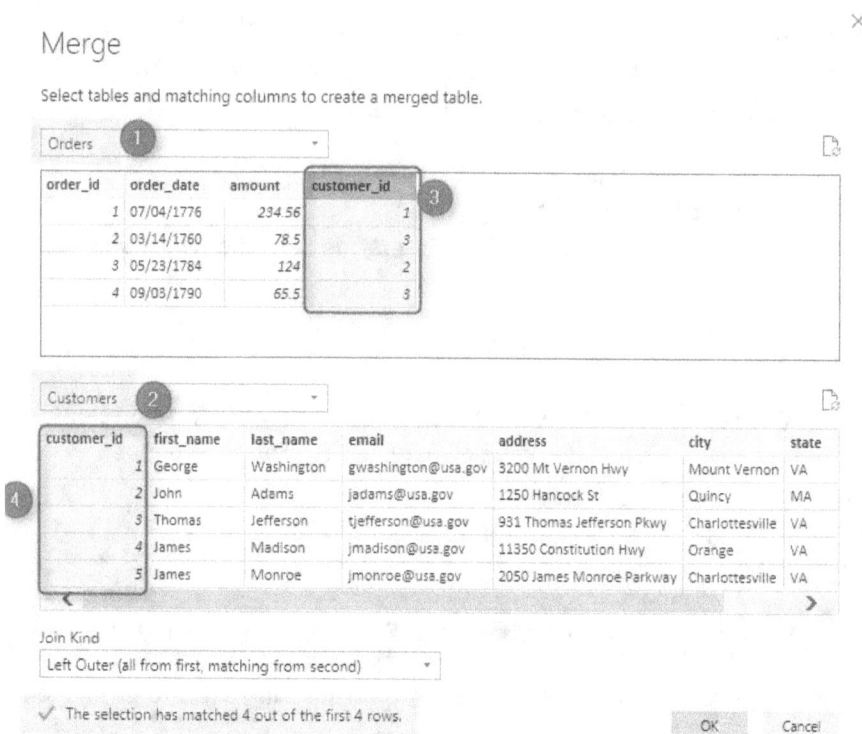

The result of this operation will be a new query named as Merge1, which has the combined result of these two queries.

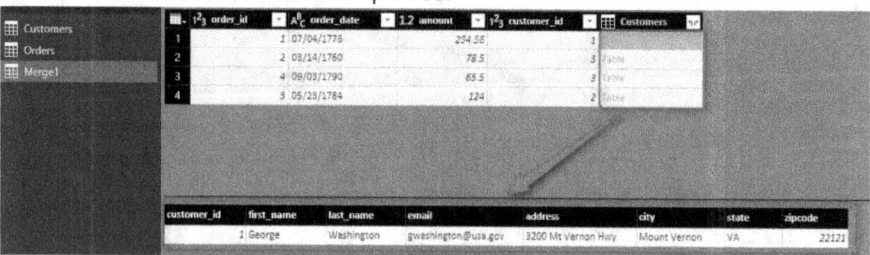

The table in Customers column is a sub table from customer table for records matching with that customer_id. You can then expand it to columns you want;

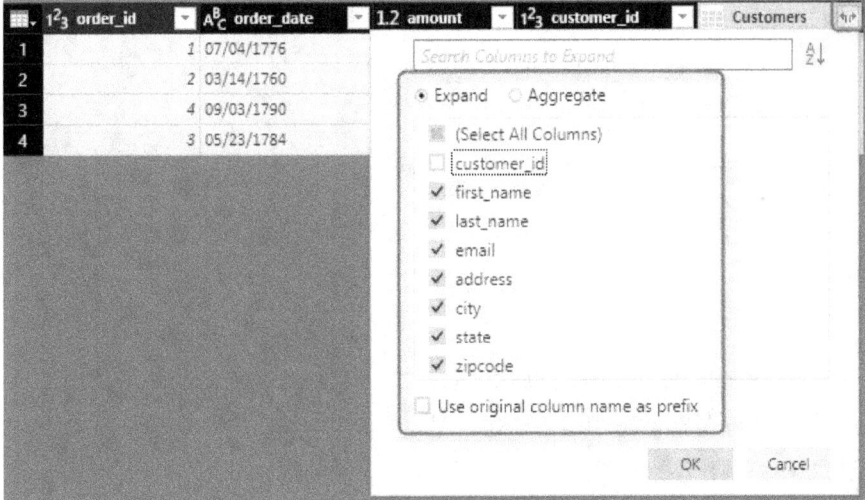

and the final result will be now all columns in one query;

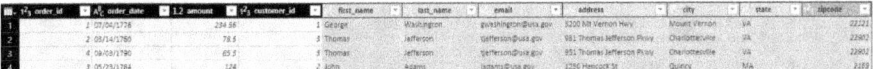

This process is called Merge Join. However, there are some configurations you can do for this;

Merging Based on Multiple Columns

You can easily use multiple columns for merging two datasets. Just select them in order with holding Ctrl key of the keyboard.

Merge

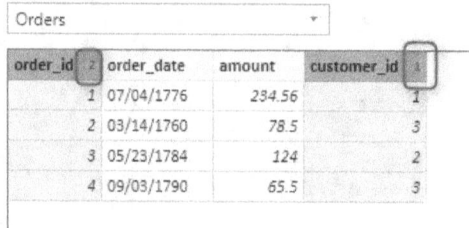

This method can be really helpful because the relationship tab in Power BI Desktop doesn't allow you to create a relationship based on multiple columns. In Power Query, however, you can create the merge and create a unique field for the relationship in Power BI Desktop. Here is my blog post about it.

Merge Types

In addition to the merging column (or joining field); the type of Merge is very important. You can get a totally different result set with choosing a different type of merge. Here is where you can see the Join Kind (or Merge Type);

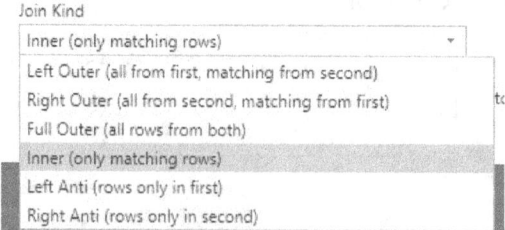

At the moment of writing this blog post, there are six types of joins. About a year ago or even before that fewer number of joins were available. However, you could always choose your Join type in Power Query M script.
Every one of these joins gets a different result set, let's see what their difference is.

Left and Right

To start, you need to know the concept of Left and Right tables (or queries). When you merge two data sets, the first query is considered as LEFT and the second as RIGHT.

In the example above; Orders is LEFT query, and Customers is the RIGHT query. You can change them if you want of course. Understanding this is important because most of Join Kinds works with the concept of left or right or both.

Left Outer (All from first, matching from second)

The first type of Join/Merge is Left Outer. This means the LEFT query is the important one. All records from this query (LEFT or FIRST) will be shown in the

Power BI from Rookie to Rock Star – Book 3: Power Query and Data Transformation in Power BI

result set plus their matching rows in the right (or second table). This type of join is the default type. If you don't specify the Join Kind, it will always be Left Outer. For example in the first Merge example we have done, you can see that the result set is four records, representing four records from the left table (orders), and their matching rows in the customer table.

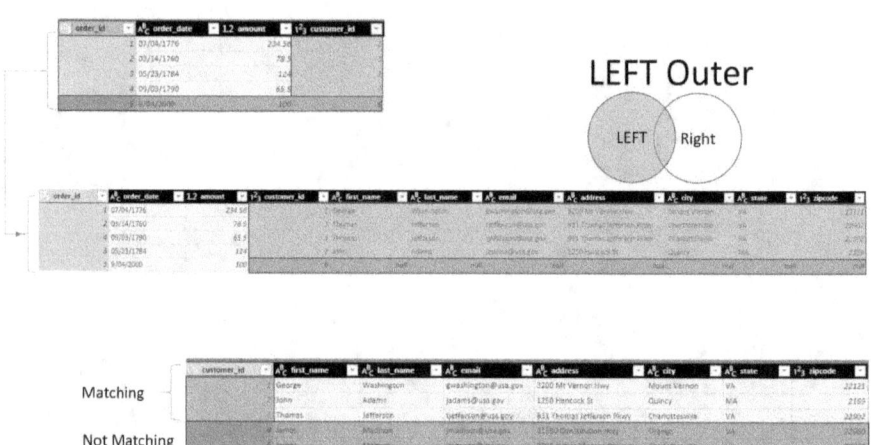

As you can see in the screenshot above; there are two customers who won't be in the result set. Customers with id 4 and 5. because these rows are not matching with the customer_id field in the orders table. In LEFT Outer merge, only records from Left table with matching rows of the right table will be selected.

Right Outer (all rows from second, matching from first)

Sometimes you need to fetch all rows from the second table, regardless if they exist in the first table or not. In that case, you would need to use another type of Join called Right Outer. With this type of Join, you get all rows from the RIGHT (or second) table, with their matching rows from left (or first table). Here is an example:

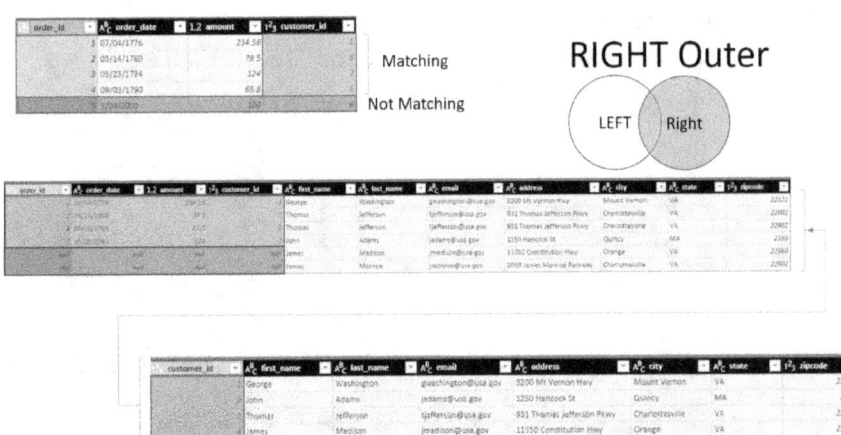

As you can see in the above screenshot; all rows from customers table is showed in the result set. However only four rows of that are matching with the orders table. If there is a record in orders table that doesn't match it will come as Null (two red rows in the result set).

Full Outer (all rows from both)

This type of join/merge is normally the safest among all. This will return all rows from both tables (matching and non-matching). You will have all rows from a first table, and all rows from the second table, and all matching rows. With this method, you won't lose any records.

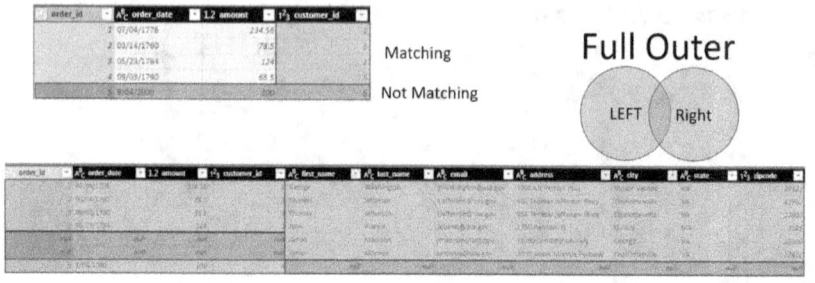

This result set as you can see is seven rows. Four rows matching in both tables. 2 rows only in the customer table, but not in the orders table. One row only in orders table, but not in the customers table.

Inner (only matching rows)

This method only selects matching rows. You will not have any record with null values (because these records generated as a result of not matching). Here is an example;

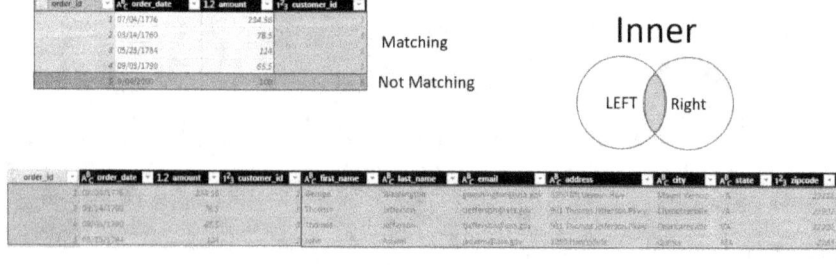

There are only four rows that are matching between two tables. Rows with customer_id 1, 2, and 3. all not matching rows will be excluded from the result set.

Let Anti (rows only in first)

If you are only interested in rows from the LEFT (first) table, then this is the option to select. This means rows that are in the first table and DO NOT match with the second table. So, only Not matching rows from the first table. With Anti options, you always get null for the second data set, because these rows don't exist there. Anti options are good for finding rows that exist in one table but not in the other one. Here is an example:

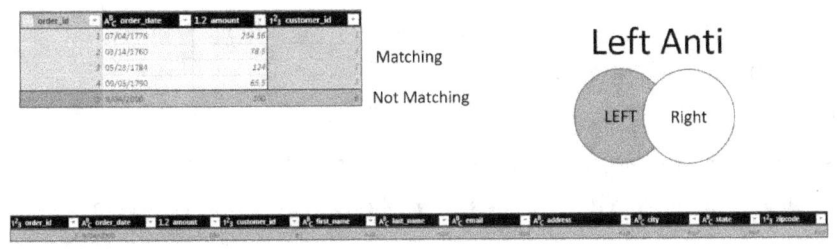

This will find the only one row that exists in the Orders table and does not match with any of the rows in the customer's table.

Right Anti (rows only in second)

Similar to Left Anti; this method will give you only not matching rows. However, this time from the second (Right) table. You can find out what rows in the right table are not matching with the left table. Here is the example;

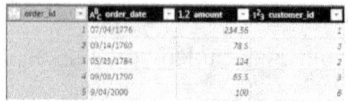
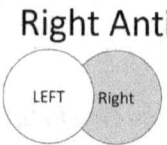

Right Anti

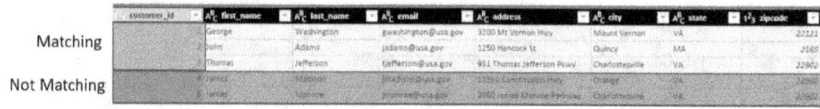

This result set is all rows from the customer table (right table) that does NOT match with orders (first table).

Summary

Different Join Kinds in Merge returns a different result set. Make sure to select the right join kind to avoid any issues later. There are six types of joins as below;

- Left Outer: Rows from left table and matching with the right
- Right Outer: Rows from right table and matching with the left
- Full Outer: Rows from both tables (matching or not matching)
- Inner: Only matching rows from both tables
- Left Anti: Not matching rows from the left table
- Right Anti: Not matching rows from the right table

LEFT Outer

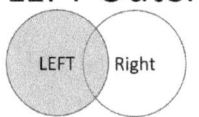

All rows from left and matching from right

Full Outer

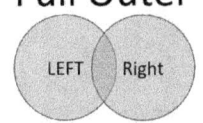

All rows from both: matching and not matching

RIGHT Outer

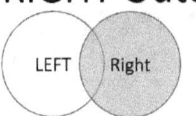

All rows from right and matching from left

Left Anti

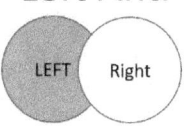

Not matching rows from left

Inner

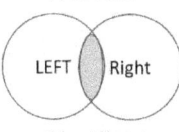

Only matching rows

Right Anti

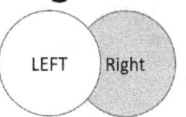

Not matching rows from right

How to Change Joining Types in Power BI and Power Query

Posted by Reza Rad on Jul 31, 2015

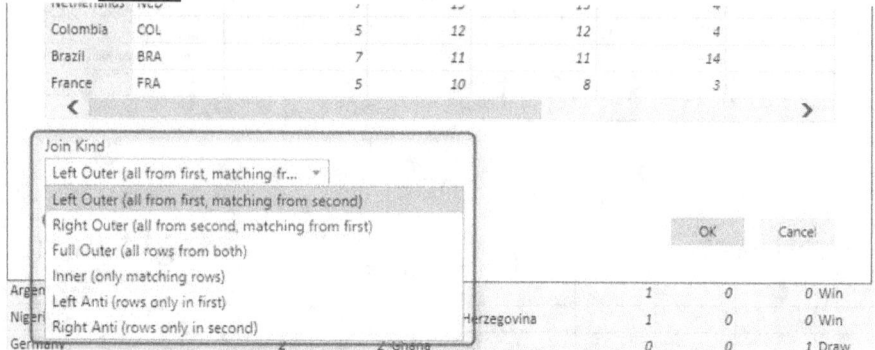

Joining tables is not a new concept, I bet all readers of my blog at least have a clue about that. However there are different types of joins, and applying these types of Joins are not all possible through Power Query GUI. Power BI recently took a step and implemented that in the GUI, however, you might like to know how to apply that in the Power Query. The trick is that M is your friend, You can do whatever you want behind the scenes with M script.

I don't want to go through the details of explaining every join type here. The picture below illustrated it perfectly;

JOINS AND SET OPERATIONS IN RELATIONAL DATABASES

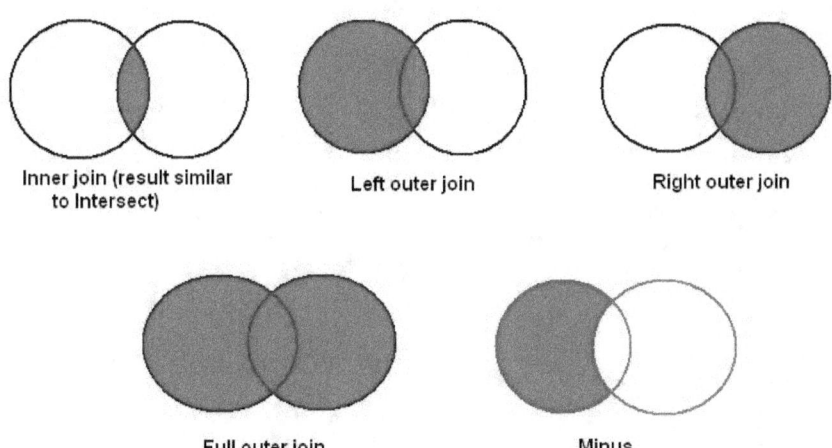

Picture referenced from http://www.udel.edu/evelyn/SQL-Class2/SQLclass2_Join.html

Now let's see how to use joins through Power BI and Power Query;

Power BI Desktop

In Power BI Desktop you can join two tables with Merge menu item in the Query Editor, in Home tab, Under Combine, Merge Queries.

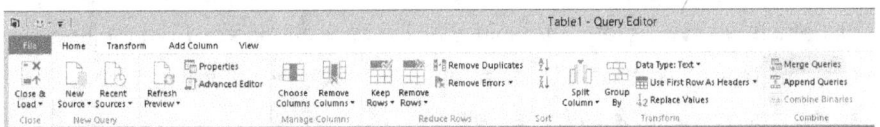

The Merge Window will appear with the ability to select the first table (Left part of the join), and the second table (Right part of the join). You can choose columns that you want to participate as joining key within an order (you can choose multiple columns with Ctrl Key). And there is join kindly that you can choose.

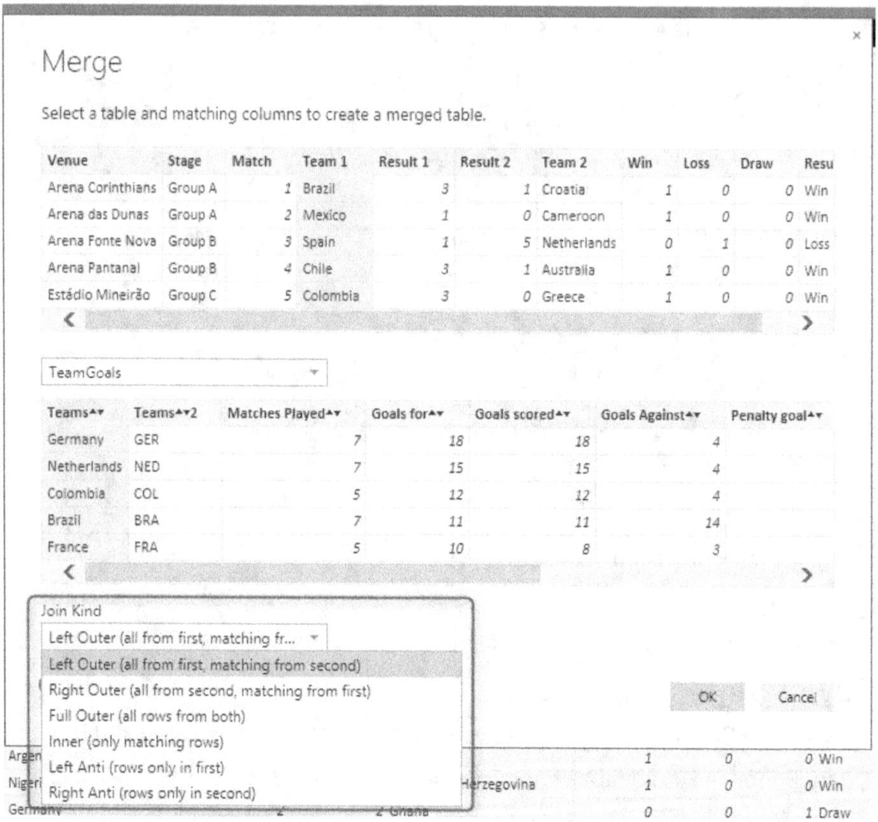

The default behavior is left outer join, which means all records from the first table if there is any record in the first table that matches record(s) in the second table it would be listed as well.

After joining tables, the second table will appear as a field that has table value in its cells. What you need to do is to select columns that you want to show in the result set.

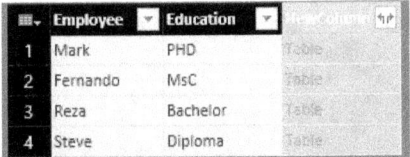

Choose columns as below:

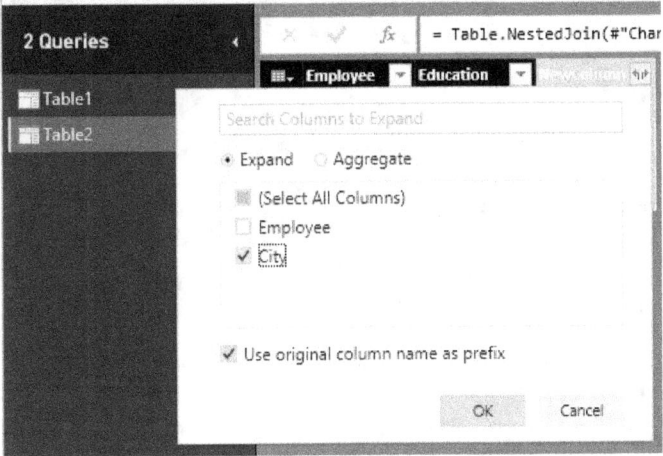

You can also choose from one of the other join types as mentioned below:
- Left Outer (all from first, matching from second): this option was the default behavior previously within Merge dialog
- Right Outer (all from second, matching from first)
- Full Outer (all rows from both)
- Inner (only matching rows); this option was available previously through "Choose only matching rows" option in Merge dialog
- Left Anti (rows only in first)
- Right Anti (rows only in second)

Power Query

At the time of writing this blog post, The Power Query Editor (GUI) only supports two types of joins mentioned above: Left Join, and Inner Join.

You should follow the same path through Merge Queries, and then you will see joining options as below:

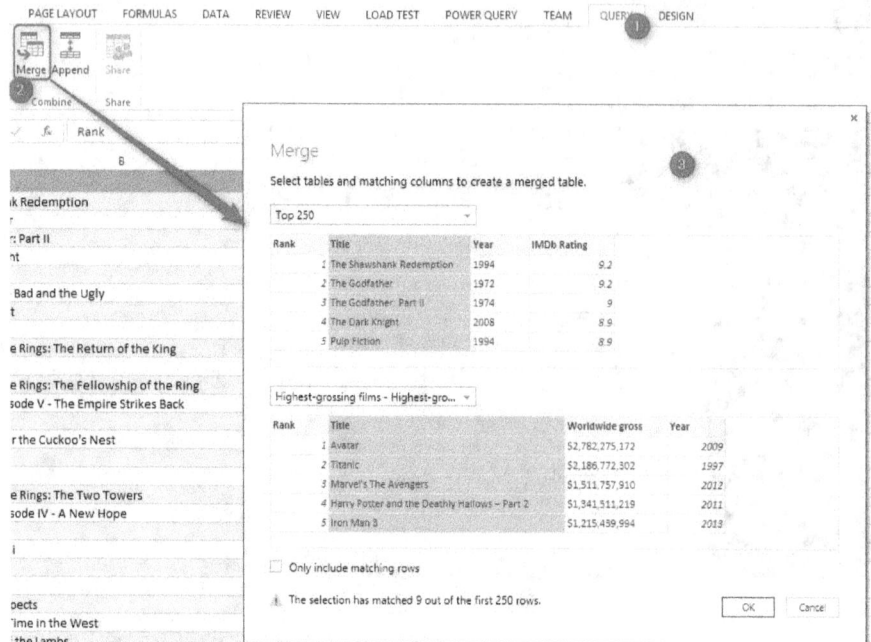

As you see the default behavior is Left join. You can change it to inner join with selecting "Only include matching rows".

Change Through M

You can apply any join type that you want simply by going to advanced editor, and changing the M script as below:

Go to View tab, and click on Advanced Editor:

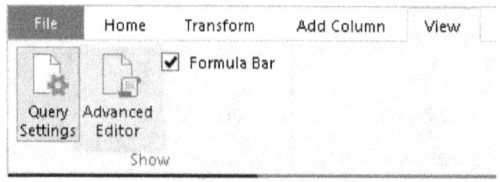

In the Advanced Editor query window, you can see the M script that builds the result set. Find the join function and change the JoinKind.

Advanced Editor

Table2

```
let
    Source = Excel.Workbook(File.Contents("C:\Users\adm_radr\Documents\join.xlsx"), null, true),
    Table2_Table = Source{[Item="Table2",Kind="Table"]}[Data],
    #"Changed Type" = Table.TransformColumnTypes(Table2_Table,{{"Employee", type text}, {"Education", type text}}),
    #"Merged Queries" = Table.NestedJoin(#"Changed Type",{"Employee"},Table1,{"Employee"},"NewColumn",JoinKind.FullOuter),
    #"Expanded NewColumn" = Table.ExpandTableColumn(#"Merged Queries", "NewColumn", {"City"}, {"NewColumn.City"})
in
    #"Expanded NewColumn"
```

JoinKind is an enumeration type that can have below values:
- JoinKind.Inner=0
- JoinKind.LeftOuter=1
- JoinKind.RightOuter=2
- JoinKind.FullOuter=3
- JoinKind.LeftAnti=4
- JoinKind.RightAnti=5

So you can change it as you want.

This feature I reckon soon will be available on Power Query Editor GUI as well, but till that time the above description hopefully helps you in any situation that you want to set a join type.

Find Mismatch Rows with Power Query in Power BI

Posted by Reza Rad on Aug 20, 2018

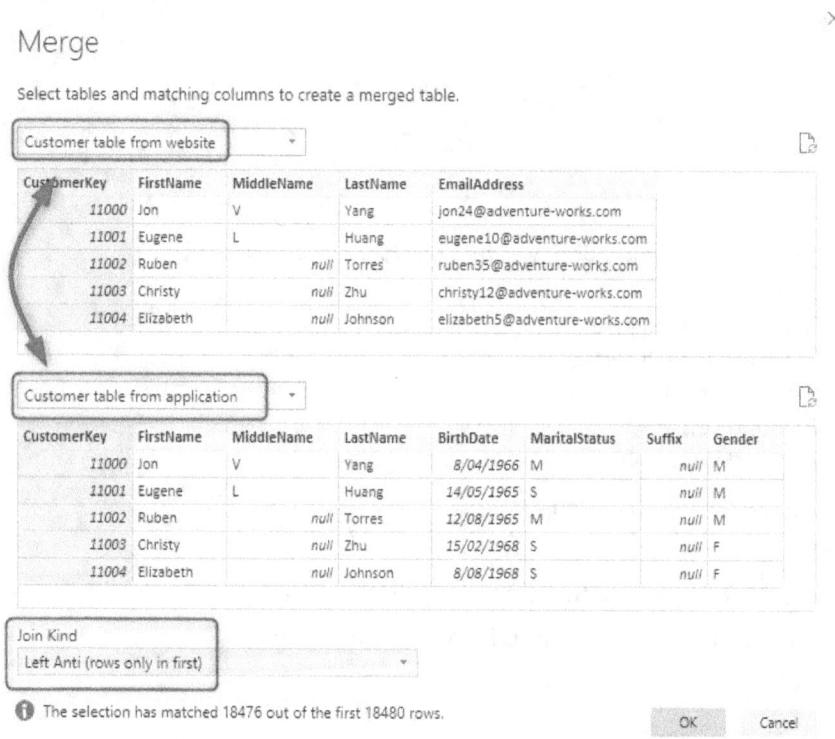

Finding rows that are in one table, but not the other is one of the most common scenarios happening in any data related applications. You may have customer records coming from two sources, and want to find data rows that exist in one, but not the other. In Power Query, you can use Merge to combine data tables. Merge can be also used for finding mismatch records. You will learn through this blog post, how in Power Query you can find out which records are missing with Merge, and then report it in Power BI. To learn more about Power BI, read Power BI book from Rookie to Rock Star.

Sample Data Tables

In this sample scenario, I have two customer tables; one customer table is coming from the website, and another customer table coming from an application. Here is the customer table from the website:

CustomerKey	FirstName	MiddleName	LastName	EmailAddress
11000	Jon	V	Yang	jon24@adventure-works.com
11001	Eugene	L	Huang	eugene10@adventure-works.com
11002	Ruben		Torres	ruben35@adventure-works.com
11003	Christy		Zhu	christy12@adventure-works.com
11004	Elizabeth		Johnson	elizabeth5@adventure-works.com
11005	Julio		Ruiz	julio1@adventure-works.com
11006	Janet	G	Alvarez	janet9@adventure-works.com
11007	Marco		Mehta	marco14@adventure-works.com
11008	Rob		Verhoff	rob4@adventure-works.com
11013	Ian	M	Jenkins	ian47@adventure-works.com
11014	Sydney		Bennett	sydney23@adventure-works.com
11015	Chloe		Young	chloe23@adventure-works.com
11016	Wyatt	L	Hill	wyatt32@adventure-works.com
11017	Shannon		Wang	shannon1@adventure-works.com

And the other table that comes from the application:

CustomerKey	FirstName	MiddleName	LastName	BirthDate	MaritalStatus	Suffix	Gender
11000	Jon	V	Yang	8/04/1966	M		M
11001	Eugene	L	Huang	14/05/1965	S		M
11002	Ruben		Torres	12/08/1965	M		M
11003	Christy		Zhu	15/02/1968	S		F
11004	Elizabeth		Johnson	8/08/1968	S		F
11005	Julio		Ruiz	5/08/1965	S		M
11006	Janet	G	Alvarez	6/12/1965	S		F
11007	Marco		Mehta	9/05/1964	M		M
11008	Rob		Verhoff	7/07/1964	S		F
11009	Shannon	C	Carlson	1/04/1964	S		M
11010	Jacquelyn	C	Suarez	6/02/1964	S		F
11017	Shannon		Wang	26/06/1944	S		F
11018	Clarence	D	Rai	9/10/1944	S		M
11019	Luke	L	Lal	7/03/1978	S		M
11020	Jordan	C	King	20/09/1978	S		M
11021	Destiny		Wilson	3/09/1978	S		F

The customer table from the website has the email address field, plus name and CustomerKey. They table coming from the application has fields such as birthdate, gender, and marital status, plus name and customer key. the link field in this scenario is CustomerKey which exists in both tables.

Merge in Power Query

Previously I have explained What the Merge is, and what is the difference of that to Append. I also explained in another blog post, about different types of Merge Kind. In this example, you would find a couple of those join kinds useful; Left Anti Join, and Right Anti Join. In Below Power Query example, I read the data from both tables, and I merge them;

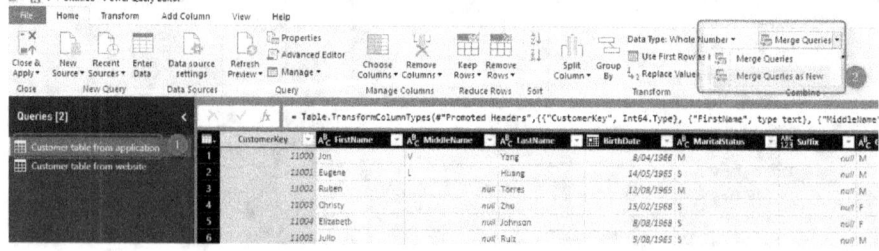

Left Anti Join: Records Only in the First Table

When I merge these two queries, I select Left Anti Join, that gives me rows that exist only in the first table (customer table from application):

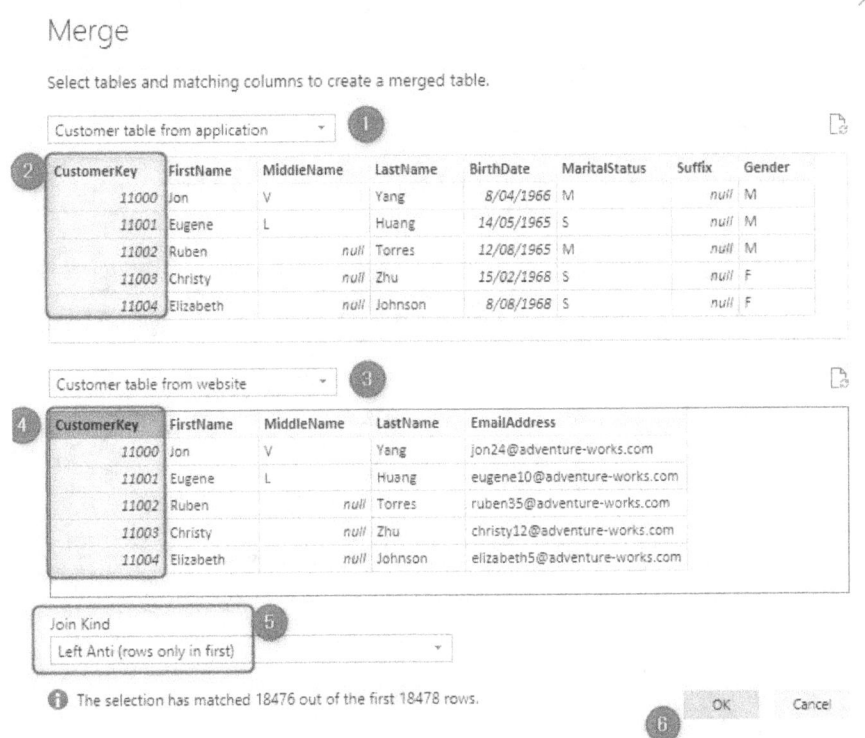

This will give you only rows that exist in the first table "Customer table from application."

Then you can remove the last column in the output because the table value would not have any rows (this are mismatch rows)

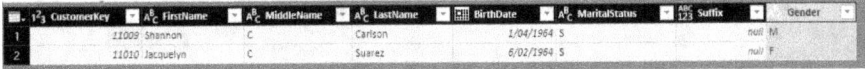

Right Anti Join: Records Only in the Second Table

The same Approach can be used for rows that exist only in the second table, using the Right Anti Join

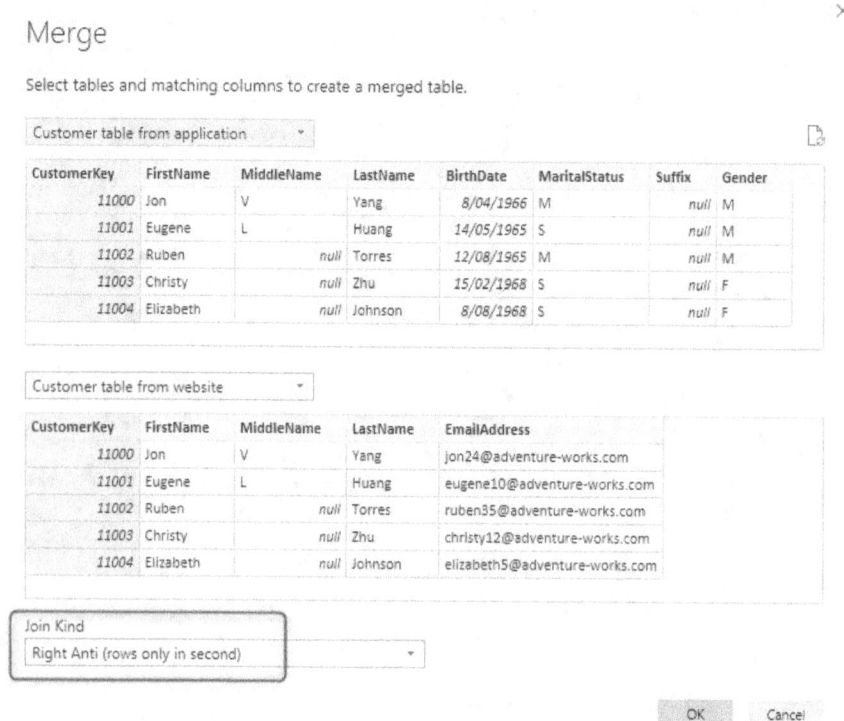

But right Anti Join will give you a result which looks a bit weird if you do not expand the table;

You DO NEED to expand the table for the second query to get mismatch rows when you use RIGHT ANIT Join. Which is an extra step, but still works fine. You can remove all columns from the first table, and expand the last column;

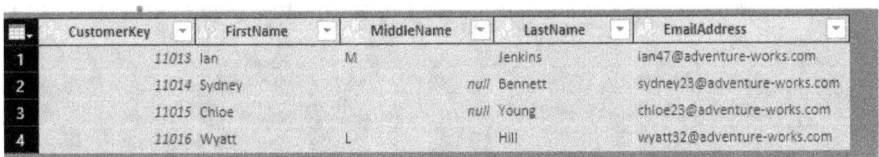

Left Anti with Changing Order of Tables; Works similar to Right Anti

Or you can switch the order of tables at the time of Merge, and use Left Anti join to get the same output;

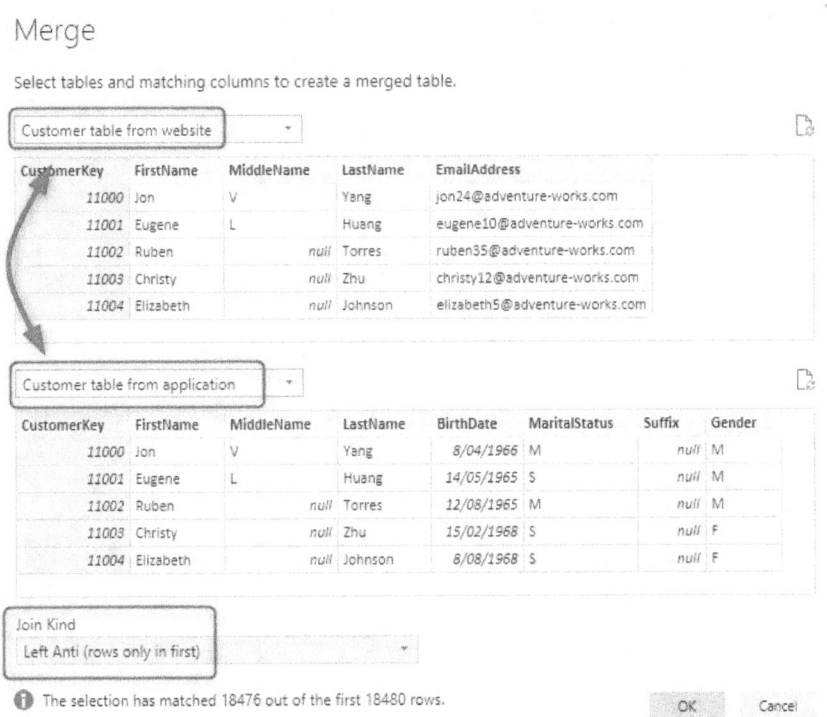

The output of this is similar to the step we have done before (it gives you the records only in the second table "customers from the website"):

	CustomerKey	FirstName	MiddleName	LastName	EmailAddress	Customer table from application
1	11013	Ian	M	Jenkins	Ian47@adventure-works.com	Table
2	11014	Sydney	null	Bennett	sydney23@adventure-works.com	Table
3	11015	Chloe	null	Young	chloe23@adventure-works.com	Table
4	11016	Wyatt	L	Hill	wyatt32@adventure-works.com	Table

Summary

In summary, this post focused on two of the least common join types in Power Query; **Left Anti** join, and **Right Anti** join. These two join types are very useful when you want to find records that exist in one of the tables, but not the other one. All you do need is to select the right order of tables and merge type in the Merge command graphical interface. If you like to know more about other types of joins, read this post.

Power BI from Rookie to Rock Star – Book 3: Power Query and Data Transformation in Power BI
Dates Between Merge Join in Power Query
Posted by Reza Rad on Aug 15, 2017

Dates Between Merge with Matching Grains

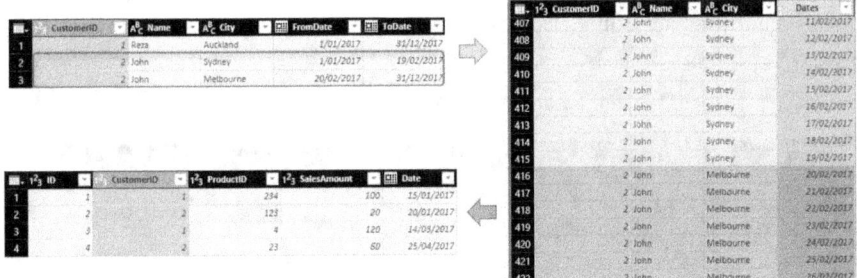

Using Merge in Power Query gives you the ability to join on an EQUAL join with one or more fields between two tables. However, in some situations, you need to do the Merge Join not based on equality of values, based on other comparison options. One of the very common use cases is to Merge Join two queries based on dates between. In this example, I am going to show you how to use Merge Join to merge based on dates between. If you want to learn more about joining tables in Power Query read this blog post. To learn more about Power BI, read Power BI book from Rookie to Rock Star.

Download Sample Data Set
Download the data set and sample from here:
Enter Your Email to download the file (required)

Download

Problem Definition

There are some situations that you need to join two tables based on dates between the not exact match of two dates. For example; consider scenario below: There are two tables; Sales table includes sales transactions by Customer, Product, and Date. And Customer table has detailed information about customer including ID, Name, and City. Here is a screenshot of Sales Table:

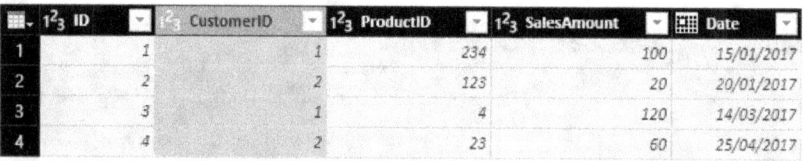

Customer's table has the history details of changes through the time. For example, the customer ID 2, has a track of change. John was living in Sydney for some time, then moved to Melbourne after that.

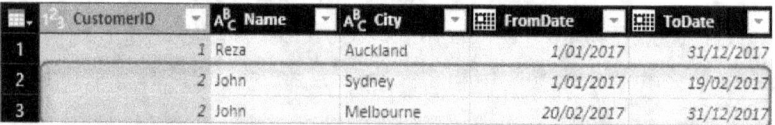

The problem we are trying to solve is to join these two tables based on their customer ID and find out the City related to that for that specific period. We have to check the Date field from Sales Table to fit into FromDate and ToDate of the Customer table.

Grain Matching

One of the easiest ways of matching two tables is to bring them both to the same grain. In this example, the Sales Table is at the grain of Customer, Product, and Date. However, the Customer table is at the grain of Customer and a change in properties such as City. We can change the grain of the customer table to be on Customer and Date. That means Having one record per every customer and every day.

Before applying this change, there is a little warning I would like to explain; with changing grain of a table to more detailed grain, the number of rows for that table will increase significantly. It is fine to do it as an intermediate change, but if you want to make this change as a final query to be loaded in Power BI, then you need to think about your approach more carefully.

Step 1: Calculating Duration

The first step in this approach is to find out how many days is the duration between FromDate and ToDate in the customer table for each row. That simply can be calculated with selecting two columns (First ToDate, then FromDate), then From Add Column Tab, under Date, Subtract Days.

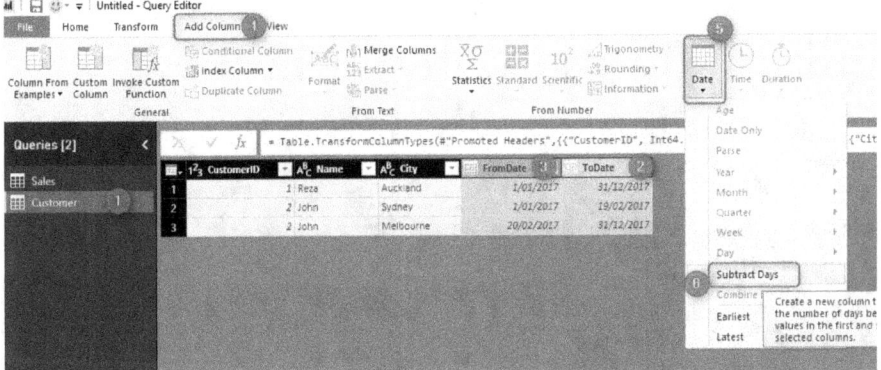

Then you will see the new column added which is the duration between From and To dates

CustomerID	Name	City	FromDate	ToDate	DateDifference
1	Reza	Auckland	1/01/2017	31/12/2017	364
2	John	Sydney	1/01/2017	19/02/2017	49
2	John	Melbourne	20/02/2017	31/12/2017	314

Step 2: Creating List of Dates

The second step is to create a list of dates for every record, starting from FromDate, adding one day at a time, for the number of occurrence in DateDifference column.

There is a generator that you can easily use to create a list of dates. List. Dates are a Power Query function which will generate a list of dates. Here is the syntax for this table;

1 List.Dates(<start date>,<occurrence>,<duration>)

- start date in this scenario will come from FromDate column
- Occurrence would come from DateDifference plus one.

Duration should be in a day Level. Duration has 4 input arguments:

1 #duration(<day>,<hour>,<minute>,<second>)

a daily duration would be: #duration(1,0,0,0)

So, we need to add a custom column to our table;

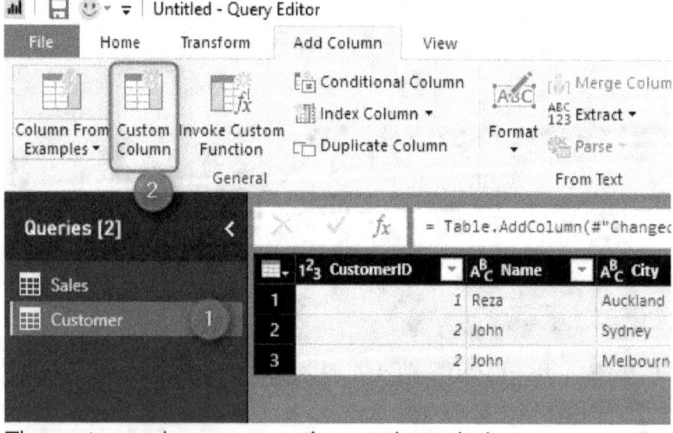

The custom column expression can be as below;
1 List.Dates([FromDate],[DateDifference]+1,#duration(1,0,0,0))

I named this column as Dates.

Here is the result:

The Dates column now has a list in every row. This list is a list of dates. Next step is to expand it.

Step 3: Expand List to Day Level

The last step to change the grain of this table, is to expand the Dates column. To expand, click on the Expand button.

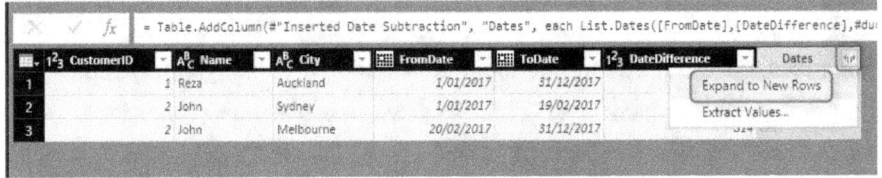

Expanding to new rows will give you a data set with all dates;

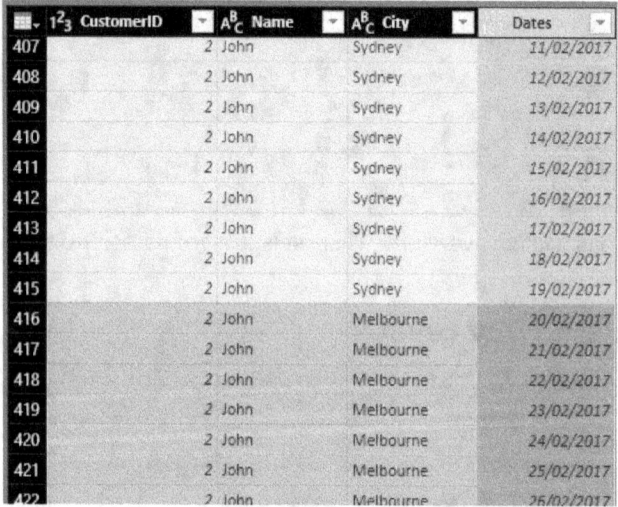

Now you can remove FromDate, ToDate, and DateDifference. We don't need these three columns anymore.

The table above is the same customer table but on different grain. We can now easily see on which dates John was in Sydney, and which dates in Melbourne. This table now can be easily merged with the sales table.

Merging Tables on the Same Grain

When both tables are at the same grain, then you can easily merge them.

Merge

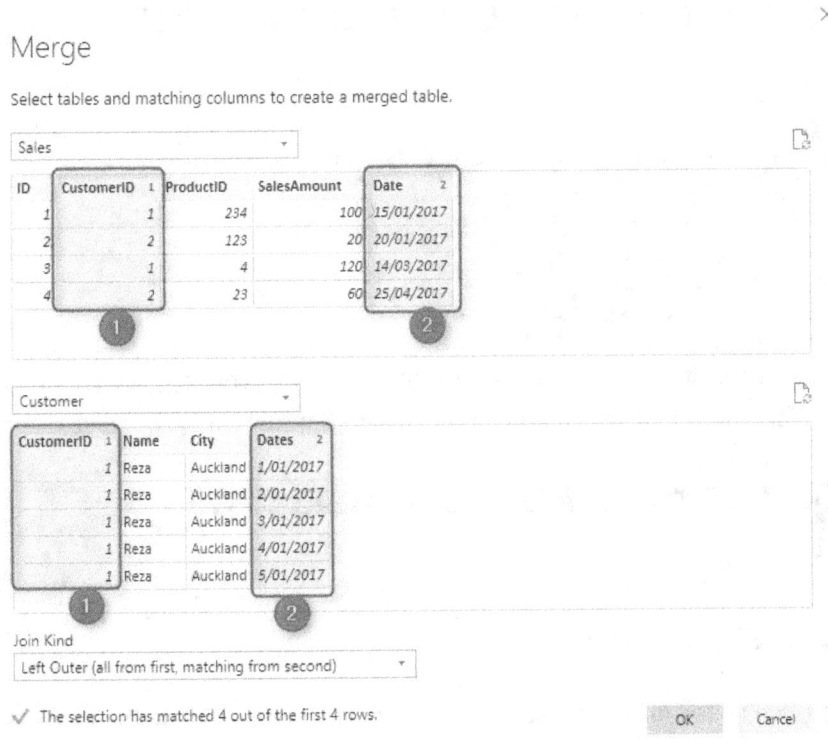

Merge should be between two tables, based on CustomerID and Dates. You need to hold Ctrl key to select more than one column. And make sure you select them in the same order in both tables. After merge then you can expand and only select City and Name from the other table;

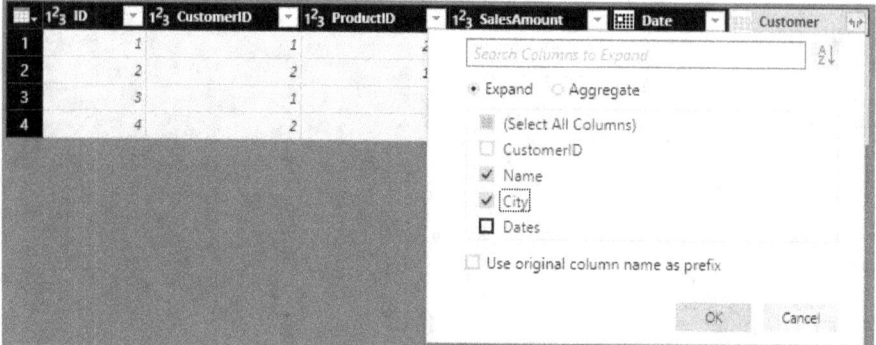

The final result shows that two sales transactions for John happened at two different times that John has been in two different cities of Sydney and Melbourne.

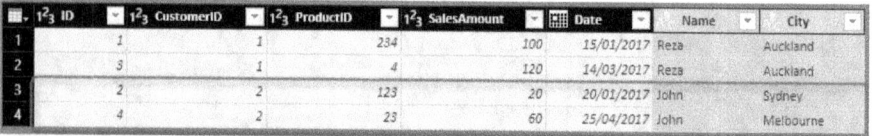

Final Step: Cleansing

You won't need the first two tables after merging them, you can disable their load to avoid extra memory consumption (especially for Customer table which should be big after grain change). To learn more about Enable Load and to solve performance issues, read this blog post.

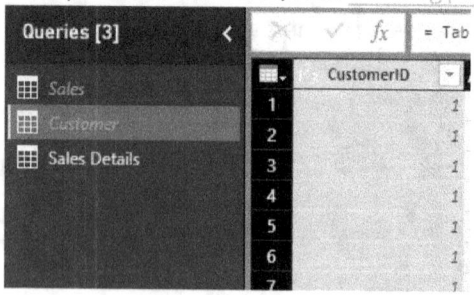

Summary

There are multiple ways of joining two tables based on the non-equality comparison. Matching grain is one of them and works perfectly fine, and easy to implement. In this post, you've learned how to use grain matching to do this joining and get the join result based on dates between comparison. With this method, be careful to disable the load of the table that you've changed the grain for it to avoid performance issues afterward.

Power BI from Rookie to Rock Star – Book 3: Power Query and Data Transformation in Power BI

Pivot and Unpivot with Power BI

Posted by Reza Rad on Apr 7, 2016

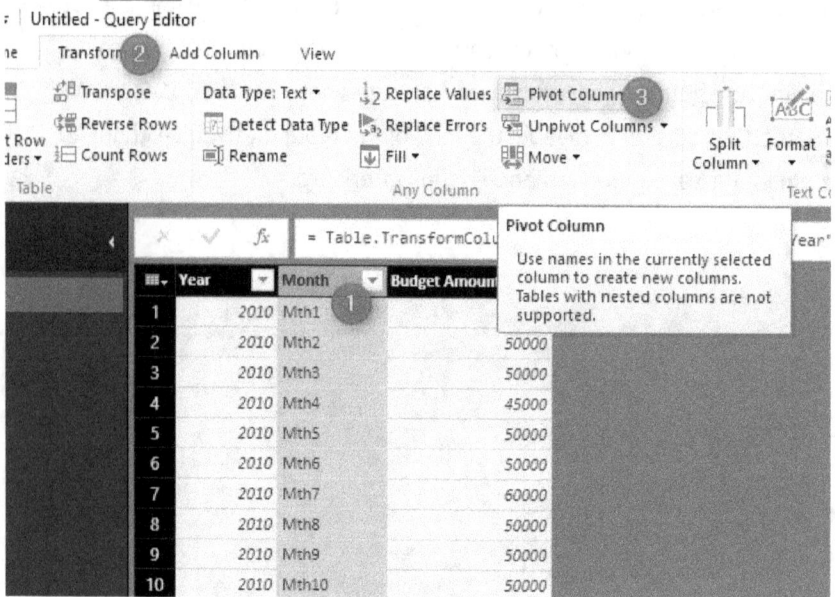

Turning columns to rows or rows to columns is easy with Power Query and Power BI. There are many situations that you get a name, value data source, and wants to convert that into columns with values underneath.

On the other hand, many times you get multiple columns and want to change it to name, value structure with a column for name, another column for value. That's why Pivot and Unpivot are for. In this post, I'll get you through the basic pivot and unpivot. If you want to read more about Power Query, read it from Power BI online book.

Pivot: Turning Name,Value Rows to Columns

Consider we have a data source like this:

	A	B	C
1	Year	Month	Budget Amount
2	2010	Mth1	50000
3	2010	Mth2	50000
4	2010	Mth3	50000
5	2010	Mth4	45000
6	2010	Mth5	50000
7	2010	Mth6	50000
8	2010	Mth7	60000
9	2010	Mth8	50000
10	2010	Mth9	50000
11	2010	Mth10	50000
12	2010	Mth11	50000
13	2010	Mth12	50000
14	2011	Mth1	50000
15	2011	Mth2	55000
16	2011	Mth3	55000
17	2011	Mth4	65000
18	2011	Mth5	55000
19	2011	Mth6	55000

(Name = Month column, Value = Budget Amount column)

above data set is budget information. If we want to spread the table with a column for every month, we can simply use Pivot as below:

first click on the column that contains *names*, in this example it would be Month column. Then from Transform menu tab, choose Pivot Column.

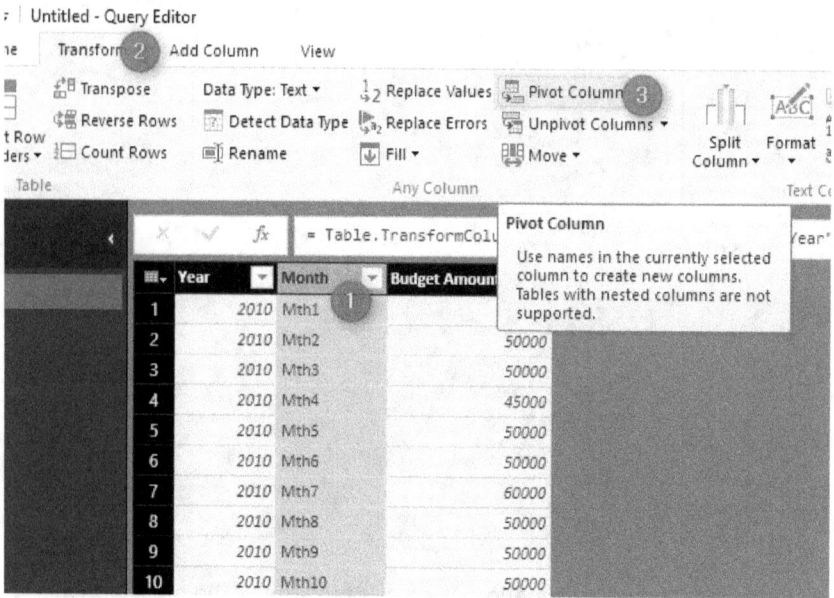

The Pivot dialog box asks you to choose the *Value* column, which is Budget Amount in this example

and then simply and easily I have the pivoted result set;

You can see that I have a column for each month now. Year column was just passed through. I can have as many as columns I want to pass through. The important factor for Pivot is that there should be a name column, and a value column. You can also see the Table.Pivot script of Power Query generated for this example in above screenshot. Now let's see what happens if name value is a bit different;

Year	Month	Budget Amount
2010	Mth1	50000
2010	Mth2	50000
2010	Mth3	50000
2010	Mth4	45000
2010	Mth5	50000
2010	Mth6	50000
2010	Mth7	60000
2010	Mth8	50000
2010	Mth9	50000
2010	Mth10	50000
2010	Mth11	50000
2010	Mth11	50000
2010	Mth12	50000
2011	Mth1	50000
2011	Mth2	55000
2011	Mth3	55000
2011	Mth5	55000
2011	Mth6	55000
2011	Mth7	55000
2011	Mth8	55000

In this example, I have two records for a single name (Mth 11 2010 is repeated). and for some names, I don't have any records at all (Mth 4 2011 is missing)

Pivot dialog has the option to choose the aggregation function, and that is especially for cases that a name appeared more than once in the data set. Default aggregation is Sum,

So the default Pivot will result as below:

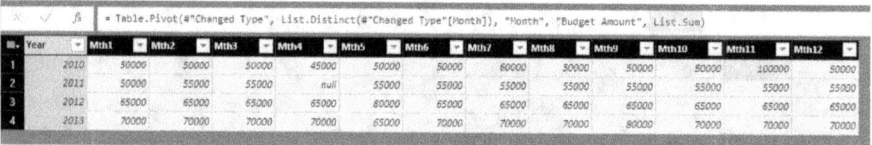

However, if the aggregation is set to Do Not Aggregate. then you will get an error when a name is repeated in the data set

Here is the error value in the result set;

Year	Mth1	Mth2	Mth3	Mth4	Mth5	Mth6	Mth7	Mth8	Mth9	Mth10	Mth11	Mth12
2010	50000	50000	50000	45000	50000	50000	60000	50000	50000	50000 Error	50000	50000
2011	50000	55000	55000	null	55000	55000	55000	55000	55000	55000	55000	55000
2012	65000	65000	65000	65000	80000	65000	65000	65000	65000	65000	65000	65000
2013	70000	70000	70000	70000	65000	70000	70000	70000	80000	70000	70000	70000

and the error would be:

Expression.Error: There were too many elements in the enumeration to complete the operation.

Details:

  List

So Pivot is easy and simple to do, but you have to be careful about the nature and quality of the source data set. If it is normal to have a name repeated in the source data, then an aggregation needs to be set properly. If you expect each name to appear once, then setting it as Do Not Aggregate works better because you can use error handling mechanism in Power Query to handle error somehow.

Unpivot; Turning Columns to Rows; Name, Values

Unpivot does the reverse. It turns multiple column headers into a single column but in rows. And store their values in another column. Here is an example of Budget data that usually you get from the finance department;

Year	Mth1	Mth2	Mth3	Mth4	Mth5	Mth6	Mth7	Mth8	Mth9	Mth10	Mth11	Mth12
2010	50000	50000	50000	45000	50000	50000	60000	50000	50000	50000	50000	50000
2011	50000	55000	55000	65000	55000	55000	55000	55000	55000	55000	55000	55000
2012	65000	65000	65000	65000	80000	65000	65000	65000	65000	65000	65000	65000
2013	70000	70000	70000	70000	65000	70000	70000	70000	80000	70000	70000	70000

You can click on Columns that you want to unpivot, and then select Unpivot columns (or you can do the reverse, select pass through columns, and select unpivot other columns);

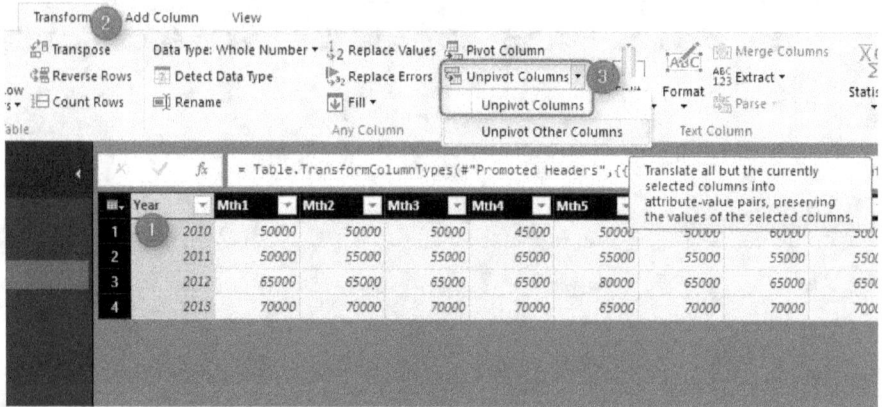

and then unpivoted result set would be as below:

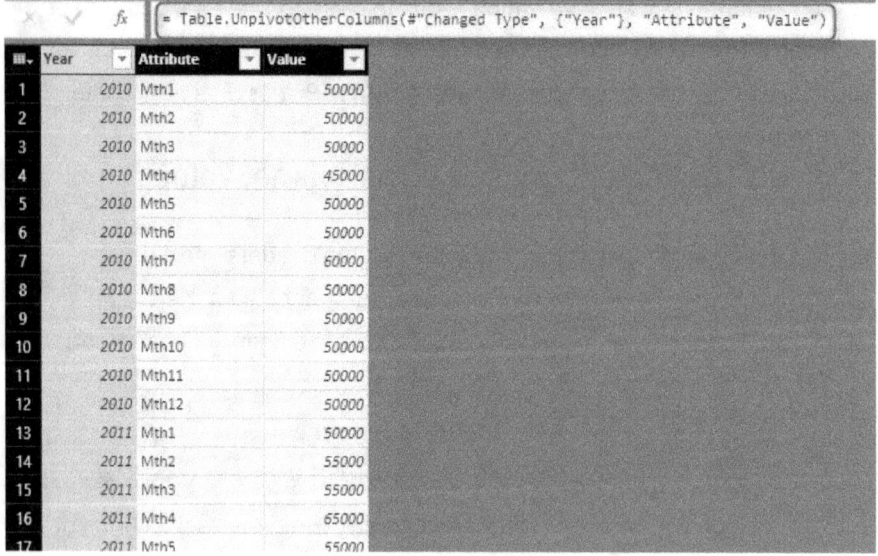

As you see columns and their values are now converted to rows split into only two columns: attribute, and value.

If you get a repetitive column in the source data like below;

	A	B	C	D	E	F	G	H	I	J	K	L	M	N
1	Year	Mth1	Mth2	Mth3	Mth4	Mth5	Mth6	Mth7	Mth8	Mth8	Mth9	Mth10	Mth11	Mth12
2	2010	50000	50000	50000	45000	50000	50000	60000	50000	50000	50000	50000	50000	50000
3	2010	50000	50000	50000	55000	50000	50000	60000	50000	50000	50000	50000	50000	50000
4	2011	50000	55000	55000	65000	55000	55000	55000	55000	55000	55000	55000	55000	55000
5	2012	65000	65000	65000	65000	80000	65000	65000	65000	65000	65000	65000	65000	65000
6	2013	70000	70000	70000	70000	65000	70000	70000	70000	70000	80000	70000	70000	70000

Then you would get that repeated in the attribute field after unpivot;

	Year	Attribute	Value
1	2010	Mth1	50000
2	2010	Mth2	50000
3	2010	Mth3	50000
4	2010	Mth4	45000
5	2010	Mth5	50000
6	2010	Mth6	50000
7	2010	Mth7	60000
8	2010	Mth8	50000
9	2010	Mth8_1	50000
10	2010	Mth9	50000
11	2010	Mth10	50000
12	2010	Mth11	50000
13	2010	Mth12	50000

So the best way to handle that is to identify the repetitive column before applying unpviot. You can do these types of checking with Power Query scripts and other functions, If you want to read more about Power Query read it from Power BI online book.

Power BI from Rookie to Rock Star – Book 3: Power Query and Data Transformation in Power BI
Warning! Misleading Power Query Filtering
Posted by Reza Rad on Dec 15, 2016

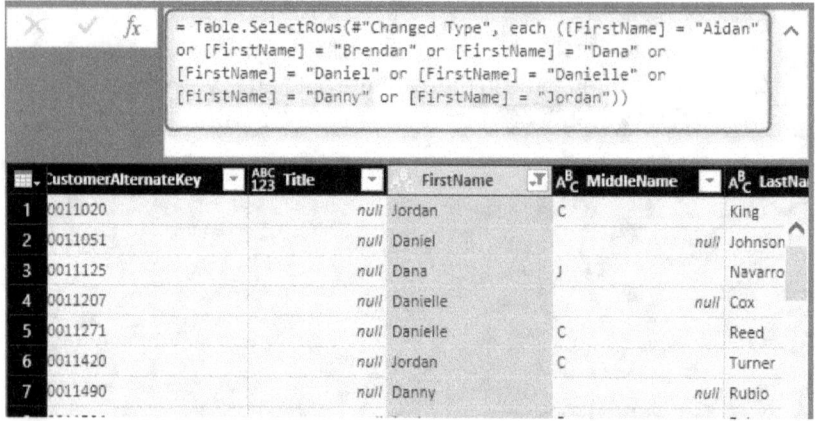

Filtering in Power Query component of Power BI is easy. However it can be misleading very easily as well. I have seen the usage of this filtering inappropriately in many cases. Many people simply believe in what they see, rather than seeing behind the scenes. Power Query filtering is totally different when you do basic filtering or advanced filtering, and the result of filtering will be different too. In this post, I'll show you through a very simple example of how misleading it can be and what it the correct way to do filtering in Power Query. This post is a must read for everyone who uses filtering in Power Query. If you like to learn more about Power BI, read the Power BI online book from Rookie to Rock Star.

Prerequisite

For this example, I'll use the AdventureWorksDW SQL Server database example. Only one table which is DimCustomer.

Filtering in Power Query

Filtering rows is one of the most basic requirements in a data preparation tool such as Power Query, and Power Query do it strongly with an Excel-like behavior for filtering. To see what it looks like open Power BI Desktop (or Excel), and Get Data from the database and table above; DimCustomer, Click on Edit to open the Query Editor window.

In the Query Editor window, there is a button on the top right-hand side of every column that gives you access to filtering rows

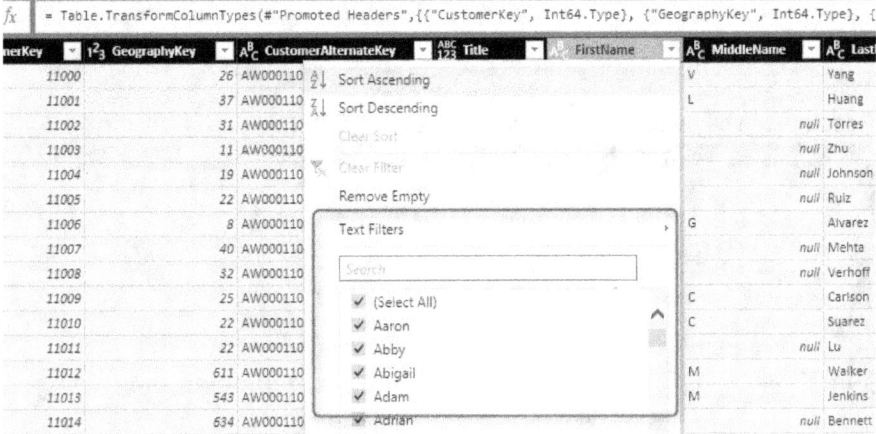

You can simply filter values in the search box provided.

Basic Filtering

For basic filtering, all you need to do is typing in the text, number, or date you want in the search box and find values to select from the list. For example, if you want to filter all data rows to be only for the FirstName of David, you can simply type it and select and click on OK.

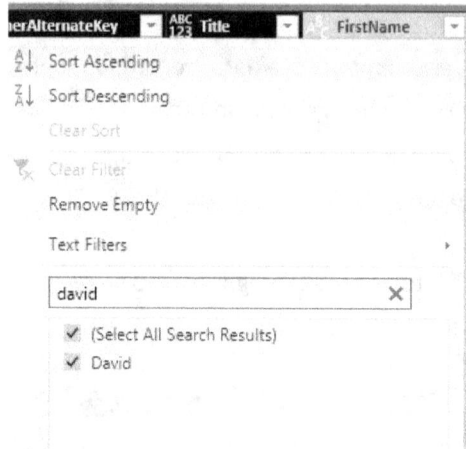

Result then will be only records with David as the first name.

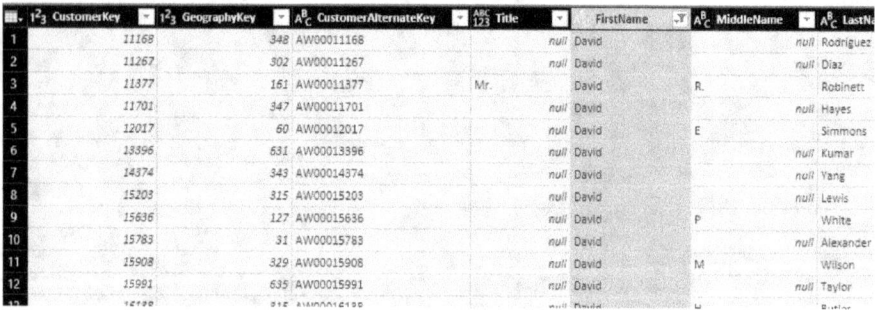

Exactly as you expect. Now let's see when it is misleading.

Misleading Behavior of Basic Filtering

If you want to do equity filtering, basic filtering is great. For example, you only want to pick David, and that's what we've done in the above example.

However what if you want to do similarity filtering? For example, let's say you are interested in FirstNames that has three characters of "Dan" in it. You can do it in the same search box of basic filtering, and this will give you a list of all first names that have "Dan" in it.

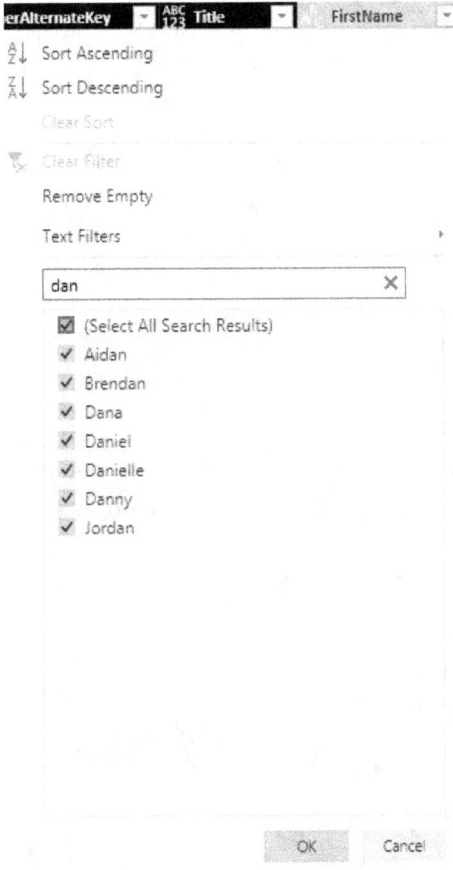

And then you can click on OK. The result will be showing you all first names with "Dan" characters in it. So everything looks exactly as expected, right?

Power BI from Rookie to Rock Star – Book 3: Power Query and Data Transformation in Power BI

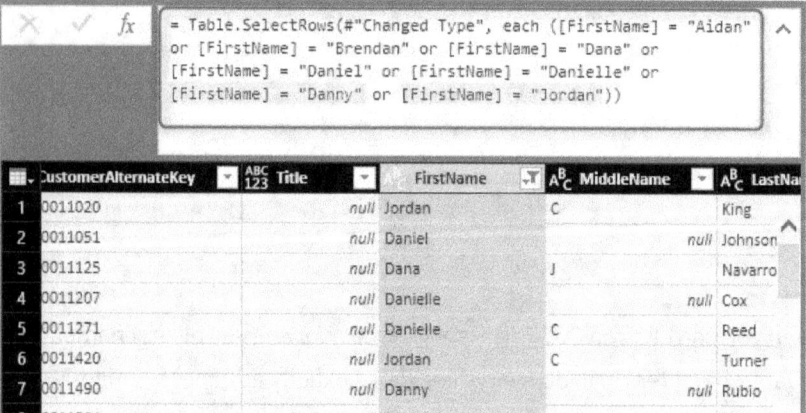

However, as a Power Query geek, I always look at the M script of each step to see what is happening behind the scene. For this case, here is the Power Query M script;

The script tells the whole story. Even though you typed in "Dan" and Power Query showed you all FirstNames that has "Dan" in it. The script still uses equity filters for every individual FirstName. For this data set, there won't be any issue obviously, because all FirstNames with "Dan" is already selected. However, if new data rows are coming into this table in the future, and they have records with FirstNames that are not one of these values, for example, Dandy, it won't be picked! As a result, the filter won't work exactly as you expect. That's why I say this is misleading.

Advanced Filtering: Correct Filtering

Basic filtering is very handy with that search box and suggestions of items while you are typing, but it is misleading easily as you have seen above, and can't give you what you expect in many real-world scenarios. Advanced Filtering is simply what you can see on top of the Search box, which depends on the data type of column can be Text Filters, Number Filters, Date Filters, etc. If we want to do the same "Dan" filter here, I can go to Text Filtering and select Contains.

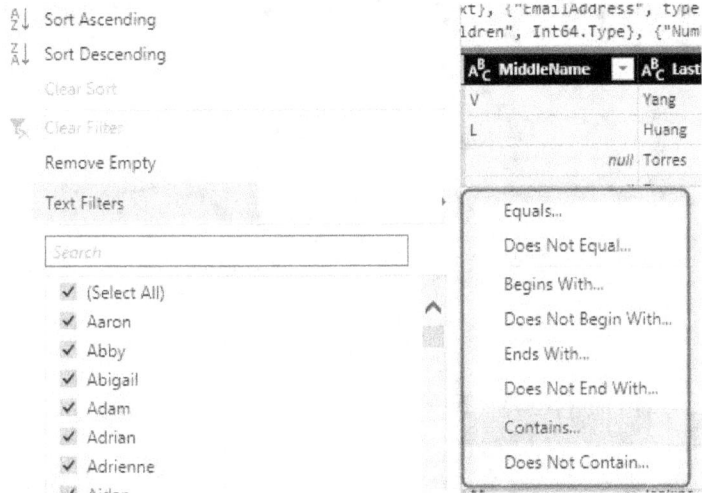

You can even choose filters such as Begins With or Ends With or many other choices. For this example, I'll select Contains, and type in Dan in the text box of Contains.

Filter Rows

○ Basic   ○ Advanced

Show rows where: FirstName

[contains ▼] [dan ▼]

● And   ○ Or

[▼] [Type or select a value ▼]

OK   Cancel

After clicking on OK, you will see the same result set (like the time that you did basic filtering with "Dan"). However the M script this time is different;

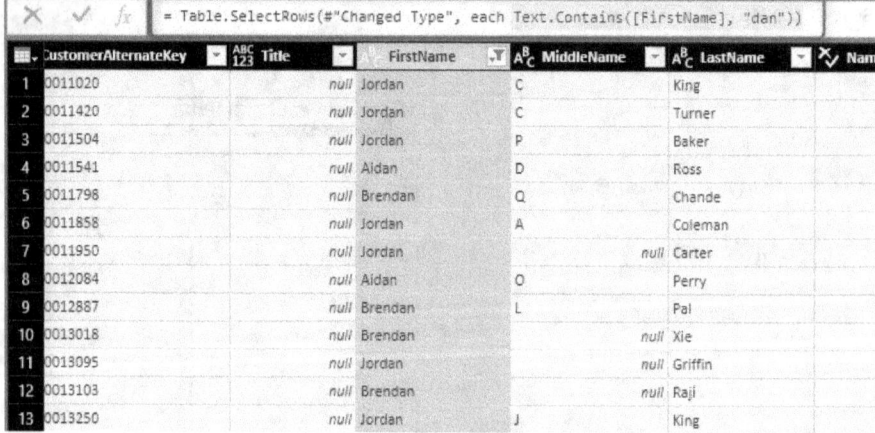

You can see the big difference now, This time M script used **Text.Contains** function. This function will pick every new value with "Dan" in the FirstName. There will be no values missing in this way. You will be amazed at how many Power Query scenarios are not working correctly because of this very simple reason. There are advanced filters for all types of data types.

Summary

Basic Filtering is good only if you want to do equity filtering for values that exist in the current data set. However it won't work correctly if you want to check ranges, or contains or things that are not an exact equity filter. Advanced Filtering is the correct way of filtering in Power Query, and there are advanced filters for all types of data types; Numbers, Text, Date.... This is a very simple fact, but not considering that will bring lots of unwanted behavior and incorrect insight to your Power BI solution.

Power BI from Rookie to Rock Star – Book 3: Power Query and Data Transformation in Power BI

Grouping in Power Query; Getting The Last Item in Each Group

Posted by Reza Rad on Aug 22, 2016

Power BI or Power Query in Excel (or Get Data and Transform as the new name of it) can do many data transformations. One of these transformations is grouping rows by a number of fields. If you use the graphical user interface in Power Query for Power BI or Excel, you have a number of options to get some aggregated results such as a count of rows, maximum or minimum, an average of each group, or sum... But there are still heaps of operations that you cannot perform through GUI, such as getting the last item in each group, or first item. Fortunately, with M (Power Query Formula Language), you can apply any of these operations you want. In this post I'll show you how to get the benefit of both; start with GUI to write the Group by the command for you, and then customize it in M script to achieve what you want. If you like to learn more about Power BI read Power BI online book; from Rookie to Rock Star. If you like to learn more about Power Query, start with the Introduction to Power Query.

Learning Objectives for this section

By completing the example of this post, you will learn;

- How to perform Group By in Power Query/Power BI
- How to leverage pre-defined aggregation functions in Group By GUI window
- How to extend grouping possibilities with changes in Power Query script

Prerequisite

For this example, I will be using AdventureWorksDW sample Microsoft SQL Server database. You can download it from here.

Scenario

The scenario that I want to solve as an example is this: FactInternetSales has sales transaction information for each customer, by each product, each order date, and some other information. We want to have a grouped table by the customer, which has the number of sales transaction by each customer, total sales amount for that customer, the first and the last sales amount for that customer. First and last defined by the first and last order date for the transaction.

Get Data

Let's start by getting data from SQL Server, Choose AdventureWorksDW as the source database, and select DimCustomer and FactInternetSales as the only tables for this example. Click on Edit to move into Power Query window.

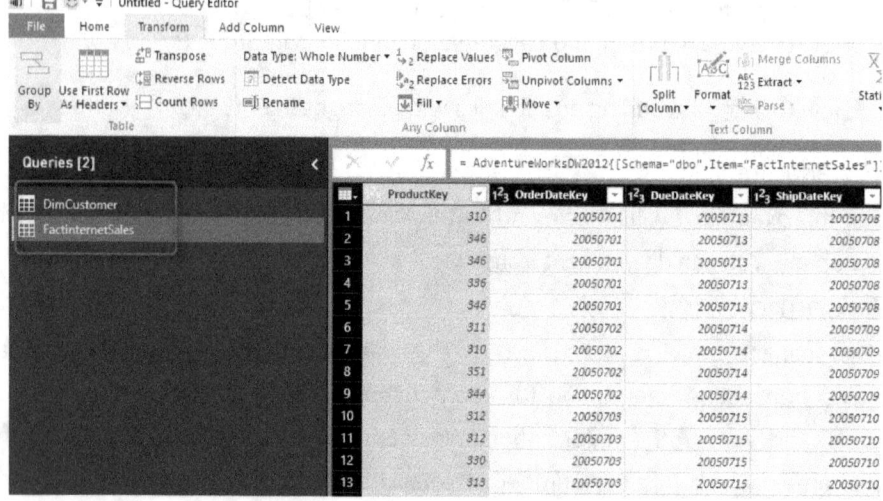

Group By Transformation

FactIntenetSales table is the one we want to apply all transformations in. So Click on FactInternetSales first, then from Transform Tab, select Group By option as the first menu option.

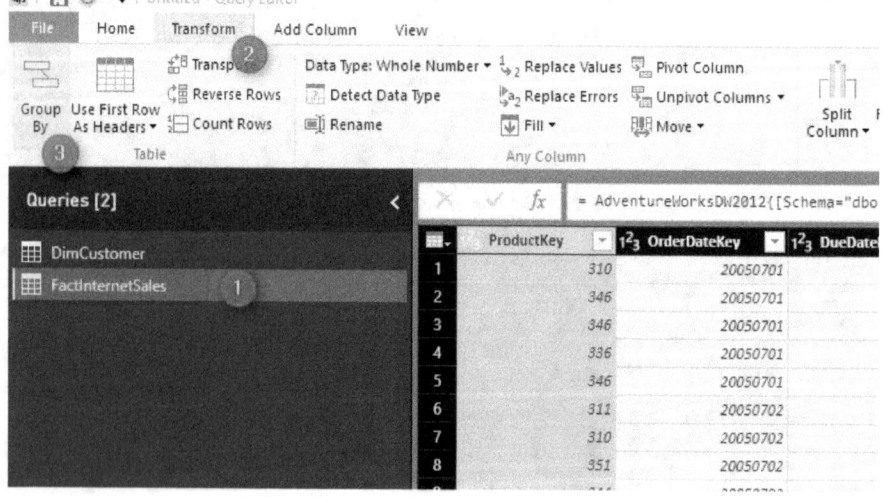

220 | Page

This will open the Group By dialog window with some configuration options

By default Group By happens on the selected columns. Because usually, the first column is the selected column (in our table ProductKey), then the column mentioned under group by section is also ProductKey. You can change this to another column and add or remove columns in this section.

Choose the Group By Field

Based on your final grain of the output table the group by field will be defined. In this example we want the final table to have one record per Customer, so CustomerKey (which is the identifier for each customer) should be our Group By Column.

Group By

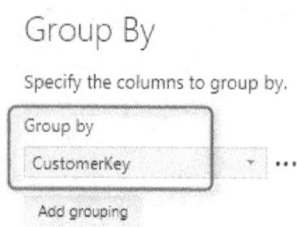

Note that you can add as many fields as you want in the Group By section. The result would be one record per combination of unique values from all these fields.

Add Aggregation Fields

Group by result would be one record per each unique combination of all fields set in the "group by" section. Also you can also have some aggregated columns. Here is a list of operations you can have by default:

Most of the items above are self-explanatory. For example; when you want to count a number of the sales transaction. You can use Count Rows. If you want total Sales amount for each group, you can choose Sum, and then in the Column section choose the column as SalesAmount. All Rows will generate a sub-table in each element of the aggregated table that contains all rows in that group.

Columns that I want to create in this section are:

Order Count (Count Rows), Total Revenue (Sum of Sales Amount), Order Details (All Rows)

Adding aggregated columns is as easy as that. Now If you click on OK, you will see the result;

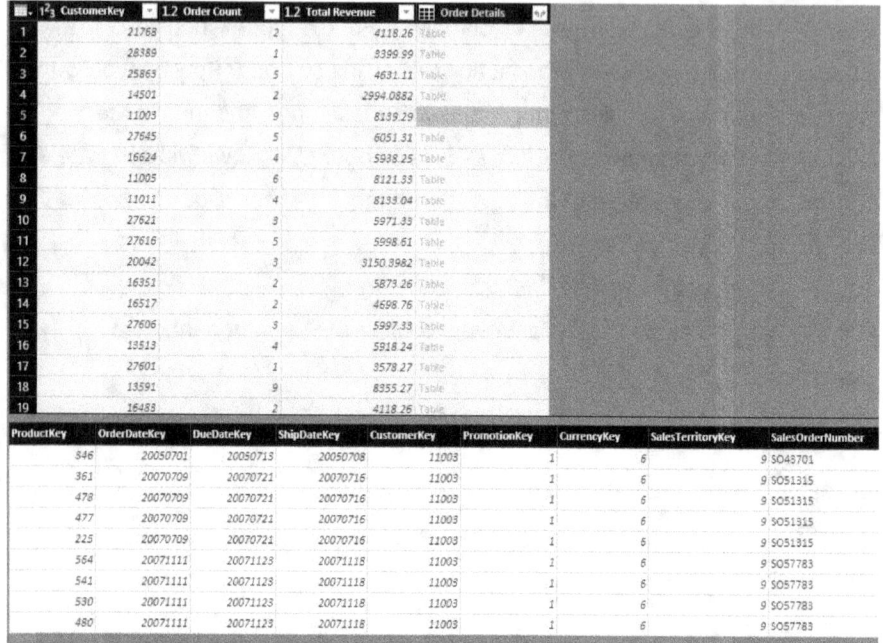

As you can see Order Count and Total Revenue show the aggregated result of each group, and Order Details (if you click not on the "Table" itself, but on a blank area on that cell) contains the actual rows in each group. This detailed view can be used for many other calculations or transformations later on. In many cases, you will find the All rows option useful.

First and Last Item in each Group

Getting some default aggregation was as easy as selecting them in Group By window. However, not all types of operations are listed there. For example in the detailed table above you can see that customer 11003 had nine sales transaction, and they happened in different Order dates, getting the first and last order date is easy with Max and Min operations. However getting the sales amount or product key associated with that record, or in other words getting the first and last item in each group isn't possible through GUI. Fortunately, we can use M (Power Query formula language) to achieve this easily.

Sort By Date

To get the first or last item in each group, I have to order the table based on that date column. Sorting is possible simply through GUI., and I have to apply that to the step before group by operation. So from the right-hand side applied steps list I'll select Navigation (which is the step before Grouped Rows);

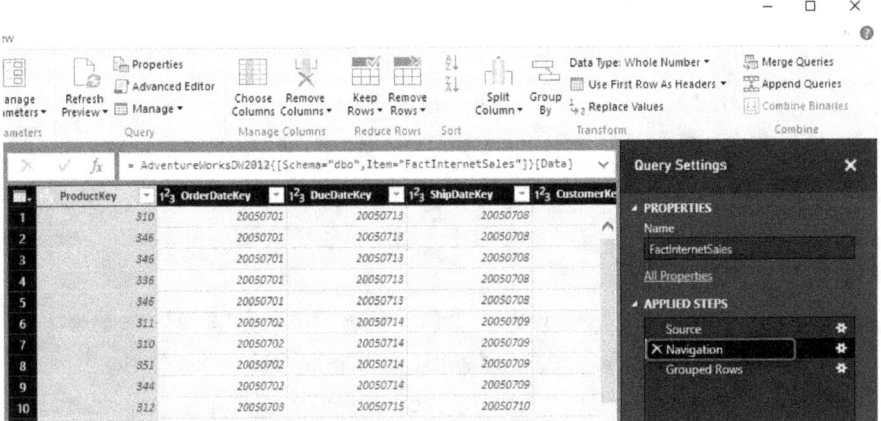

Now in this view, you can order simply by clicking on OrderDateKey and Choose Sort Ascending.

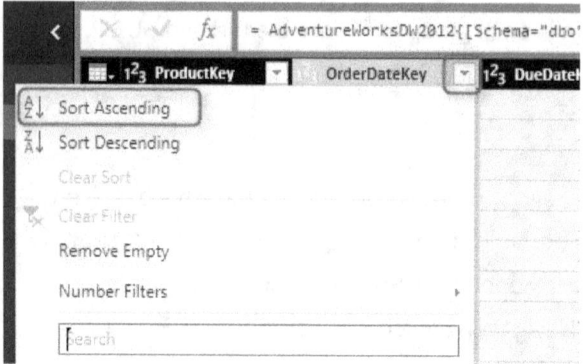

This will create another step, and asks you do you want to INSERT this step here?

Click on Insert to confirm you want to insert it here before the Grouped Rows. And then you will see a Sorted Rows step added before Grouped Rows. This means Grouped Rows will use the output of Sorted Rows step as the input for grouping (which is exactly what we want).

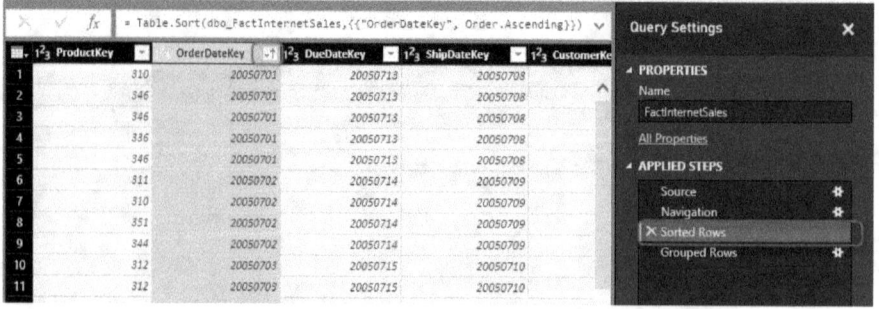

Now you can go to the Grouped Rows step to see the result hasn't changed, but the sub-tables are sorted now. All we need from here is to get the first and last item in the subtable.
** If you want to sort based on multiple columns go to the Advanced Editor and add as many as sections you want to Table.Sort input parameters.
List.First and List.Last

Fortunately, Power Query has a bunch of operations on List that we can use. List.First will return the first item in the list (based on the order defined in the list), and List.Last will return the last item. So let's use them in the Group By operation to fetch the first and last sales amount. To make changes, you need to go to script editor in Power Query which can be achieved via Advanced Editor option in the Home tab. You have to make sure that you are in the FactInternetSales Query first.

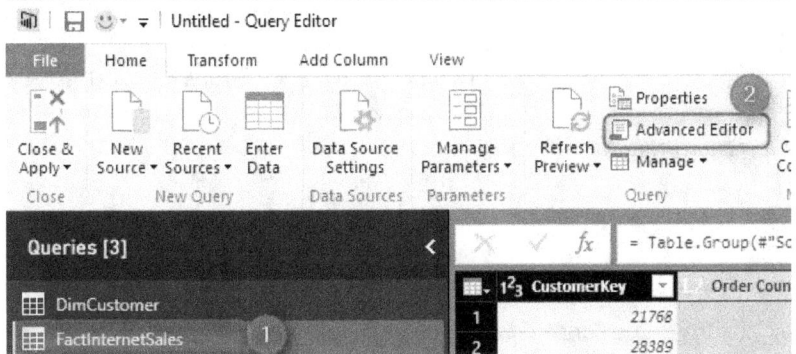

Advanced Editor will show you M script that builds the output and the group by the command as well.

```
1  let
2      Source = Sql.Databases("."),
3      AdventureWorksDW2012 =
4          Source{[Name="AdventureWorksDW2012"]}[Data],
5
```

```
6    dbo_FactInternetSales =
7 AdventureWorksDW2012{[Schema="dbo",Item="FactInternetSales"]}[Data]
8,
    #"Sorted Rows" = Table.Sort(dbo_FactInternetSales,{{"OrderDateKey",
    Order.Ascending}}),
    #"Grouped Rows" = Table.Group(#"Sorted Rows", {"CustomerKey"},
    {{"Order Count", each Table.RowCount(_), type number}, {"Total Revenue",
    each List.Sum([SalesAmount]), type number}, {"Order Details", each _, type
    table}})
in
    #"Grouped Rows"
```

The script in above code section created automatically when you did transformations through GUI. The line with Table.Group is the line that does all the grouping and aggregation. It is a long line, so let me format it better for easier understanding;

```
      #"Grouped Rows" = Table.Group(#"Sorted Rows",
6 7 8 9               type              {"CustomerKey"},
number},                                {
                                          {"Order Count", each Table.RowCount(_),
                                          {"Total Revenue", each
10    11   List.Sum([SalesAmount]),     type
number}, 12 13
                                          {"Order Details", each _, type table}
                                        }
                                      )
```

Script below is the same script. I just put some enters and tabs to format it better for reading. The above section shows Table.Group section of the script. As you can see Table.Group gets a table as input, which is the #"Sorted Rows" table from the previous step. The group by field is "CustomerKey". and then a set of aggregated columns one after each other (which is highlighted in the code above). Each column has the name of the column, type of transformation (or aggregation), and the data type of the column. For example:

```
                                {"Total Revenue", each
10
    List.Sum([SalesAmount]), type number},
```

Total Revenue is the name of the column. Calculation for this column is the Sum of [SalesAmount] which is one of the fields in the table, and the output is of type number.

So by now you should thinking of how each is to create a new aggregated column here; by adding similar column in the script. I add the new column after Order Details column, so I need an extra comma (,) after that line, and the new lines would be;

```
1  let
2      Source = Sql.Databases("."),
3      AdventureWorksDW2012 =
4  Source{[Name="AdventureWorksDW2012"]}[Data],
5      dbo_FactInternetSales =
6  AdventureWorksDW2012{[Schema="dbo",Item="FactInternetSales"]}[Dat
7  a],
8      #"Sorted Rows" = Table.Sort(dbo_FactInternetSales,{{"OrderDateKey",
9  Order.Ascending}}),
10     #"Grouped Rows" = Table.Group(#"Sorted Rows",
                           {"CustomerKey"},
11                         {
                               {"Order Count", each Table.RowCount(_),
12 type number},      {"Total Revenue", each
13 List.Sum([SalesAmount]), type number},
                           {"Order Details", each _, type table},
14                         {"First SalesAmount", each
   List.First([SalesAmount]), type number},
15                         {"Last SalesAmount", each
   List.Last([SalesAmount]), type number}
                           }
16                     )
17 in
   #"Grouped Rows"
```

Marked lines above use List.First and List.Last on the same structure that List.Sum worked. Because we have already sorted the table based on OrderDate so the first item would be the first sales transaction, and the last item would be the last.

Here is the output of this change:

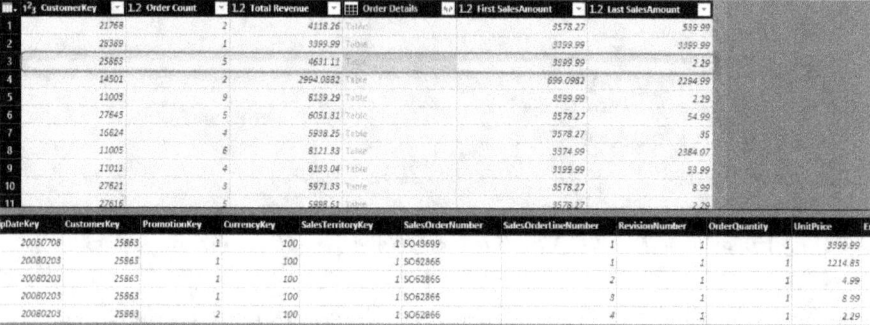

You can see that the first and the last SalesAmount picked correctly from each group as two new columns.

** Note that with adding some changes in script editor that are not supported through GUI, you will lose the GUI configuration window section. As a result of the change here you cannot change Grouping configuration in GUI anymore, if you want to change it, you have to go to Advanced Editor for this section. So if you are a GUI fan, better to apply all required configuration first, and then add extra logic in the code.

Fuzzy Matching in Power BI and Power Query; Match based on Similarity Threshold

Posted by Reza Rad on Oct 23, 2018

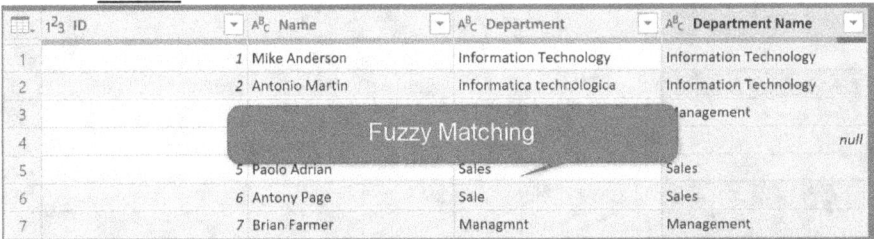

After a long wait, in the October 2018 release of Power BI Desktop, we saw the fuzzy matching feature added finally. Yay! Have you ever wanted to match two tables together but not on exact matches, but also a threshold of similarity? If your answer to this question is yes, then this feature is built for you. Let's explore in details how the fuzzy matching works in Power BI. To learn more about Power BI, read Power BI from Rookie to Rock Star.

Enable the Preview Feature

At the time of writing this blog post, Fuzzy matching is a preview feature, and you have to enable it in Power BI Desktop -> Files -> Options and Settings -> Options;

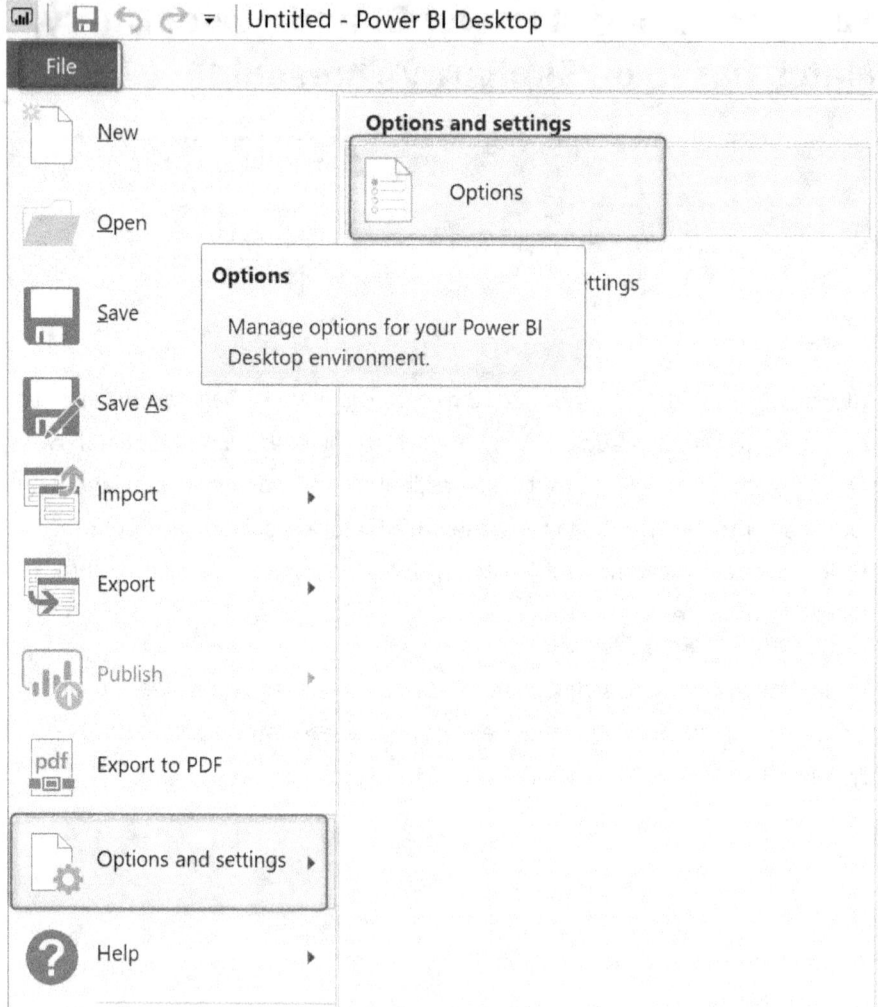

In the Options window, under Preview Features, select the checkbox beside "Enable fuzzy merge"

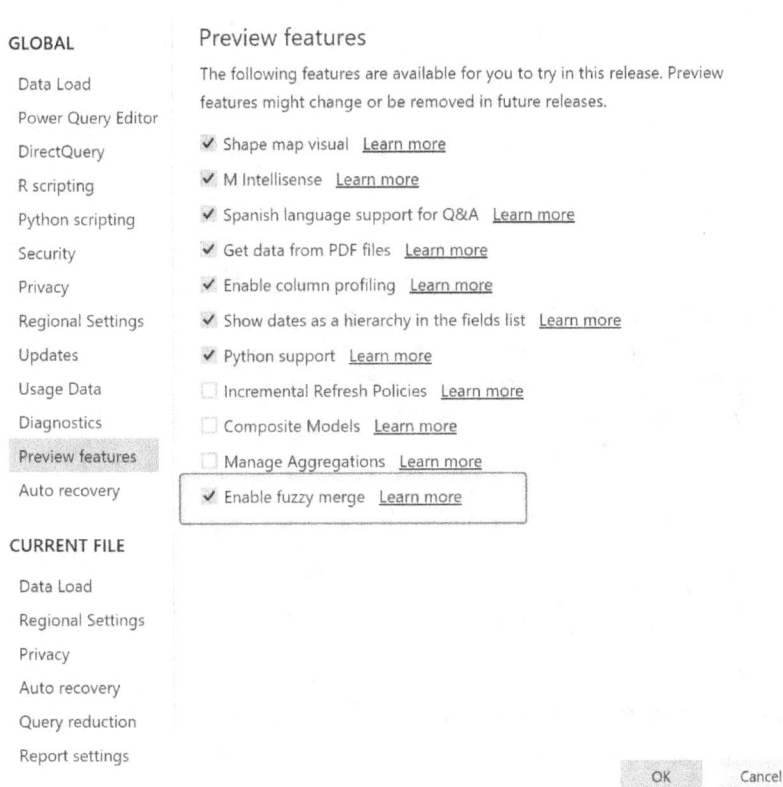

After this step, you'll need to close the Power BI Desktop and open it again.
Sample Dataset

for this example; I will be using a sample dataset which has two very simple tables below;

A "source" table which is the data of employees and their departments. Notice that the Department field has data quality issues. We have department values such as "Sales" and "Sale". Or another example is "Management" and "Management".

ID	Name	Department
1	Mike Anderson	Information Technology
2	Antonio Martin	informatica technologica
3	John Jefferson	Management
4	Joe McCarthy	Mangmt
5	Paolo Adrian	Sales
6	Antony Page	Sale
7	Brian Farmer	Managmnt

A "Department" table which has a list of all departments;

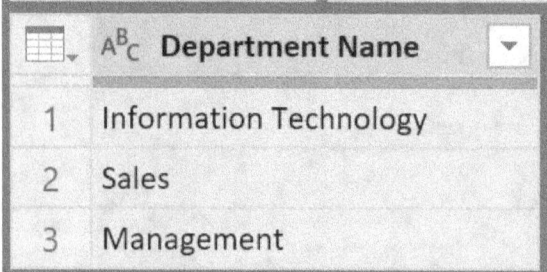

As you can see the list of Department Names are clean in this table, and this is the table that should be used to clean the "source" table. Now let's see how this is possible?

Fuzzy Merge

Fuzzy Merge is a way of joining two tables together, but not on exact matching criteria, on the similarity threshold. If you want to learn what is the Merge operation itself and the difference of that with Append, read my blog post here. If you want to learn more details about what is Merge and the different types of join or merge, read my other blog post here. Merge or Join is simply the act of combining two tables with different structures, but with link/join columns, to access columns from one of the tables in the other one. To use Merge operation on the "source" query, You can click on the Merge Queries as New option in the Home tab of Power Query Editor window.

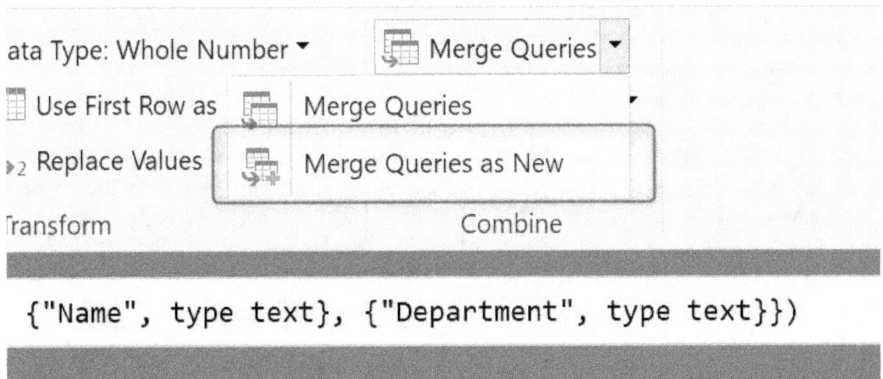

Then you can select the second table and choose Department as the joining field

Merge

This process will give you the output below: (result below is after expanding the merge's column output);

You can see that the Merge operation only finds the EXACT Matching scenarios. Department "Sale" doesn't match with the Department table, because it is missing an "S" at the end to match with the "Sales".
Now, let's see how Fuzzy match works here. To use the Fuzzy Merge, select the checkbox under the Merge tables dialog box;

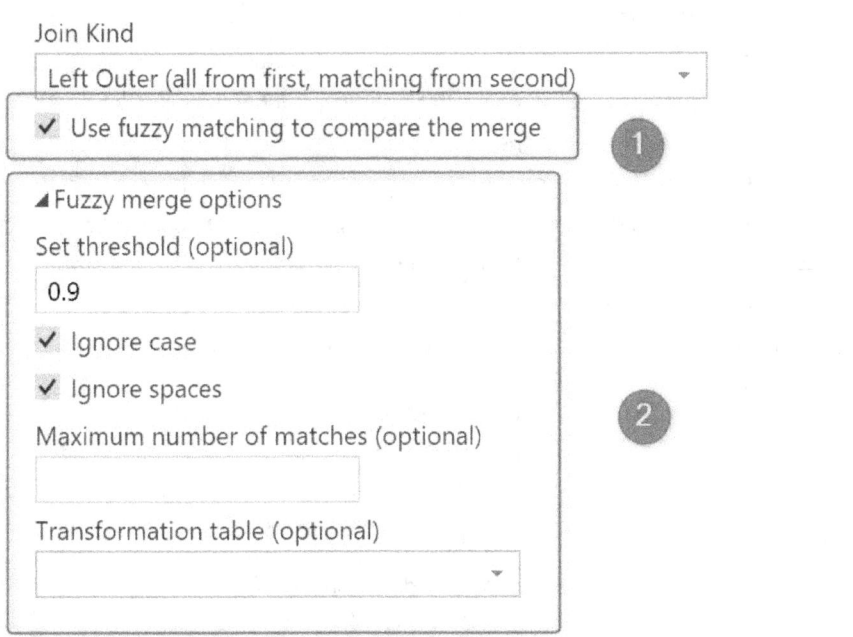

When you enable the fuzzy matching, then you can configure it in the "fuzzy merge operations". You can leave everything optional. Or set values. Let's first see the sample output of this operation and then see what the options are. This is the sample output of Fuzzy Merge:

ID	Name	Department	Department Name
1	Mike Anderson	Information Technology	Information Technology
2	Antonio Martin	informatica technologica	Information Technology
3	John Jefferson	Management	Management
4	Joe McCarthy	Mangmt	null
5	Paolo Adrian	Sales	Sales
6	Antony Page	Sale	Sales
7	Brian Farmer	Managmnt	Management

You can see the three highlighted records, which was not recognized as the exact match in the normal merge operation, is not matching the output of the fuzzy merge. Fuzzy merge will check the similarity between joining fields, and if their similarity is more than the threshold configuration, it will pass it as a successful match. You can see that "Managmnt" can match with "Management" with this threshold configuration, but the "Mangmt" doesn't, it shows that the threshold of similarity is higher than the similarity rate of these two text values with each other.

You can play with Options of Fuzzy Merge and get different outputs. Here is an explanation of these options:

Option	Acceptable Value	Description
Threshold	a value between 0.00 to 1.00	if the similarity of the two text values is more than the threshold, it will be considered as a successful match. Value 1.00 means exact match.
Ignore Case	true/false	If you want the similarity algorithm to work regardless of the upper or lower case letters, then select this option.
Ignore Space	true/false	If you want the similarity algorithm to work regardless of the number of spaces in

a numeric positive value, between 0 to 2147483647		the text, then select this option.
Transformation Table	table	The number of rows that can be matched to one value. This is like a mapping table, let's check it out a bit later in this post. It gives you the option to use your mapping table. This table should have at least two columns of "To" and "From".

Power Query Functions

In addition to the option added in the graphical interface of Power Query, we also have two Power Query Functions that do the Fuzzy Merge, Functions are:

Table.FuzzyJoin

Table.FuzzyNestedJoin

Functions above both do have the same fuzzy configurations. Their only difference is that one of them gives you the expanded output (FuzzyJoin), the other one gives you the same output as the one that you see in the graphical interface with the table column output after merge (FuzzyNestedJoin). If you use these two functions directly in M script, you will have a couple of more parameters to set, which are for concurrency and culture settings.

These are parameters of the two functions above;

table1

key1 (optional)

table2

key2 (optional)

newColumnName

Example: abc

joinKind (optional)

▲ joinOptions (optional)

ConcurrentRequests (optional)

Example: 123

Culture (optional)

Example: abc

IgnoreCase (optional)

Example: true

IgnoreSpace (optional)

Transformation Table

Sometimes in the merge operation, you need a mapping table. This table is called here as Transformation Table. Here is an example of a mapping table:

From	To
Information Technology	IT
Sales	Sales
Management	Board

Note that this table should have at least the two columns of "To" and "From". And don't forget that Power Query is case sensitive!

Now you can select this table in your Merge operation in the Fuzzy configuration as below;

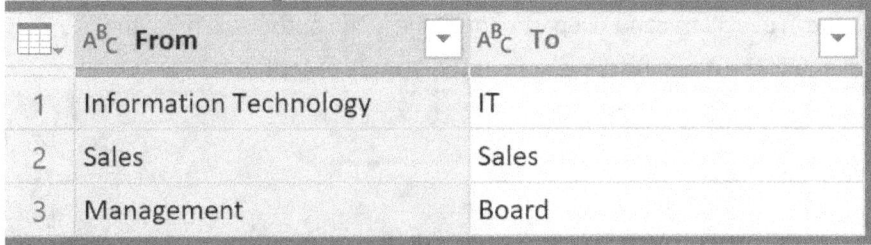

This process is like merging "source" table, which is the first table in our Merge, with the "Department" table based on the "Department" and then "Department Name" column, then merging it with the "mapping" table, based on the "To" column and "Department Name". The output will bring the "To" column of the mapping table. Here is the sample output:

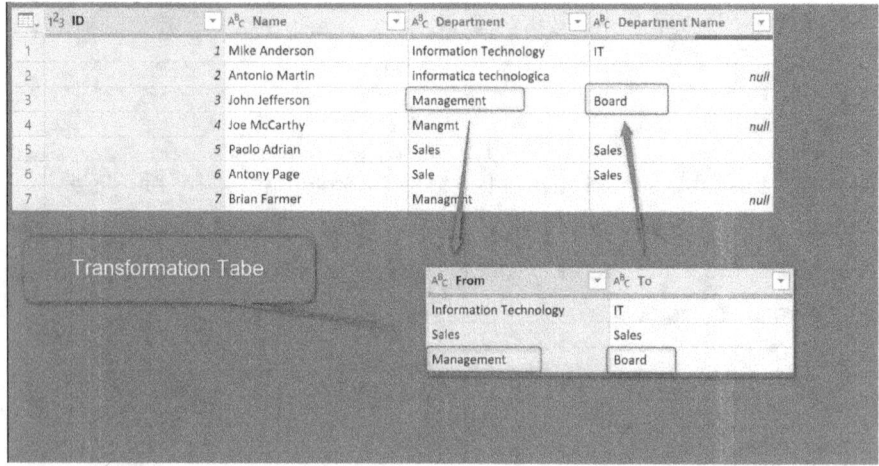

Summary

Matching based on similarity threshold, or Fuzzy matching is a fantastic feature added to Power Query and Power BI, however, it is still a preview feature, and it may have some more configuration coming up. Please try it in your dataset, and let me know if you have any questions in the comment below.

Fetch Files and/or Folders with Filtering and Masking: Power Query

Posted by Reza Rad on Aug 3, 2015

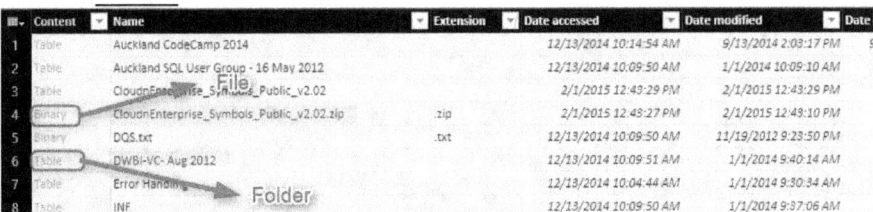

Fetching list of Files in a folder is easy with Power Query. It is one of the built-in source types. However, fetching a list of folders is not a built-in function. In this post, I'll show you how to fetch a list of files, and also fetch the only a list of folders. The method explained in a way that you can customize the code and apply any conditions as you want later on — conditions such as File or folder name masking to fetch only names that contain special character strings.

Fetch All Files in a Folder

For fetching all files in a folder you can simply use the GUI Get Data, and under File, choose Folder

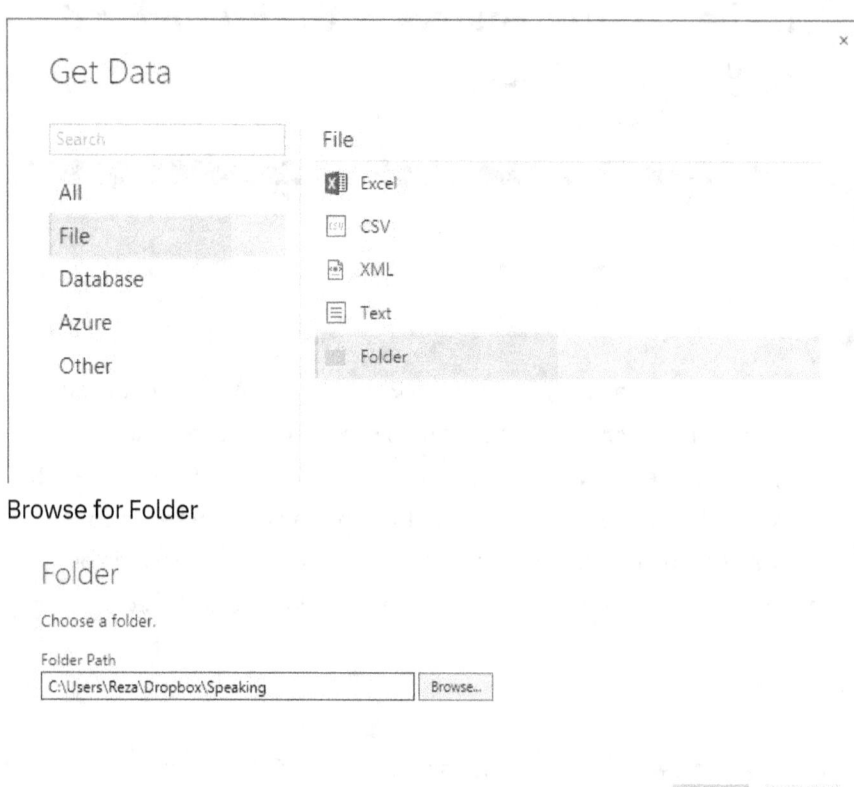

and then simply you will see the list of all files.

As you see in the above table extracted, there is a column named Content, which has the content of the file. You can click on that to see the content of the file if you want.

What is the M Code Written Behind the Scenes
The code behind the scenes for this transformation used Folder.Files function

```
1 let
2    Source = Folder.Files("C:\Users\Reza\Dropbox\Speaking")
3 in Source
4
```

Fetch All Files and Folders
There is another M function to fetch all files and folders listed under a folder, named Folder.Contents. This function returns the Content column with a data type of the record and content of it. For Files data type usually is Binary, and for Folders it is a table. So it can be easily distinguished and separated. Here is a list of all files and folders fetched:

```
1 let
2    Source = Folder.Contents("C:\Users\Reza\Dropbox\Speaking")
3 in Source
4
```

The result set contains both files and folders

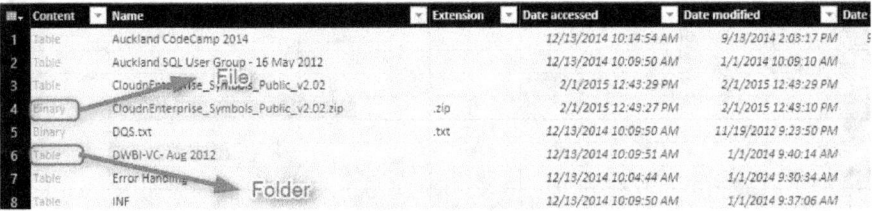

As you see the Content column shows the data type of the value. To check if a record is Folder or not, we have to compare its data type to Table. We can add a column to the table to check the data type of the content column in each record. The data type can be checked with Value.Is function.

```
1 let
2   3Source = Folder.Contents("C:\Users\Reza\Dropbox\Speaking"),
4   inTypeAdded=Table.AddColumn(Source,"Type",each Value.Is([Content],type table))
5   TypeAdded
```

And the result set shows if the record is folder or not

Power BI from Rookie to Rock Star – Book 3: Power Query and Data Transformation in Power BI

Attributes	Folder Path	Type
6 AM Record	C:\Users\Reza\Dropbox\Speaking\	TRUE
7 AM Record	C:\Users\Reza\Dropbox\Speaking\	TRUE
9 PM Record	C:\Users\Reza\Dropbox\Speaking\	TRUE
7 PM Record	C:\Users\Reza\Dropbox\Speaking\	FALSE
0 AM Record	C:\Users\Reza\Dropbox\Speaking\	FALSE
5 AM Record	C:\Users\Reza\Dropbox\Speaking\	TRUE
5 AM Record	C:\Users\Reza\Dropbox\Speaking\	TRUE
5 AM Record	C:\Users\Reza\Dropbox\Speaking\	TRUE
5 AM Record	C:\Users\Reza\Dropbox\Speaking\	FALSE
6 PM Record	C:\Users\Reza\Dropbox\Speaking\	TRUE

To fetch only folders, we can filter the data set with Table.SelectRows function. I've sorted the result set descending by creating date of the folder. Here is the code:

```
1  let
2      Source = Folder.Contents("C:\Users\Reza\Dropbox\Speaking"),
3      TypeAdded=Table.AddColumn(Source,"Type",each Value.Is([Content],type table)),
4      Folders=Table.SelectRows(TypeAdded, each [Type]=true),
5      Sorted=Table.Sort(Folders,{"Date created", Order.Descending})
6  
7  in
8      Sorted
```

And the result:

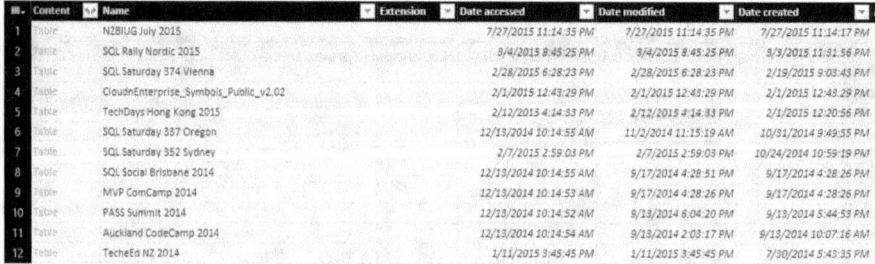

Fetch Files and Folders with Masking

Now that you've got through the M code, it would be really easy to apply any masking option to this. Here are a couple of examples:

1- Fetch Only Folders Created after Specific Date

```
1  let
2      Source = Folder.Contents("C:\Users\Reza\Dropbox\Speaking"),
```

```
    3  4TypeAdded=Table.AddColumn(Source,"Type",each Value.Is([Content],type table)),
    5  6Folders=Table.SelectRows(TypeAdded, each [Type]=true),
    7  8Sorted=Table.Sort(Folders,{"Date created", Order.Descending}),
in  9  Filtered=Table.SelectRows(Sorted, each [Date created]>DateTime.FromText("2015-1-1"))
```

Filtered

Result

Content	Name	Extension	Date accessed	Date modified	Date created
Table	NZBIUG July 2015		7/27/2015 11:14:35 PM	7/27/2015 11:14:35 PM	7/27/2015 11:14:17 PM
Table	SQL Rally Nordic 2015		3/4/2015 8:45:25 PM	3/4/2015 8:45:25 PM	3/5/2015 11:31:56 PM
Table	SQL Saturday 374 Vienna		2/28/2015 6:28:23 PM	2/28/2015 6:28:23 PM	2/19/2015 9:03:43 PM
Table	CloudnEnterprise_Symbols_Public_v2.02		2/1/2015 12:43:29 PM	2/1/2015 12:43:29 PM	2/1/2015 12:43:29 PM
Table	TechDays Hong Kong 2015		2/12/2015 4:14:33 PM	2/12/2015 4:14:33 PM	2/1/2015 12:20:56 PM

2- Fetch Only Files with .txt extension and name similar to "amp"

```
1  let
2    3Source = Folder.Files("C:\Users\Reza\Dropbox\Speaking"),
4    5Sorted=Table.Sort(Source ,{"Date created", Order.Descending}),
6  inFiltered=Table.SelectRows(Sorted, each [Extension]=".txt" and Text.Contains([Name],"amp"))
7
```

Filtered

Result:

Content	Name	Extension	Date accessed	Date modified
Binary	M sample.txt	.txt	7/27/2015 11:14:38 PM	2/10/201·
Binary	M sample.txt	.txt	2/19/2015 9:23:56 PM	2/10/201·
Binary	M sample.txt	.txt	12/13/2014 10:15:07 AM	2/10/201·
Binary	M sample.txt	.txt	12/13/2014 10:15:04 AM	2/10/201·
Binary	M sample.txt	.txt	12/13/2014 10:09:55 AM	2/10/201·

Part IV: Dealing with Errors

Exception Reporting in Power BI: Catch the Error Rows in Power Query

Posted by Reza Rad on Nov 23, 2018

Exception Report: Error Rows

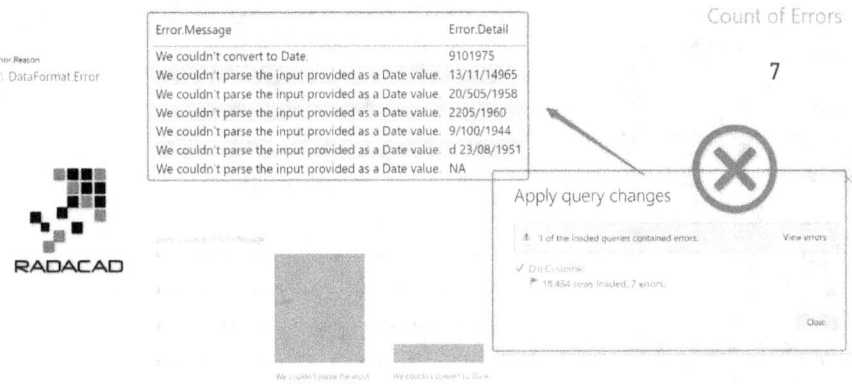

To build a robust BI system, you need to cater for errors and handle errors carefully. If you build a reporting solution that the refresh of that fails everytime an error occurs, it is not a robust system. Errors can happen by many reasons. In this post, I'll show you a way to catch potential errors in Power Query and how to build an exception report page to visualize the error rows for further investigation. The method that you learn here will save your model from failing at the time of refresh. Means you get the dataset updated, and you can catch any rows caused the error in an exception report page. To learn more about Power BI, read Power BI book from Rookie to Rock Star.

Sample Dataset

I will use a sample Excel file as a data source which has 18,484 customer rows in it. In the sample Dataset, we have a BirthDate field beside all other fields, which supposed to have a date value in it. Here is what the data looks like when I bring it into Power Query:

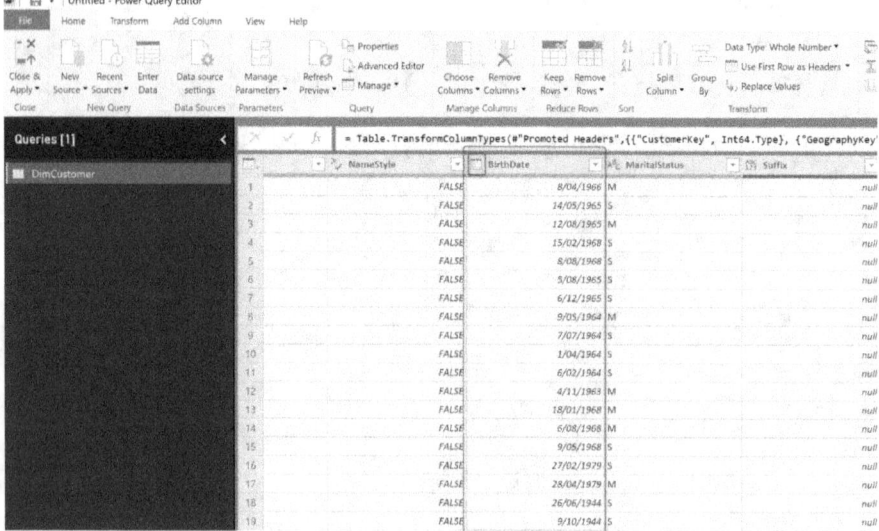

Error Happens

When I get this dataset in my Power Query Editor window (as you see in the above screenshot), Power Query automatically converts the data type of the BirthDate column to Date. You can see this automatic data type conversion in the list of Steps;

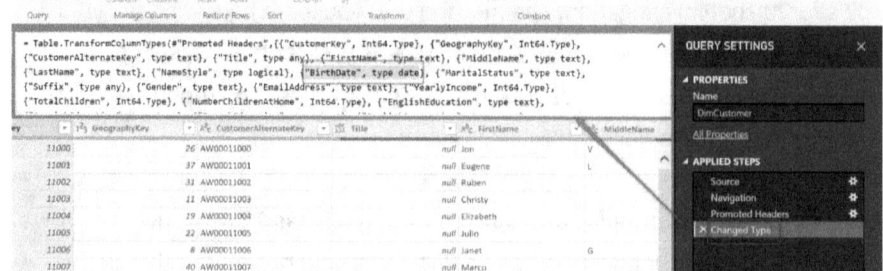

Of course, you can turn off this automatic data type detection of Power Query, but that is not my point. I want the dataset to fail to show you how to deal with it. Errors happen in Power Query in the real world, and I'm here to show you how to find them.

As you can see in the Power Query Editor, I see no errors for this data type change, and everything looks great;

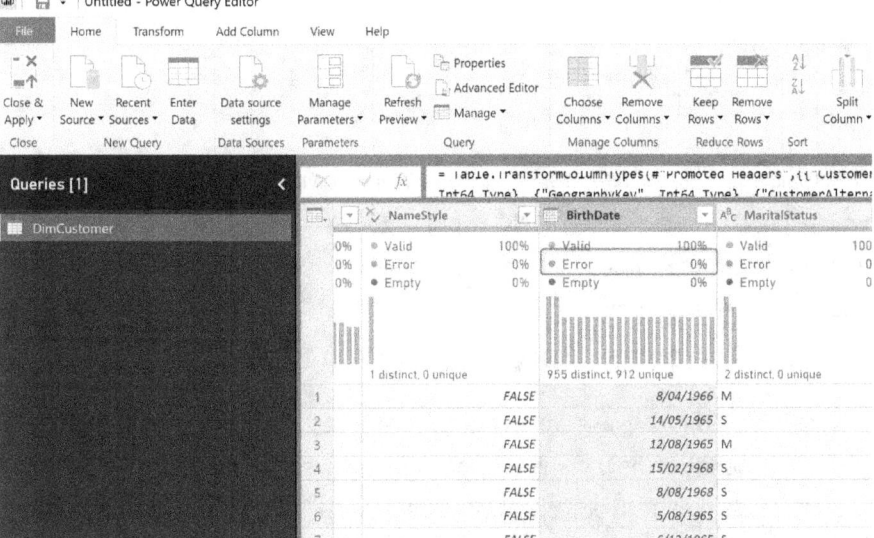

Now I load this dataset into Power BI, by using Close and Apply in the Query Editor window, and I expect everything to load successfully, however, this is coming out of the blue!

Apply query changes

> ⚠ 1 of the loaded queries contained errors.   View errors
>
> ✓ DimCustomer
>   ⚑ 18,484 rows loaded. 7 errors.
>
>   Close

Does this sound familiar? Yes, if you have worked with Power BI for a while, you might have experienced it. No errors in Power Query Editor, but when we load the data into Power BI, there are errors! How is that possible? Let's first find out why this happens.

Why didn't Power Query Editor Catch the Error?

Power Query Editor always work with a preview of the dataset, the size of the preview depends on how many columns you have, sometimes it is 1000 rows, sometimes 200 rows. If you click on a Query in the Power Query editor window, you can see this stated down below in the status bar;

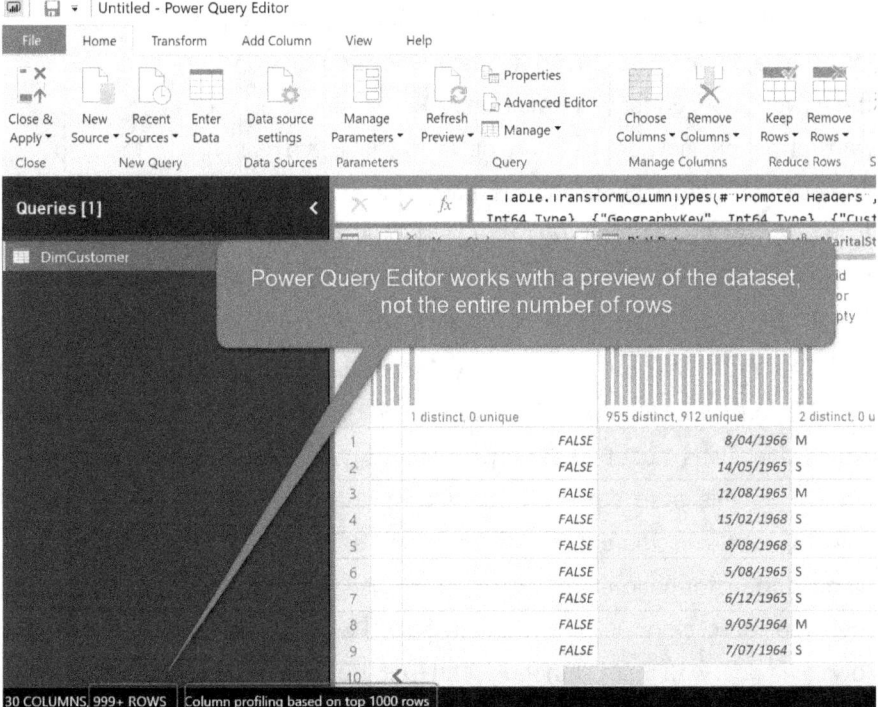

The reason for Power Query to use the preview dataset is mainly because of speeding up the transformation development process. Imagine if you have a table with 10 million rows, every single transformation that you want to apply on that dataset would take a long time, and you have to wait for it before you start doing the next step. The wait for the response each time will slow down your development process. This is the reason why working on a preview on the dataset is a preferred option. You can apply all transformations you want on the preview, and when you are happy with it, then apply it to the entire dataset. Usually, the first 1000 rows or the first 200 rows are a good sample of the entire dataset, and you can expect to see most of the data challenges there. Usually, not always of course.

How will the transformation be applied to the entire dataset then? When you load the data into Power BI. That means when you click on Close and APPLY in the Power Query Editor window. That APPLY means apply those transformations now on the entire dataset. That is the reason, why the load process may take longer especially if the dataset is big.

Power Query Editor always works with a preview of the data, to make the development process fast. When you load the data in Power BI, transformations will be applied on the entire dataset.

Now that you know how Power Query Editor deals with the preview of the data, you can guess why the error above happened? The reason is; The preview of the data (which was about 1000 rows) had no issues with the transformations applied (in this case automatic data type change to Date for the BirthDate column). However, the entire dataset (which is about 18K rows) have problems with that transformation! When you see the error above in the Power BI Desktop, then you can click on View errors and go to Power Query editor and see those rows, and deal with them somehow, and fix it. However, that is not enough.

What if the error doesn't happen in Power BI Desktop, but happens in a scheduled refresh in the Power BI Service?

True! Fixing errors in Power BI Desktop is easy, but consider that the error didn't happen in the desktop too, and you got your Power BI report published to the website, and scheduled it to refresh. Then the next day you see the report failed to refresh with an error! You have to learn how to deal with the error rows beforehand before it cause the scheduled refresh to fail. Let's see how to deal with it then.

Dealing with Errors: Catching the Error Rows

To deal with errors, you have to catch the error before it loads into Power BI. One way to do it is to create two references of the same table, one as the final query, and the other one as Error Rows.

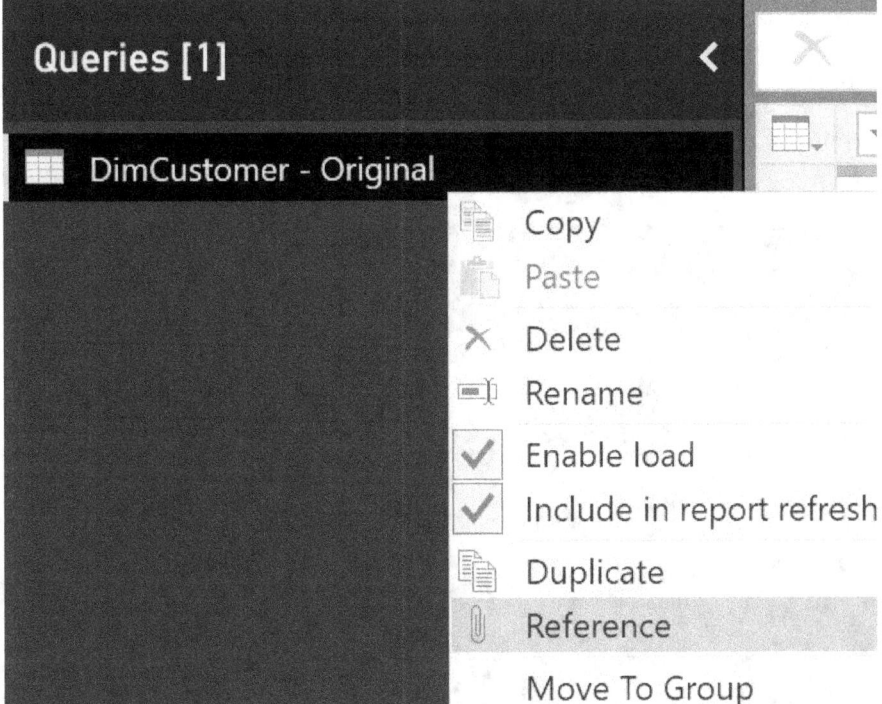

in the screenshot above, I renamed the DimCustomer table to DimCustomer – Original and then created a Reference from it. If you would like to learn what Reference is, read my article about Reference vs. Duplicate here. The new referenced query can be called as DimCustomer. This would be the clean query with no errors (we will remove errors from it in the next step);

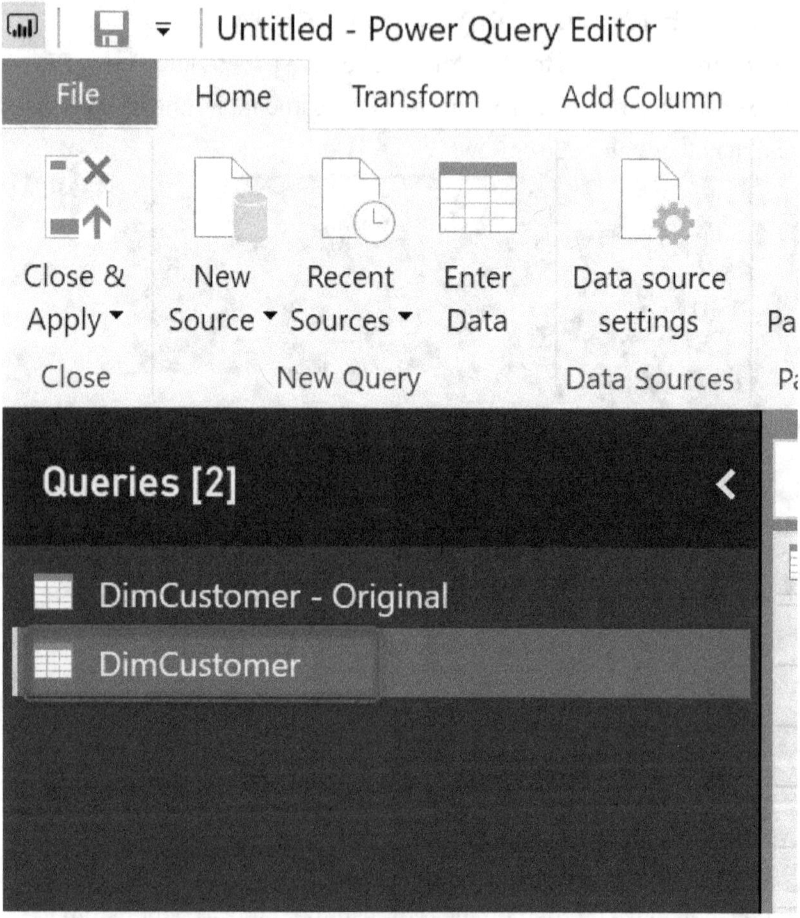

The new table is the table that would be clean with no errors, and we can use it in the report. Let's clean this from any errors

Remove Errors from the Table loading into Power BI

As DimCustomer would be the final query for us, I want to remove errors from it. Removing errors is a simple option in the Home tab, under Reduce Rows ->

Remove Rows -> Remove Errors. Make sure that you select the BirthDate column before that.

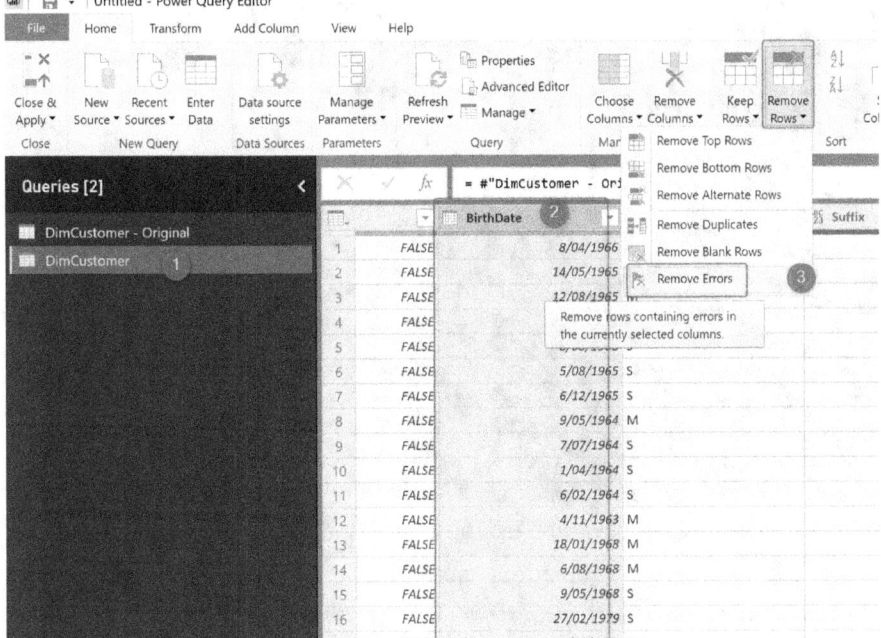

You can also do this for all columns if you want; by selecting all columns and then using Remove Errors. This post is just a sample on one column and can be extended to all for sure.

Remove Errors will be a step in the data transformations step, and it means that when you click on APPLY, it will apply on the entire dataset, so as a result, when the data type change cause an error, the next step after that which is Remove Errors, will wipe the rows that caused the error. But the DimCustomer – Original still may cause the error, so we have to uncheck the Enable Load of that query.

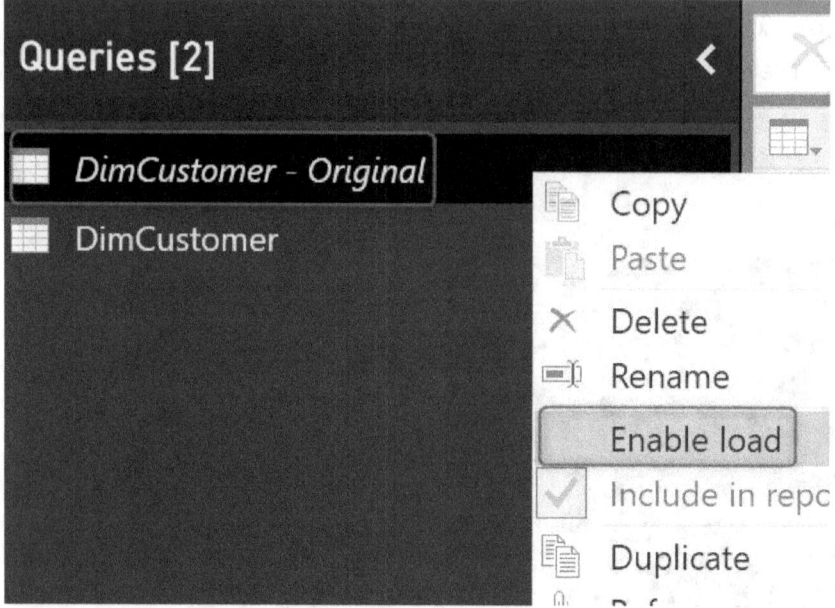

Now we have successfully removed the errors, and if we load the data into Power BI. There would be no errors happening.

But wait! What about those error rows? How can we catch them? We need to catch those rows and investigate what happened and think about an action plan to fix them, right? So, we do need another query reference from the original query, but to keep the error rows.

Keep Errors in the Exception Table

Similar to the Remove Errors option, there is also an option to Keep Errors. If you have seen this option before, you may have wondered what the use of such a thing is? Well, here is the exact use case scenario. Keep Errors will help to catch the error rows in an exception table.

Create another reference from the DimCustomer – Original.

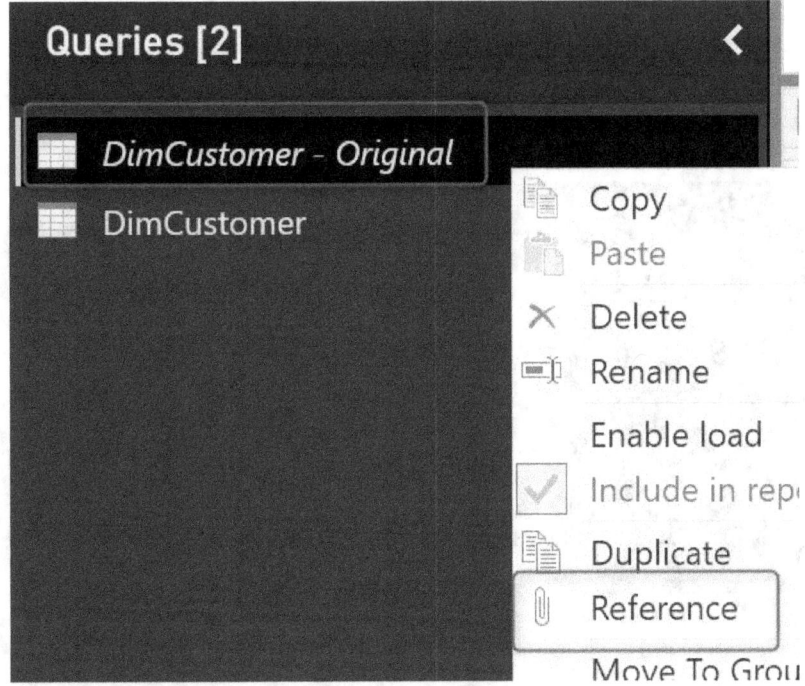

Rename this new query as DimCustomer Error Rows. For this query, we have to Keep Errors, which can be found close to where the Remove Errors is, but under Keep Rows.

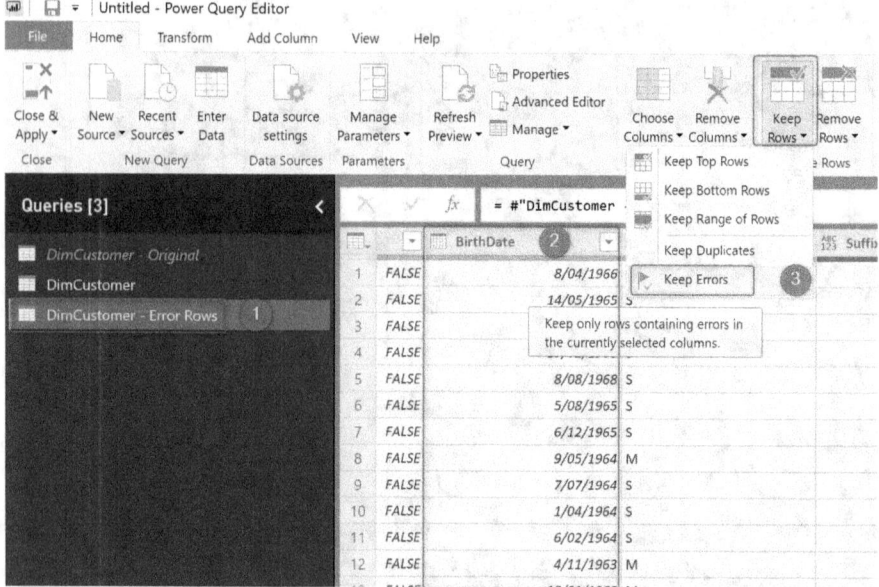

Now this table would only keep rows that cause an error. Here is a sample set;

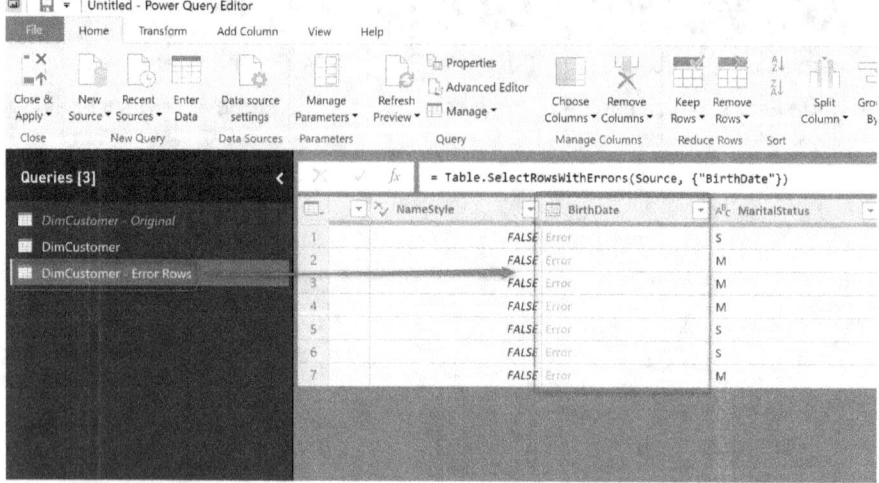

This is not the end of the story. If you load this new table of DimCustomer – Error Rows in Power BI, you will end up with the same error again. Why? Well, because this query is going to return error rows! You need to remove the Error occurred from this dataset.

Getting Error Details

If you remove the error column from the exception table we have created, then you would have no details about the error happened, and it would be hard to track it back and troubleshoot. The best would be catching the error details. The error message and the value that caused the error are important details that you don't want to miss. Follow steps below to get that information. In the Error Rows table, add a Custom Column.

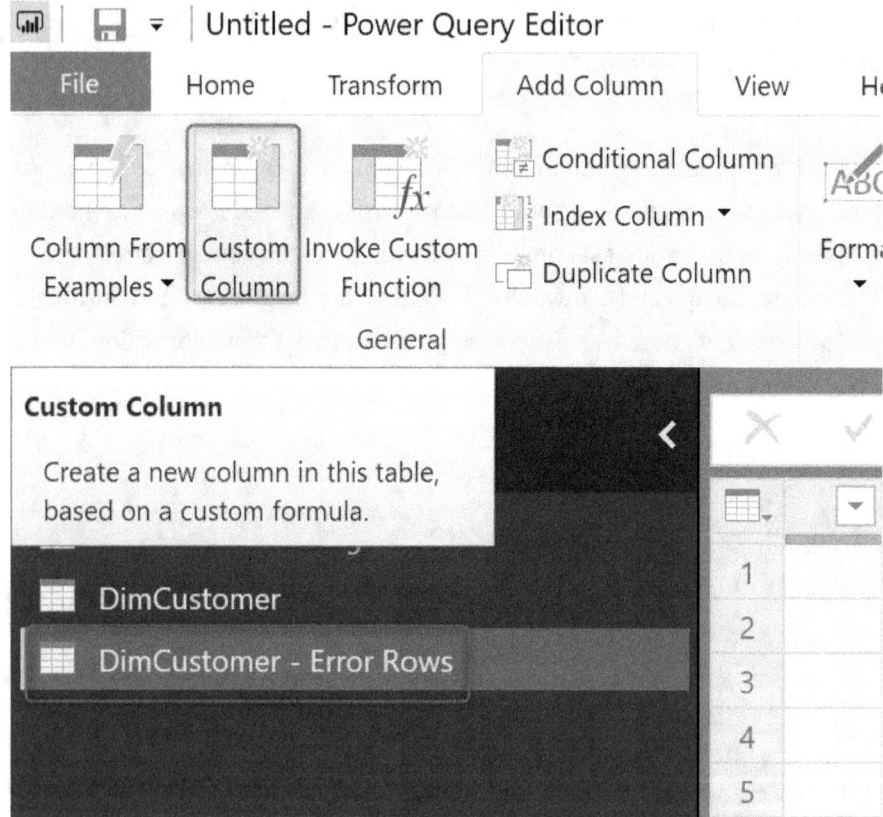

In the Custom Column editor, write **"try"** and then after a space, the name of the field that caused the error. In our example: BirthDate;

1 try [BirthDate]

Custom Column

try (all lowercase), is a keyword in M that will catch the error details. Instead of returning just an error, it will return a record containing the error details such as the source value and the error message. Below screenshot shows how the output of *try* would come;

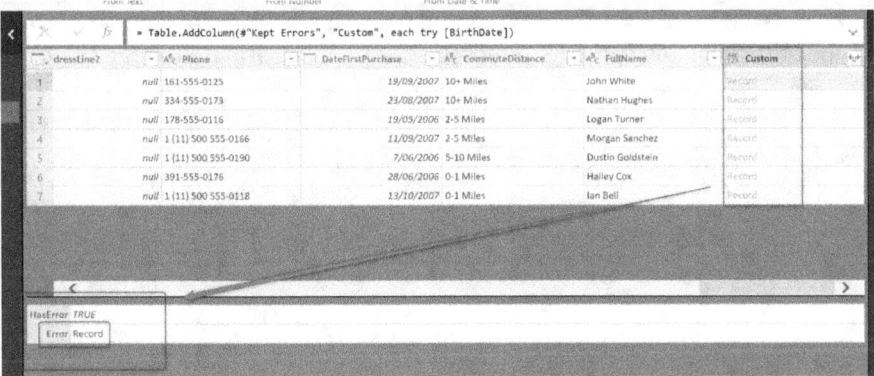

The Record output of the "try" will have two fields; HasError (which we already know it is going to be true), and the Error. The Error is another record with more details. Click on Expand on the Custom column, and select Error.

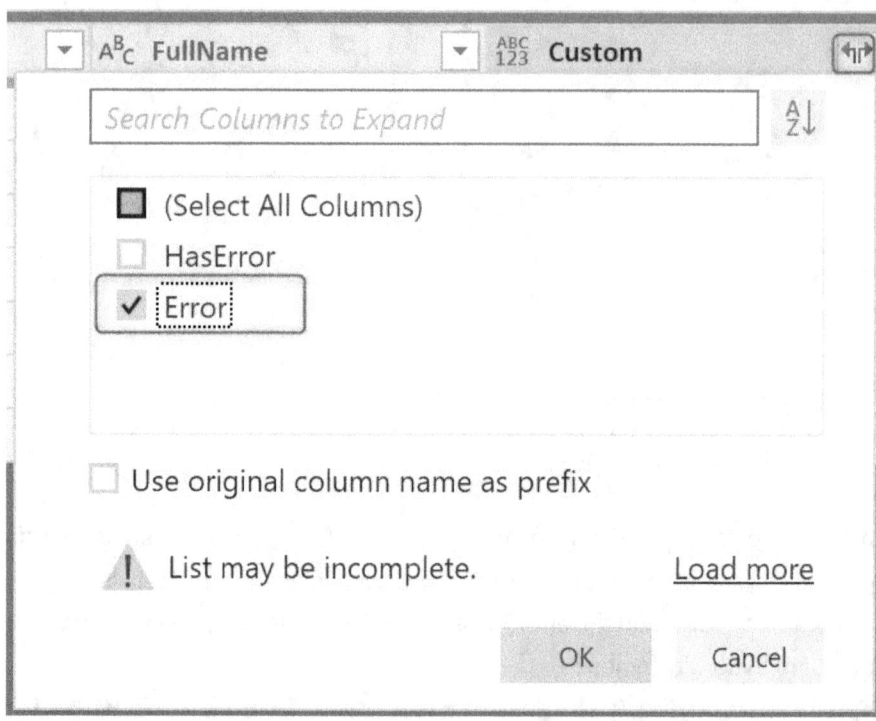

In the output column named Error, click on Expand again and this time select all columns;

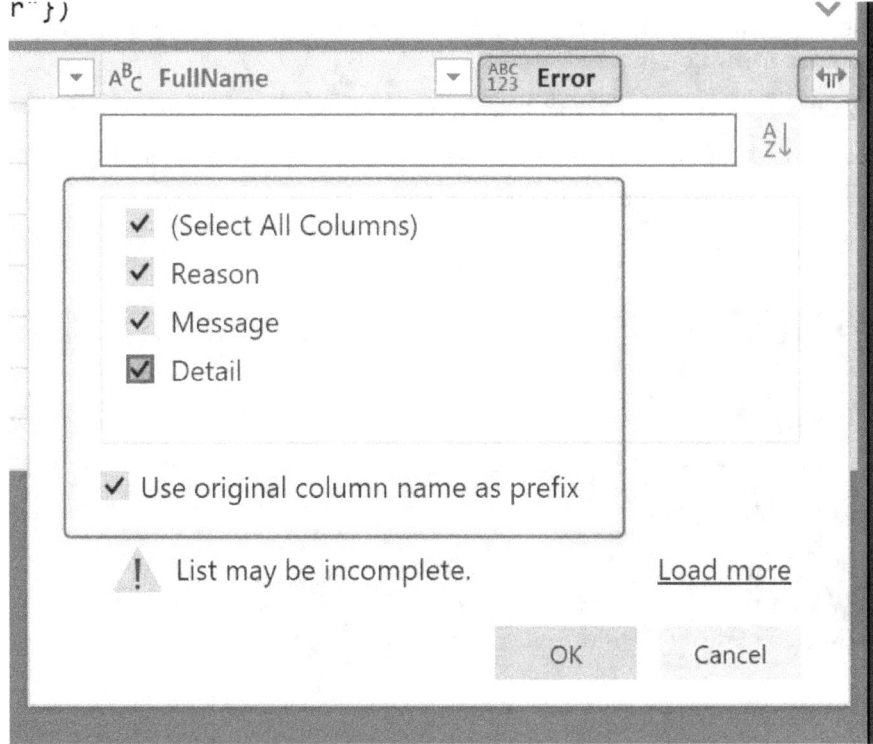

It is good to have the original column name as a prefix because then you would know that these are error detail columns.

Now you would get the full details of the error as below;

Error.Reason	Error.Message	Error.Detail	
DataFormat.Error	We couldn't parse the input provided as a Date value.	9/100/1944	
DataFormat.Error	We couldn't parse the input provided as a Date value.	d 23/08/1951	
DataFormat.Error	We couldn't parse the input provided as a Date value.	13/11/14965	
DataFormat.Error	We couldn't parse the input provided as a Date value.	2205/1960	
DataFormat.Error	We couldn't convert to Date.		9101975
DataFormat.Error	We couldn't parse the input provided as a Date value.	20/505/1958	
DataFormat.Error	We couldn't parse the input provided as a Date value.	NA	

The information above is your most valuable asset for the exception reporting.

Remove Error Column

Now the last step before loading the data into Power BI is to remove the column that causes the Error. In our example; the BirthDate Column should be removed (otherwise the refresh will fail again);

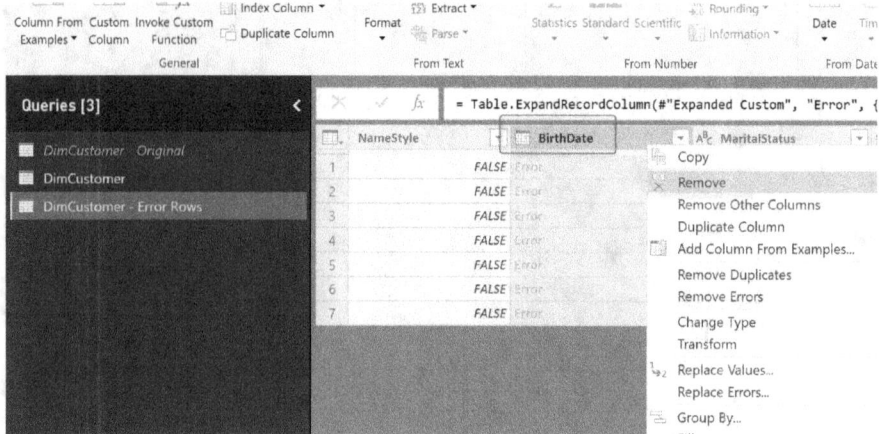

Exception Report

You can now load the data into Power BI. You will have two tables; DimCustomer, and DimCustomer – Error Rows. DimCustomer is the table that you can use for your normal reporting. DimCustomer – Error Rows is the table that you can use for exception reporting. The exception report is the report that can be used for troubleshooting and will list all the errors to users for further investigation. Make sure that there is no relationship between these two tables.

Here is a sample report visual I created that shows the errors;

Exception Report: Error Rows

Summary

Errors happen, and you have to deal with them. Instead of waiting for the error to happen and then finding it a month after it caused, it is better to catch them as soon as they happen. In this article, you learned a way to deal with error rows. In RADACAD we always create an exception report for Power BI reports. That way, we are always sure that the refresh won't fail because of the error, and we would also have a place for investigating the errors, which is called the Exception Report. Do you have an exception report? If not, go and create one, If yes, tell us about your experience down below in the comments.

Power BI from Rookie to Rock Star – Book 3: Power Query and Data Transformation in Power BI
Flawless Date Conversion in Power Query
Posted by Reza Rad on Jan 6, 2017

	Date1	Date2	Date3	Date4
1	1/1/2017	1/1/2017	1/1/2017	1/1/2017
2	1/2/2017	1/2/2017	1/2/2017	2/1/2017
3	1/3/2017	1/3/2017	1/3/2017	3/1/2017
4	1/4/2017	1/4/2017	1/4/2017	4/1/2017
5	1/5/2017	1/5/2017	1/5/2017	5/1/2017
6	1/6/2017	1/6/2017	1/6/2017	6/1/2017
7	1/7/2017	1/7/2017	1/7/2017	7/1/2017
8	1/8/2017	1/8/2017	1/8/2017	8/1/2017
9	1/9/2017	1/9/2017	1/9/2017	9/1/2017
10	1/10/2017	1/10/2017	1/10/2017	10/1/2017
11	1/11/2017	1/11/2017	1/11/2017	11/1/2017
12	1/12/2017	1/12/2017	1/12/2017	12/1/2017
13	1/13/2017	1/13/2017	1/13/2017	Error
14	1/14/2017	1/14/2017	1/14/2017	Error
15	1/15/2017	1/15/2017	1/15/2017	Error
16	1/16/2017	1/16/2017	1/16/2017	Error
17	1/17/2017	1/17/2017	1/17/2017	Error
18	1/18/2017	1/18/2017	1/18/2017	Error
19	1/19/2017	1/19/2017	1/19/2017	Error
20	1/20/2017	1/20/2017	1/20/2017	Error
21	1/21/2017	1/21/2017	1/21/2017	Error
22	1/22/2017	1/22/2017	1/22/2017	Error
23	1/23/2017	1/23/2017	1/23/2017	Error
24	1/24/2017	1/24/2017	1/24/2017	Error
25	1/25/2017	1/25/2017	1/25/2017	Error
26	1/26/2017	1/26/2017	1/26/2017	Error
27	1/27/2017	1/27/2017	1/27/2017	Error
28	1/28/2017	1/28/2017	1/28/2017	Error
29	1/29/2017	1/29/2017	1/29/2017	Error
30	1/30/2017	1/30/2017	1/30/2017	Error
31	1/31/2017	1/31/2017	1/31/2017	Error

Date Conversion is one of the simplest conversions in Power Query, however, depends on locale on the system that you are working with Date Conversion might return a different result. In this post, I'll show you an example of an issue with date conversion and how to resolve it with Locale. In this post, you'll learn that Power Query date conversion is dependent on the system that this conversion happens on, and can be fixed to a specific format. If you want to learn more about Power BI; Read Power BI online book; from Rookie to Rock Star.

Prerequisite

The sample data set for this post is here: book1

Different Formats of Date

Most of the countries use YMD format. However some of them use MDY or DMY more frequently. This Wikipedia page explains different formats of date in each country. Dataset below have different formats in it;

Date1	Date2	Date3	Date4
2017-1-1	2017/1/1	1-1-2017	1-1-2017
2017-1-2	2017/1/2	1-2-2017	2-1-2017
2017-1-3	2017/1/3	1-3-2017	3-1-2017
2017-1-4	2017/1/4	1-4-2017	4-1-2017
2017-1-5	2017/1/5	1-5-2017	5-1-2017
2017-1-6	2017/1/6	1-6-2017	6-1-2017
2017-1-7	2017/1/7	1-7-2017	7-1-2017
2017-1-8	2017/1/8	1-8-2017	8-1-2017
2017-1-9	2017/1/9	1-9-2017	9-1-2017
2017-1-10	2017/1/10	1-10-2017	10-1-2017
2017-1-11	2017/1/11	1-11-2017	11-1-2017
2017-1-12	2017/1/12	1-12-2017	12-1-2017
2017-1-13	2017/1/13	1-13-2017	13-1-2017
2017-1-14	2017/1/14	1-14-2017	14-1-2017
2017-1-15	2017/1/15	1-15-2017	15-1-2017
2017-1-16	2017/1/16	1-16-2017	16-1-2017
2017-1-17	2017/1/17	1-17-2017	17-1-2017
2017-1-18	2017/1/18	1-18-2017	18-1-2017
2017-1-19	2017/1/19	1-19-2017	19-1-2017
2017-1-20	2017/1/20	1-20-2017	20-1-2017
2017-1-21	2017/1/21	1-21-2017	21-1-2017
2017-1-22	2017/1/22	1-22-2017	22-1-2017
2017-1-23	2017/1/23	1-23-2017	23-1-2017
2017-1-24	2017/1/24	1-24-2017	24-1-2017
2017-1-25	2017/1/25	1-25-2017	25-1-2017
2017-1-26	2017/1/26	1-26-2017	26-1-2017
2017-1-27	2017/1/27	1-27-2017	27-1-2017
2017-1-28	2017/1/28	1-28-2017	28-1-2017
2017-1-29	2017/1/29	1-29-2017	29-1-2017
2017-1-30	2017/1/30	1-30-2017	30-1-2017
2017-1-31	2017/1/31	1-31-2017	31-1-2017

In the above table, first two columns (Date1, and Date2) are in YYYY-MM-DD and YYYY/MM/DD format, which is the most common format of the date. Date3 is MM-DD-YYYY format (very common in the USA and some other countries), and Date4 is DD-MM-YYYY format, which is most common in New Zealand, Australia, and some other countries. Now let's see what happens if we load this data into Power BI.

Automatic Type Conversion

Power BI leverages automatic data type conversion. This automatic action sometimes is useful, sometimes not! If you open a Power BI Desktop file and get data from the specified data set. In Query Editor you will see the data types converted automatically at some level. Here is the data loaded into the Query Editor window with automatic data type conversion;

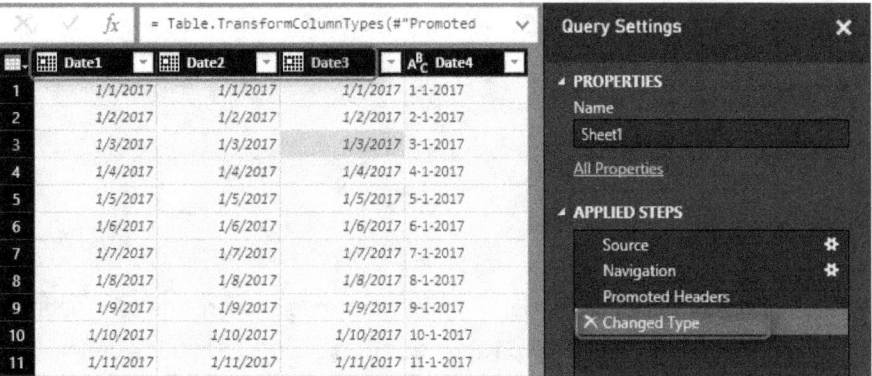

You can see the Changed Type step that applied automatically and converted the first three columns in the data set to the data type of Date and left the Date4 as data type Text. Automatic Date type conversion understand characters like / or -, and apply conversion correctly in both cases (Date1, and Date2)

* If you are running this example on your machine you might see a different result because Power Query uses the locale of the machine to do data type conversion. Locale of my machine is US format, so it understands the format of USA and converts it automatically. If you have different locale, the conversion might result differently. We will go through that in a second.

If the automatic data type conversion is not something you want, you can remove that step. Or if you want to disable the automatic type conversion, Go to File, Options, and Settings, then Options.

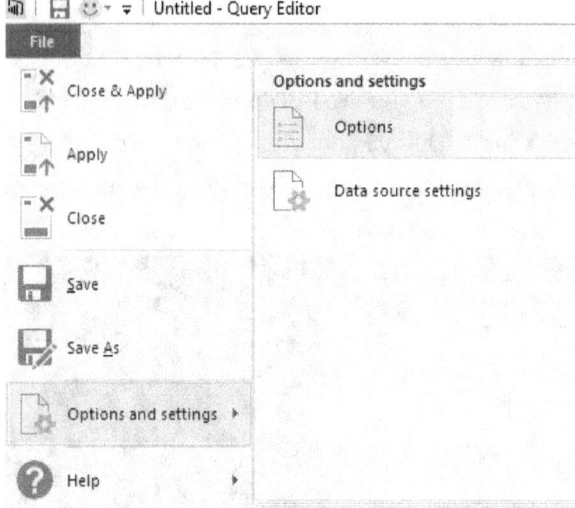

In the Options window, under Current File, Data Load section. You can enable or disable the automatic data type detection if you wish to. (In this example I'll keep it enabled)

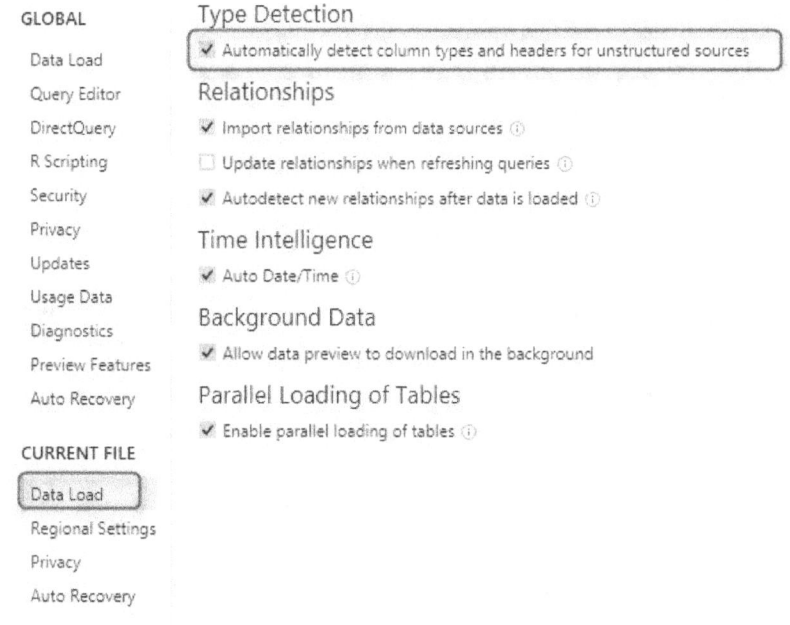

You can also check the Locale of your current machine in the Regional Settings section of Options Window;

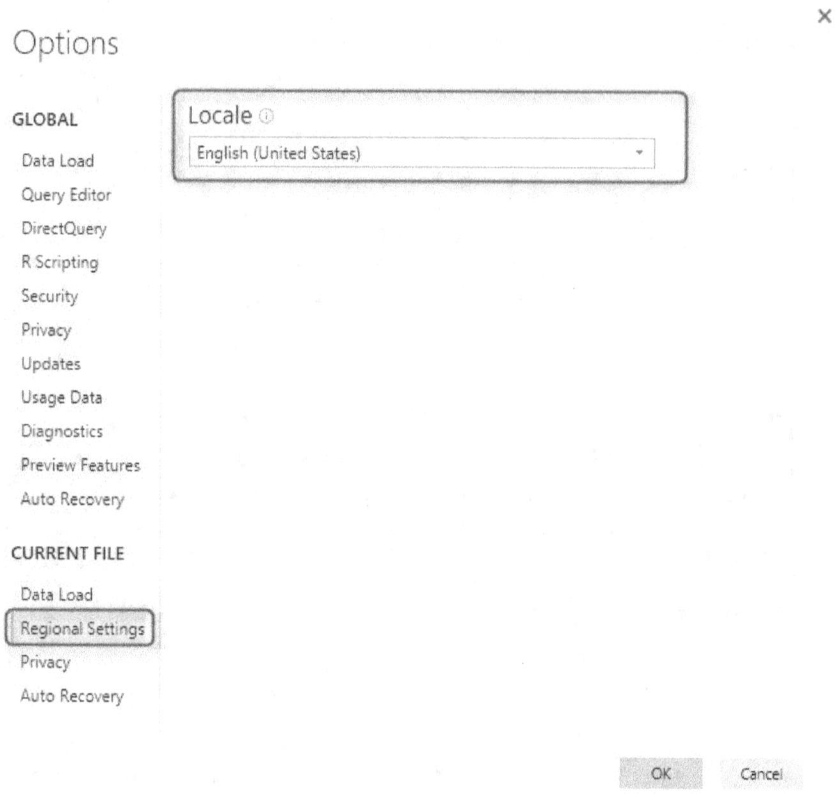

Options

GLOBAL
Data Load
Query Editor
DirectQuery
R Scripting
Security
Privacy
Updates
Usage Data
Diagnostics
Preview Features
Auto Recovery

CURRENT FILE
Data Load
Regional Settings
Privacy
Auto Recovery

Locale
English (United States)

OK   Cancel

Date Conversion Issue

Date4 in the data set isn't converted properly, and that's because the Locale of the current system (my machine) is English (United States). I can change the locale to English (New Zealand) in the Options window and Refresh the data, but this will corrupt the existing Date Conversion of Date3 column. If I try to change the data type of Date4 column myself, the result will not be correct, and I'll see some errors;

Date1	Date2	Date3	Date4
1/1/2017	1/1/2017	1/1/2017	1/1/2017
1/2/2017	1/2/2017	1/2/2017	2/1/2017
1/3/2017	1/3/2017	1/3/2017	3/1/2017
1/4/2017	1/4/2017	1/4/2017	4/1/2017
1/5/2017	1/5/2017	1/5/2017	5/1/2017
1/6/2017	1/6/2017	1/6/2017	6/1/2017
1/7/2017	1/7/2017	1/7/2017	7/1/2017
1/8/2017	1/8/2017	1/8/2017	8/1/2017
1/9/2017	1/9/2017	1/9/2017	9/1/2017
1/10/2017	1/10/2017	1/10/2017	10/1/2017
1/11/2017	1/11/2017	1/11/2017	11/1/2017
1/12/2017	1/12/2017	1/12/2017	12/1/2017
1/13/2017	1/13/2017	1/13/2017	Error
1/14/2017	1/14/2017	1/14/2017	Error
1/15/2017	1/15/2017	1/15/2017	Error
1/16/2017	1/16/2017	1/16/2017	Error
1/17/2017	1/17/2017	1/17/2017	Error
1/18/2017	1/18/2017	1/18/2017	Error
1/19/2017	1/19/2017	1/19/2017	Error
1/20/2017	1/20/2017	1/20/2017	Error
1/21/2017	1/21/2017	1/21/2017	Error
1/22/2017	1/22/2017	1/22/2017	Error
1/23/2017	1/23/2017	1/23/2017	Error
1/24/2017	1/24/2017	1/24/2017	Error
1/25/2017	1/25/2017	1/25/2017	Error
1/26/2017	1/26/2017	1/26/2017	Error
1/27/2017	1/27/2017	1/27/2017	Error
1/28/2017	1/28/2017	1/28/2017	Error
1/29/2017	1/29/2017	1/29/2017	Error
1/30/2017	1/30/2017	1/30/2017	Error
1/31/2017	1/31/2017	1/31/2017	Error

You can see that conversion didn't happen correctly, and also it returned Error in some cells because my machine is expecting MM/DD/YYYY, but the date format in the column is DD/MM/YYYY which is not that format. So it can convert first 12 records because it places the day as a month in the result! And the rest it can't because there is no month 13 or more.

Date Conversion Using Locale

Fortunately, you can do date conversion using specific Locale. All you need to do is to go through right click and data type conversion using Locale;

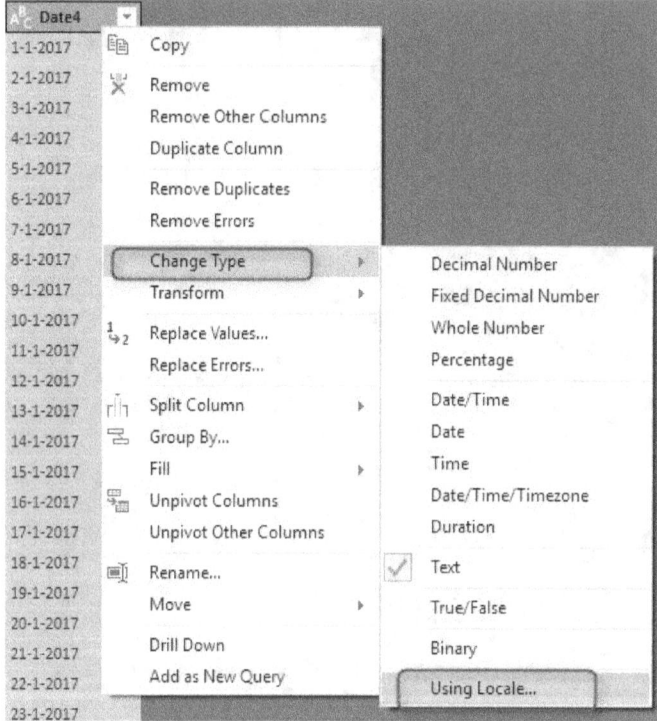

In the Change Type with Locale, choose the Data Type to be Date (Normally Locale is for Date, Time, and Numbers). And then set Locale to be English (New Zealand). You can also see some sample input values for this locale there.

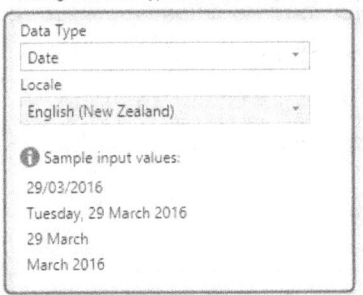

With this simple change, you can now see the Date4 column converted correctly. You still see that in MM/DD/YYYY format in Query Editor window, and that's because my machine's date format is this. The actual column data type is Date, however, which is the correct format to work with.

```
let
    Source = Excel.Workbook(File.Contents("C:\Users\Reza\SkyDrive\Blog\DateConversion\Book1.xlsx"), null, true),
    Sheet1_Sheet = Source{[Item="Sheet1",Kind="Sheet"]}[Data],
    #"Promoted Headers" = Table.PromoteHeaders(Sheet1_Sheet),
    #"Changed Type" = Table.TransformColumnTypes(#"Promoted Headers",{
        {"Date1", type date},
        {"Date2", type date},
        {"Date3", type date},
        {"Date4", type text} }
    ),
    #"Changed Type with Locale" = Table.TransformColumnTypes(#"Changed Type", {{"Date4", type date}}, "en-NZ")
in
    #"Changed Type with Locale"
```

In the script, you can see the difference of data type change using Locale which uses locale as the last parameter, instead of without locale. This brings a very important topic in mind; correct date type conversion is locale-dependent, and you can get it always works if you mention Locale in date type conversion.

Summary

Date Type conversion can be tricky depends on the locale of system you are working on. To get the correct Date Type conversion recommendation is to use Locale for type conversion. Some of the formats might work even without using Locale. For example, I have seen YYYYMMDD is working fine in all locales I worked with so far, but DDMMYYYY or MMDDYYYY might work differently.

Make Your Numeric Division Faultless in Power Query

Posted by Reza Rad on Jun 20, 2016

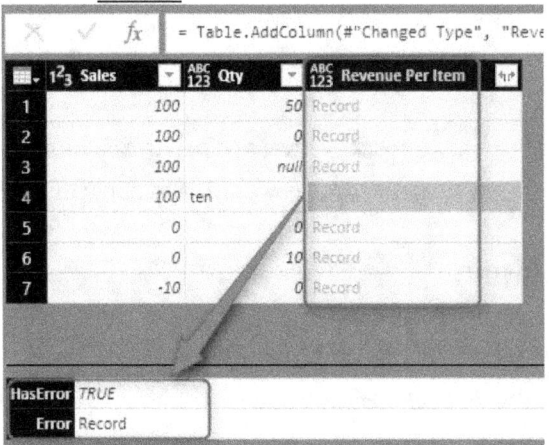

When you work with data, it is normal that you apply numeric calculations. Numeric calculations in Power Query depends on the nature of data returns different results. One of the most error-prone calculations is division. Power Query behaves differently when you divide a number by zero, zero by zero, number by null, and non-numeric values. One of the most frustrating facts is that not all of these calculations end up to an error. So you can't just remove error rows. In this post, I'll explain some examples of output for the division and a method to find these rows.

Sample Data Set

For this post, I'll use a sample excel file which has most of the possible combinations that I might face in a division calculation. The table below is some records with Sales Amount and Quantity. And as a simple calculation, I want to find out Revenue Per Item which would be the result of [Sales]/[Quantity].

A	B
Sales	Qty
100	50
100	0
100	
100	ten
0	0
0	10
-10	0

In the table above there are nulls, texts, zeros, negative, and positive values. Now let's bring the table into Power Query (Excel or Power BI) and apply the division

Simple Division Calculation

Here is the data set loaded into Power Query. As you can see the Quantity column shows the data type as numeric and text.

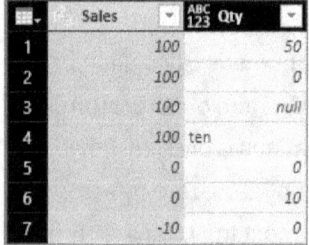

Now If I apply a simple division calculation as a new custom column

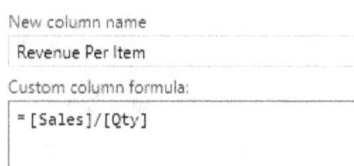

The result would be as below;

```
= Table.AddColumn(#"Changed Type", "Revenue Per Item", each [Sales]/[Qty])
```

#	Sales	Qty	Revenue Per Item
1	100	50	2
2	100	0	Infinity
3	100	null	null
4	100	ten	Error
5	0	0	NaN
6	0	10	0
7	-10	0	-Infinity

As you see the result set has different outputs depends on the inputs. If the number is divided by a zero value result would be positive or negative infinity (depends on the number). If one of the values be null, the result set would be null. If zero divided by zero, then the result would be NaN! And in case of dividing a number by string or reverse there will be an error raised. Now Let's look at each output separately.

Error Output

Error in the sample above happened when one of the values is not number. Fortunately, errors can be simply found by TRY keyword. Here is how I change the calculation of Revenue Per Item:

```
1 = try [Sales]/[Qty]
```

Add Custom Column

New column name
Revenue Per Item

Custom column formula:
```
= try [Sales]/[Qty]
```

Result set this time would be a Record for each calculation.

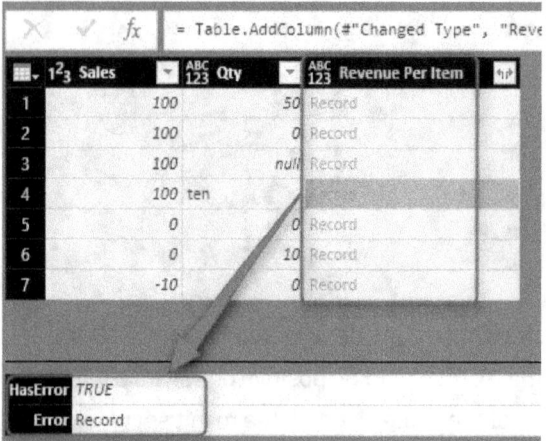

The record has two columns: HasError (which says does this record contains error or not), and Error Record (which would be the error happened in details). So I can add a custom column with a condition on HasError to see if the record contains error or not. In expression below, if I find an error, I will return zero as a result.

1 = if [Revenue Per Item][HasError] then 0 else [Revenue Per Item][Value]

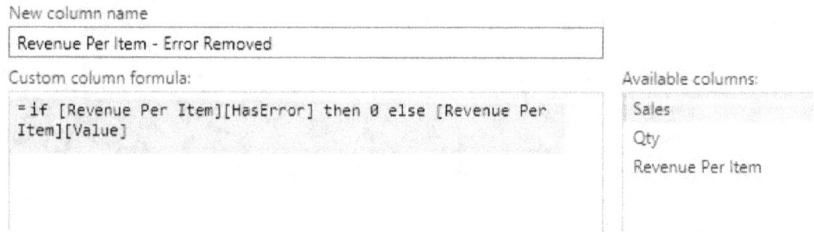

The result set this time would be:

Sales	Qty	Revenue Per Item	Revenue Per Item - Error Removed
100	50	Record	2
100	0	Record	Infinity
100	null	Record	null
100	ten	Record	0
0	0	Record	NaN
0	10	Record	0
-10	0	Record	-Infinity

In this example, I just returned zero if I find the error. But you can return an error message if you like with [Revenue Per Item][ErrorMessage]. This method is great error handling method when an error out of the blue happens in your data set. I always recommend using TRY method to get rid of errors that might stop the whole solution to work properly.

I have to mention that steps above are separated to show you how the output of try expression looks like. You can combine both steps above in single step with TRY OTHERWISE as below (Thanks to Maxim Zelensky for pointing this out);

1 = try [Sales]/[Qty] otherwise 0

Infinity

Error output can be handled with TRY. However, Infinity and -Infinity are not errors! These are numerical values in Power Query, named Number.PositiveInfinity and Number.NegativeInfinity.

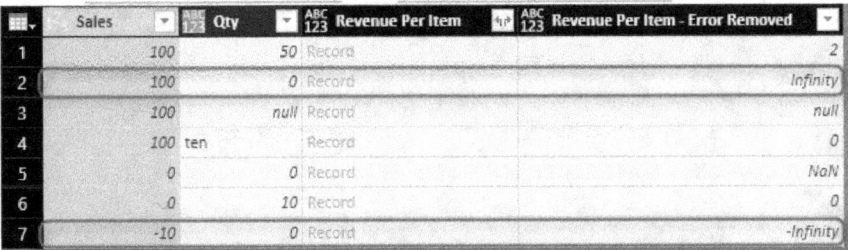

- PositiveInfinity happens when a positive number divided by zero
- NegativeInfinity happens when a negative number divided by zero

You can't find these with error handling because as I mentioned earlier, these are not error values! You can, however, check these values to see if a value is NegativeInfinity or PositiveInfinity with sample code below:

```
1 Pinfinity=(if x=Number.PositiveInfinity then false else true),
2 Ninfinity=(if x=Number.NegativeInfinity then false else true)
```

NaN

NaN is another output which happens when zero is divided by zero. NaN is a number value like positive and negative infinity. So you can't use error handling to spot them out of millions of records.

#	Sales	Qty	Revenue Per Item	Revenue Per Item - Error Removed
1	100	50	Record	2
2	100	0	Record	Infinity
3	100	null	Record	null
4	100	ten	Record	0
5	0	0	Record	NaN
6	0	10	Record	0
7	-10	0	Record	-Infinity

You can find it with Number.IsNaN function which works as below;

```
1 Nan=(if Number.IsNaN(x) then false else true)
```

Null Check

Null values always happen in the data, and best practice is always to replace them with default values. In numeric calculations, if a null value appears in one of the values, the result of the calculation will be null.

#	Sales	Qty	Revenue Per Item	Revenue Per Item - Error Removed
1	100	50	Record	2
2	100	0	Record	Infinity
3	100	null	Record	null
4	100	ten	Record	0
5	0	0	Record	NaN
6	0	10	Record	0
7	-10	0	Record	-Infinity

You can find nulls with if a condition such as below;

```
1 Null=(if x=null then false else true)
```

Function to Check All Anomalies

Anomalies in outputs such as the above examples happen in most of the cases, and I found it useful to have a function to check all these options. The function below checks Null, NaN, PositiveInfinity, and NegativeInfinity. It doesn't check errors, however. Error handling is best to be applied on the calculation level as we've done earlier in this post. Here is the code for the function:

```
1  let
2      Source = (x as any) =>
3          let
4              Null=(if x=null then false else true),
5              Pinfinity=(if x=Number.PositiveInfinity then false else true),
6              Ninfinity=(if x=Number.NegativeInfinity then false else true),
7              Nan=(if Number.IsNaN(x) then false else true)
8          in
9              Null and Pinfinity and Ninfinity and Nan
10 in
11     Source
```

ValidateDivisionResult

```
let
    Source = (x as any) =>
        let
            Null=(if x=null then false else true),
            Pinfinity=(if x=Number.PositiveInfinity then false else true),
            Ninfinity=(if x=Number.NegativeInfinity then false else true),
            Nan=(if Number.IsNaN(x) then false else true)
        in
            Null and Pinfinity and Ninfinity and Nan
in
    Source
```

With function above, now I can add a custom column to my data set, and validate rows;

Add Custom Column

New column name

Validation Result

Custom column formula:

`=ValidateDivisionResult([#"Revenue Per Item - Error Removed"])`

Final result set shows me which record is validated and which one is not. Note that the row containing error has been handled previously, so it is validating as true here.

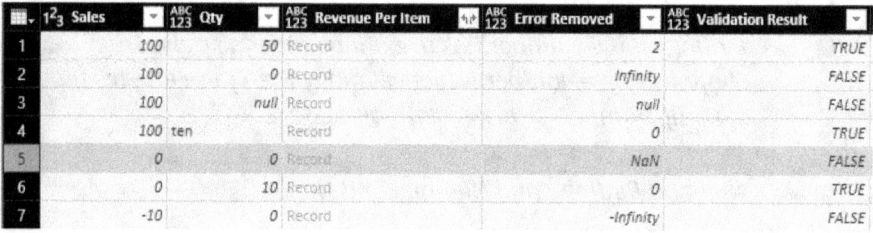

Summary

Divide by zero is not the only error that happens in Power Query. Power Query returns different results such as Error, NaN, Positive Infinity, Negative Infinity, and Null. For a proper faultless calculation, you have to consider all these exceptions. In this post, You've learned how to spot these exceptions easily and make your calculation faultless with a small amount of effort. If you like to learn more about Power Query and Power BI read Power BI online book; from Rookie to Rock Star.

Part V: Power Query Formula Language: M

Power Query Formula Language: M

Posted by Reza Rad on Feb 7, 2014

```
let
    TableA = #table({"CustomerId", "TranDate","TranCount"},
        {
        {1,DateTime.FromText("2014-01-01 01:00:00.000"),10},
        {1,DateTime.FromText("2014-01-01 02:00:00.000"),5},
        {1,DateTime.FromText("2014-01-03 01:00:00.000"),5},
        {1,DateTime.FromText("2014-01-04 02:00:00.000"),80}
        }),

    TableB = #table({"CustomerId", "TranDate","TranCount"},
        {
        {1,DateTime.FromText("2014-01-01 02:00:00.000"),10},
        {1,DateTime.FromText("2014-01-01 03:00:00.000"),5},
        {1,DateTime.FromText("2014-01-02 01:00:00.000"),20},
        {1,DateTime.FromText("2014-01-02 03:00:00.000"),15},
        {2,DateTime.FromText("2014-01-01 01:00:00.000"),5},
        {2,DateTime.FromText("2014-01-01 02:00:00.000"),80}
        }),
    TableATransformed=Table.Sort(
            Table.AddColumn(TableA,"Date",each Date.From([TranDate]))
            ,{"CustomerId","TranDate"}
            )
in
    Table.Group(TableATransformed,{"CustomerId","Date"},{"Total",each List.Last([TranCount])})
```

In the previous post, I described what Power Query is, and how we can use that for self-service ETL. You've how to work with Power Query menus and connect to different data sources, and apply multiple transformations on the data. In this post, I'll go one step closer to the core of Power Query Formula Language known as M. In this post, you will learn about the structure of M language with demo samples.

As you've learned in the previous section, Power Query uses a GUI in Excel Add-In to fetch data from different sources and transform it with some functions. Every change that you apply on the dataset through GUI will be translated to the formula language "M". M is a functional language. M is a powerful language, and the good news is that M is much more powerful than what you see in the Excel GUI of Power Query. The GUI doesn't implement all functionality of M. So for advanced use of Power Query you would require to work with M directly. So as much as you expert yourself in M would result in better use of Power Query. So I dare to say learning M is not only the fundamental step but also the most important step in learning Power Query. Follow these steps to get into the Query mode of Power Query;

Open Query Editor (In the previous post you've learned that you can open query editor from Excel's Power Query tab). In the Query Editor window go to View tab, and click on Advanced Editor menu item.

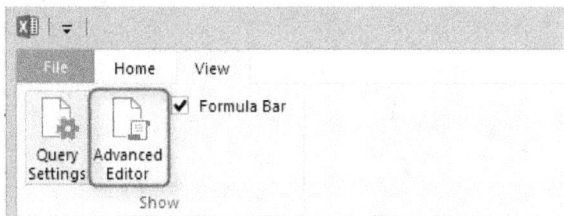

You will see the Query script window opens.

Now let's go through some features of M language with a sample; In this sample, I don't use an external data sources, I use static tables to show you how we can do everything with just script.

1- Open an empty excel sheet, and in the Power Query tab, In the "Get External Data" section click on "From Other Sources" and then choose "Blank Query".

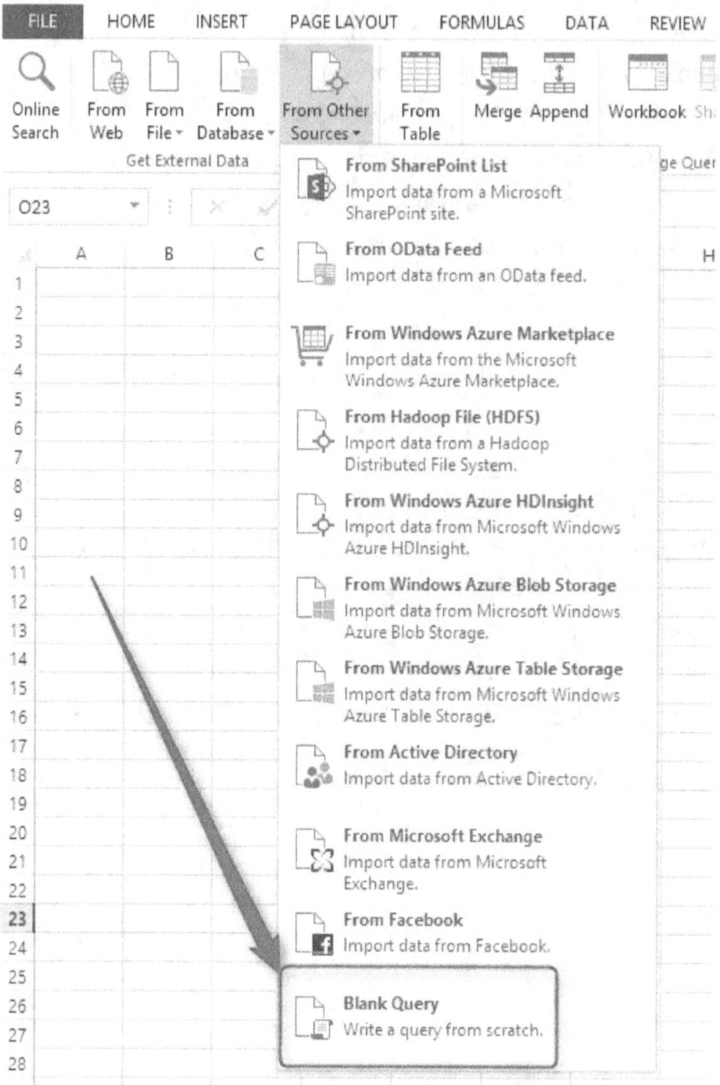

Power BI from Rookie to Rock Star – Book 3: Power Query and Data Transformation in Power BI

2- In the Query Editor window, go to the View tab, and click on Advanced Editor. You will see the script below in advanced editor window:

```
let
    Source = ""
in
    Source
```

3- Type inside double quotes the string "Hello World!", And then click OK. you will see the result in the Query Editor window as screenshot below illustrates

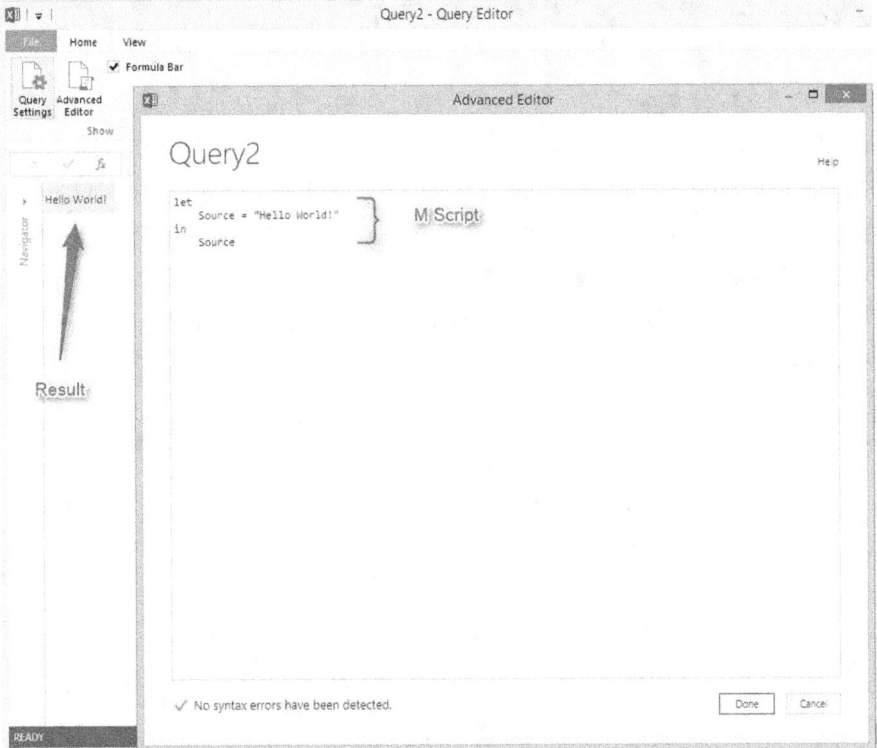

Wow, That was your first M script. And it was a very simple script. You see that script editor is not that much powerful like Visual Studio or SSMS, So the editor only is the location for writing the script with a very high-level validation bar in the left down part of the window.

The script that you've written has two parts; Let, and In.

Let; is the definition area. Here we define variables, records, lists, etc. as you see in this example we defined a variable named "Source", and we assigned a string to it: "Hello World!".

If you define more than one variable, record, or list, you can separate them by a single comma.

For example:

let

x=12,

Source="Hello World!"

IN; is the functional area. You can write the result out to the output with this section. In our example, we write down the value of "Source" variable into the Power Query editor window.

4- **M is case sensitive**. You can check that with the script showed in below screenshot.

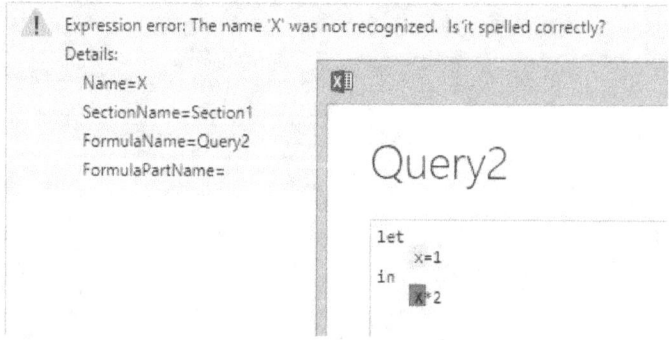

5- M contains Literals or Values. Values can be used as below;

1 // number

"Hello World!" // string

true //logical

6- Comments; Comments can be determined as a single line or multiple lines.

// this is comment markup for single line comments
/* this is multiple lines comment markup */

7- Variables define simply in the "let" section with naming the variable and assigning it. For example "Source" variable in the example above.

let
  // This is single line comment
  x=1,
  y=2
in
  /* this is
multiple lines
comment */
  x+y

8- Defining records and tables; You can define records in let section within two brackets { }, columns in the record will be separated by comma.
a sample record can be defined as following: {1,"Reza","Rad"}
For defining a table you can follow this structure:
TableX=#table({"Column A","Column B"} ,{ {1,11},{2,22} })

9- Now let's do a real sample with data.
Define a table as below:

let
  TableA = #table({"CustomerId", "TranDate","TranCount"},
  {   {1,DateTime.FromText("2014-01-01 01:00:00.000"),10}, {1,DateTime.FromText("2014-01-01 02:00:00.000"),5}, {1,DateTime.FromText("2014-01-03 01:00:00.000"),5}, {1,DateTime.FromText("2014-01-04 02:00:00.000"),80} })

in

   TableA

The result set of TableA would be as below:

As you see, we've used the function **DateTime.FromText** in this example. This function converts text to DateTime data type.

The table defined in this example has three columns; CustomerId, TranDate, TranCount

10- Define second table as below:

TableB = #table({"CustomerId", "TranDate","TranCount"},

   {

   {1,DateTime.FromText("2014-01-01 02:00:00.000"),10},

   {1,DateTime.FromText("2014-01-01 03:00:00.000"),5},

   {1,DateTime.FromText("2014-01-02 01:00:00.000"),20},

   {1,DateTime.FromText("2014-01-02 03:00:00.000"),15},

   {2,DateTime.FromText("2014-01-01 01:00:00.000"),5},

   {2,DateTime.FromText("2014-01-01 02:00:00.000"),80}

   })

this is an illustration of the second table

CustomerId	TranDate	TranCount
1	1/1/2014 2:00:00 AM	10
1	1/1/2014 3:00:00 AM	5
1	1/2/2014 1:00:00 AM	20
1	1/2/2014 3:00:00 AM	15
2	1/1/2014 1:00:00 AM	5
2	1/1/2014 2:00:00 AM	80

11- the purpose of this part of the example is to group TableA by date. For grouping this table, we transform it to another table with a new column: date. Date column would only contain the date part of TranDate column (not the time portion of it). We use **Table.AddColumn** function for this purpose.
TableATransformed= Table.AddColumn(TableA,"Date",each Date.From([TranDate]))

Table.AddColumn(<table name>,<new column name>, expression for new column)

here is the full script for this example:
let

    TableA = #table({"CustomerId", "TranDate","TranCount"},

{

{1,DateTime.FromText("2014-01-01 01:00:00.000"),10},

{1,DateTime.FromText("2014-01-01 02:00:00.000"),5},

{1,DateTime.FromText("2014-01-03 01:00:00.000"),5},

{1,DateTime.FromText("2014-01-04 02:00:00.000"),80}

}),

TableB = #table({"CustomerId", "TranDate","TranCount"},

{

{1,DateTime.FromText("2014-01-01 02:00:00.000"),10},

{1,DateTime.FromText("2014-01-01 03:00:00.000"),5},

{1,DateTime.FromText("2014-01-02 01:00:00.000"),20},

{1,DateTime.FromText("2014-01-02 03:00:00.000"),15},

{2,DateTime.FromText("2014-01-01 01:00:00.000"),5},
    {2,DateTime.FromText("2014-01-01 02:00:00.000"),80}
    }),
    TableATransformed= Table.AddColumn(TableA,"Date",each Date.From([TranDate]))
in
    TableATransformed

And the result is:

	CustomerId	TranDate	TranCount	Date
1	1	1/1/2014 1:00:00 AM	10	1/1/2014
2	1	1/1/2014 2:00:00 AM	5	1/1/2014
3	1	1/3/2014 1:00:00 AM	5	1/3/2014
4	1	1/4/2014 2:00:00 AM	80	1/4/2014

12- in this step, we sort records with **Table.Sort** function as below:

TableATransformed=Table.Sort(
        Table.AddColumn(TableA,"Date",each Date.From([TranDate]))
            ,{"CustomerId","TranDate"}
)

Table.Sort works in this structure;

Table.Sort (<table>,<columns to be sorted>)

Columns to be sorted can be defined in order like a record. For our example, we used {"CustomerId","TranDate"}, which means sorting will be applied on CustomerId first and then on TranDate. this expression is similar to this T-SQL order by clause; order by CustomerId, TranDate

13- We use **Table.Group** function to group records by the Date Column.

Table.Group(TableATransformed,{"CustomerId","Date"},{"Total",each List.Last([TranCount])})

Table.Group(<table>,<group key columns>,{<name of the new aggregated column>,<expression>})

List.Last([TranCount]) function will return the last record's TranCount. The result would be as below:

	CustomerId	Date	Total
1	1	1/1/2014	5
2	1	1/3/2014	5
3	1	1/4/2014	80

14- Now repeat the same expression for Table B.

TableBTransformed=Table.Sort(

      Table.AddColumn(TableB,"Date",each Date.From([TranDate]))

        ,{"CustomerId","TranDate"}

          ),

TableBGrouped=Table.Group(TableBTransformed,{"CustomerId","Date"},{"Total", each List.Last([TranCount])})

15- In this step we want to join TableA and TableB on two fields; CustomerId, and Date. we will use Table.Join function for this purpose.

Table.Join works with this syntax:

Table.Join(<first table>,<first table keys>,<second table>,<second table keys>,JoinKind optional, JoinAlgorithm optional)

The important things to note before applying join in Power Query is that the Table.Join works only on datasets with different column names. So if there be a column with a similar name in both tables, it would return an error. In this example, both tables have a similar structure with similar column names, so we use **Table.PrefixColumns** to change the name of columns for one of the tables.

Table.PrefixColumns(<table>,"Prefix")

The result of Table.PrefixColumn would be the same table with the "Prefix" at the beginning of each column name.

so this expression

Table.PrefixColumns(TableAGrouped,"TableA")

will result

TableA.CustomerId	TableA.Date	TableA.Total
1	1/1/2014	5
1	1/3/2014	5
1	1/4/2014	80

now we can join two tables based on the CustomerId and Date column, as below:

in

Table.Join(Table.PrefixColumns(TableAGrouped,"TableA"),{"TableA.CustomerId","TableA.Date"},TableBGrouped,{"CustomerId","Date"},JoinKind.FullOuter)

Join kind can have any of these values:

JoinKind.Inner=0

JoinKind.LeftOuter=1

JoinKind.RightOuter=2

JoinKind.FullOuter=3

JoinKind.LeftAnti=4

JoinKind.RightAnti=5

(Left Anti and Right Anti will return only records from a table that doesn't have a match in the other table -based on left/right respectively)

you can use codes instead of enumeration. this means that expression below would return same result as previous one:

Table.Join(Table.PrefixColumns(TableAGrouped,"TableA"),{"TableA.CustomerId","TableA.Date"},TableBGrouped,{"CustomerId","Date"},3)

But it is highly recommended to use enumeration because it is much easier to read.

result of above expression would be as below:

TableA.CustomerId	TableA.Date	TableA.Total	CustomerId	Date	Total
1	1/1/2014	5	1	1/1/2014	5
null	null	null	1	1/2/2014	15
null	null	null	2	1/1/2014	80
1	1/3/2014	5	null	null	null
1	1/4/2014	80	null	null	null

Here is the full script for this example:

```
let
    TableA = #table({"CustomerId", "TranDate","TranCount"},
    { {1,DateTime.FromText("2014-01-01  01:00:00.000"),10},
    {1,DateTime.FromText("2014-01-01       02:00:00.000"),5},
    {1,DateTime.FromText("2014-01-03       01:00:00.000"),5},
    {1,DateTime.FromText("2014-01-04  02:00:00.000"),80} }),
    TableB = #table({"CustomerId", "TranDate","TranCount"},
    { {1,DateTime.FromText("2014-01-01  02:00:00.000"),10},
    {1,DateTime.FromText("2014-01-01       03:00:00.000"),5},
    {1,DateTime.FromText("2014-01-02       01:00:00.000"),20},
    {1,DateTime.FromText("2014-01-02       03:00:00.000"),15},
    {2,DateTime.FromText("2014-01-01       01:00:00.000"),5},
    {2,DateTime.FromText("2014-01-01  02:00:00.000"),80} }),
    TableATransformed=Table.Sort(




            Table.AddColumn(TableA,"Date",each Date.From([TranDate]))
                ,{"CustomerId","TranDate"}
                        ),
    TableBTransformed=Table.Sort(
```

```
            Table.AddColumn(TableB,"Date",each Date.From([TranDate]))
              ,{"CustomerId","TranDate"}
                        ),
      TableAGrouped=Table.Group(TableATransformed,{"CustomerId","Date"},{"T
otal",each List.Last([TranCount])}),
      TableBGrouped=Table.Group(TableBTransformed,{"CustomerId","Date"},{"T
otal",each List.Last([TranCount])})
in
Table.Join(Table.PrefixColumns(TableAGrouped,"TableA"),{"TableA.CustomerId","
TableA.Date"},TableBGrouped,{"CustomerId","Date"},JoinKind.FullOuter)
```

We will go through more data transformation in next blog posts.

Power BI from Rookie to Rock Star – Book 3: Power Query and Data Transformation in Power BI

M or DAX? That is the Question!

Posted by Reza Rad on Mar 3, 2017

What is the main difference between M and DAX? Why can we do a calculated column in two different places? What are the pros and cons of each? Which one should I use for creating a profit column? Why I cannot do all of it in only one; DAX or M! Why two different languages?! Why the structure of these two are so different? ... If any of these are your questions, then you need to read this post. In this post, I'll go through differences of these two languages, and explain why, when, where of it. Normally I don't get this question asked from students of my Power BI course, because I elaborate the difference in details. However, if you have this question, this is a post for you. If you would like to learn more about Power BI; read Power BI book; from Rookie to Rock Star.

What is M?

M is the scripting language behind the scene for Power Query. M is the informal name of this language. The formal name is Power Query Formula Language! Which is long, and even Microsoft refer it to M. M stands for many things, but one of the most common words of it is Mashup. Which means this language is capable of data mashup, and transformation. M is a functional language. And structure of M script can be similar to this:

```
let
    FirstAndLastDayOfTheMonth = (date) =>
        let
            dated=Date.FromText(date),
            year=Date.Year(dated),
            month=Date.Month(dated),
            FirstDateText=Text.From(year)&"-"&Text.From(month)&"-01",
            FirstDate=Date.FromText(FirstDateText),
            daysInMonth=Date.DaysInMonth(dated),
            LastDateText=Text.From(year)&"-"&Text.From(month)&"-"&Text.From(daysInMonth),
            LastDate=Date.FromText(LastDateText),
            record=Record.AddField([],"First Date of Month",FirstDate),
            resultset=Record.AddField(record,"Last Date of Month",LastDate)
        in
            resultset
in
    FirstAndLastDayOfTheMonth("30/07/2015")
```

Source: Day Number of Year Function in Power Query

M is a step by step language structure. Usually (Not always), every line in M script is a data transformation step. And the step after that will use the result of the previous step. It is usually easy to follow the structure of M language for a programmer. Because it is understandable with programming blocks of Let and In, and some other programming language features alike.

What is DAX?

DAX is Data Analysis Expression Language. This is the common language between SQL Server Analysis Services Tabular, Power BI, and Power Pivot in Excel. DAX is an expression language, and unlike M, it is very similar to Excel functions. DAX has many common functions with Excel. However, DAX is much more powerful than Excel formula in many ways. Here is an example DAX expression:

```
Sales Rolling 12 Months =
CALCULATE(
    SUM(FactInternetSales[SalesAmount]),
    DATESBETWEEN
        (DimDate[FullDateAlternateKey],
            NEXTDAY(SAMEPERIODLASTYEAR(LASTDATE(DimDate[FullDateAlternateKey]))),
            LASTDATE(DimDate[FullDateAlternateKey])
        ),
    ALL(DimDate)
)
```

Source: Secret of Time Intelligence Functions in Power BI

DAX calculations are built in a way that makes sense mostly for Excel users. Normally Excel users are very comfortable with this language. Everything goes through functions. DAX doesn't have programming blocks in it and is a combination of function uses, filters, and expressions.

Example Usage of M

M can be used in many data transformation scenarios. As an example, it can be used to Pivot or Unpivot Data, To Group it based on some columns. Here is how a Pivot/Unpivot can work in Power Query;

Pivot / Unpivot

- Pivot: Turning Name/Value; Rows to Columns

- Unpivot: Turning Columns to Rows; Name/Values

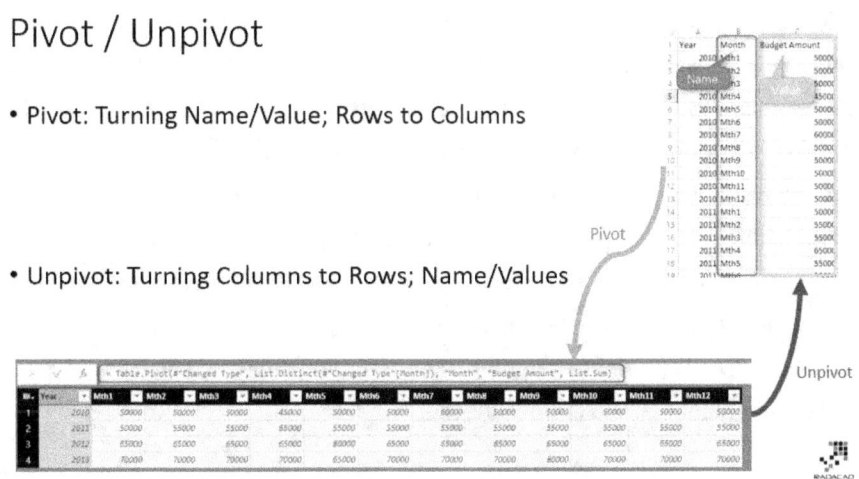

Example Usage of DAX?

DAX can be used for many calculations for analyzing data. For example, calculating Year To Date, Calculating Rolling 12 Months Average, or anything like that. Here is an example which based on selection criteria in the report and few simple DAX expressions we can do a customer retention case with DAX;

Calculated Column Dilemma

The main question of choosing between DAX and M comes from calculated column dilemma in my opinion. You can create many calculated columns in both M or DAX, and it is confusing where is the best place to do it, or why there are two different places to do it?! As an example; you can create a full name which is concatenated of FirstName and LastName column. You can do that in M, and also in DAX. So this question comes up that: Why two different places? Which one is best to use? Can we always use one language? To answer this question, I would like to use another example; There are many types of knives, and you can use almost all of them to cut the cheese!

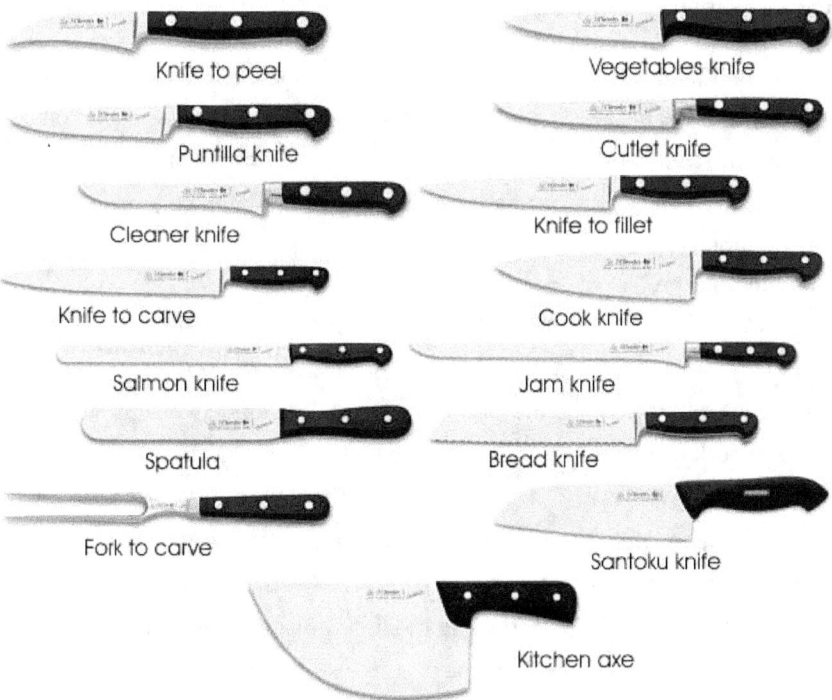

reference: http://forkitchen.blogspot.co.nz/2008/10/what-are-different-types-of-kitchen.html

Almost every knife in the above picture can be used for cutting cheese except one of them! So why there are so many knives for cutting cheese?! The answer is that; these are not knives for cutting cheese! Each knife is good for doing one special case. For cutting bread, bread knife gives you the best result. For cutting a fillet, you normally need another type of knife. But as you agree, for some cases (such as cutting cheese!) you can use many of these knives. Let's know to go back to the original question;

Why can I create a same calculated column in DAX or M?

These two languages are built independently. They built in a way that they can handle most of the business-related solutions. So, as a result, there are some use cases that both languages are capable of doing it. As an example, both of these languages can easily be used to create a concatenated column of two other columns.

Which one is best?

The quick answer is Depends! Depends on the type of usage. If you want to create a concatenated column; Power Query (M) is a better option in my view, because that is normally like the ETL part of your BI solution, you can simply build your model and data sets in a way you like it to be. But if you want to create something like Year To Date; you can do that in Power Query or M, but it will be lots of code, and you have to consider many combinations of possibilities to create a correct result, while in DAX you can simply create that with the usage of TotalYTD function. So the answer is; there is no best language between these two. The type of usage identifies which one is best. Normally any changes to prepare the data for the model is best to be done in M, and any analysis calculation on top of the model is best to be done in DAX.

Two Languages for Two Different Purposes

There are many programming languages in the world; each language has its pros and cons. JavaScript is a language of web scripting, which is very different from ASP.NET or PHP. The same thing happens here. When M born, it meant to be a language for data transformation, and it is still that language. DAX was created to answer business analysis questions.

What Questions Can DAX Answer?

DAX is the analytical engine in Power BI. It is the best language to answer analytical questions which their responses will be different based on the selection criteria in the report. For example; You might want to calculate Rolling 12 Months Average of Sales. It is really hard if you want to calculate that in M, because you have to consider all different types of possibilities; Rolling 12 months for each product, for every customer, for every combinations, etc. However if you use a DAX calculation for it, the analytical engine of DAX take care of all different combinations selected through Filter Context in the report.

What Questions Can M Answer?

M is Data Transformation engine in Power BI. You can use M for doing any data preparation and data transformation before loading that into your model. Instead of bringing three tables of DimProduct, DimProductSubcategory, and DimProductCategory, you can merge them all in Power Query, and create a single DimProduct including all columns from these tables, and load that into the model. Loading all of these into the model and using DAX to relate these to each other means consuming extra memory for something that is not required to be in the model. M can combine those three tables and based on "Step Based" operational structure of M, they can be simply used to create a final data set.

As a Power BI Developer Which Language Is Important to Learn?

Both! With no hesitation! M is your ETL language, and DAX is the analytical language. You cannot live with only one. If you want to be an expert in Power BI, you should be an expert in both of these languages. There are some cases that one of the languages will be used more than the other one. However, you will need a very good understanding of both languages to understand which one is best for which purpose, and easily can use it in real-world scenarios.

Basics of M: Power Query Formula Language

Posted by Reza Rad on Jul 10, 2017

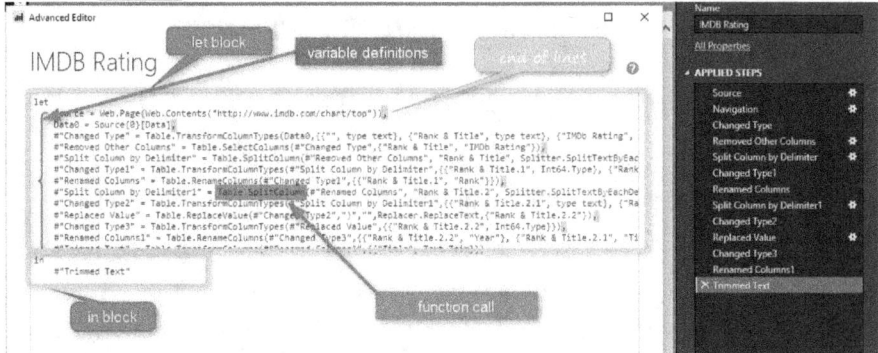

M is the powerful language behind the scene of Power Query. Any transformation you apply will be written in M language. For many, M looks like a scary language. In this post, I like to explain a bit of basic of M. Not mentioning any functions. Mainly I want to explain to you how the M language syntax is structured. Once you know the syntax, then everything becomes simple. M is a language that you can learn it's syntax easily. As a Power Query developer; I highly recommend you to spend time on M, because there are MANY operations that you can with M, but you might not be able to do it simply with the graphical interface. If you would like to learn more about Power BI, read Power BI book from Rookie to Rock Star.

What is M?

M is an informal name of Power Query Formula Language. The formal name is so long that no one uses that, everyone calls it M! M stands for Data Mashup, some say stands for Data Modeling. M is a functional language, and it is important to know functions of it. However, each language has a structure and syntax which is the beginner level of learning that language. In this post, I will explain the syntax of M. Before learning M; I would like you to read this sentence loud;

M is much more powerful than the graphical interface of Power Query

Yes, you read it correct! The graphical interface of Power Query is changing every month. Every month new functionality comes to this graphical interface. But the fact is all of these functionalities has been in the language for many years! If you knew the language, you could easily use them, instead of waiting for graphical interface option for it. There are heaps of examples for it. One very small example is here: you can extend your Grouping ability in Power Query with a minor change in M script of it.

Syntax of M

The syntax of this language is simple. It always has two blocks of programming: LET expression block, and IN expression block. Here is the most simple M syntax;

```
1 let
2    x=1
3 in x
4
```

let and **in** are reserved words. Before going even one step further, the first and foremost thing you need to know;

M (Power Query Formula Language) is Case Sensitive. There is a difference between x and X.

What are these two programming blocks:

let: definition of all variables

in: output! Yes, it means out! just named as in. Everything you put in this block will be the output of your query.

So basically, the query below means defining a variable named as x, assigning the value 1 to it, and showing it as the result set. So the query will return 1.

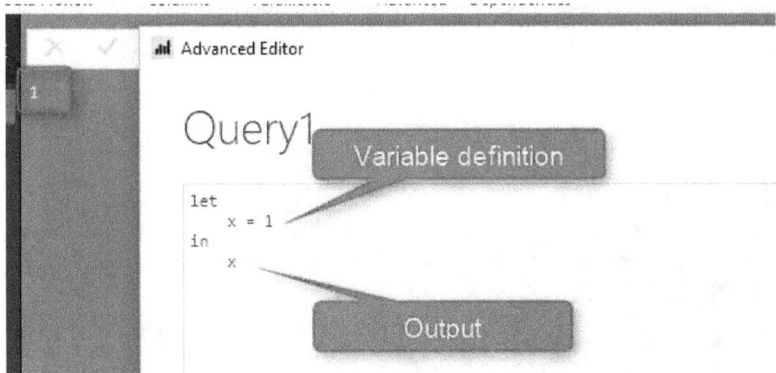

to run this example, you need to Open Power BI Desktop. Go to getting Data, start with New Blank Query.

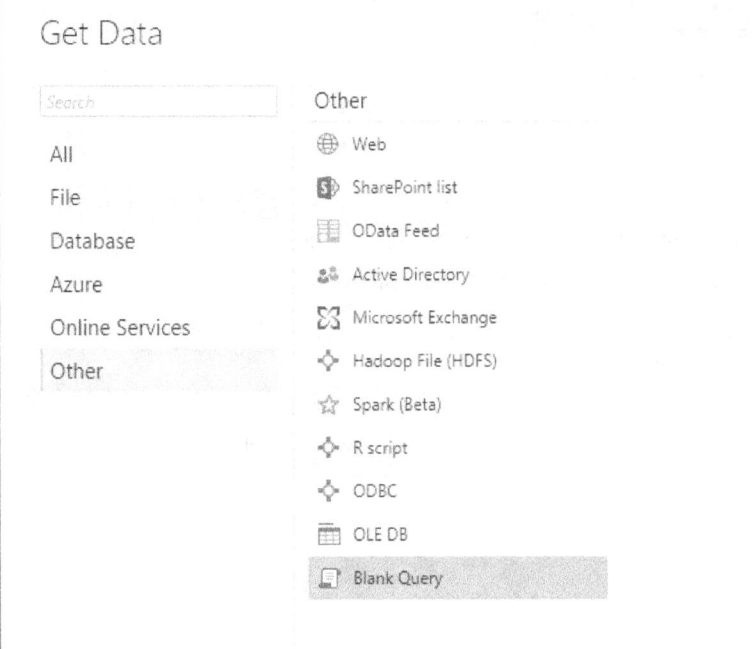

then in View tab, select advanced Editor;

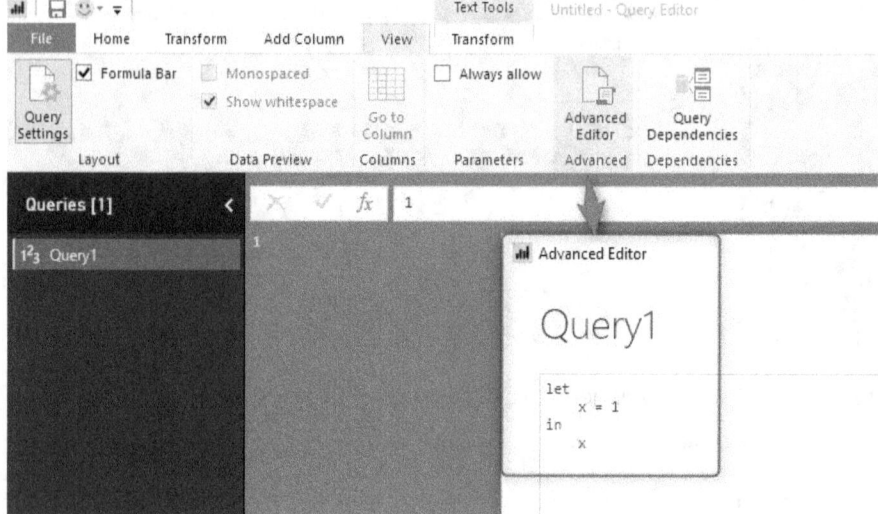

Make sure when you write the script that you put reserved words such as let and in all lowercase. Also your variable name should be the same case in both let and section.

As you can see, there is no need to define data types for the variable. It will be automatically assigned when the first assignment occurs.

If you specify a text value, then variable would be a text data type automatically.

End of the Line

Lines of codes in M continues if you don't put the end of the line character.

As you can see in the above example, the line continues, and x will be equal to x=1+1. If you want to put an end for a line use comma(,). Example here:

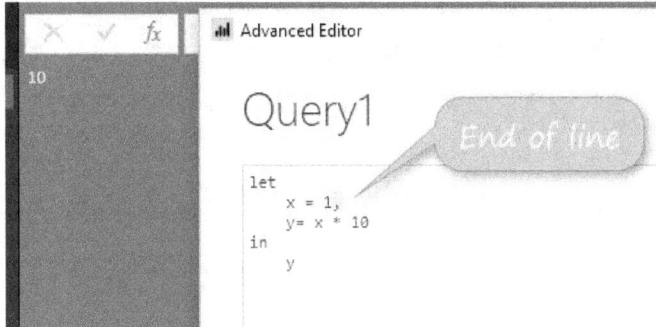

every line needs a comma(,) to finish. Except the last line before **"in"**.

Variable Names

Name of variables can be all one word, like Source. Or it can have spaces in it. In case that you have some characters such as space, then you need to put the name inside double quote (") and put a hashtag at the beginning of it(#). Something similar to:

```
1 #"This is a variable name"
```

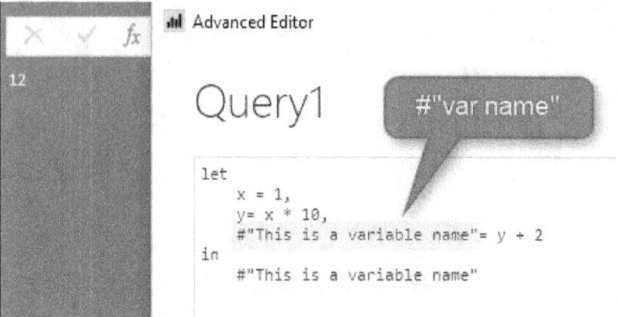

A variable name can contain special characters, here is an example:

Special characters

Variable names can have a special character, as you can see below variable has all types of characters in it and still runs well.

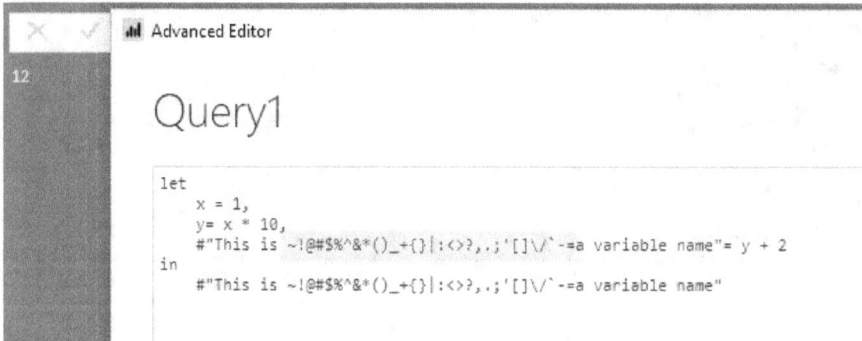

Escape character

Double quote (") is escape character. You can use it to define variables with names that have another double quote in it. Here is an example:

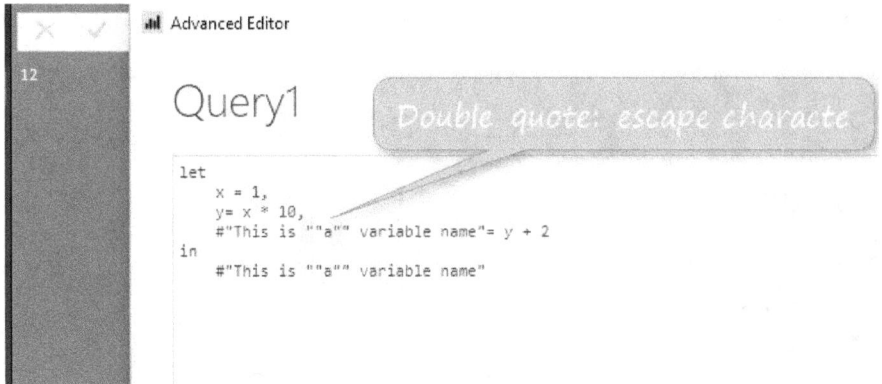

first double quote (highlighted) above is necessary to be before the second double quote (which is part of the variable name).

Step by Step Coding

Power Query is a step by step transformation. Every transformation usually happens in step. While you are writing the code, you can also notice that in the right-hand side, you will see every variable form a step.

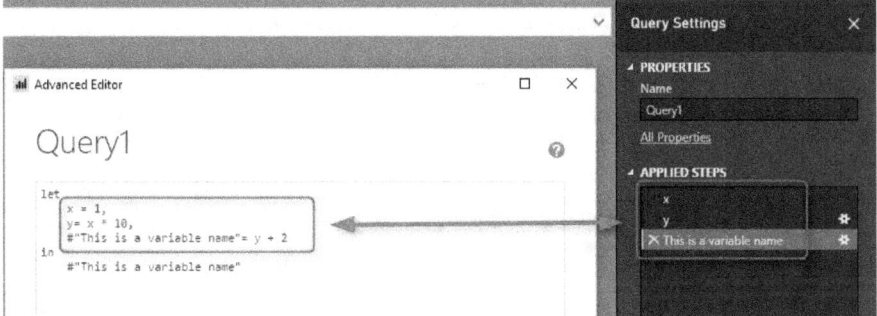

in the screenshot above, you can see every variable is determined as a step. And if the variable has space in the name, it will show it with spaces in the list of applied steps.

The last variable is always specified in the **in** section.

Literals

There are different ways of defining every literal in Power Query. For example, if you want to define a date variable, here is how to do it;

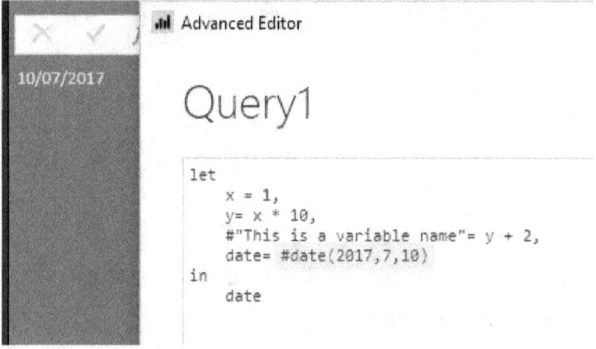

for defining all other types of literals, here is the reference table to use:

Kind	Literal
Null	null
Logical	true false
Number	0 1 -1 1.5 2.3e-5
Time	#time(09,15,00)
Date	#date(2013,02,26)
DateTime	#datetime(2013,02,26, 09,15,00)
DateTimeZone	#datetimezone(2013,02,26, 09,15,00, 09,00)
Duration	#duration(0,1,30,0)
Text	"hello"
Binary	#binary("AQID")
List	{1, 2, 3}
Record	[A = 1, B = 2]
Table	#table({"X","Y"},{{0,1},{1,0}})
Function	(x) => x + 1
Type	type { number } type table [A = any, B = text]

* for function and type; I'll write another post later to explain how these types work.

Function Call

M is a functional language, and for doing almost everything, you need to call a function for it. Functions can be easily called with the name of the function and specifying parameters for it.

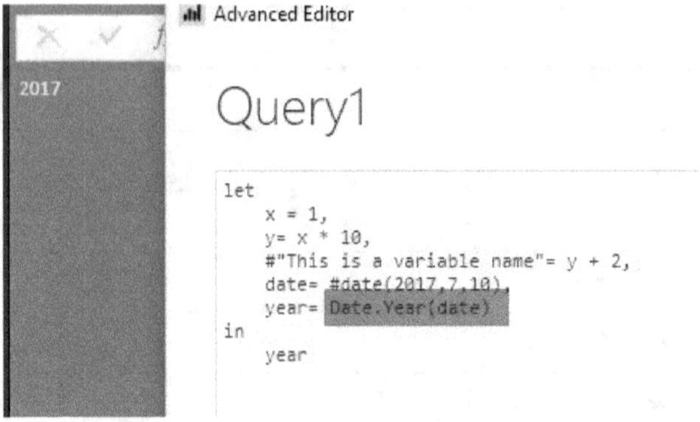

```
let
    x = 1,
    y= x * 10,
    #"This is a variable name"= y + 2,
    date= #date(2017,7,10),
    year= Date.Year(date)
in
    year
```

the screenshot above uses Date.Year function, which fetches the year part of a date. Functions names start always with capital letters: **D**ate.**Y**ear()

Comments

Like any programming language, you can put some comments in your code. It can be in two forms;

Single line commentary with a double slash (//)

```
let
// this is a comment line and will not be executed
    x = 1,
    y= x * 10,
    #"This is a variable name"= y + 2,
    date= #date(2017,7,10),
    year= Date.Year(date)
in
    year
```

Multi-line commentary between slash and starts (/* comments */)

```
let
/* this is a
multi
lin
comment and will not be executed
*/
    x = 1,
    y= x * 10,
    #"This is a variable name"= y + 2,
    date= #date(2017,7,10),
    year= Date.Year(date)
in
    year
```

A real-world example

Now that you know some basics let's look at an existing query in advanced editor mode and understand it.

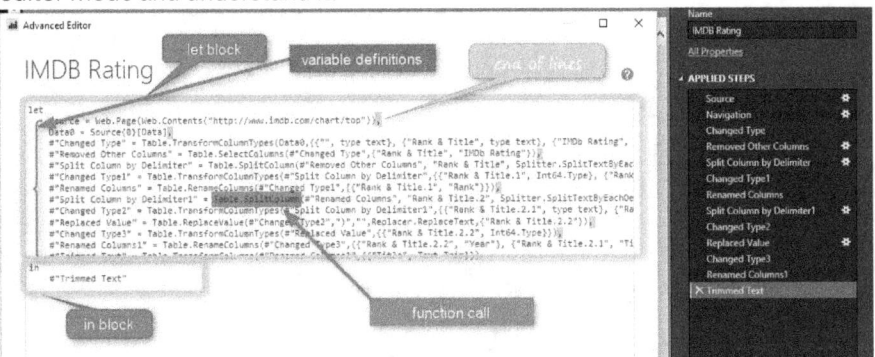

in the screenshot above, you can see all the basics mentioned so far:
1. let and in block
2. variable names matching steps applied in the query
3. some variable names with the hashtag and double quote: #"var name"
4. end of the line characters: comma
5. calling many functions

There are still many parts of this query that you might not understand. Specially when using functions. You need to learn what functions are doing to understand the code fully. I have written a blog post, that explains how to use the #shared keyword to get documentation of all functions in Power Query. In next posts, I'll explain another level of structures in M.

Basics of Value Structures in M – Power Query Formula Language

Posted by Reza Rad on Sep 21, 2017

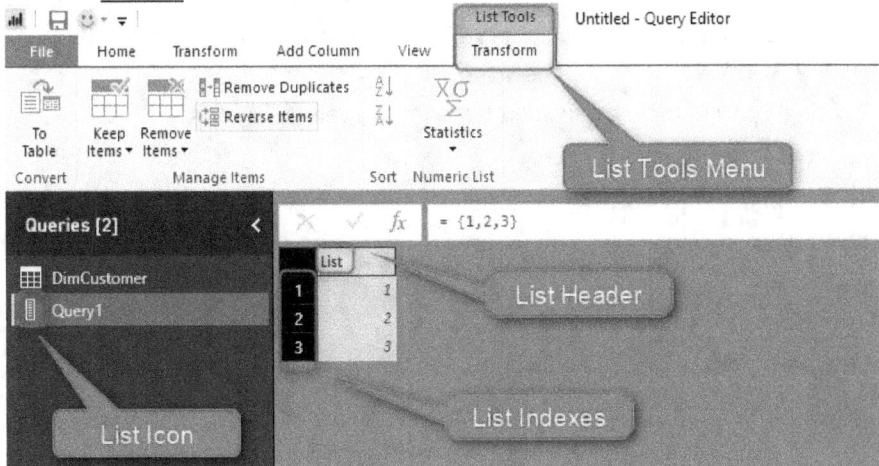

A couple of months ago, I've written a blog post about the Basics of M and explained few basics about this language. In this post, I'm going to the next step and will explain a few other structure definitions in this language. In this post, you will learn about Tables, Records, Lists, and how to navigate through structures. These structures are main value structures in Power Query and M. Every data value in Power Query is in one of these value structures, and it is important that you can work with these structures. To learn more about Power BI; read Power BI book from Rookie to Rock Star.

Prerequisite

To understand parts of code from this post, you might need first to read Basics of M post.

Five Main Value Structures in Power Query

Power Query has five structures for values. Data is either in one of these five structure types. By structure type, I don't mean the data type. I mean the way that data is stored. Sometimes data stored as a simple value like text, date, or number. Sometimes it is a complex value like a table, record, list, or function.

Primitive Value

Any single part data type considered a primitive value. Examples:

12 – a number value

"text sample" – text value

2017/09/21 – date value

null – null value

List

A list is a structure that has only one column, but multiple rows. Each row identified with an index. Example of a list in Power Query window;

The M script to define a list is as below;

1 Source = {1,2,3}

List Definition is always started with { and ends with }, items placed in between with a comma separator;

1 List = {<item 1>,<item 2>,<item 3>}

There are some ways to understand if a structure is a list or not. in the screenshot below all mentioned;

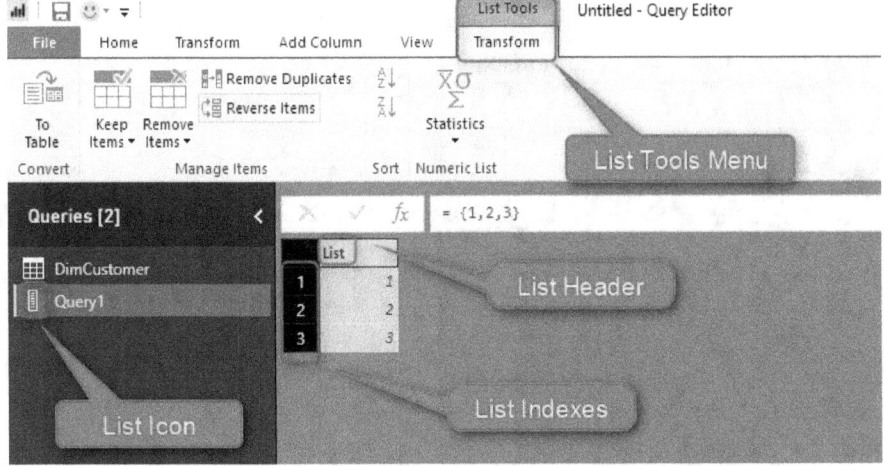

- List Icon: There will be a specific icon for the list in the Queries pane.
- List Tools: When you select a list, you will see List Tools menu. This menu gives you some options later on for changing and transforming the list.
- List Header: At the top of the list column, you will see "List" name.
- List Indexes: Every row in the list should have a numeric index starts from zero.

A list can have items that are different in data types. Here is an example;

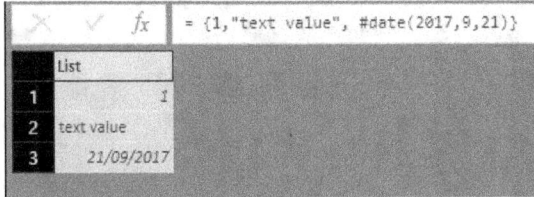

Here is the line definition for this list;
1 Source = {1,"text value", #date(2017,9,21)}

Record

A record is a structure with a single row, but multiple columns. However, the way that record is showed in Query editor is vertical! The main reason is that scrolling to the right is always harder than scrolling to down. So, Record is only visualized similarly to list. However, it is a totally different structure. This is how a record looks like in Power Query;

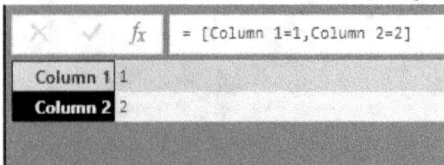

As you can see the record showed vertically, but every column header is visible there.

Here is the script for defining the record;

1 Source = [Column 1=1,Column 2=2]

Record definition always starts with [and ends with]. for every column you will have the column name before = sign, and the value of that after the = sign.

1 Record = [Column 1 = <value>, Column 2 = <value>]

Screenshot below shows how you can identify that the structure is a record;

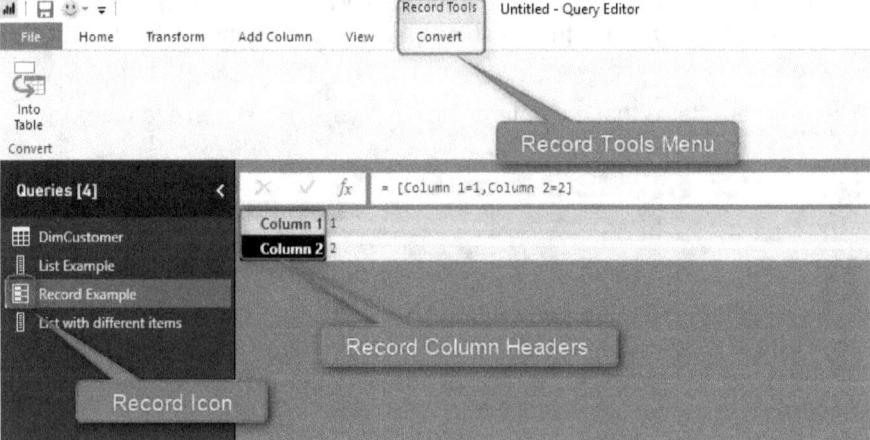

- Record Icon: There is a specific Icon that determines the object is a Record.
- Record Column Headers: You can see column headers in the record. In a list, you can see only numbers, but in a record, you see column names.
- Record Tools Menu: Every time you select a record object, you will see Record Tools which gives you the option to convert it to a table.

A record also can have different types of items. It is different columns.

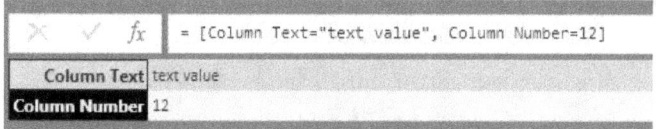

Here is the definition of the record above;

1 Source = [Column Text="text value", Column Number=12]

Table

A table is a structure that is most well known among others. A table is a combination of multiple rows and multiple columns. Here is a table sample;

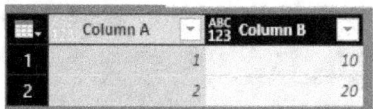

To create a table through M script, you can run a script such as below;

```
1  Source  =  #table( 2
{"Column A","Column B"}, 3
{ 4 {1,10}, 5 {2,20} 6 } 7 )
```

Table definition always starts with #table, then inside the bracket, you have to set of brackets; one set for defining headers, and the other set for all row values. Here is how this works;

```
1 Source = #table(
2 {"Column A","Column B"}, // all column headers
3 { // start of row values
4 {1,10}, // row one
5 {2,20} // row two
6 } // end of row values
7 )
```

If you see a table, then you can recognize it immediately. Because the table is the only structure that has multiple rows and multiple columns in it.

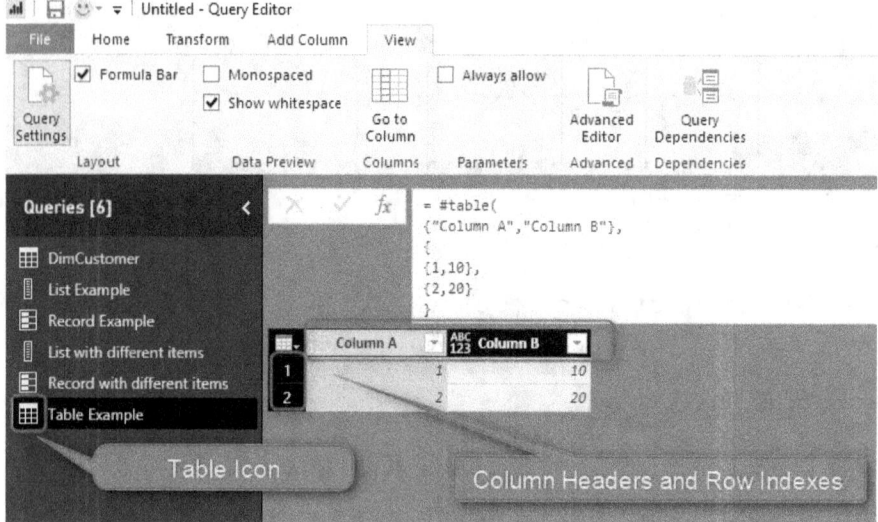

Table Icons shows that this is a table, and multiple columns and rows are only possible in a table.

You can also have a table with different items in each cell.

Function

A function is a data type that performs an operation and gives you a result. Here is an example of how function looks like in the query editor window;

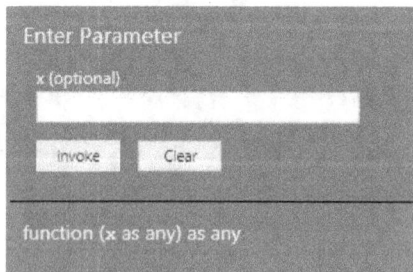

A function can be defined based on Lambda language as below;

1 Source = (x) => x+1

Function Definition has many details in it. I'll talk about it separately in another post. For now, just knowing this is enough that function has an input and output. Input and output are separated from each other with => signs.

```
1 Source = (<input of function>) => <output of function>
```

You can easily understand a function based on its specific icon, and also the function call dialog box.

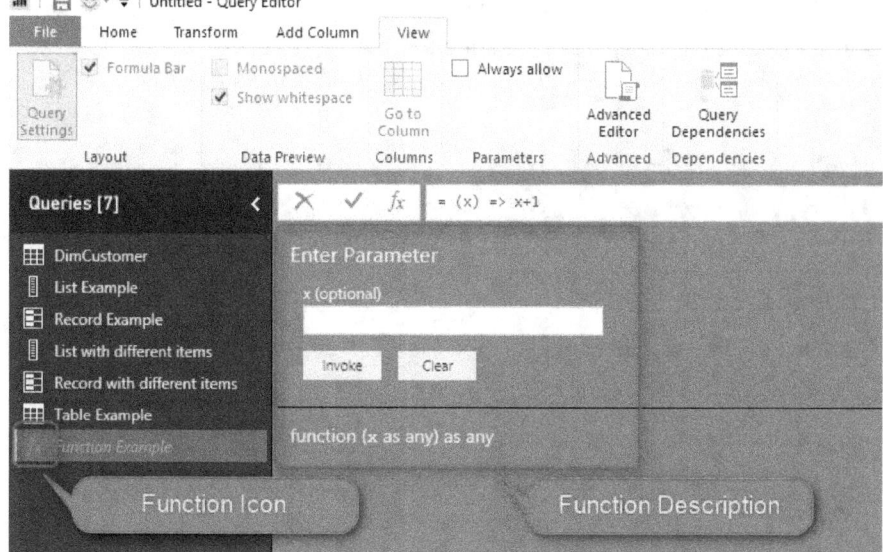

A function is one of the most powerful features in Power Query, and can't be explained only in few paragraphs. Stay tuned, and I'll write more details about functions in other posts separately.

Navigating Through List

Now that you know what list is, and how to define it, let's look at how you can navigate through the list. Each list item has a row index. You can easily navigate to that item using that index.

```
1 let
2   3Source = {1,2,3},
4   inSource1 = Source{1}
5   Source1
```

For navigating through a list, simply use a bracket and put the index of the item in the bracket. Now here is the tricky part:

Index starts from zero

When you look at the list in the query editor window, the index starts from 1. However, the actual index starts from zero. So if you want to drill down to a specific item in the list, you have to use a zero-based index to get to that. The example above will navigate to the **second item** in the list.

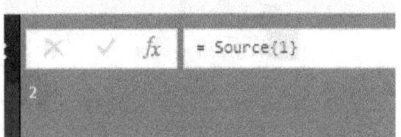

So this is simply the syntax to navigate through the list;

```
1 List{<item index starting from zero>}
```

List Functions

There are also some functions that work on a list. For example, you can get the count of items in a list, with List.Count() function.

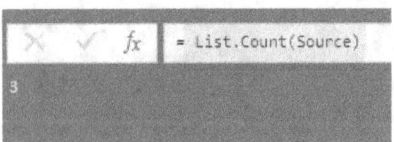

I will write more about List functions in the future separately.

Navigating Through Record

To navigate through a record, you need to use the column name for that record.

```
1 let
2     Source = [Column 1=1,Column 2=2],
3     #"Column 2" = Source[Column 2]
4 in #"Column 2"
5
```

You can simply put the column name inside bracket [and], and as a result, you will have the item;

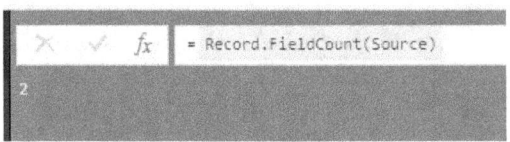

Record Functions

The Record also has a lot of functions. For example, you can use the Record.FieldCount() to get the count of columns in a record.

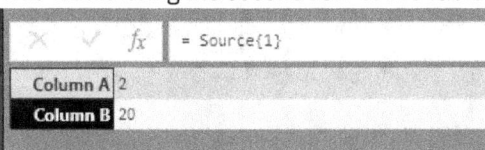

I will write another post about functions for Record.

Navigating Through Table

Navigating through a table happens a lot in real world scenarios when you want to drill down into a specific area of the table. For the table, you can use different methods to navigate;

Navigate with Record Index: Drill Down to Record

You can navigate to any records in the table simply with putting the record's index (zero-based) inside { and }. Here is an example;

```
1 let
2     Source = #table(
3 {"Column A","Column B"},
4 {
5 {1,10},
6 {2,20}
7 }
8 ),
9 record=Source{1}
10 in
11    record
```

This would bring the second row of the table as a Record structure;

Navigate with Column Name: Drill Down to List

You can also fetch every column of the table with referring to that column name inside [and]. The result would be a list.

```
1 let
2    Source = #table(
3 {"Column A","Column B"},
4 {
5 {1,10},
6 {2,20}
7 }
8 ),
9    #"Column A" = Source[Column A]
10 in #"Column A"
11
```

Navigating to a column will result in a list;

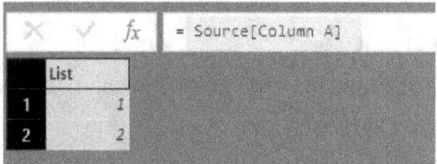

Navigate with Row Index and Column Name: Drill Down to individual Value

Sometimes you want to drill down to a specific cell, for that you need row index (zero-based), and column name both.

```
1 let
2    Source = #table(
3 {"Column A","Column B"},
4 {
5 {1,10},
6 {2,20}
7 }
8 ),
9    #"Column B" = Source{1}[Column B]
10 in #"Column B"
11
```

The script above navigates to the second row (Index 1 belongs to the second row), and column B. Result would be a primitive value in this case;

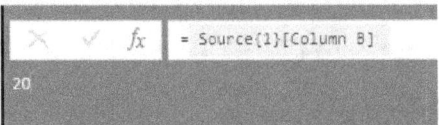

You can also do this navigation the other way around. Navigate to column first, and then to row. An example below;

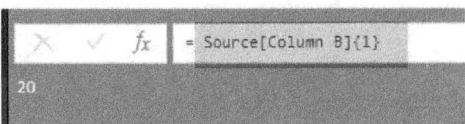

Navigate with Filter Criteria

For the majority of the cases, you want to navigate based on criteria. For example, you want to get the Column B value of the row that Column A value for that row is something specific. Like writing a SQL Statement clause. In the table below. For example; we want to navigate to the column B where column A is 1. You cannot do that search based on an index. However, you can search based on criteria.

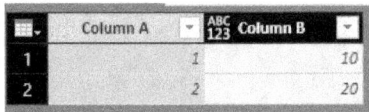

in the table below. For example; we want to navigate to the column B where column A is 1. You cannot do that search based on an index. However, you can search based on criteria.

Here is how you can search;

```
1 let
2    Source = #table(
3 {"Column A","Column B"},
4 {
5 {1,10},
6 {2,20}
7 }
8 ),
9 filtered=Source{[Column A=1]}[Column B]
10 in
11    filtered
```

The result would be 10 as expected;

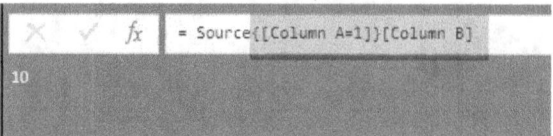

The structure simply is as below;
1 = <Table Name>{[Column Name="criteria 1", Column Name="criteria 2"]}[Output Column]

This is similar to SQL Where and Select Clause.

Concatenate List or Records

You can concatenate list or records together with ampersand (&) character.

Here is an example for list concatenation;

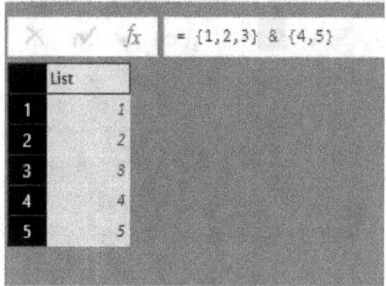

and here is an example for record concatenation;

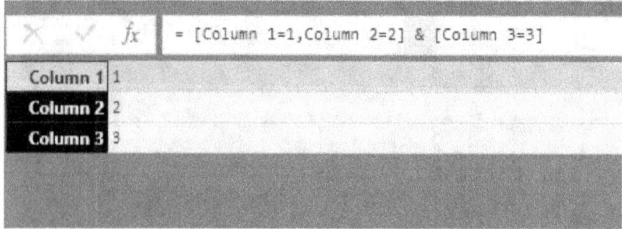

For concatenating tables; you need to use either Append or Merge. I explained fully in details about Append and Merge in this post.

Summary

In this post, you learned some of the basics about different value structures in Power BI; Primitive values, list, record, table, and function. You learned how to navigate through list, record, and table with different methods with M script. In future posts, I'll explain more details about each value structure and functions related to that structure.

Power BI from Rookie to Rock Star – Book 3: Power Query and Data Transformation in Power BI

Power Query Formula Language M: Table Functions Part 1

Posted by Reza Rad on Feb 10, 2014

CustomerId	Date	TableA.Total	TableB.Total
1	1/1/2014	5	5
1	1/2/2014	0	15
1	1/3/2014	5	15
1	1/4/2014	80	15
2	1/1/2014	0	80

In a previous post, you've learned about the Formula language of the Power Query known as "M". You've learned that M is a functional language that applies data transformations through the script. In examples of the previous post, you've learned some of the table functions such as Table.AddColumn, Table.Sort, Table.Join, and Table.PrefixColumns. In this post, we will discover more table functions through an example.

In this post you will learn these functions:

Table.AddColumn

Table.RemoveColumns

Table.ReorderColumns

Table.SelectColumns

Table.Sort

Table.ReplaceValue

Table.FillDown

Table.AddIndexColumn

Table.RenameColumns

This function renames one or more columns of a table to desired name(s).

Let's apply this function on a sample table. Here is the sample table generated from the previous example:

TableA.CustomerId	TableA.Date	TableA.Total	CustomerId	Date	Total
1	1/1/2014	5	1	1/1/2014	5
null	null	null	1	1/2/2014	15
null	null	null	2	1/1/2014	80
1	1/3/2014	5	null	null	null
1	1/4/2014	80	null	null	null

this is the script that generates above table:

```
let
    TableA = #table({"CustomerId", "TranDate","TranCount"},
    {  {1,DateTime.FromText("2014-01-01  01:00:00.000"),10},
    {1,DateTime.FromText("2014-01-01    02:00:00.000"),5},
    {1,DateTime.FromText("2014-01-03    01:00:00.000"),5},
    {1,DateTime.FromText("2014-01-04 02:00:00.000"),80}  }),
    TableB = #table({"CustomerId",  "TranDate","TranCount"},
    {  {1,DateTime.FromText("2014-01-01  02:00:00.000"),10},
    {1,DateTime.FromText("2014-01-01    03:00:00.000"),5},
    {1,DateTime.FromText("2014-01-02    01:00:00.000"),20},
    {1,DateTime.FromText("2014-01-02    03:00:00.000"),15},
    {2,DateTime.FromText("2014-01-01    01:00:00.000"),5},
    {2,DateTime.FromText("2014-01-01  02:00:00.000"),80}  }),
    TableATransformed=Table.Sort(
        Table.AddColumn(TableA,"Date",each Date.From([TranDate]))
        ,{"CustomerId","TranDate"}
```

```
        ),
    TableBTransformed=Table.Sort(
        Table.AddColumn(TableB,"Date",each Date.From([TranDate]))
        ,{"CustomerId","TranDate"}
            ),
    TableAGrouped=Table.Group(TableATransformed,{"CustomerId","Date"},{"T
otal",each List.Last([TranCount])}),
    TableBGrouped=Table.Group(TableBTransformed,{"CustomerId","Date"},{"T
otal",each List.Last([TranCount])}),
ResultTable=Table.Join(Table.PrefixColumns(TableAGrouped,"TableA"),{"Table
A.CustomerId","TableA.Date"},TableBGrouped,{"CustomerId","Date"},JoinKind.Ful
lOuter)
in
    ResultTable
```

Now we want to rename last three column of the table with a new prefix "TableB.". Here is how we can do that with Table.RenameColumns

```
let
.....
,RenamedTable=Table.RenameColumns(ResultTable,{
{"CustomerId","TableB.CustomerId"},{"Date","TableB.Date"},{"Total","TableB.Total
"}})
in
    RenamedTable
```

The result would be the below table

	TableA.CustomerId	TableA.Date	TableA.Total	TableB.CustomerId	TableB.Date	TableB.Total
1	1	1/1/2014	5	1	1/1/2014	5
2	null	null	null	1	1/2/2014	15
3	null	null	null	2	1/1/2014	80
4	1	1/3/2014	5	null	null	null
5	1	1/4/2014	80	null	null	null

Here is the structure of Table.RenameColumns

Table.RenameColumns(<table>,({<column name before change>,<column name after change>},{repeat for more columns} })

Table.AddColumn

This function adds a column to the table. You would assign the name of the new column and the script to generate a new column. The new column generator can be a static value or an expression.

In this example, we want to add three columns that be generated based on expressions from existing columns of RenamedTable. We want a new CustomerId Column to be generated from TableA.CustomerId, but if it is null, then it should get its value from TableB.CustomerId.

Here is the script to generate the new CustomerId Column:

,CustomerColumnAddedTable=Table.AddColumn(RenamedTable,"CustomerId",each if [TableA.CustomerId] is null then [TableB.CustomerId] else [TableA.CustomerId])

in

    CustomerColumnAddedTable

Result table showed below:

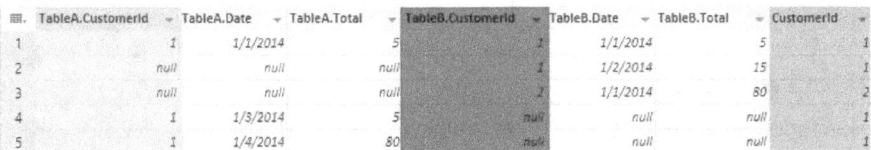

As you see in the above expression we used IF structure which is the very handy conditional structure in M. the <IF> structure is simply as below:

If <condition>
then <if true>

else <if false>

The good thing about If is that it can be used within expressions to build the table/record/lists, etc (as you seen in this example).

The **EACH** keyword is required to generate expression for each record of the dataset.

here is structure of Table.AddColumn function:

Table.AddColumn(<table>,<new column name>,<new column generator>,<data type optional>)

we use AddColumn function to add another column as below:

,CustomerColumnAddedTable=Table.AddColumn(RenamedTable,"CustomerId",each if [TableA.CustomerId] is null then [TableB.CustomerId] else [TableA.CustomerId])

   ,DateColumnAddedTable=Table.AddColumn(CustomerColumnAddedTable, "Date",each if [TableA.Date] is null then [TableB.Date] else [TableA.Date])
in
   DateColumnAddedTable

The result showed below:

Ⅲ.	TableA.CustomerId	TableA.Date	TableA.Total	TableB.CustomerId	TableB.Date	TableB.Total	CustomerId	Date
1	1	1/1/2014	5	1	1/1/2014	5	1	1/1/2014
2	null	null	null	1	1/2/2014	15	1	1/2/2014
3	null	null	null	2	1/1/2014	80	2	1/1/2014
4	1	1/3/2014	5	null	null	null	1	1/3/2014
5	1	1/4/2014	80	null	null	null	1	1/4/2014

Table.RemoveColumns

This function removes one or more columns from the table.

We can use this function to remove extra columns such as TableA.CustomerId, TableB.CustomerId, TableA.Date, and TableB.Date from the table.

Here is the script:

,ColumnsRemoved=Table.RemoveColumns(DateColumnAddedTable,{"TableA.CustomerId","TableB.CustomerId","TableA.Date","TableB.Date"}) in

    ColumnsRemoved

Result would be as below:

TableA.Total	TableB.Total	CustomerId	Date
5	5	1	1/1/2014
null	15	1	1/2/2014
null	80	2	1/1/2014
5	null	1	1/3/2014
80	null	1	1/4/2014

structure of Table.RemoveColumns is as below:

Table.RemoveColumn(<table>,{columns to remove separated by comma})

Table.ReorderColumns

changes order of columns in table.

here is the expression that we used to reorder columns of this table:

    ,ColumnsOrdered=Table.ReorderColumns(ColumnsRemoved,{"CustomerId","Date","TableA.Total","TableB.Total"})

in

    ColumnsOrdered

Result would be as below:

CustomerId	Date	TableA.Total	TableB.Total
1	1/1/2014	5	5
1	1/2/2014	null	15
2	1/1/2014	null	80
1	1/3/2014	5	null
1	1/4/2014	80	null

here is the structure of Table.ReorderColumns

Table.ReorderColumns(<table>,{order of columns as desired in output})

Table.SelectColumns

This function selects specific columns from a table with the order defined. This function is a combination of Table.RemoveColumns and Table.ReorderColumns.

this script will result same table as above but with only a single function Table.SelectColumns instead of using Table.RemoveColumns and Table.ReorderColumns.

,ColumnsSelected=Table.SelectColumns(DateColumnAddedTable,{"CustomerId", "Date","TableA.Total","TableB.Total"})

in

    ColumnsSelected

Result would be the same

CustomerId	Date	TableA.Total	TableB.Total
1	1/1/2014	5	5
1	1/2/2014	null	15
2	1/1/2014	null	80
1	1/3/2014	5	null
1	1/4/2014	80	null

Table.Sort

Sorts a table on the desired ordering list

,SortedTable=Table.Sort(ColumnsSelected,{"CustomerId","Date"})

in

    SortedTable

Result would be as below:

CustomerId	Date	TableA.Total	TableB.Total
1	1/1/2014	5	5
1	1/2/2014	null	15
1	1/3/2014	5	null
1	1/4/2014	80	null
2	1/1/2014	null	80

Here is the Table.Sort function structure

Table.Sort(<table>,{sorting criteria})

Table.ReplaceValue

This function replace all old values with new value from the specific column in the table.

the expression below would replace all NULL values in TableA.Total with 0.

,ValueReplaced=Table.ReplaceValue(SortedTable,null,0,Replacer.ReplaceValue,{"TableA.Total"})

in

    ValueReplaced

Result showed below:

	CustomerId	Date	TableA.Total	TableB.Total
1	1	1/1/2014	5	5
2	1	1/2/2014	0	15
3	1	1/3/2014	5	null
4	1	1/4/2014	80	null
5	2	1/1/2014	0	80

Here is the structure of Table.ReplaceValue function

Table.ReplaceValue(<table>,<old value>,<new value>,<replacer function>,{column name})

replacer function can be Replacer.ReplaceValue or Replacer.ReplaceText

Table.FillDown

This function will fill the value from upper record down to the null values of the records after that.

Here is the example: (we want to fill down the values of columns TableB.Total, that means if a record has a null value for this column, then the value would be fetched from the most recent top record that has a not null value)

    ,FilledDown=Table.FillDown(ValueReplaced,"TableB.Total")

in

    FilledDown

result would be as below:

	CustomerId	Date	TableA.Total	TableB.Total
1	1	1/1/2014	5	5
2	1	1/2/2014	0	15
3	1	1/3/2014	5	15
4	1	1/4/2014	80	15
5	2	1/1/2014	0	80

Here is the structure of Table.FillDown function

Table.FillDown(<table>,<Column>)

Table.AddIndexColumn

This function adds an identity auto-increment column to the table. You can specify the column name, initial value, and the increment seed.

This is a sample expression:

   ,IndexAdded=Table.AddIndexColumn(FilledDown,"Index",10000,10)

in

   IndexAdded

Result is as below:

	CustomerId	Date	TableA.Total	TableB.Total	Index
1	1	1/1/2014	5	5	10000
2	1	1/2/2014	0	15	10010
3	1	1/3/2014	5	15	10020
4	1	1/4/2014	80	15	10030
5	2	1/1/2014	0	80	10040

Here is the structure for this function:

Table.AddIndexColumn(<table>,<column name>,<initial value>,<increment seed>)

Here is the full script for this example:

let

   TableA = #table({"CustomerId", "TranDate","TranCount"},

   {

   {1,DateTime.FromText("2014-01-01 01:00:00.000"),10},

   {1,DateTime.FromText("2014-01-01 02:00:00.000"),5},

```
    {1,DateTime.FromText("2014-01-03 01:00:00.000"),5},
    {1,DateTime.FromText("2014-01-04  02:00:00.000"),80}  }),
    TableB = #table({"CustomerId", "TranDate","TranCount"},
    {  {1,DateTime.FromText("2014-01-01  02:00:00.000"),10},
    {1,DateTime.FromText("2014-01-01       03:00:00.000"),5},
    {1,DateTime.FromText("2014-01-02       01:00:00.000"),20},
    {1,DateTime.FromText("2014-01-02       03:00:00.000"),15},
    {2,DateTime.FromText("2014-01-01       01:00:00.000"),5},
    {2,DateTime.FromText("2014-01-01  02:00:00.000"),80}  }),
    TableATransformed=Table.Sort(



           Table.AddColumn(TableA,"Date",each Date.From([TranDate]))
             ,{"CustomerId","TranDate"}
                       ),
    TableBTransformed=Table.Sort(
           Table.AddColumn(TableB,"Date",each Date.From([TranDate]))
             ,{"CustomerId","TranDate"}
                       ),
      TableAGrouped=Table.Group(TableATransformed,{"CustomerId","Date"},{"T
otal",each List.Last([TranCount])}),
         TableBGrouped=Table.Group(TableBTransformed,{"CustomerId","Date"},{"T
otal",each List.Last([TranCount])}),
ResultTable=Table.Join(Table.PrefixColumns(TableAGrouped,"TableA"),{"Table
A.CustomerId","TableA.Date"},TableBGrouped,{"CustomerId","Date"},JoinKind.Ful
lOuter)
    ,RenamedTable=Table.RenameColumns(ResultTable,{
```

{"CustomerId","TableB.CustomerId"},{"Date","TableB.Date"},{"Total","TableB.Total"} })

    ,CustomerColumnAddedTable=Table.AddColumn(RenamedTable,"CustomerId",each if [TableA.CustomerId] is null then [TableB.CustomerId] else [TableA.CustomerId])

    ,DateColumnAddedTable=Table.AddColumn(CustomerColumnAddedTable,"Date",each if [TableA.Date] is null then [TableB.Date] else [TableA.Date])

    ,ColumnsRemoved=Table.RemoveColumns(DateColumnAddedTable,{"TableA.CustomerId","TableB.CustomerId","TableA.Date","TableB.Date"})

    ,ColumnsOrdered=Table.ReorderColumns(ColumnsRemoved,{"CustomerId","Date","TableA.Total","TableB.Total"})

    ,ColumnsSelected=Table.SelectColumns(DateColumnAddedTable,{"CustomerId","Date","TableA.Total","TableB.Total"})

    ,SortedTable=Table.Sort(ColumnsSelected,{"CustomerId","Date"})

    ,ValueReplaced=Table.ReplaceValue(SortedTable,null,0,Replacer.ReplaceValue,{"TableA.Total"})

    ,FilledDown=Table.FillDown(ValueReplaced,"TableB.Total")

    ,IndexAdded=Table.AddIndexColumn(FilledDown,"Index",10000,10)
in
    IndexAdded

There are many other table functions in Power Query which we will go through them with more samples in next blog posts.

List.Accumulate Hidden Gem of Power Query List Functions in Power BI

Posted by Reza Rad on Dec 12, 2017

There are some List transformations available in Power Query's graphical interface. However, the number of functions in the graphical interface is very limited. In this post, I'm going to explain about a function that is powerful and is not yet listed in the graphical interface. List.Accumulate is a function that loops through items of a list and applies a transformation. This function at the time of writing this post is only available through Power Query M scripting. If you like to learn more about Power BI, read Power BI book from Rookie to Rock Star.

List Transformations in Graphical Interface of Power Query

If you have a list, you can see what transformations are available to be applied to it using the graphical interface. You can create a list with a simple M script as below;

1 = {1..12}

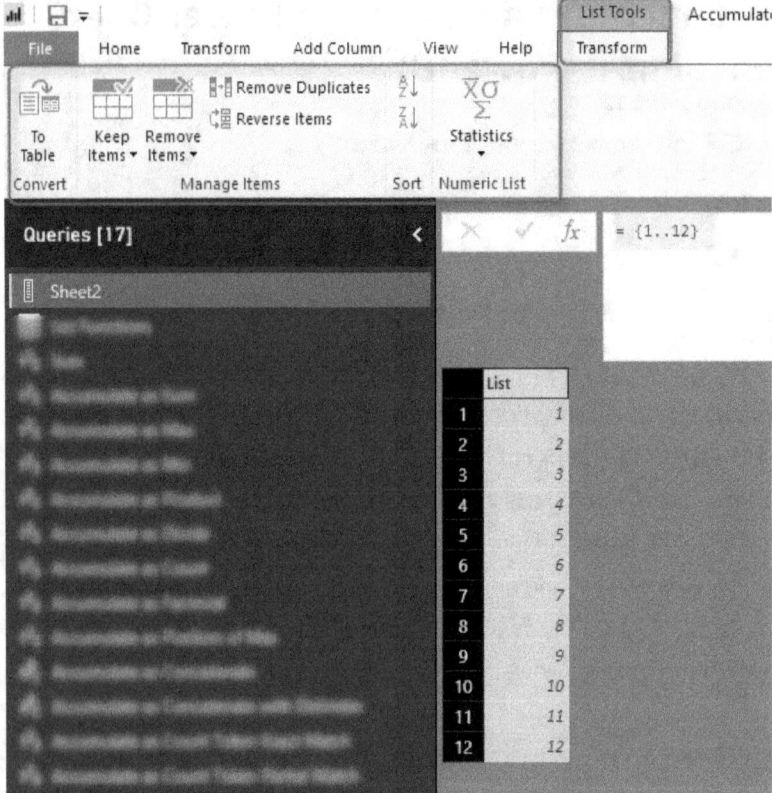

This code generates a list of numbers from 1 to 12. Now you can see in the top menu under List Tools, that there are some transformations available for List. These items are very few options such as; convert to a table, keep items, remove items, etc. Altogether considering all options in every element this list is not more than 20 functions. However, let's look at the number of List functions in M script.

List Functions in M; Power Query Formula Language

I have written previously about the usage of the #shared key to finding all functions available in M. you can then filter it to only "List." Functions and then

346 | Page

you will end up with a bit list of functions; 69 functions! More than three times of what you see in the graphical interface.

#	Name	Value
1	List.Accumulate	Function
2	List.AllTrue	Function
3	List.Alternate	Function
4	List.AnyTrue	Function
5	List.Average	Function
6	List.Buffer	Function
7	List.Combine	Function
8	List.Contains	Function
9	List.ContainsAll	Function
10	List.ContainsAny	Function
11	List.Count	Function
12	List.Covariance	Function
13	List.DateTimeZones	Function
14	List.DateTimes	Function
15	List.Dates	Function
16	List.Difference	Function
17	List.Distinct	Function
18	List.Durations	Function
19	List.FindText	Function
20	List.First	Function
21	List.FirstN	Function
22	List.Generate	Function
23	List.InsertRange	Function
24	List.Intersect	Function
25	List.IsDistinct	Function
26	List.IsEmpty	Function
27	List.Last	Function
28	List.LastN	Function
29	List.MatchesAll	Function

Some of these functions Some of the functions in this list are very useful and powerful. Example of those functions is List.Dates, List.Numbers, List.Generate, List.Accumulate and many others. We cannot go through all functions in one blog post. In this post, I'll be covering List.Accumulate and in future posts; I'll talk about other functions.

List.Accumulate Function

List.Accumulate is a function that can easily save some steps in your Power Query transformations, instead of applying multiple steps, you can simply use List.Accumulate to overcome what you want. List.Accumulate function loops through the list and accumulate value as a result. This function usually needs three parameters; the list itself, seed, and accumulator. Here are parameters explained in details;

- List; the list that we want to apply the transformation to it.
- Seed; is the initial value.
- Accumulator; is a function. This function determines what accumulation calculation happens on items of the list. The way that this function is defined is exactly the way that you write a function in Power Query M script using Lambda expressions.

Best way to learn about seed and accumulator is through some examples, let's apply some transformations with List.Accumulate and see how these two parameters are working.

Accumulate to Calculate Sum

The sum is a function that is accumulating every two values in the list till the end of the list. If you want to write Sum with List.Accumulate, you can do it with this expression:

1 = List.Accumulate(Source,0,(state,current)=>state+current)

The function part of this expression is: *(state, current)=>state+current*
state is the value accumulated in the calculation. current is the current item in the list. seed is the initial value of the state

Let's see how the calculation works. To clarify it more in details, I explained the value of the state, current, and accumulator in every step;

List	state	current	(state,current)=>state+current
1	0	1	1
2	1	2	3
3	3	3	6
4	6	4	10
5	10	5	15
6	15	6	21
7	21	7	28
8	28	8	36
9	36	9	45
10	45	10	55
11	55	11	66
12	66	12	78
13	78	13	91
14	91	14	105
15	105	15	120
16	120	16	136
17	136	17	153
18	153	18	171
19	171	19	190
20	190	20	210

List.Accumulate loops through every item in the list and run accumulator function. The very first time, the state value is equal to seed. Which in this case is zero. Current is the current value in the list. For the very first item that value is 1. so accumulator result is state+current=0+1=1. this value then will be the state of the next item on the list. For the next item, the state is 1 (calculated from the previous row), and current is 2. state+current becomes 1+2=3. This process continues through the whole list, so the final state value for a list from 1 to 20, becomes 210, which is equal to the sum of those values. In every row of the list, we added that to the previous row's result.

Accumulate to Calculate Max

Learning how the accumulate function can cover basic tasks, help you to understand how accumulator function works. For applying Max, you need to compare every two items in the list and pick the one which is bigger. Here is the script;

$_1$ = List.Accumulate(Source,0,(state,current)=>if state>current then state else current)

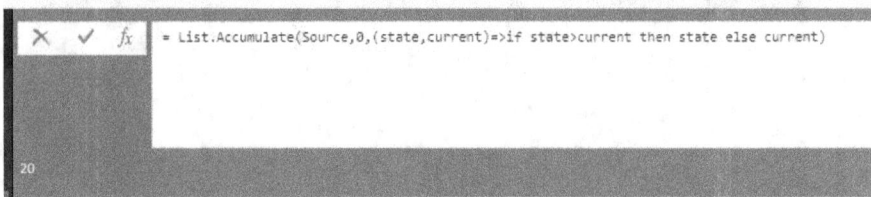

remember the same thing about the state, current, and seed; this is how the calculation works;

List	state	current	(state,current)=>if state>current then state else current	
1	0	1		1
2	1	2		2
3	2	3		3
4	3	4		4
5	4	5		5
6	5	6		6
7	6	7		7
8	7	8		8
9	8	9		9
10	9	10		10
11	10	11		11
12	11	12		12
13	12	13		13
14	13	14		14
15	14	15		15
16	15	16		16
17	16	17		17
18	17	18		18
19	18	19		19
20	19	20		20

the function **(state, current)=>if state>current then state else current** will run on every row and give you the result. Remember that seed value should be a value less than any other values for this case.

Accumulate as Product or Divide

you can use the same logic with a different accumulator to calculate Product or Divide, Here is the calculation for Product;

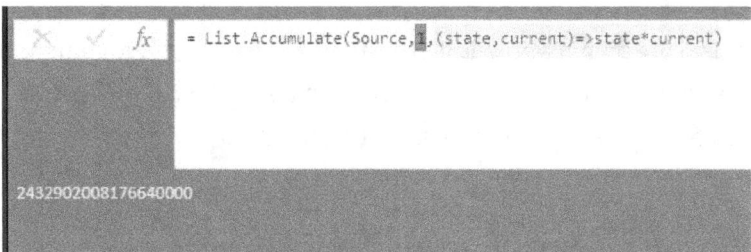

for Product or Divide, you need to set the seed as 1, because if it is zero, then divide or multiply considering zero will end up zero always. Here is the calculation for Divide;

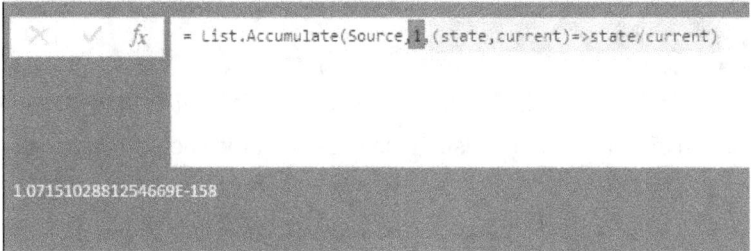

Accumulate as Count

Count of a list is the number of items in a list. This can be achieved with no need of the current item, just using seed and state as below;

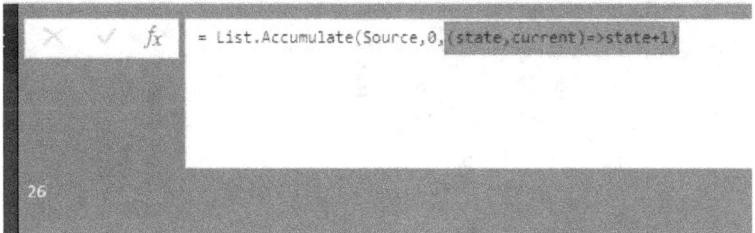

in every row, the value would be plus one of the state value from previous row's calculation. As a result, you get the count.

Accumulate as Concatenate (with a delimiter or without)

So far, we applied to accumulate on lists which had a number in every item. Now, let's apply it to a list of text items. To concatenate two items you need to add them one after each other with concatenation character which is the ampersand (&).

```
= List.Accumulate(Source,"",(state,current)=>state&current)
```

abcdefghijklmnopqrstuvwxyz

This worked on a list of items which are text values {"a".."z"}, and the result is the concatenation of all items in the list. Please note that the seed, in this case, is an empty text.

If you want to add a delimiter between items, you can add the delimiter plus a condition to check if this is the very first item or not.

```
= List.Accumulate(Source,"",
    (state,current)=>
        if state=""
        then state&current
        else state&","&current
)
```

a,b,c,d,e,f,g,h,i,j,k,l,m,n,o,p,q,r,s,t,u,v,w,x,y,z

Accumulate as Count Token Exact Match

Now that you've learned the logic of the accumulator, you can apply it to do any expressions. For example, if you want to calculate the count of items in the list which their value matches exactly with a value, you can write this expression;

```
= List.Accumulate(Source,0,
(state,current)=>
            if current="a"
            then state+1
            else state
)
```

```
1 = List.Accumulate(Source,0,
2 (state,current)=>
3        if current="a"
4
5        then state+1
6
)        else state
```

the logic is simple, if the item matches with "a" (which in this case is our token), then count it, otherwise don't

Accumulate as Count Token Partial Match

Similar to the previous calculation. However this time we want to count the item, even it partially matches the text. This can be done with the help of Text.Contains function. and because of Text.Contains might not find the lower case or upper case matches, we convert it to lower case beforehand.

```
= List.Accumulate(Month,0,
(state,current)=>
            if Text.Contains(Text.Lower(current),"a")
            then state+1
            else state
)
```

```
1 = List.Accumulate(Month,0,
2 (state,current)=>
3 
4         if Text.Contains(Text.Lower(current),"a")
5         then state+1
6         else state
)
```

Accumulate as Conditions on Records

So far, we went through a lot of use cases and examples of List.Accumulate function. You understand that this function can be so powerful and useful in many scenarios. However, the main use cases of List.Accumulate is to apply to scenarios which other functions cannot resolve easily. List.The sum might be better used than List.Accumulate which only calculates the sum. However, there are many scenarios that many steps are needed to get the result you want with normal functions. In those cases, List.Accumulate is your friend. For example; consider the situation that you have a list, and this list is a list of records! Every record might have a different set of fields; you want to fetch only records that have a specific field on their list, and get their position as a concatenated result. This process, using other list functions might take some steps, however, with List.Accumulate that is easy. Here is the sample input list;

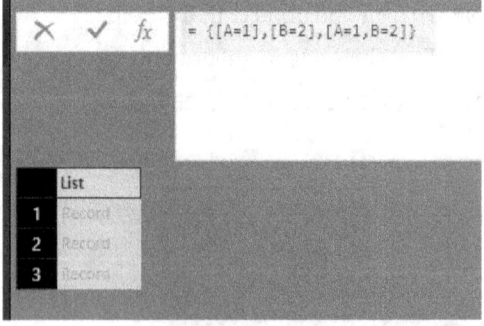

As you can see the list includes records, and to find out what each record has, you need to expand it. A list of records cannot be expanded because it will add the number of columns and list can have only one column. So you have to convert it to a table, and then expand it. As you feel now; there are some steps required to get the result we wanted. However, List.Accumulate can be a big help in this scenario. Here is the calculation with List.Accumulate;

```
= List.Accumulate(Source,"",
(state,current)=>
if Record.HasFields(current,"A")
then state&","&Text.From(List.PositionOf(Source,current))
else state
)
```

,0,2

```
1 = List.Accumulate(Source,"",
2 (state,current)=>
3 if Record.HasFields(current,"A")
4 then state&","&Text.From(List.PositionOf(Source,current))
5 else state
6 )
```

Record.HasFields used to determine if a record contains a field ("A" in this example).

List.PositionOf used to get the position of that record which satisfy the criteria above.

Summary

This post explained how List.Accumulate works. List.Accumulate is a very powerful function, that can easily save many steps in your Power Query transformations. In this post, you've learned basics of this function with using it for simple operations such as Sum, Divide, Product, Max, Count, etc. You also learned that the main power of this function is when basic functions cannot operate easily. You learned that the accumulator function gives you full power to write exactly what you want. In future posts, I'll write about other List functions that can be very powerful, but you still don't have it in the graphical interface.

Have you liked the List.Accumulate function as I do? If yes, please share your story that how this function can be helpful for you in the comments below.

Power BI from Rookie to Rock Star – Book 3: Power Query and Data Transformation in Power BI

Power Query; Convert Time Stamp to Date Time

Posted by Reza Rad on May 31, 2016

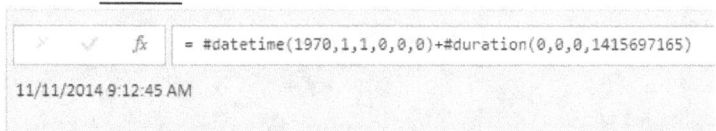

Power Query has a number of Date and Time functions that convert values to date and time. However, I haven't found a function that converts a timestamp value. Fortunately, it is easy to calculate a date-time from a timestamp value. In this post, I'll explain an easy way of converting the timestamp to date time. To Learn more about Power Query read Power BI online book; from Rookie to Rock Star.

What is Timestamp

The timestamp is a whole number value, which is the number of seconds from date 1970-01-01 00:00:00. For example; timestamp 100 means 1970-01-01 00:01:40, or timestamp 86400 means 1970-01-02 00:00:00. So the calculation is easy; We have to add the timestamp as seconds to the date/time 1970-01-01 00:00:00.

Power Query Convert Timestamp to Date Time

Once we know what is definition of timestamp, and how to calculate date/time from it; easily we can use **#duration(0,0,0,<timestamp value>)** to show duration in seconds, and add it to the **#datetime(1970,1,1,0,0,0)** which is date time 1970-01-01 00:00:00.
So as a result, here is the code to convert timestamp to date time;

```
1 DateTimedValue=#datetime(1970,1,1,0,0,0)+#duration(0,0,0,1415697165)
```

the above query will respond 11/11/2014 9:12:45 AM.

Please note that you have to replace the 1415697165 number with the field name containing timestamp values, or with your static timestamp value in the query.

Power BI from Rookie to Rock Star – Book 3: Power Query and Data Transformation in Power BI

Get List of Queries in Power BI

Posted by Reza Rad on Jan 16, 2017

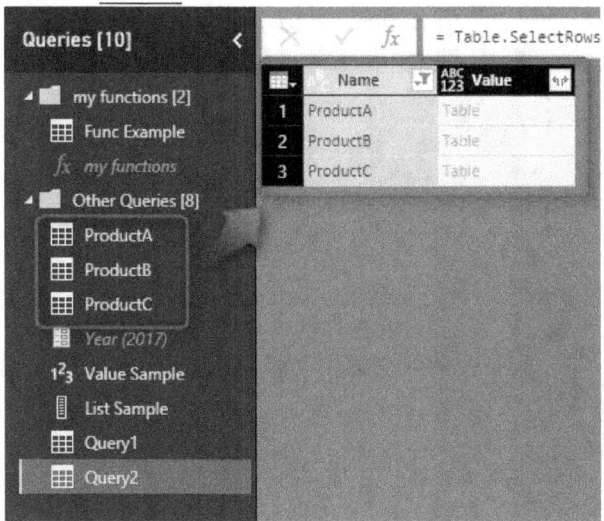

Power Query is the component of getting data in Power BI. But have you used Power Query to get metadata of the Power BI queries itself? In this post, I'll show you a quick and simple way of using Power Query to get metadata (name of queries and the data in queries) from all queries in Power BI. I have previously explained how to use a #shared keyword to get a list of all functions in Power Query; this post shows how to use #shared or #sections to get all queries (and parameters, and functions, and lists...) from Power BI. If you want to learn more about Power BI; read Power BI online book from Rookie to Rock Star.

* Thanks to Alex Arvidsson who brought this question, and was the cause of writing this blog post.

Question: How to Fetch Name of All Queries into One Query?

Consider below Power BI file that has functions, parameters, and queries. Queries also return tables, values, and lists;

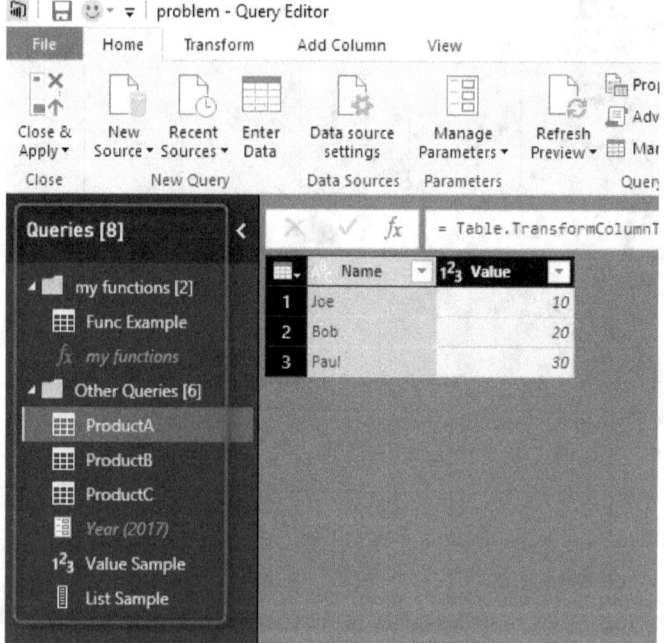

The question is how I can get a list of all these queries and their values as a new query? Let's see the answer

Answer: Using #shared or #sections Keywords
#shared to Get Current File's Queries Plus All Functions

I have previously explained what #shared keyword does; it is a keyword that returns a list of all functions, and enumerators in Power Query. It can be used as a document library in the Power Query itself. It will also fetch all queries in the existing Power BI file. Here is how you can use it:

Create a New Source, from Blank Query.

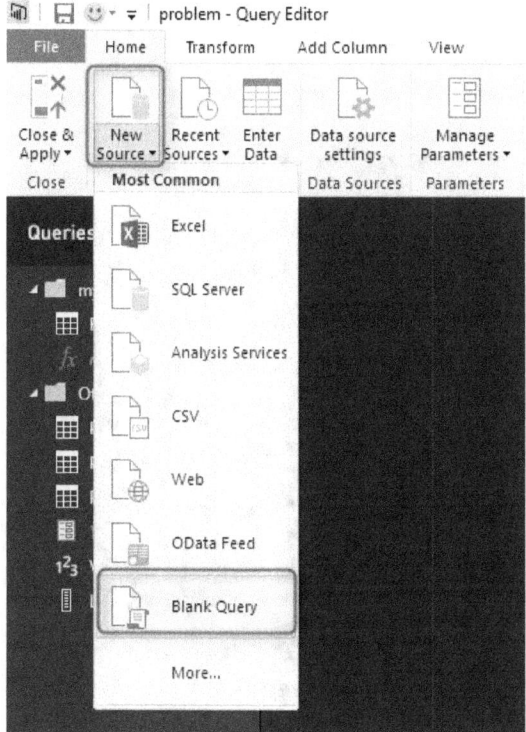

Then go to Advanced Editor of that query (from Home tab or View tab)

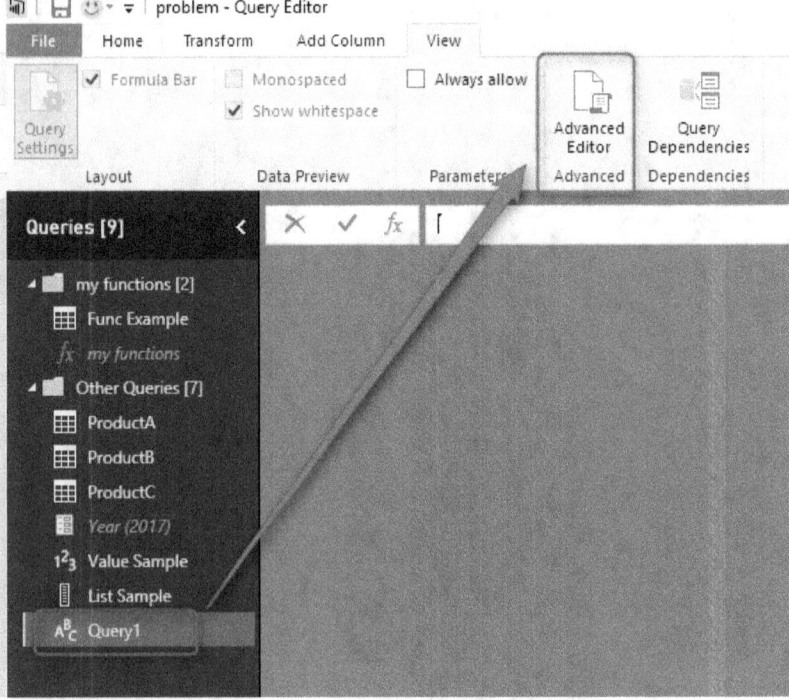

write only one keyword in the Advanced Editor: **#shared**

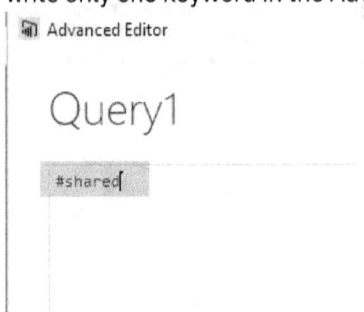

And Click on Done. The result will come up quickly;

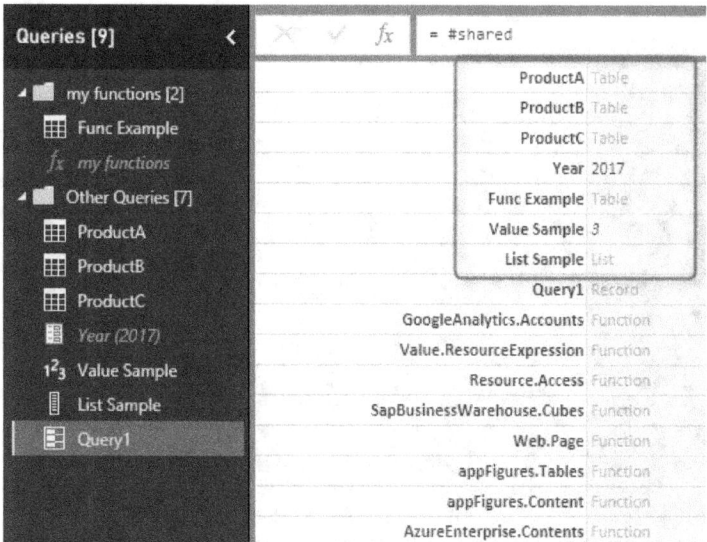

You can see in the result that #shared fetch all existing queries, plus all built-in functions in Power Query. The section which is marked in the above result set in where you can find queries from the current file. Note that the Query1 itself (which includes the #shared keyword) is listed there. The limitation of this method is that it won't return your custom function; "my function" in this example. The next method, however, would pick that as well.

#sections To Get Current File's Queries

The other way of a fetching list of queries is using the #sections keyword. The #sections keyword will give you a list of all sections in Power Query (This post is then't right place to explain what sections are, but for now, consider every query here as a section). so same method this time using #sections will return result below;

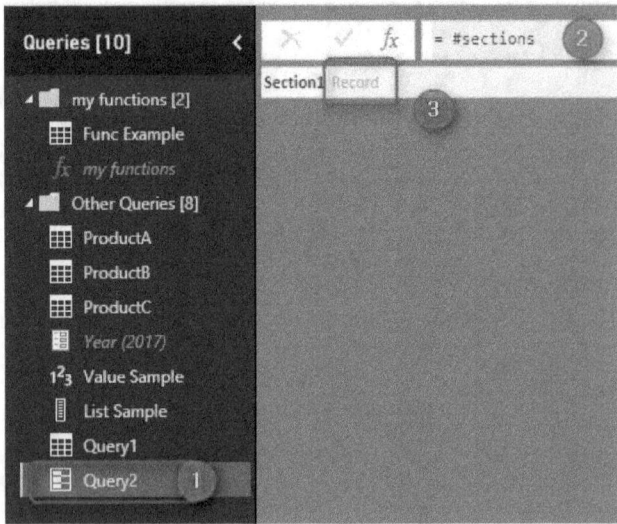

The result is a record that you can simply click on the Record to see what are columns in there. Columns are queries in the current file:

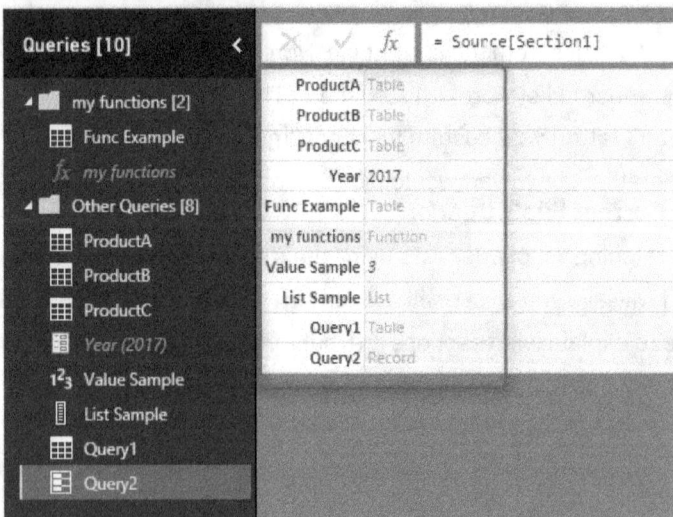

This method also returns functions in the current file, which the previous method with #shared didn't. So this is a better method if you are interested in fetching function's names as well.

The result is a record which can be converted to a table (this gives you better filtering options in the GUI). You can find the Convert Into Table under Record Tools Convert Section menu.

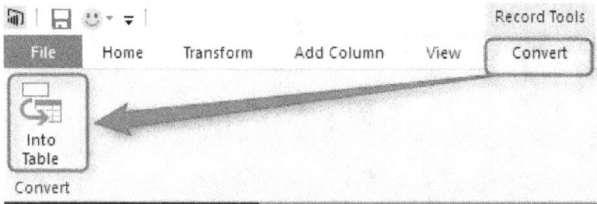

After having this as a table, then you can apply any filters you want;

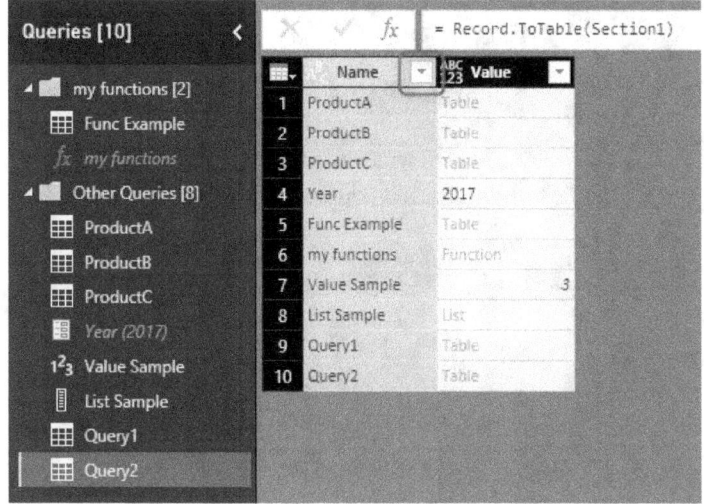

Sample Scenario of Usage

There are many usages of getting the name of queries in another query. One sample usage of that can be getting different queries coming from different places, and the only way to identify the source is query name. In this case, instead of manually adding a column to each query and then combining them, you can use this method to get the query name dynamically. In the screenshot below ProductA, ProductB, and ProductC are coming as source queries, and you can simply do filtering to get them all with their product names.

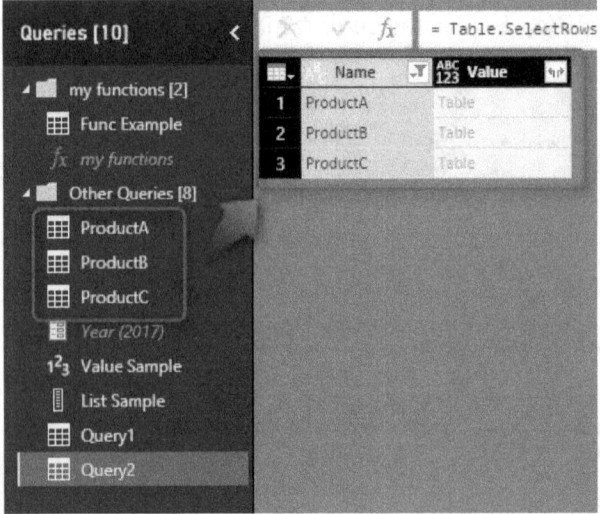

And you can expand it to tables underneath if you want to (this would work if they all have same data structure);

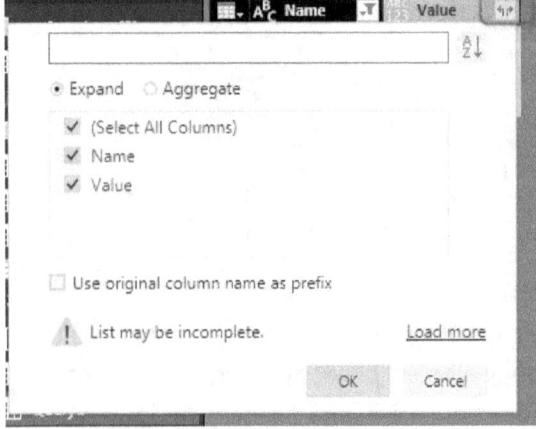

and as a result you have combined result of all queries, with the query name as another column;

Name	Name.1	Value.1
ProductA	Joe	10
ProductA	Bob	20
ProductA	Paul	30
ProductB	Joe	30
ProductB	Bob	60
ProductB	Paul	90
ProductC	Joe	1
ProductC	Bob	2
ProductC	Paul	3

Power Query Library of Functions; Shared Keyword

Posted by Reza Rad on Jun 20, 2016

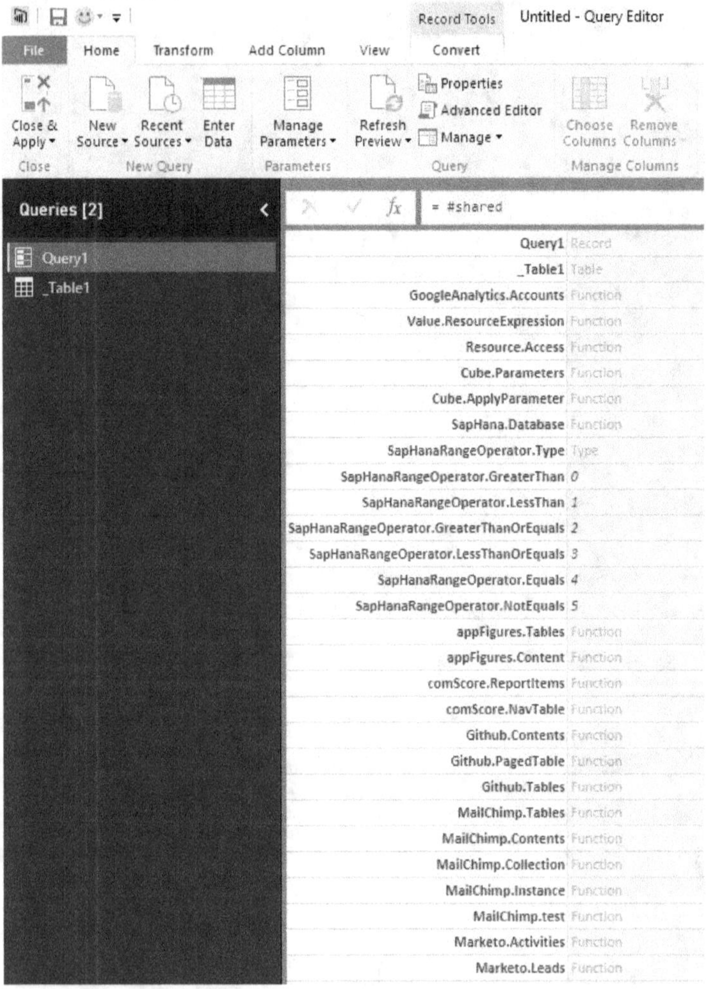

As I mentioned earlier in Power BI online book, Power Query is a functional language. Knowing functions is your best helper when you work with a functional language. Fortunately, Power Query both in Excel and Power BI can use the shared keyword to reveal a document library of all functions. I wrote about shared keyword almost 2.5 years ago when it was only an add-in for excel. However, I still see people in my webinars who are new with #shared keyword functionality and amazed how helpful this little keyword is. So I decided to explain it with the new Power BI. With the method in this post, you can find any function you want easily in Power Query, and you won't need an internet connection to search in functions.

#shared Keyword

Shared is a keyword that loads all functions, and enumerators in the result set. You can simply create a blank query in Power BI (or Excel)

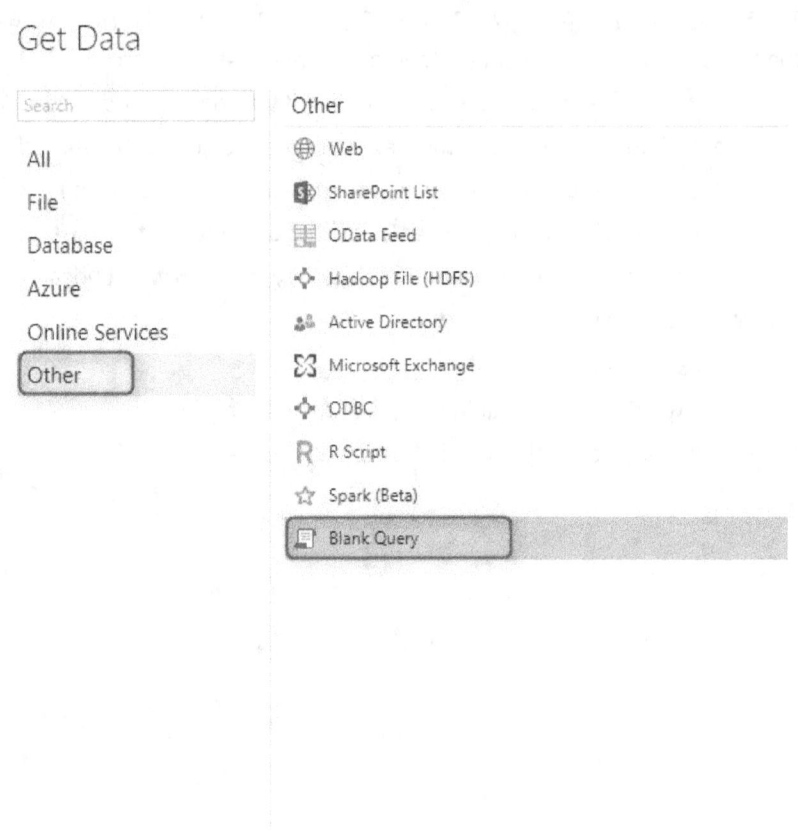

After opening a blank query, go to Advanced Editor

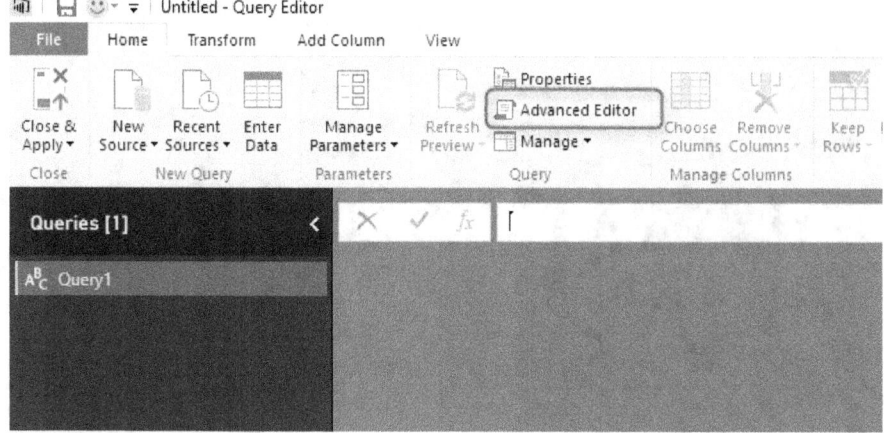

Here in the script editor is where you usually write or modify power query script. Now delete all script here and only type in: #shared

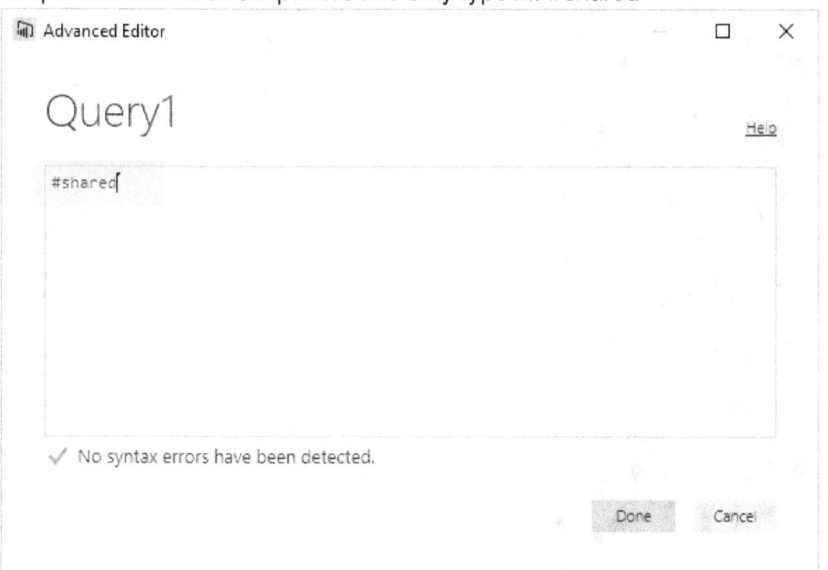

After clicking on Done, you will see a list of all functions and enumerators in power query. You will also see other queries in your Power BI solution or workbook plus other custom functions.

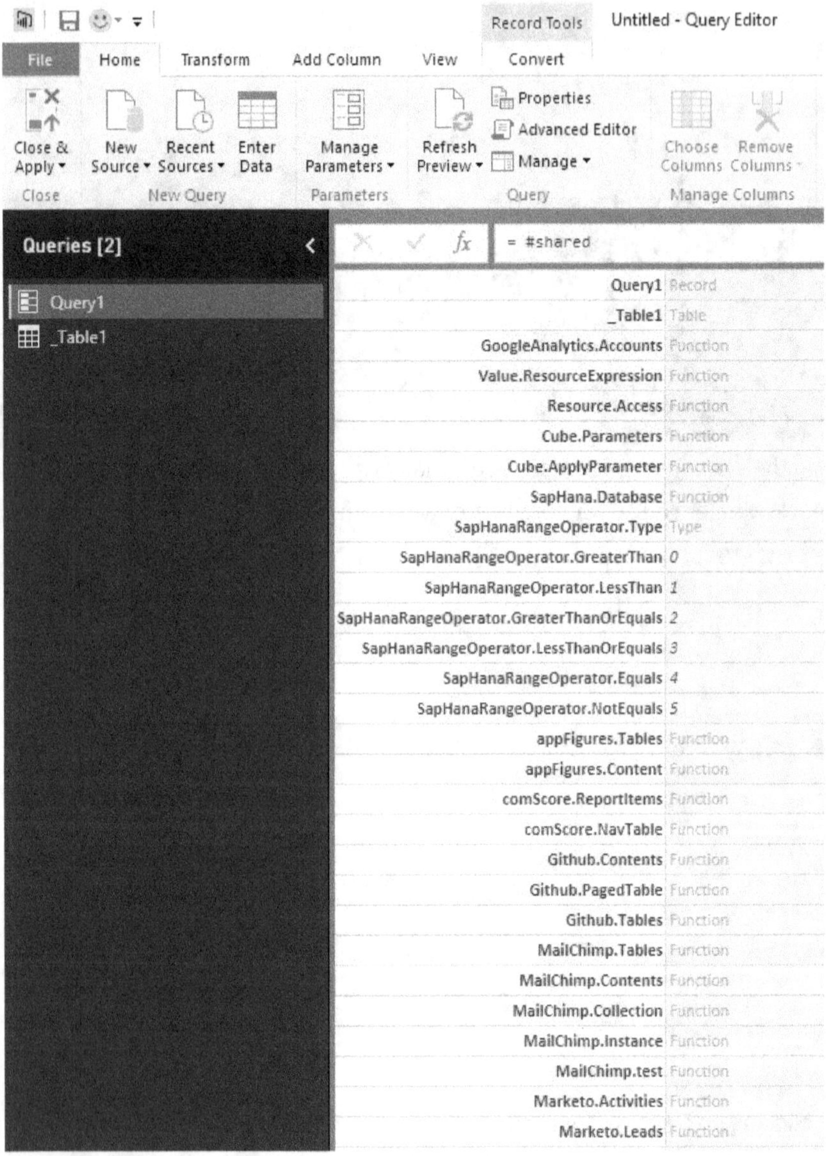
Record Tools
Untitled - Query Editor
File
Home
Transform
Add Column
View
Convert
Close & Apply
New Source
Recent Sources
Enter Data
Manage Parameters
Refresh Preview
Properties
Advanced Editor
Manage
Choose Columns
Remove Columns
Close
New Query
Parameters
Query
Manage Columns
Queries [2]
Query1
_Table1
= #shared
Query1 Record
_Table1 Table
GoogleAnalytics.Accounts Function
Value.ResourceExpression Function
Resource.Access Function
Cube.Parameters Function
Cube.ApplyParameter Function
SapHana.Database Function
SapHanaRangeOperator.Type Type
SapHanaRangeOperator.GreaterThan 0
SapHanaRangeOperator.LessThan 1
SapHanaRangeOperator.GreaterThanOrEquals 2
SapHanaRangeOperator.LessThanOrEquals 3
SapHanaRangeOperator.Equals 4
SapHanaRangeOperator.NotEquals 5
appFigures.Tables Function
appFigures.Content Function
comScore.ReportItems Function
comScore.NavTable Function
Github.Contents Function
Github.PagedTable Function
Github.Tables Function
MailChimp.Tables Function
MailChimp.Contents Function
MailChimp.Collection Function
MailChimp.Instance Function
MailChimp.test Function
Marketo.Activities Function
Marketo.Leads Function

Result set here is a Record structure that has functions, enumerators, and queries in each item of the record. Now let's explore the record more in details.

Use the Result set as a Table

The result above is loaded in Power Query, and that is the greatest feature of Power Query itself that can turn this result into a table.

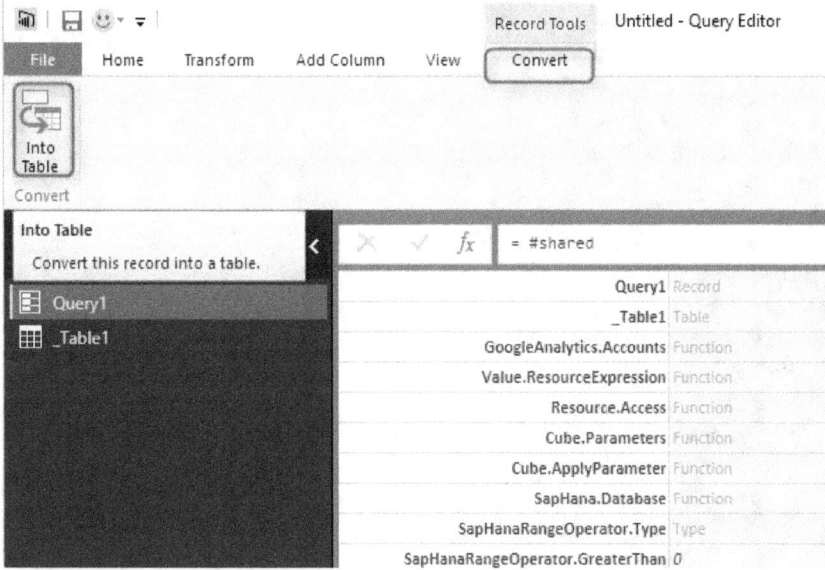

This will convert the result set record to a table. And the table is really easy to search in as you know.

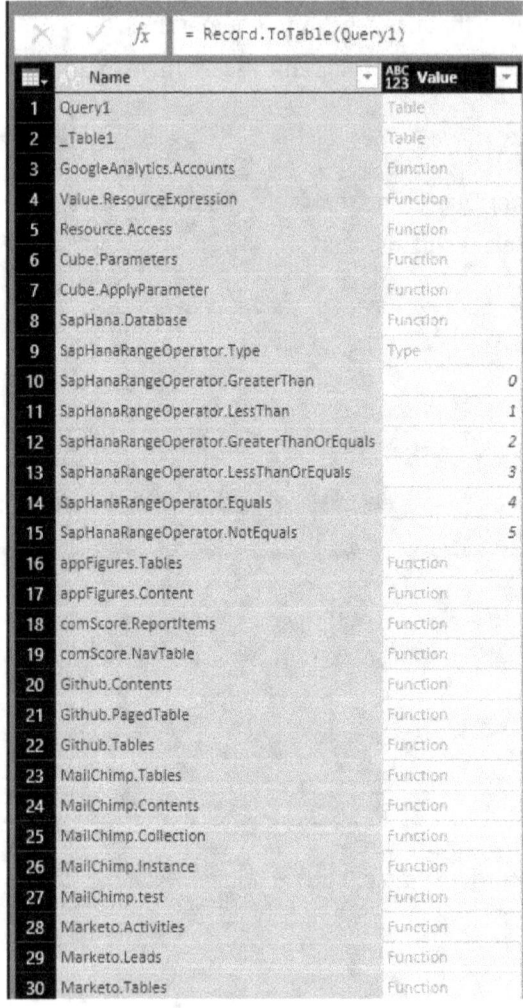

I can now simply search in the function list. Let's see for example what function I can find for working with WEEK;

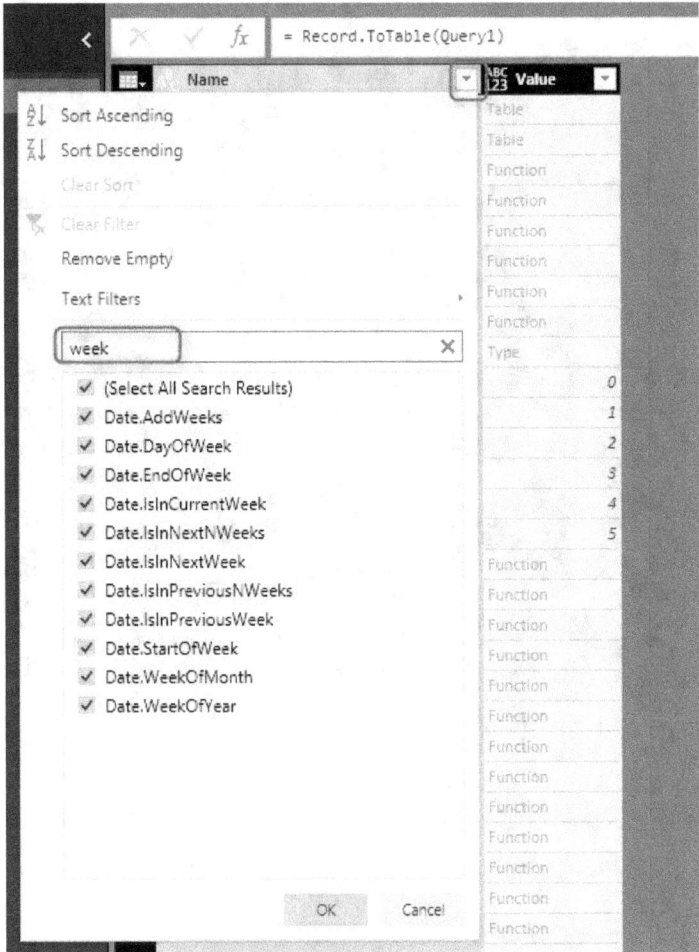

This will filter the table to a subset that I can see only functions with WEEK in the name of it.

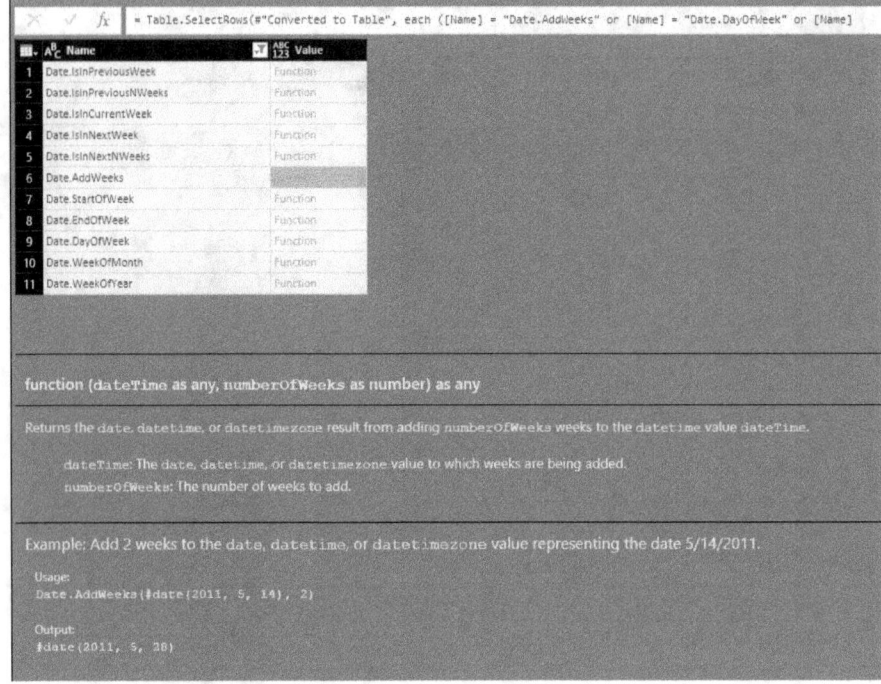

Documentation of Function

Now for example if I want to see the Date.AddWeeks function I can click on the "function" link of it in the value column and this will redirect me to the documentation of this function, and will bring a dialog box to invoke the function!

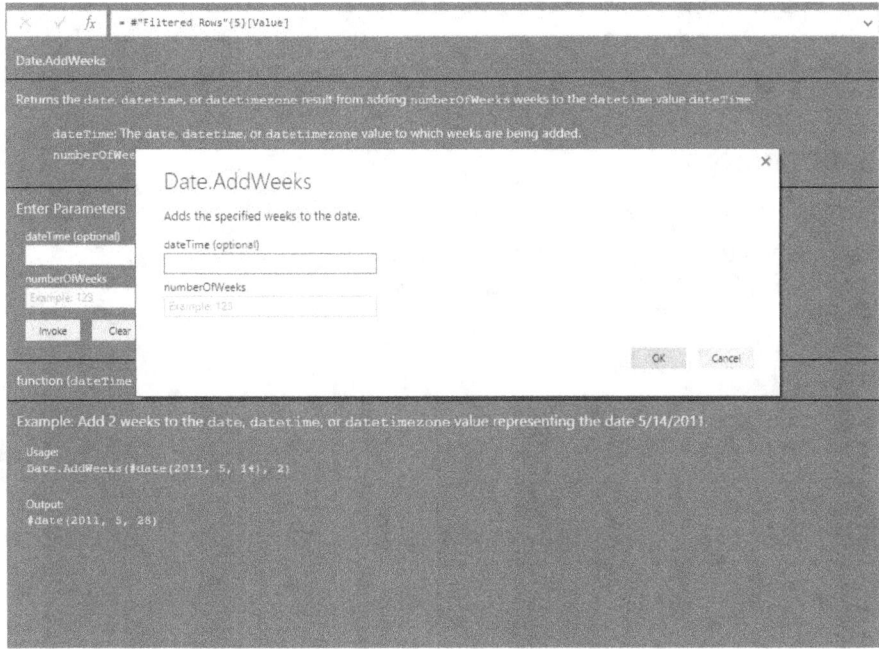

You can see the documentation in grey that also includes examples of how to call this function. For invoking the function, I can simply provide parameters, and click OK or Invoke;

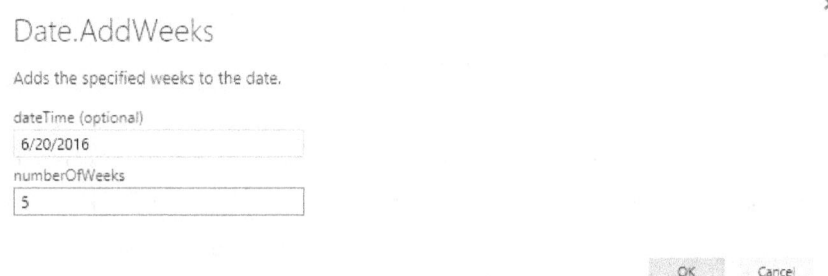

And it calls the function and shows me the result as below;

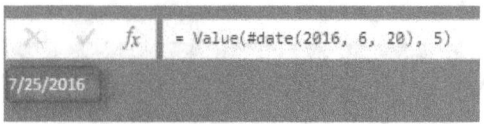

7/25/2016

Enumerators

Finding enumerators is also easy with the help of #shared keyword. Here I can see enumerators for JoinKind and JoinAlgorithm;

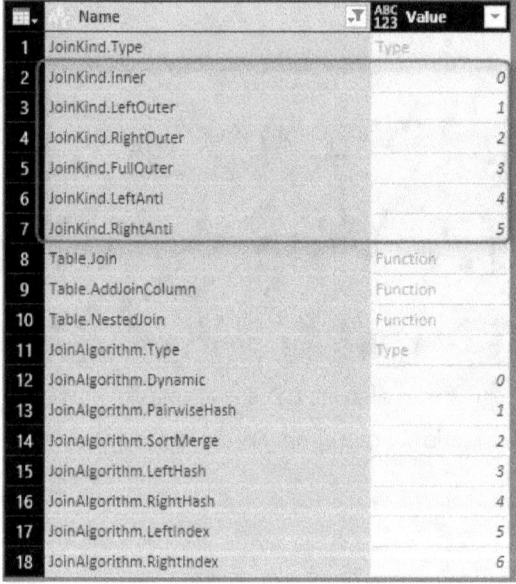

Summary

You've learned how #shared keyword can be helpful for getting the list of all functions and enumerators in Power Query. You learned you could convert the result set into a table and filter that to find the particular function you are looking for. This is superb, especially for people like myself who can't remember things well. You know how I look for functions? This post explained my method! I use the #shared keyword to find the function I want and start working on that. For me, the #shared is the keyword that I use more than any other queries in Power query side of Power BI.

Power BI from Rookie to Rock Star – Book 3: Power Query and Data Transformation in Power BI

Writing Custom Functions in Power Query M

Posted by Reza Rad on Feb 12, 2014

One of the most powerful features of M is that you can write custom functions to re-use part of your code. Custom functions can be single or multiple liners, they will be written in Lambda style syntax. In this post, you will learn how to write functions and invoke them in M.

Custom functions and some of the other features of M such as error handling, completely distinguish this language from expressions in SSIS. I'm saying this because I've heard questions like: Is the M similar to SSIS expressions? The answer is: NO! I am a big fan of SSIS (those of you who know me would agree that), But SSIS expressions are just for calculation and creating transformations based on expressions. SSIS expressions is not a language, it is an expression. M in the other hand is a language, and it is a functional language, that means you don't need to write Main function, etc, M would handle most of them. and you have features such as writing custom functions and error handling (You cannot find most of these advanced features through Power Query GUI, So start scripting M   )

Basic Syntax

Functions in M can be written in this format:

(x) => x+1

This is lambda syntax (that previously used in LINQ if you come from .NET development background). The line above is equal to pseudo-code below:

Function anonymous (x)
{
return x+1
}

As you see lambda made it much simpler to define the function with just that single line. So the function above get a parameter from the input and adds 1 to it. Please note that datatype of the parameter not defined, so that means if a text is input, then an error would occur, so you would require to imlement the error handling as well (I'll describe Error Handling in M in future blog posts).

So let's see how this function works and how we can call this function. Script below shows how to define the function and invoke it with a parameter:

let

   Add = (x) => x+1

in

   Add(10)

The result of the above expression is: 11

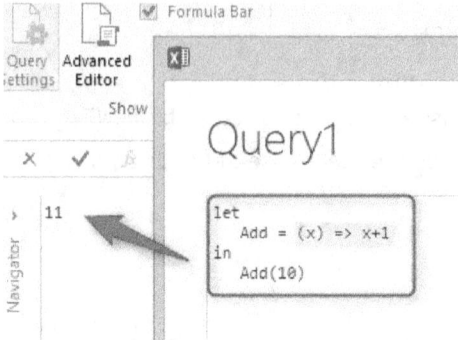

In the example above we've named the function as "Add" and then we call that with Add(inputparam).

Parameters

If you want to define a function with more parameters, then add parameters as below:

(x,y,z) => x+y+z

you can also define a function without parameters, as below:

() => "sample function without parameter"

This function gets no parameters and returns the text "sample function without parameter".

Optional Parameters

Parameters are defined as Required by default. That means you should specify the parameter at the time of invoking the function. So if you want to define an optional parameter, use the Optional keyword as below:

let

    Func = (optional x) => if x is null then "nothing" else x

in

    Func(5)

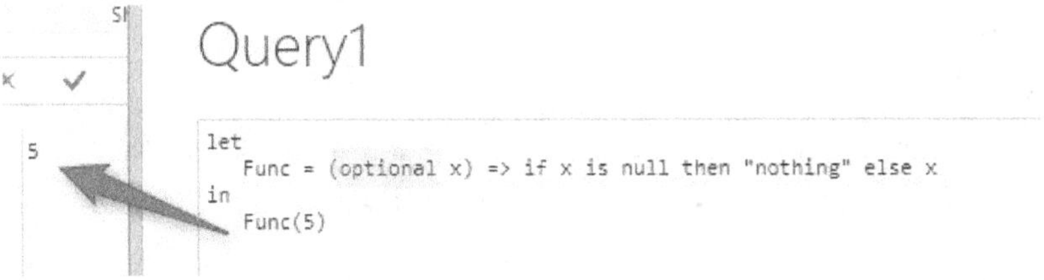

Variables in Function

Samples above showed how to write single line expression function, but in most of the cases, you would require to write multiple line function that contains variables inside the function. In that case, you can define the function within the LET / IN structure as below:

let

    Func = (x) =>

        let

            <body>

        in

            <return value>

in

    Func(5)

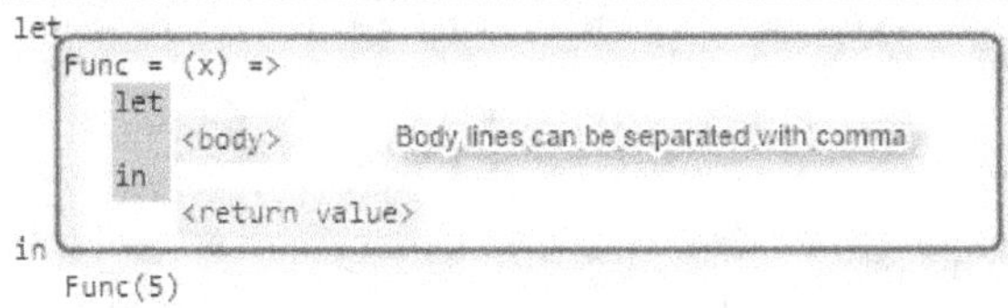

Power BI from Rookie to Rock Star – Book 3: Power Query and Data Transformation in Power BI

As you see in the above script, another set of Let/In added inside the function. You can write the body of the function in the LET clause. And if you want to add multiple lines there, or if you want to define variables, do this as usual with a single comma at the end of each line. Finally, you can return value in the IN clause.

Example
Following example show how we can use structure above to create a function that return number of days passed from the start of the year until that date.

```
let
   DayPassedInYear = (x) =>
      let
         MonthList=List.Numbers(1,Date.Month(DateTime.FromText(x))-1),
         Year=Date.Year(DateTime.FromText(x)),
         DaysInMonthList=List.Transform(MonthList,each Date.DaysInMonth(DateTime.FromText(Text.From(Year)&"-"&Text.From(_)&"-01")))
      in
         Date.Day(DateTime.FromText(x))+List.Sum(DaysInMonthList)
in
   DayPassedInYear("5/14/2014")
```

Line by Line Description
Let's go through the script line by line;

```
DayPassedInYear = (x) =>
```

In above line we define the function name as "DayPassedInYear", this function require a single parameter, definition of the body would come in next lines.

let

MonthList=List.Numbers(1,Date.Month(DateTime.FromText(x))-1),

We used Let to define a multi-line body. The first line of the body is defining a variable that creates a list of Month numbers from the first month (1) to the previous month of the input date. For calculating the previous month of the input date, we used this expression: *Date.Month(DateTime.FromText(x))-1* . And this part generates a list based on numbers from a beginning number (1) to ending number (which would be the result of previous month function): *List.Numbers(1,.....)*

So as a result, the MonthList would be a variable that contains a list of months from the first month up to a prior month in the current year. Let's see how that single line would return the result:

Next line in the script calculates year of the input date and store that into a variable named "Year":

Year=Date.Year(DateTime.FromText(x)),

Consider that you should end each line with a single comma (if you don't want to logic of two lines to be parsed together).

The final line of the body combined from multiple expressions, I'll describe the one by one;

DateTime.FromText(Text.From(Year)&"-"&Text.From(_)&"-01")

Above expression will return the first day of a month. Please note that there is a single underscore in the expression. That underscore would be used in EACH expression. EACH is a single parameter function. We used EACH in this example to apply a transformation to every item in the list. Actually we want to replace each month number in the list, with the number of days in that month. So we use EACH single liner function to fetch a number of days in that month. When you use EACH, you can use underscore as the parameter marker. In simpler words, if you have a list as below:

ListA

1

2

3

And if you transform that list with List.Transform function as below:

*List.Transform(ListA,each _ *10)*

The result would be:

ListA

10

20

30

So the result of This line below:

DaysInMonthList=List.Transform(MonthList,each Date.DaysInMonth(DateTime.FromText(Text.From(Year)&"-"&Text.From(_)&"-01")))

Would be:

As you see each list item which had the month number earlier, now replaced (transformed) with the number of days in that month.

In the final step of the function we return the result;

in

Date.Day(DateTime.FromText(x))+List.Sum(DaysInMonthList)

IN clause used to return the result, and we use Date.Day function to return the day part of input date. And we add that with the sum of all values form the list. As a result, we would see the number of days passed from the first of the year to the input date.

Summary

In this blog post, you've learned how to define functions and how to invoke them. You've learned that you can define optional or required parameters. You can also define multi-line functions that contain variables inside the body. You've seen a sample function that shows how useful are functions in the real world. You've also learned about EACH keyword which can be used as a single parameter function (especially in lists and tables).

Power BI from Rookie to Rock Star – Book 3: Power Query and Data Transformation in Power BI

Day Number of Year, Power Query Custom Function

Posted by Reza Rad on Jul 28, 2015

```
let
    DayNumberOfYear= (date) =>
        let
            dated= try DateTime.FromText(date),
            month=Date.Month(dated[Value]),
            MonthList=List.Numbers(1,month-1),
            year=Date.Year(dated[Value]),
            TransformedMonthList=List.Transform
                    (MonthList,
                    each Text.From(year)&"-"&Text.From(_)&"-1"),
            DateList=List.Transform(
                    TransformedMonthList,
                    each DateTime.FromText(_)),
            DaysList=List.Transform(
                    DateList,
                    each Date.DaysInMonth(_))
        in
            if dated[HasError]
                then dated[Error]
                else List.Sum(DaysList)+Date.Day(dated[Value])
in
    DayNumberOfYear("07/28/2015")
```

There are some Date and DateTime built-in functions in Power Query which are helpful. There is also a function for DayNumberOfYear. However, I've thought it would be a good example to go through writing a function that uses Generators, Each singleton function, and error handling all inside a custom function. Through this post you will also learn;
- how to create Custom Function
- how to use Generators as a loop structure
- and how to user Error Handling.

Let's consider this date as today's date: 28th of July of 2015 (this is the date of this blog post)

There might be a number of methods to calculate the day number of year for this date (which is 209). I use one of them here. Steps are as below;
- fetch a number of days for each month from January of this year (of the date above) to the previous month (of the date above).

- Calculate the sum of values above will give me the number of days in all month prior than this month.
- Add the day number of the date to the calculated sum above.

Some of the calculations can be helped through with Power Query Date functions. So let's start;

1 – Create a function in Power Query called DayNumberOfYear as below

If you don't know where to write below code:

- Open Excel, Go to Power Query Tab, Click On Get Data from Source, Blank Query, In the Query Editor window go to View tab, and click on Advanced Editor.

Open Power BI, click on Edit Queries, In the Query Editor window go to View tab, and click on Advanced Editor.

```
let                              //start of the code
    DayNumberOfYear= (date) =>   //Function name, and input parameter
    let                          //start of function body
        dated=DateTime.FromText(date) //date conversion from text
    in                           //start of function output
        dated                    //function body output
in                               //start of output lines generated
    DayNumberOfYear("07/28/2015")    //call function by a value
```

I've put some comments in above script to help you understand each line. In general, DayNumberOfYear is the name of the function. It accepts an input parameter "date". and convert the parameter from text value to DateTime. The last line of the code calls the function with a specific date ("07/28/2015").

** Note that Date Conversion function is locale dependent. So if the date time of your system is no MM/DD/YYYY then you have to enter date as it formatted in your system (look below the clock on right-hand side bottom of your monitor to check the format).

The result of the above script will be:

07/28/2015 12:00:00 a.m.

2 – Fetch Month Number and generate a list of all prior months.

Fetching month number is easily possible with Date.Month function. The remaining part is looping through months from January of this year to the previous month (of the given date). Unfortunately there is no loop structure in Power Query M language yet, but fortunately, we can use Generator functions for that. A generator function is a function that produces/generate a list based on some parameters. For example, you can generate a list of dates from a start date, based on the given occurrence of a period. Or you can generate a list of numbers. For this example, we want to generate a list of numbers, starting from 1 (month January) to the current month number minus 1 (previous month).

Here is the code:

```
let
    DayNumberOfYear= (date) =>
        let
            dated=DateTime.FromText(date),
            month=Date.Month(dated),//month number
            MonthList=List.Numbers(1,month-1) // generate list of months from Jan to previous month
        in
            MonthList
in
    DayNumberOfYear("07/28/2015")
```

The result is a list of month numbers as below:

List
1
2
3
4
5
6

Generator Function used in the above code is List.Numbers. This function generate a list of numbers starting from a value.

3 – Transform list to full date list

We have to calculate a number of days for each month in the function. A number of days in each month can be fetched by Date.DaysInMonth function. However this function accepts a full DateTime data type, and the value that we have in our list members are text. So we have to produce a DateTime value from it. For generating a full date we need the year portion as well, we use Date.Year function to fetch that.

Here is the code to transform the list:

```
let
    DayNumberOfYear= (date) =>
        let
            dated=DateTime.FromText(date),
            month=Date.Month(dated),
            MonthList=List.Numbers(1,month-1),
            year=Date.Year(dated), // fetch year
            TransformedMonthList=List.Transform // transform list
            
                (MonthList,
                    each Text.From(year)&"-"&Text.From(_)&"-1") // generate full text value
        in
            TransformedMonthList
in
    DayNumberOfYear("07/28/2015")
```

The result is:

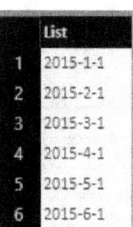

As you see the above result is not still of DateTime data type, we've only generated full date as a text value. Now we can convert values to DateTime data type
Here is the code:

```
1  let
2      DayNumberOfYear= (date) =>
3          let
4              dated=DateTime.FromText(date),
5              month=Date.Month(dated),
6              MonthList=List.Numbers(1,month-1),
7              year=Date.Year(dated),
8              TransformedMonthList=List.Transform
9                  (MonthList,
10                 each Text.From(year)&"-"&Text.From(_)&"-1"),
11             DateList=List.Transform(
12                 TransformedMonthList,
13                 each DateTime.FromText(_))//transform to DateTime value
14         in
15             DateList
16 in
17     DayNumberOfYear("07/28/2015")
```

and the result:

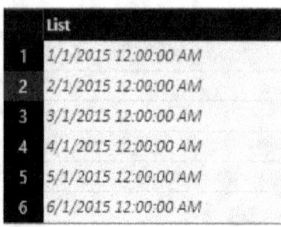

4 – Transform the list to List of DaysNumberOfMonths

We use DaysInMonth function to fetch the number of days in each month from the list. Here is the code:

```
1  let
2      DayNumberOfYear= (date) =>
3          let
4              dated=DateTime.FromText(date),
5              month=Date.Month(dated),
6              MonthList=List.Numbers(1,month-1),
7              year=Date.Year(dated),
8              TransformedMonthList=List.Transform
9                  (MonthList,
10                 each Text.From(year)&"-"&Text.From(_)&"-1"),
11             DateList=List.Transform(
12                 TransformedMonthList,
13                 each DateTime.FromText(_)),
14             DaysList=List.Transform(
15                 DateList,
16                 each Date.DaysInMonth(_))
17         in
18             DaysList
19 in
20     DayNumberOfYear("07/28/2015")
```

and the result:

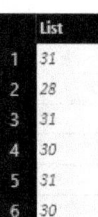

5 – Calculate the Sum of Dates and Add day number of this month to it

The list is ready to use; we need to sum it up only. And then add the current day Date.Day from the given date to it.

Here is the code:

```
1  let
2      DayNumberOfYear= (date) =>
3          let
4              dated=DateTime.FromText(date),
5              month=Date.Month(dated),
6              MonthList=List.Numbers(1,month-1),
7              year=Date.Year(dated),
8              TransformedMonthList=List.Transform
9                  (MonthList,
10                 each Text.From(year)&"-"&Text.From(_)&"-1"),
11             DateList=List.Transform(
12                 TransformedMonthList,
13                 each DateTime.FromText(_)),
14             DaysList=List.Transform(
15                 DateList,
16                 each Date.DaysInMonth(_))
17         in
18             List.Sum(DaysList)//sum of values in the list
19             +Date.Day(dated)//current date's day number
20 in
21     DayNumberOfYear("07/28/2015")
```

and the result is:

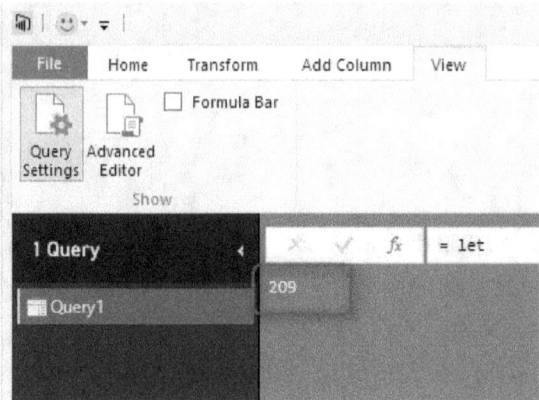

6- Error Handling

The function is working, but if the given date format is wrong then we will face an error such as below:

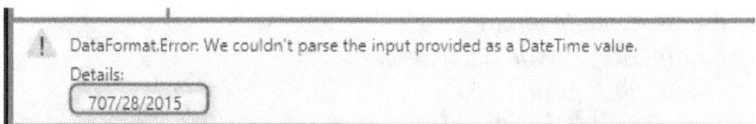

So let's add few lines of error handling to the code. We can simply use Try clause to the code as below:

```
1  let
2      DayNumberOfYear= (date) =>
3          let
4              dated= try DateTime.FromText(date),
5              month=Date.Month(dated[Value]),
6              MonthList=List.Numbers(1,month-1),
7              year=Date.Year(dated[Value]),
8              TransformedMonthList=List.Transform
9                  (MonthList,
10                 each Text.From(year)&"-"&Text.From(_)&"-1"),
11             DateList=List.Transform(
12                 TransformedMonthList,
13                 each DateTime.FromText(_)),
14             DaysList=List.Transform(
```

```
15              DateList,
16              each Date.DaysInMonth(_))
17      in
18          if dated[HasError]
19              then dated[Error]
20              else List.Sum(DaysList)+Date.Day(dated[Value])
21  in
22  DayNumberOfYear("707/28/2015")
```

Result for a bad formatted given date is :

```
         fx   = let
Reason  DataFormat.Error
Message We couldn't parse the input provided as a DateTime value.
Detail  707/28/2015
```

Here is the full code of the script:

```
1  let
2      DayNumberOfYear= (date) =>
3          let
4              dated= try DateTime.FromText(date),
5              month=Date.Month(dated[Value]),
6              MonthList=List.Numbers(1,month-1),
7              year=Date.Year(dated[Value]),
8              TransformedMonthList=List.Transform
9                  (MonthList,
10                 each Text.From(year)&"-"&Text.From(_)&"-1"),
11             DateList=List.Transform(
12                 TransformedMonthList,
13                 each DateTime.FromText(_)),
14             DaysList=List.Transform(
15                 DateList,
16                 each Date.DaysInMonth(_))
17         in
18             if dated[HasError]
19                 then dated[Error]
```

20   else List.Sum(DaysList)+Date.Day(dated[Value])
21 in
22   DayNumberOfYear("707/28/2015")

In this post you've learned:
• A Function that calculates Day Number of Year for a given date
• Creating a Custom Function
. using Generators as Loop structure
• Error Handling

Power Query Function that Returns Multiple Values

Posted by Reza Rad on Jul 30, 2015

```
let
    FirstAndLastDayOfTheMonth = (date) =>
        let
            dated=Date.FromText(date),
            year=Date.Year(dated),
            month=Date.Month(dated),
            FirstDateText=Text.From(year)&"-"&Text.From(month)&"-01",
            FirstDate=Date.FromText(FirstDateText),
            daysInMonth=Date.DaysInMonth(dated),
            LastDateText=Text.From(year)&"-"&Text.From(month)&"-"&Text.From(daysInMonth),
            LastDate=Date.FromText(LastDateText),
            record=Record.AddField([],"First Date of Month",FirstDate),
            resultset=Record.AddField(record,"Last Date of Month",LastDate)
        in
            resultset
in
    FirstAndLastDayOfTheMonth("30/07/2015")
```

Yesterday in NZ BI user group meeting, I had been asked that does Power Query custom functions return only one value as the result set? Or they can return multiple values. I've answered. Yes, and I've explained that through a sentence how to do it with Records, List, or Table. Then I thought this might be a question of many people out there. So I've written this blog post to illustrate how to return multiple values from a custom function in Power Query.

If you don't know how to create a custom function, please read my other blog post with an example of Day Number of Year function for Power Query. In this post, I'll show you through an example of how to return multiple results from a Power Query function.

As you probably know Power Query function return single value by default, and that is the value result of the operation in the "*in*" clause of the function. Now how to return multiple values? Simply by returning different type of object. The trick is that Power Query custom function can return any single object. And that *object* can be simple structure object such as Date, Text, Number. Or it can be multiple value objects such as Record, List, and Table.

To understand the difference between Record, List, and Table:
- Record: Is a single record structure with one or more fields. Each field has a field name and a field value.
- List: Is a single column structure with one or more rows. Each row contains a value.
- Table: Multiple rows and columns data structure (as you probably all know it)

Above objects can hold multiple values. So the only thing you need to do in return one of the above objects based on your requirement. In the example below, I've returned a Record. As a result set, but you can do it with other two data types.

Return First and Last Dates of Month

As an example, I would like to write a function that fetches both first and last date of a month, the input parameter of this function is a date value with text data types, such as "30/07/2015".

** Note that Date Conversion function is locale dependent. So if the date time of your system is no DD/MM/YYYY then you have to enter date as it formatted in your system (look below the clock on right-hand side bottom of your monitor to check the format).

Let's start by calculation of the First Date of the Month

First Date of the Month

We need to fetch the year, and the month, and then built a date string for the first day (day 1) of that month and year, and finally convert it to Date datatype. Here is the script:

```
1 let
2    FirstAndLastDayOfTheMonth = (date) => //function definition
```

```
3    let
4        dated=Date.FromText(date),//convert input text to Date
5        year=Date.Year(dated),//fetch year
6        month=Date.Month(dated),//fetch month
7        FirstDateText=Text.From(year)&"-"&Text.From(month)&"-
8   01",//generate text value of the first date
9        FirstDate=Date.FromText(FirstDateText)//convert text value to
10  date
11
12   in
         FirstDate//return result of the function
in
    FirstAndLastDayOfTheMonth("30/07/2015")//function call
```

and the Result:

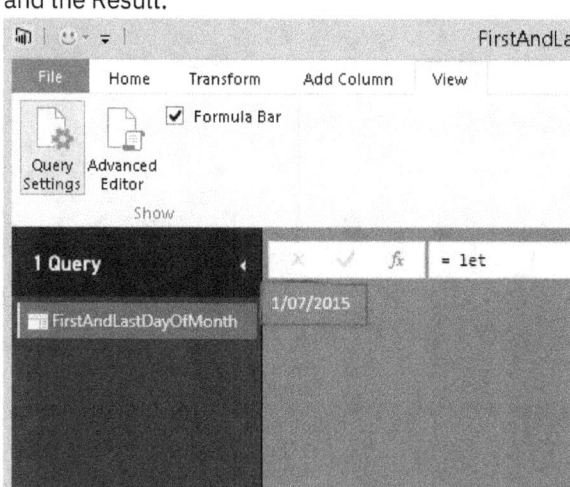

Last Date of the Month

For fetching the last date of the month, we use the same method of the first date, except one change. Which is the day part of the calculation should be the number of days in the month, which comes from Date.DaysInMonth function.

Here is the script:

```
let
    FirstAndLastDayOfTheMonth = (date) =>
        let
            dated=Date.FromText(date),
            year=Date.Year(dated),
            month=Date.Month(dated),
            FirstDateText=Text.From(year)&"-"&Text.From(month)&"-01",
            FirstDate=Date.FromText(FirstDateText),
            daysInMonth=Date.DaysInMonth(dated),//fetch number of days in month
            LastDateText=Text.From(year)&"-"&Text.From(month)&"-"&Text.From(daysInMonth),
            LastDate=Date.FromText(LastDateText)
        in
            LastDate
in
    FirstAndLastDayOfTheMonth("30/07/2015")
```

and the result:

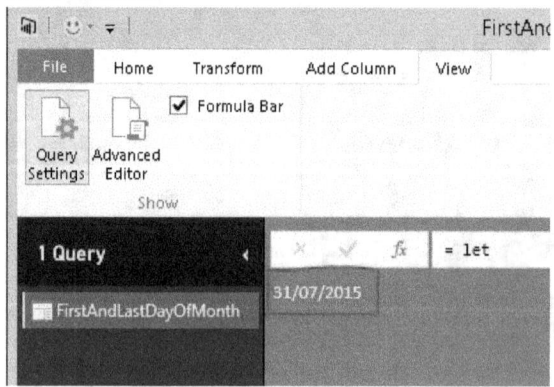

Combining both values into a Record and returning Record as a Result
Now we have both values, and we want to return them both. I'll create an empty record first. An Empty record can be created simply with this : [] .

Then I used Record.AddField function to add fields one by one.

Record.AddField gets three parameters: the record that field will be added to it, the name of the new field, and value of the new field.

Here is the script:

```
let
    FirstAndLastDayOfTheMonth = (date) =>
        let
            dated=Date.FromText(date),
            year=Date.Year(dated),
            month=Date.Month(dated),
            FirstDateText=Text.From(year)&"-"&Text.From(month)&"-01",
            FirstDate=Date.FromText(FirstDateText),
            daysInMonth=Date.DaysInMonth(dated),
            LastDateText=Text.From(year)&"-"&Text.From(month)&"-"&Text.From(daysInMonth),
            LastDate=Date.FromText(LastDateText),
            record=Record.AddField({},"First Date of Month",FirstDate),
            resultset=Record.AddField(record,"Last Date of Month",LastDate)
        in
            resultset
in
    FirstAndLastDayOfTheMonth("30/07/2015")
```

and the result:

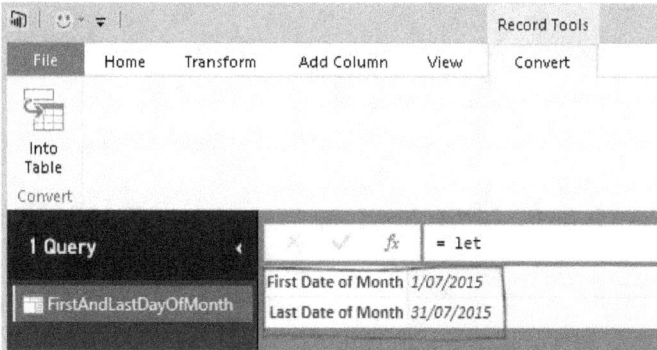

How to access this Record's values

As you see in above, the function returns a record with two fields. Now we can access fields by name, with a script like this:

1 FirstAndLastDayOfTheMonth("30/07/2015")[Last Date of Month]

and the result would be a single value

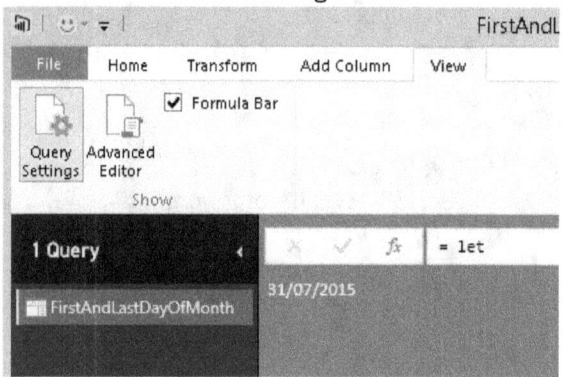

Here is the full code of example if you want to try it yourself.

Don't Limit Yourself

You can have another record in a field's value, you can have a list in a field's value, and you can have a table in a field's value. So you can create any data structure that you want as the result set of your function.

Custom Functions Made Easy in Power BI Desktop

Posted by Reza Rad on Dec 6, 2016

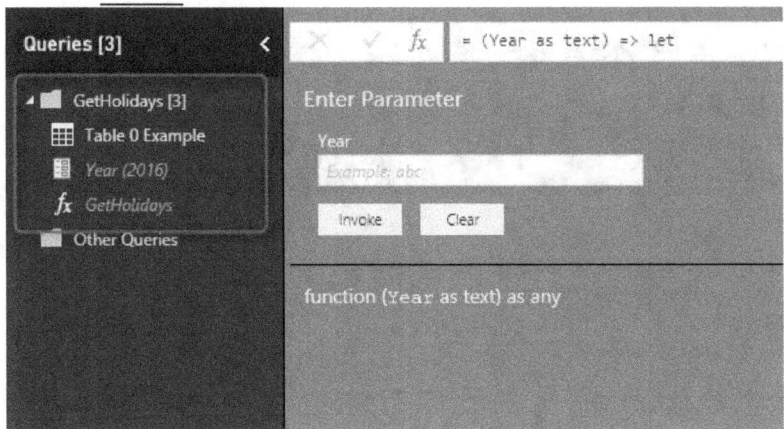

I have written a lot about Power Query M scripting language, and how to create custom functions with that. With recent updates of Power BI Desktop, creating custom functions made easier and easier every month. This started with bringing Parameters a few months ago and adding source query for the function in November update of Power BI Desktop. In this blog post you will learn how easy it is to create a custom function now, what are benefits of doing it in this way, and limitations of it. If you like to learn more about Power BI; read Power BI online book from Rookie to Rock Star.

What is Custom Function?

Custom Function in the simple definition is a query that runs by other queries. The main benefit of having a query to run by other queries is that you can repeat some steps on the same data structure. Let's see that as an example: Website below listed public holidays in New Zealand:

http://publicholiday.co.nz/

For every year, there is a page, and pages are similar to each other, each page contains a table of dates and descriptions of holidays. Here is, for example, public holidays of 2016:

You can simply use Power BI Get Data from Web menu option of Power Query to get the public holidays of this page. You can also make some changes in the date format to make it a proper Date data type. Then you probably want to apply same steps on all other pages for other years (2015, 2017, 2018...), So instead of repeating the process, you can reuse an existing query. Here is where the Custom Function comes to help.

Benefits of Custom Function

- Re-Use of Code
- Increasing Consistency
- Reducing Redundancy

With a Custom function, you can re-use a query multiple times. If you want to change part of it, there is only one place to make that change, instead of multiple copies of that. You can call this function from everywhere in your code. And you are reducing redundant steps which normally causes extra maintenance of the code.

How to Create a Custom Function?

Well, that's the question I want to answer in this post. Previously (about a year ago), creating custom functions was only possible through M scripting, with lambda expressions, that method still works, but you need to be comfortable with writing M script to use that method (To be honest I am still a fan of that method). Recently Power BI Desktop changed a lot; you can now create a function without writing any single line of code.

Through an example, I'll show you how to create a custom function. This example is fetching all public holidays from the website above, and appending them all in a single table in Power Query. We want the process to be dynamic, so if a new year's data appear in that page, that will be included as well. Let's see how it works.

Building the Main Query

For creating a custom function you always need to build the main query and then convert that to a function. Our main query is a query that will be repeated later on by calling from other queries. In this example, our main query is the query that processes the holiday's table in every page, and return that in the proper format of Date data type and Text for a description of the holiday. We can do that for one of the years (doesn't matter which one). I start with the year 2016 which has this URL:

http://publicholiday.co.nz/nz-public-holidays-2016.html

Open a Power BI Desktop and start by getting Data from Web

Use the 2016's web address in the From Web page;

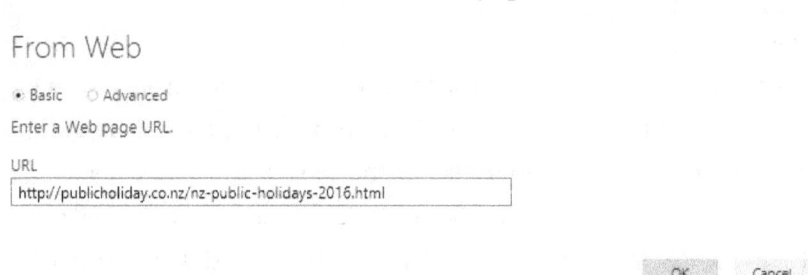

In the Navigator, you can see that Table 0 is the table containing the data we are after. Select this table and click Edit.

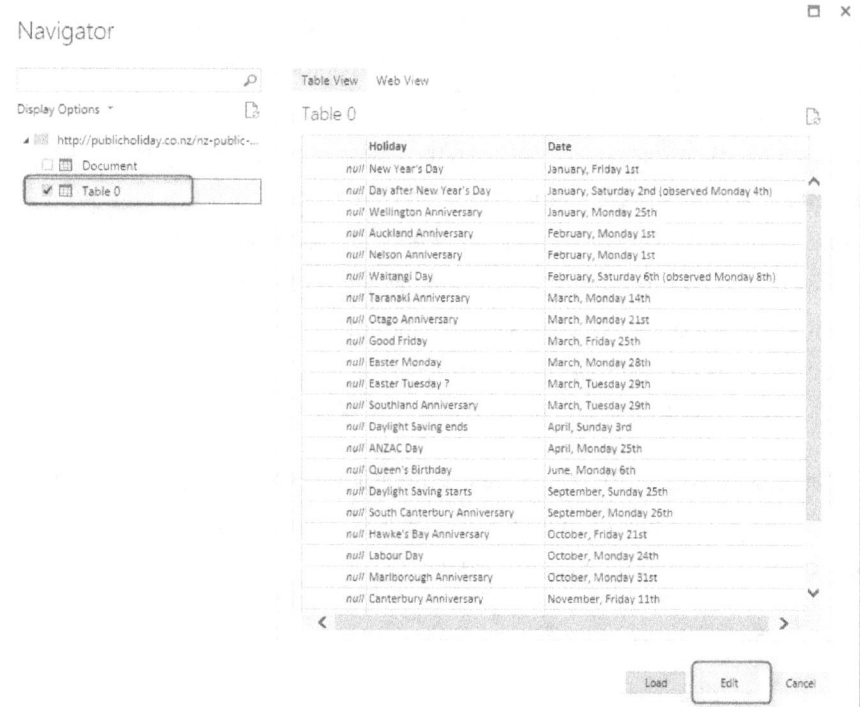

This will open Query Editor Window for you; You can now make some changes in the query, For example, remove the first column.

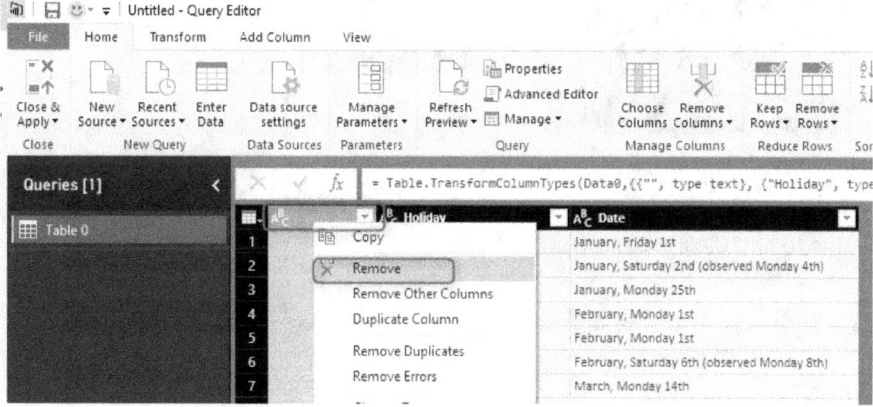

The first column was an empty column which we removed. Now you can see two columns; Holiday (which is the description of the holiday), and Date. Date column is a Text data type, and it doesn't have year part in it. If you try to convert it to Date data type, you will either get an error in each cell or incorrect date as a result (depends on the locale setting of your computer). To convert this text to a date format, we need to bring a Year value in the query. The year value for this query can be statistically set to 2016. But because we want to make it dynamic so let's use a Parameter. This Parameter later will be used as input of the query.

Parameter Definition

Parameters are ways to pass values to other queries. Normally for custom functions, you need to use parameters. Click on Manage Parameters menu option in Query Editor, and select New Parameter.

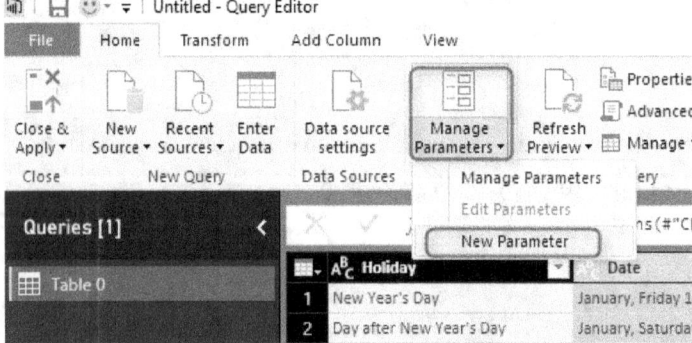

There are different types of parameters you can use, but to keep it simple, create a parameter of type Text, with all default selections. Set the Current Value to be 2016. And name it as Year.

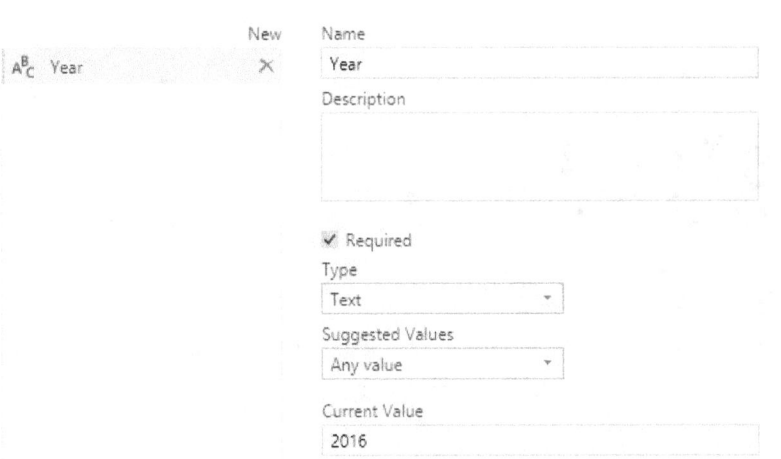

After creating the Parameter, you can see that in Queries pane with a specific icon for the parameter.

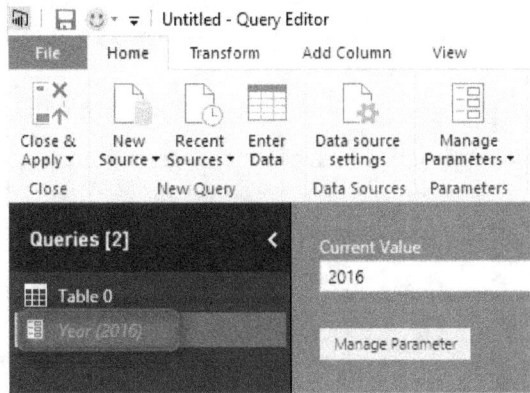

Now we can add a column in Table 0 with the value from this parameter. Click on Table 0, and from Add Column menu option, click on Add Custom Column.

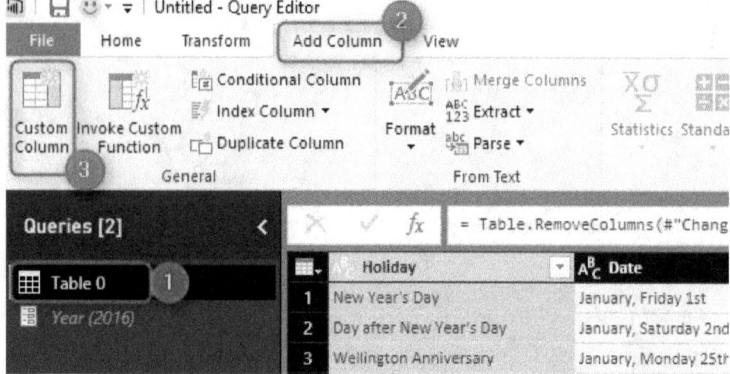

Name the Custom column as Year, and write the expression to be equal Year (remember names in Power Query are case sensitive)

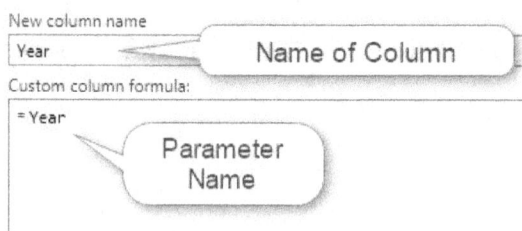

Now you can see year value added to the table. I have also changed its data type to be Text

Holiday	Date	Year
1 New Year's Day	January, Friday 1st	2016
2 Day after New Year's Day	January, Saturday 2nd (observed Monday 4th)	2016
3 Wellington Anniversary	January, Monday 25th	2016
4 Auckland Anniversary	February, Monday 1st	2016
5 Nelson Anniversary	February, Monday 1st	2016
6 Waitangi Day	February, Saturday 6th (observed Monday 8th)	2016
7 Taranaki Anniversary	March, Monday 14th	2016
8 Otago Anniversary	March, Monday 21st	2016
9 Good Friday	March, Friday 25th	2016
10 Easter Monday	March, Monday 28th	2016
11 Easter Tuesday ?	March, Tuesday 29th	2016
12 Southland Anniversary	March, Tuesday 29th	2016
13 Daylight Saving ends	April, Sunday 3rd	2016
14 ANZAC Day	April, Monday 25th	2016
15 Queen's Birthday	June, Monday 6th	2016
16 Daylight Saving starts	September, Sunday 25th	2016
17 South Canterbury Anniversary	September, Monday 26th	2016
18 Hawke's Bay Anniversary	October, Friday 21st	2016

Now that we have created Parameter we can use that parameter as an input to the query's source URL as well.

URL Parameterization

One of the main benefits of Parameters is that you can use that in a URL. In our case, the URL which contains 2016 as the year, can be dynamic using this parameter. Also for converting a query to a custom function using parameters is one of the main steps. Let's add Parameter in the source of this query then; While Table 0 query is selected, in the list of Steps, click on the Setting icon for Source step

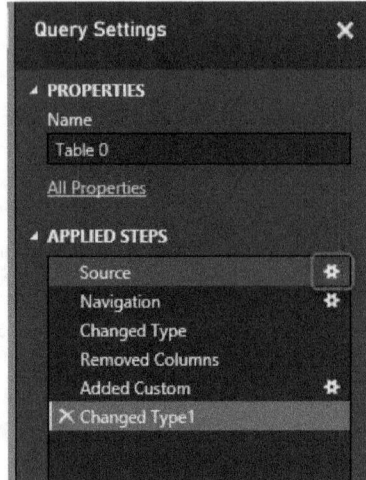

This will bring the very first step of the query where we get data from Web and provided the URL. Not in the top section change the From Web window to Advanced.

From Web

○ Basic ● Advanced

Enter a Web page URL.

URL parts

A^B_C ▼ | http://publicholiday.co.nz/nz-public-holida

A^B_C ▼ |

Add Part

URL preview

http://publicholiday.co.nz/nz-public-holidays-2016.html

Open file as

Html Page

Command timeout in minutes (optional)

HTTP Request Header Parameters (optional)

Type or select a value

Add Header

OK   Cancel

The advanced option gives you the ability to split the URL into portions. What we want to do is to put Text portions for beginning and end of the string, and make the year part of it dynamic coming from URL. So Add another part, and put setting as below;

From Web

The configuration above means that in the first part of URL we put everything before 2016 which is:

http://publicholiday.co.nz/nz-public-holidays-

The second part of URL is coming from the parameter, and we use Year parameter for that

the third part of URL is the remaining part after the year which is:

.html

altogether these will make the URL highlighted above which instead of {Year} it will have 2016, or 2015 or other values.

Click on OK. You won't see any changes yet, even if you click on the last step of this query, because we have used same year code as the parameter value. If you change the parameter value and refresh the query, you will see changes, but we don't want to do it in this way.

Convert Query to Function

After using a parameter in the source of query, we can convert it to function. Right click on the Table 0 query and select Create Function.

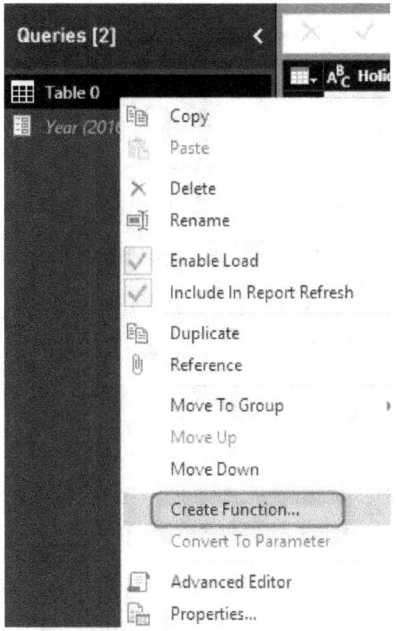

Name the function as GetHolidays and click on OK.

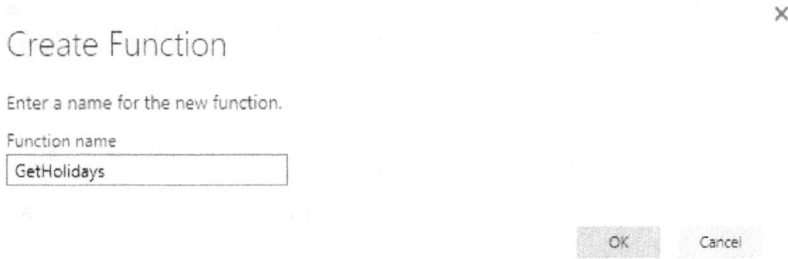

You will now see a group (folder) created with the name of GetHolidays including three objects; main query (Table 0), Parameter (year), and function (GetHolidays).

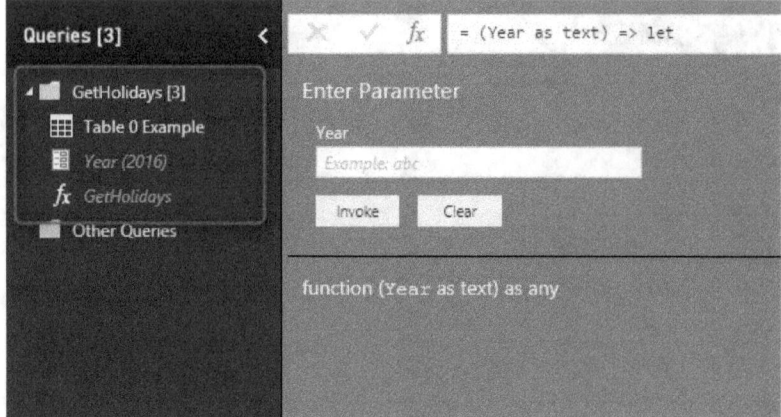

The function itself marked with *fx* icon, and that is the function we will use to call from other queries. However, the main query and parameter are still necessary for making changes in the function. I will explain this part later. All happened here is that there is a copy of the Table 0 query created as a function. And every time you call this function with an input parameter (which will be year value), this will give you the result (which is public holidays table for that year). Let's now consume this table from another query, but before that let's create a query that includes a list of years.

Using Generator

Generators are a topic of its own and can't be discussed in this post. All I can tell you for now is that Generators are functions that generate a list. This can be used for creating loop structure in Power Query. I'll write about that in another post. For this example, I want to create a list of numbers from 2015 for five years. So I'll use List.Numbers generator function for that. In your Query Editor Window, create a New Source from Home tab, and choose Blank Query.

This will create a Query1 for you. Click on Query1 in Queries pane, and in the Formula bar type in below script:

1 = List.Numbers(2015,5)

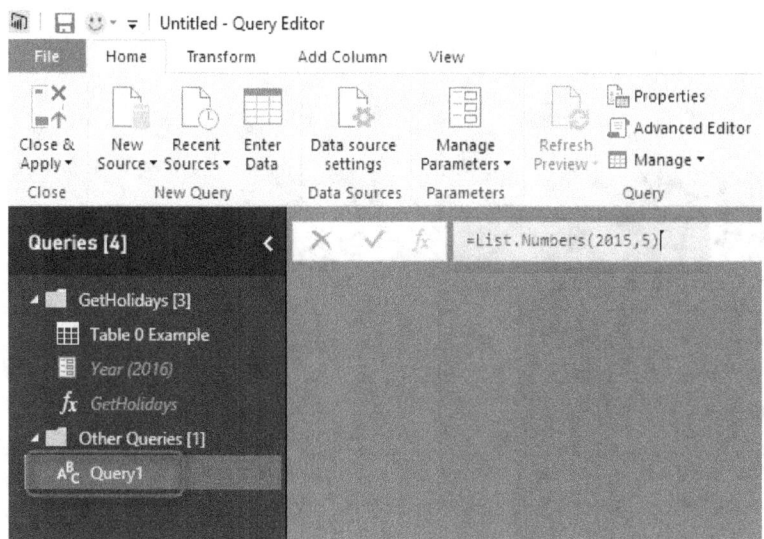

After entering the expression press Enter and you will see a list generated from 2015 for five numbers. That's the work done by a generator function.

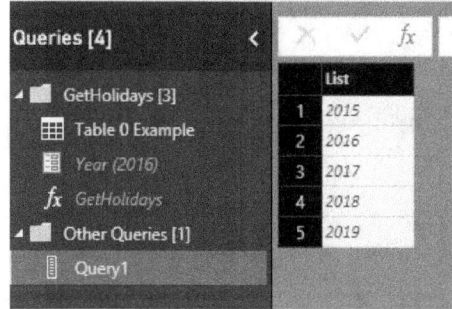

This is a List and can be converted to Table simple from List Tools menu option.

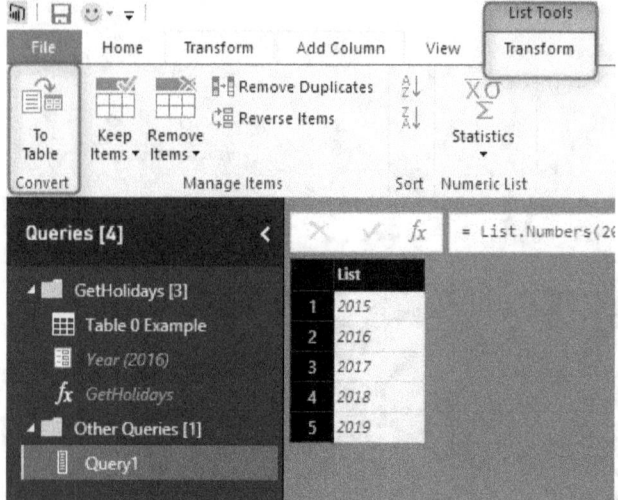

Convert this to Table with all default settings, and now you can see a table with Column1 which is year value. Because the value is the whole number, I have changed it to Text as well (to match the data type of parameter).

Consuming Function

Consuming a function in Query Editor from a table is easy. Go to Add Columns, and click on Invoke Custom Function option.

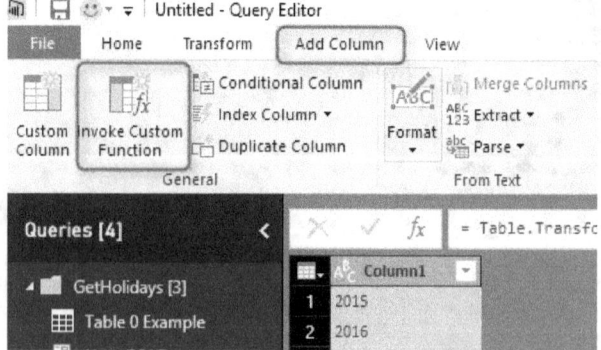

In the Invoke Custom Function window, choose the function (named GetHolidays), the input parameter is from the table column name Column1, and name the output column as Holidays.

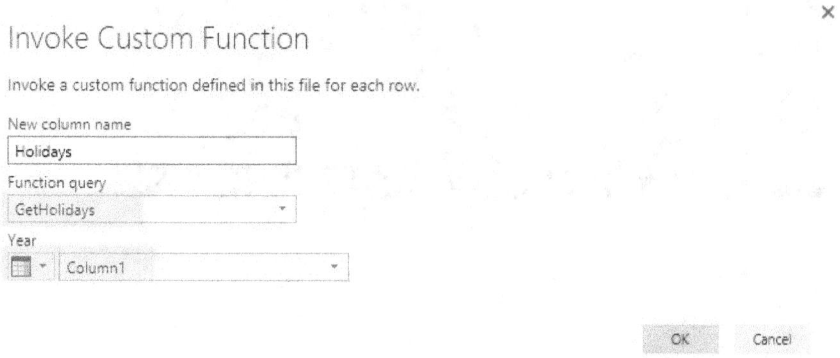

Now when you click on OK, you will see a new column added with a table in each cell. These tables are results of calling that function with the input parameter which is the value of Column1 in each row. If you click on a blank area of a cell with Table hyperlink, you will see the table structure below it.

Interesting, isn't it? It was so easy to implement. All done from GUI, not a single line of code to run this function or pass parameters, things made easy with custom functions.

Editing Function

If you want to make modifications in function, you can simply modify the main query (which is Table 0 Example). For example, let's create a full date format from that query in this way;

Click on Table 0 Example query and split the Date column with delimiter Comma, you will end up having a column now for Month values and another for Day (Note that I have renamed this column respectively);

#	Holiday	Month	Day	Year
1	New Year's Day	January	Friday 1st	2016
2	Day after New Year's Day	January	Saturday 2nd (observed Monday 4th)	2016
3	Wellington Anniversary	January	Monday 25th	2016
4	Auckland Anniversary	February	Monday 1st	2016
5	Nelson Anniversary	February	Monday 1st	2016
6	Waitangi Day	February	Saturday 6th (observed Monday 8th)	2016
7	Taranaki Anniversary	March	Monday 14th	2016
8	Otago Anniversary	March	Monday 21st	2016
9	Good Friday	March	Friday 25th	2016
10	Easter Monday	March	Monday 28th	2016
11	Easter Tuesday ?	March	Tuesday 29th	2016
12	Southland Anniversary	March	Tuesday 29th	2016
13	Daylight Saving ends	April	Sunday 3rd	2016
14	ANZAC Day	April	Monday 25th	2016
15	Queen's Birthday	June	Monday 6th	2016
16	Daylight Saving starts	September	Sunday 25th	2016
17	South Canterbury Anniversary	September	Monday 26th	2016
18	Hawke's Bay Anniversary	October	Friday 21st	2016
19	Labour Day	October	Monday 24th	2016
20	Marlborough Anniversary	October	Monday 31st	2016
21	Canterbury Anniversary	November	Friday 11th	2016
22	Westland Anniversary	November	Monday 28th	2016
23	Chatham Islands Anniversary	November	Monday 28th	2016
24	Christmas Day	December	Sunday 25th (observed Tuesday 27th)	2016
25	Boxing Day	December	Monday 26th	2016

Now if you go back to Query1, you will see changes in the results table immediately.

Power BI from Rookie to Rock Star – Book 3: Power Query and Data Transformation in Power BI

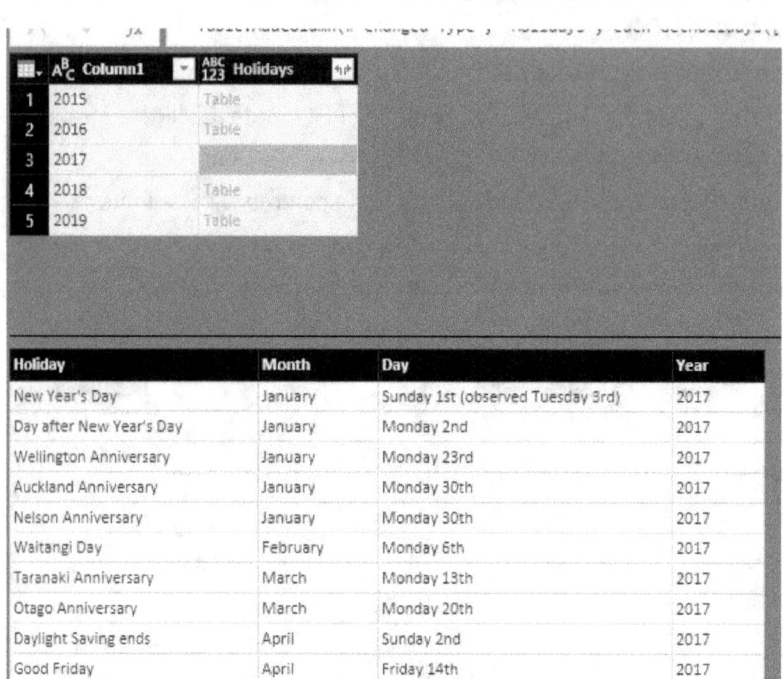

Holiday	Month	Day	Year
New Year's Day	January	Sunday 1st (observed Tuesday 3rd)	2017
Day after New Year's Day	January	Monday 2nd	2017
Wellington Anniversary	January	Monday 23rd	2017
Auckland Anniversary	January	Monday 30th	2017
Nelson Anniversary	January	Monday 30th	2017
Waitangi Day	February	Monday 6th	2017
Taranaki Anniversary	March	Monday 13th	2017
Otago Anniversary	March	Monday 20th	2017
Daylight Saving ends	April	Sunday 2nd	2017
Good Friday	April	Friday 14th	2017
Easter Monday	April	Monday 17th	2017
Easter Tuesday ?	April	Tuesday 18th	2017
Southland Anniversary	April	Tuesday 18th	2017
ANZAC Day	April	Tuesday 25th	2017
Queen's Birthday	June	Monday 5th	2017
Daylight Saving starts	September	Sunday 24th	2017
South Canterbury Anniversary	September	Monday 25th	2017
Hawke's Bay Anniversary	October	Friday 20th	2017
Labour Day	October	Monday 23rd	2017
Marlborough Anniversary	October	Monday 30th	2017

Limitations
Edit Script for the Function
Changes are fine as long as you don't want to edit the M script of the function if you want to do so, then the function definition and the query definition split apart. And you will get below message:

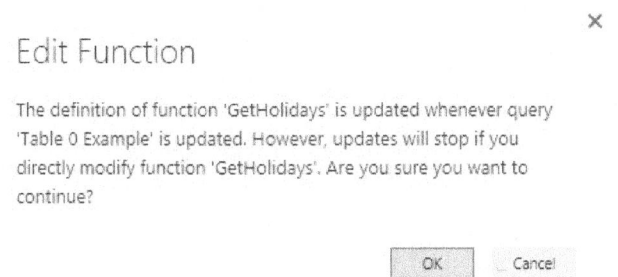

It is alright to make changes in the Advanced Editor of the source query, and then the function will be updated based on that, but if you want to change the function itself, then the query will be separated.
Disable Load of the Source Query
If you have read my blog post about Enable Load in Power Query, you already know that queries that are not used in the model should not be loaded. By Default, the source query (in this example named as Table 0 Example) will be loaded into the model. This means one extra table, and consuming more memory. So remember to uncheck the Enable Load for this query;

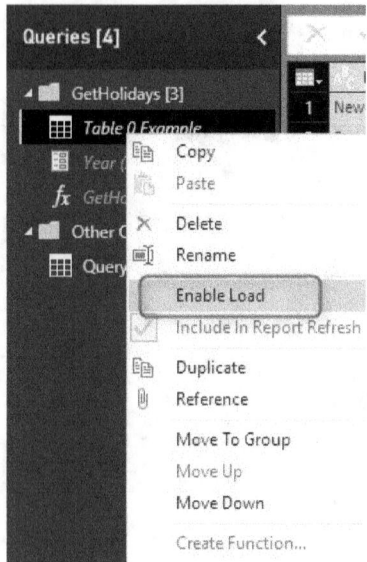

Parameterized URLs

Custom Functions that use parameterized URLs (like this example) cannot be scheduled to refresh in Power BI. That's a big limitation which I hope to be lifted very quickly.

Example at the End

I have done some other changes and changed the data type to Date format. Now the final query which is expanded table from all underlying queries include all public holidays. I'll leave that part to you to continue and build rest of the example. For that functionality you need to use Expand;

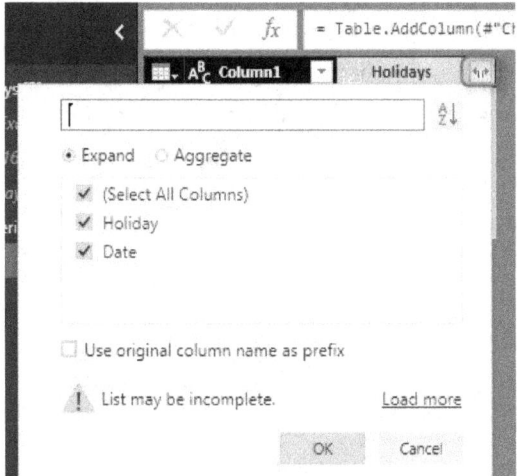

and here is the final result;

Summary

In this post, you have learned how easy it is to create a custom function from a query, all from the graphical interface. You have seen that I haven't wrote any single line of code to do it. and all happened through GUI. You have seen that you can change the definition of function simply by changing the source query. and you also have seen how easy it is to call/consume a function from another query. This method can be used a lot in real world Power Query scenarios.

Search for a Column in the Entire Database with Table.ColumnNames in Power Query and Power BI

Posted by Reza Rad on Jul 10, 2018

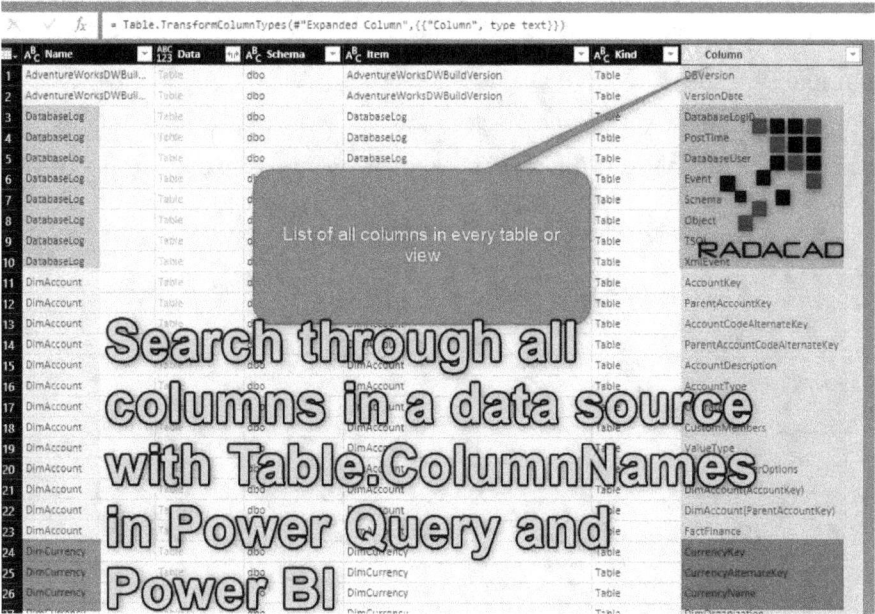

Sometimes for tables with too many columns, and also for databases with too many tables, you do need a bit of help to explore the data. As an example; you know that you are looking for a column named "account status", but the column does not exists in the accounts table. You need to search through all database tables for that column and find out which table has that value in it. Power Query has a great function that can help in such a scenario. Table.ColumnNames is a function that we are going to check out in this post. If you want to learn more about Power BI, read Power BI book from Rookie to Rock Star.

The Problem

You have a database with hundreds of tables or even more, and each table has many columns. You are looking for a specific column in the database and want to find out tables that such column exists in. Power Query has a function named Table.ColumnNames which gives you a list of all columns in a table as the output. Let's see how this function works.

Sample Dataset

For this example; you can connect to the AdventureWorksDW database. Then select any of the tables to import data from the source database.

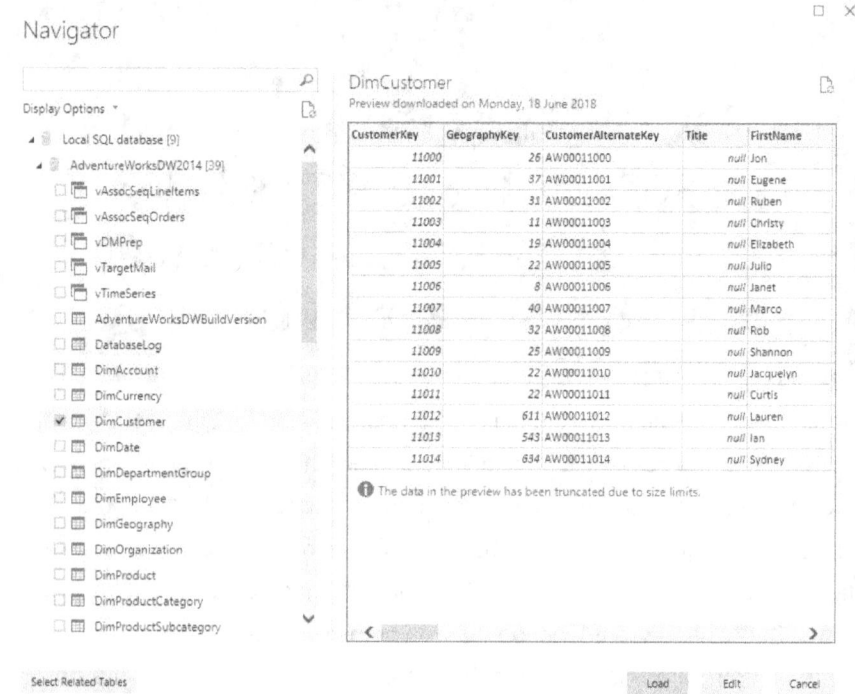

In the list of steps; you will find one step named as Navigation. This is the step that we have navigated to the table. Remove this step.

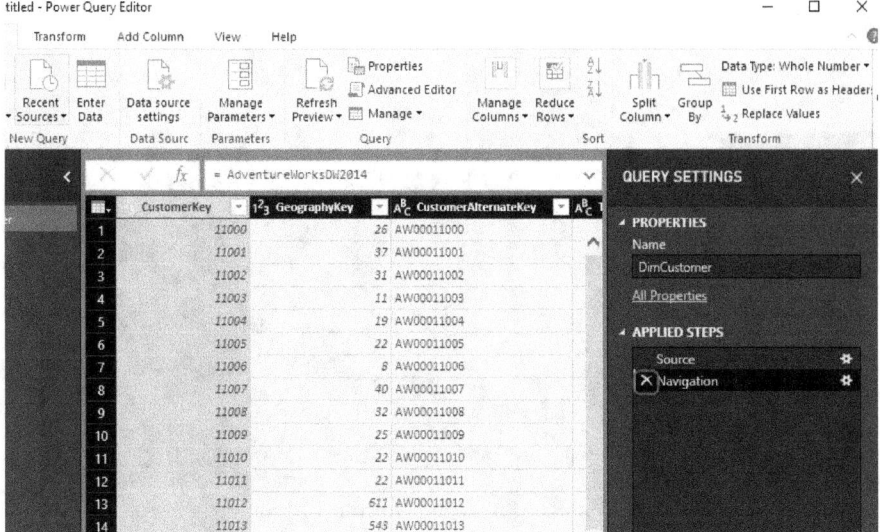

Then you will most probably see the list of all databases that you have access to (if you haven't chosen a specific database at the connect to SQL Server section). Click on the "Table" in the Data row of the database of AdventureWorks2014 (or any other databases that you want to explore columns in it).

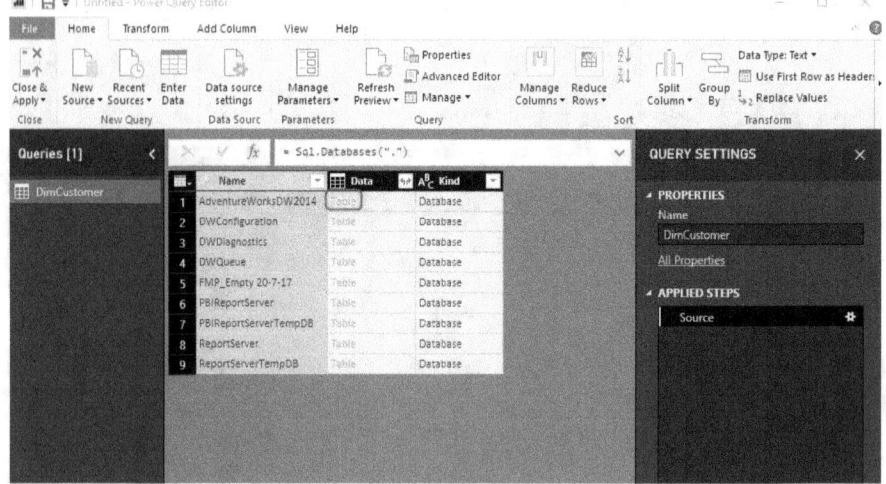

This action will give you the list of all tables under that database.

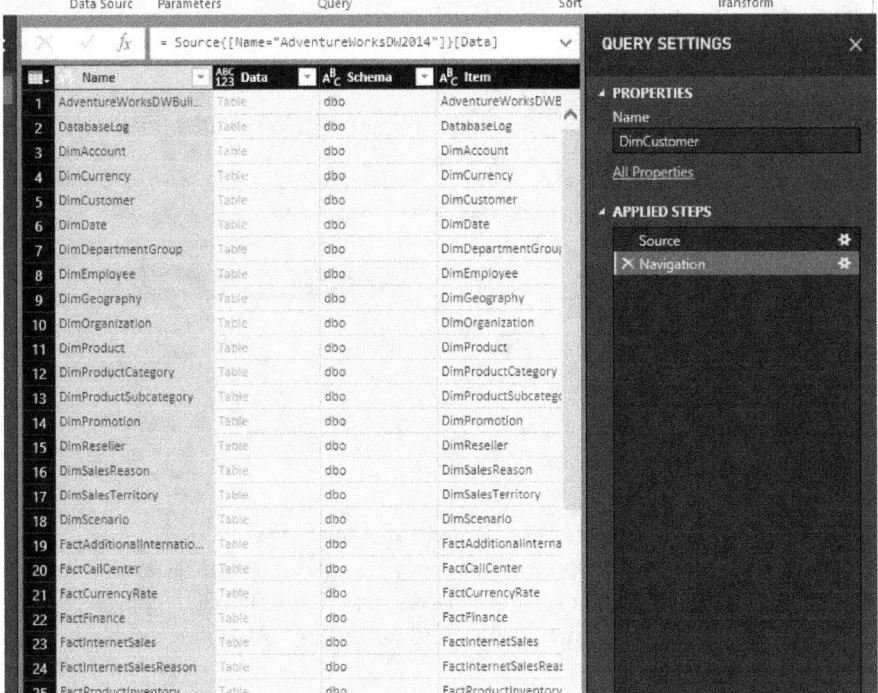

Now let's assume we want to search for Account column in the entire database. Let's see how this is possible.

Table.ColumnNames

The Table.ColumnNames function in Power Query will give you the list of all the columns in any given table. All you need to do is to call this function by passing the table as the input, and you will get a list of column names as the output. To use it in the existing example, click on Add Column, and then Add Custom Column.

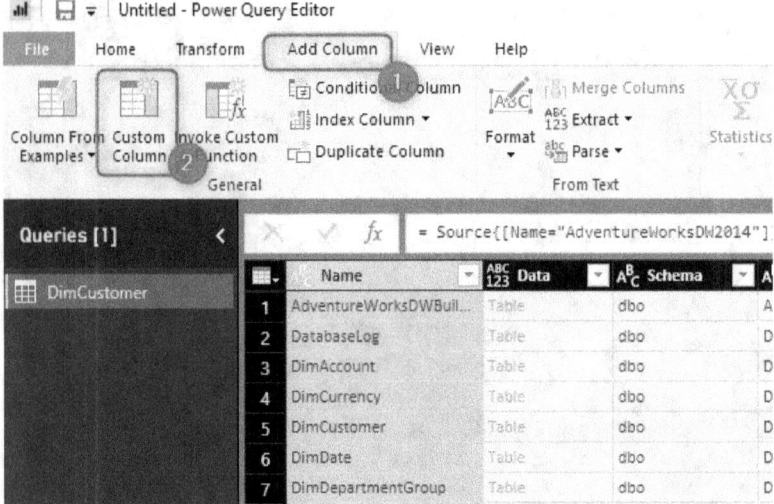

In the Custom Column expression section; you can write the Table.ColumnNames function with the input parameter of Data (Data is the column that includes the data table). Please note that Power Query is case sensitive, and Table.ColumnNames should be written exactly as mentioned here in this blog post.

1 =Table.ColumnNames([Data])

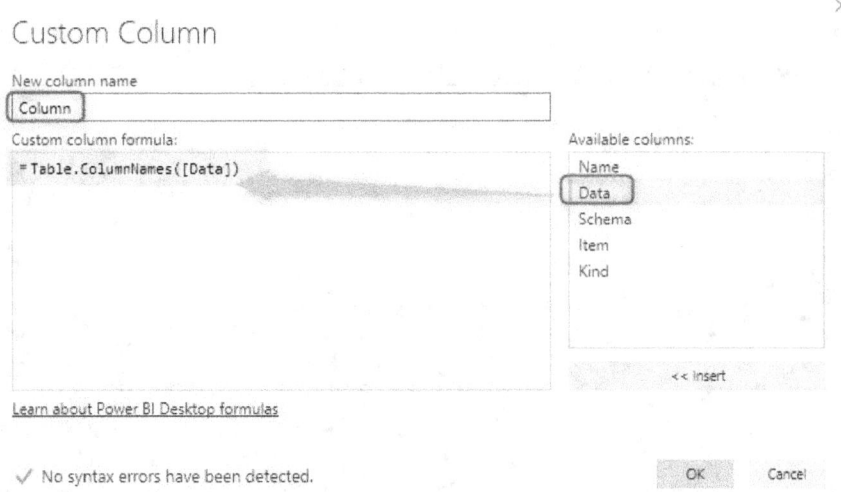

This action will give you a new column with a list in every cell. This list is the list of column names for every table.

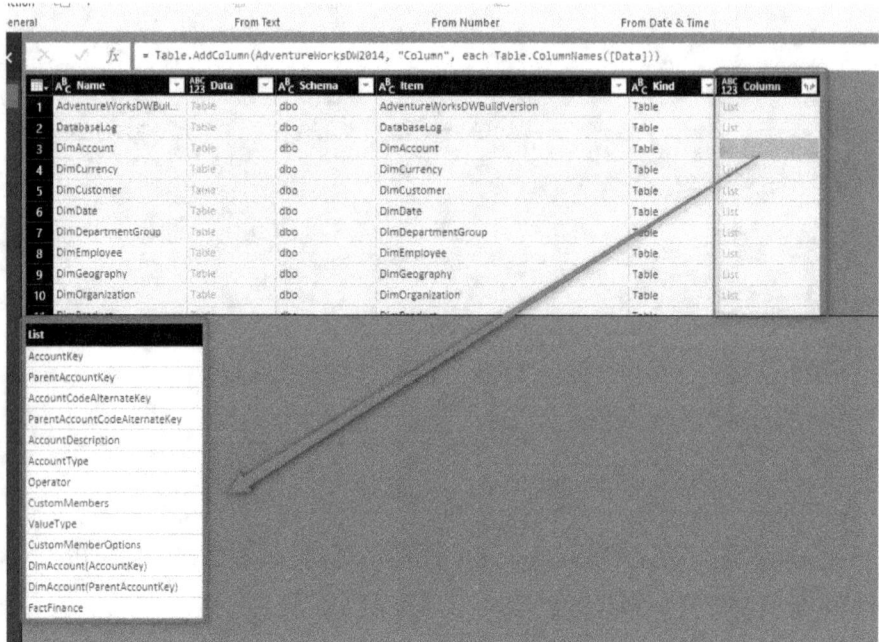

Now to get the list of all columns in all tables, you need to expand this column;

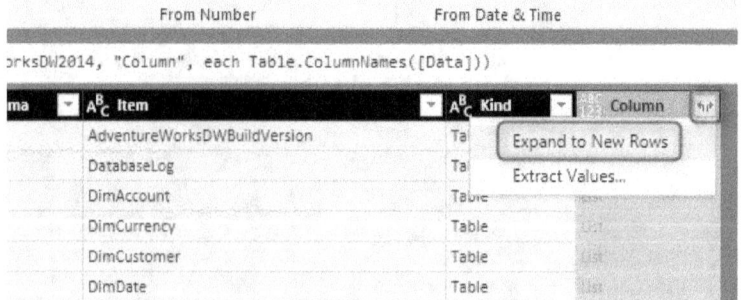

After expanding, you will have all columns in all tables listed under this "Column" field. You can convert it to Text data type.

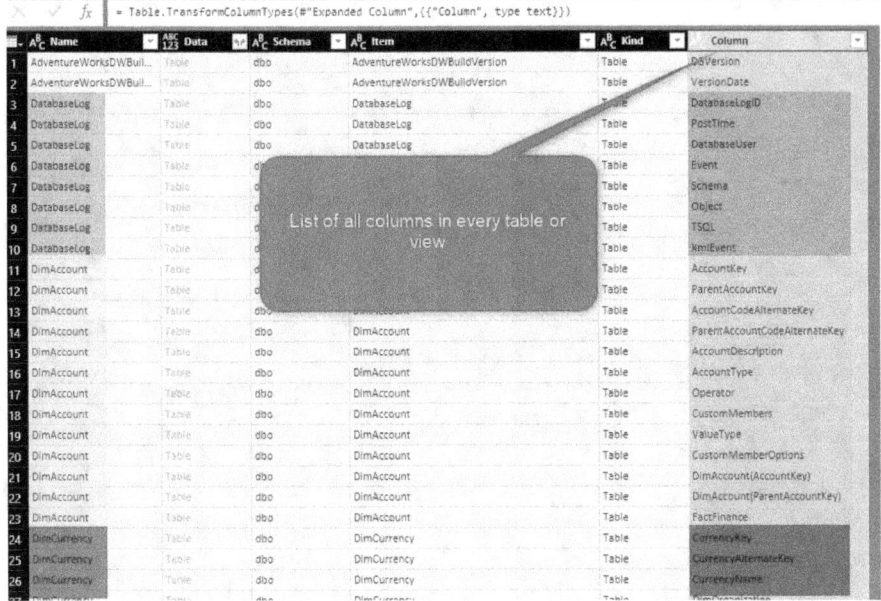

Search through Columns

Now that we got the list of all column names, then searching through it is very simple. You can use the basic search, but remember if you have more than 1000 columns in your data source, this will show you a limited list.

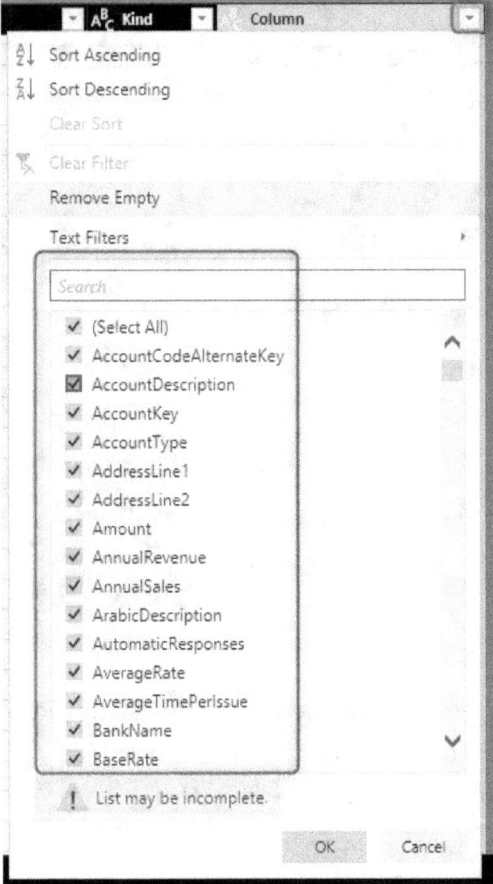

The best way to search into this list is using Advanced Search options. There you can choose criteria such as Contains, Equals, Begins With, or Ends With, etc.

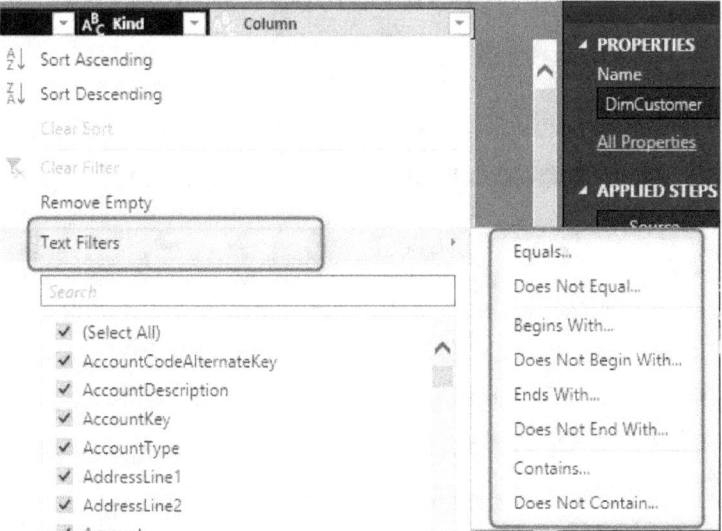

For example, a search for Contains... "Account" will end up with below result:

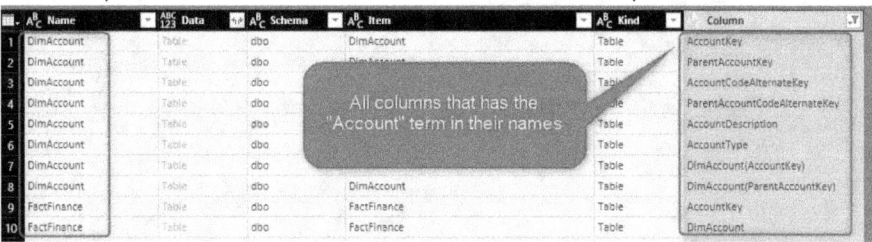

Be Careful of Case Sensitivity

Power Query is a case-sensitive language. There is a difference between "Account" as a text, and "account" as a text. One is using capital A, and the other one; lowercase a. To make sure you can always search for an item, regardless of the case sensitivity of that; you can first convert the column names all to lower case or upper case. To do that, select the "Column" field, and from the Transform tab, select transform to Lower.

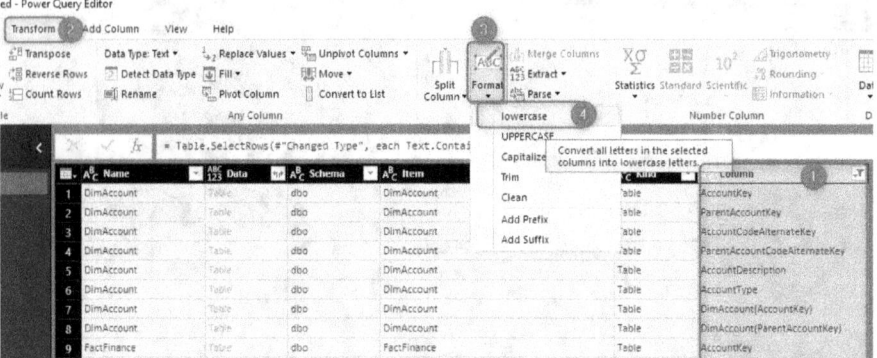

now the whole column names list will be lowercase, and you can search through it only with lowercase values;

Summary

Sometimes simple transformations such as getting the list of columns from a table can be a big help for data exploration. In this post, you've seen how this can be helpful to search through all columns in a database. This approach can be used for any data sources, regardless if they are SQL Server databases or anything else. As long as the data source has a table structure, then you can get the list of all columns from that table. This approach is particularly useful when you connect to databases with thousands of tables, and each table has hundreds of columns; CRM or Dynamics data sources is one of those examples.

Power BI Custom Connector: Connect to Any Data Sources. Hello World!

Posted by Reza Rad on Jul 27, 2017

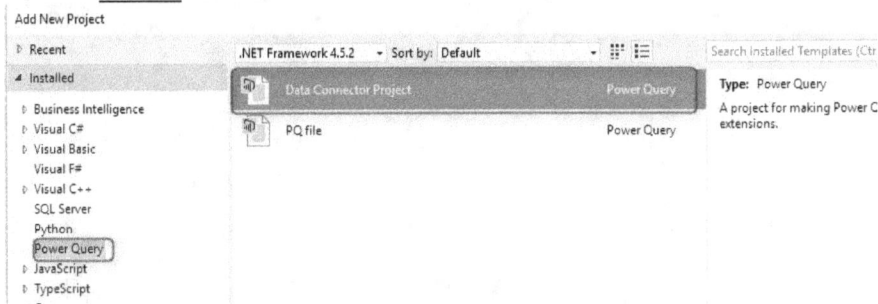

One of the recent features in Power BI Desktop is the ability to create your custom connector and use it when connecting to the data source. This feature looks just one feature, but it opens doors to many possibilities. With this feature, you can write your custom connector to any types of data source that is not already available. Many of you want to connect to some data sources already and waiting for the connector for it. With Customer Connector, you can write your component for it, and use it as many times you want. Custom Connectors should be created in Visual Studio with M script. This post is the first post of blog series about creating custom connectors. In this first post, I'll explain what Custom Connector is and how to create a very basic custom connector. If you want to learn more about Power BI; read Power BI online book from Rookie to Rock Star.

What is a Custom Connector?

Power BI has a set of existing connectors which you can find them in the Get Data section of Power BI (or Power Query).

Get Data

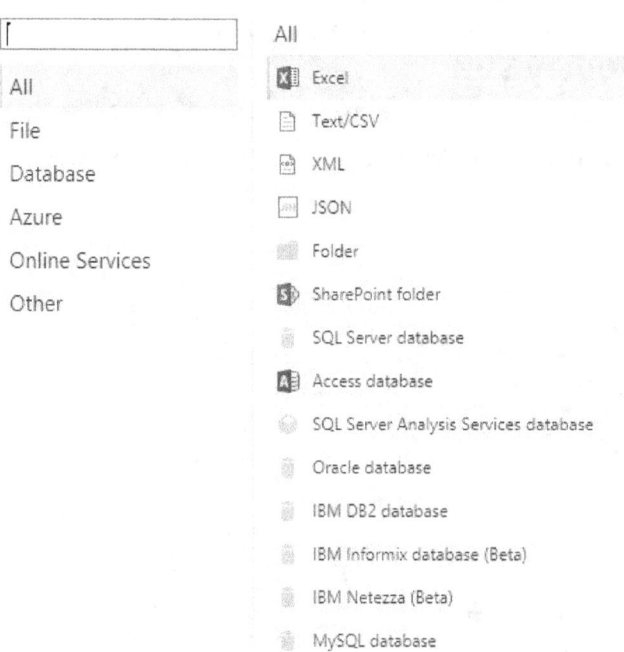

Connectors in this list are connections to the major types of data sources, such as SQL Server, Oracle, some software as a service, such as SalesForce, CRM Online, etc. However, this list is not including all types of data sources. There are always data sources that you want to connect, and is not available on this list. Power BI recently introduced a feature called Custom Data Connector, or simpler Custom Connector. With Custom Connector you can code your connection provider and re-use it multiple times. Your custom connector will appear in the list of getting Data in Power BI, similar to other connectors. Let's have a look at how this custom connector can be built.

Prerequisites

For running examples of this post, you need to have Visual Studio installed. You can download the community edition of that for free.

Install Power Query SDK

You need to install Power Query SDK on Visual Studio as the very first action. This SDK easily can be found in the Visual Studio Tools menu -> Extensions and Updates

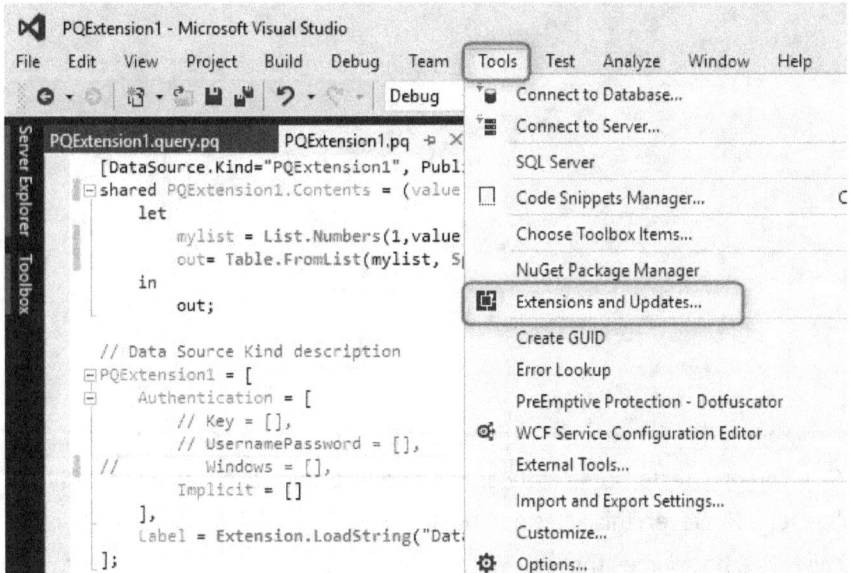

In the list of Online search for Power Query and you will easily find Power Query SDK. simply download and install it.

Create the First Project

After installing the SDK, then you should be able to create a project of type Data Connector. From List of Installed templates choose Power Query, and then select the Data Connector Project.

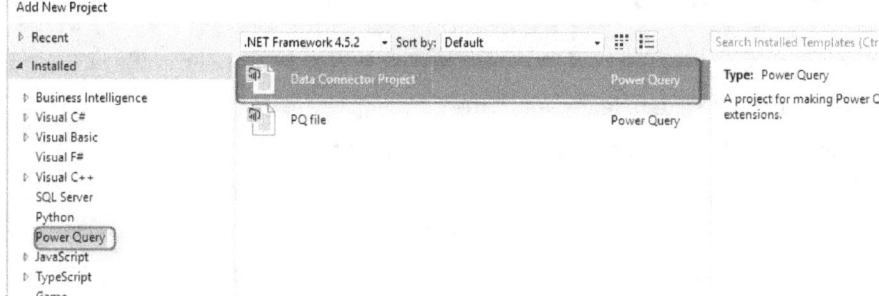

I just left the name as default PQExtension1. You can call it anything.

Project Structure

Data Connector project has a simple structure. It has some files as below;

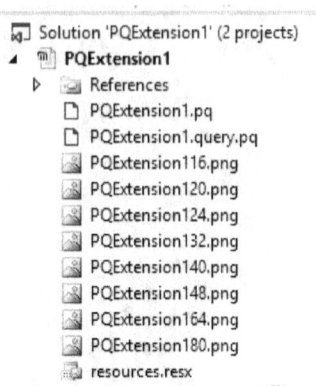

- `<connector name>.pq` file: The code and metadata of the script and connection to the data source. Majority of the development is happening in this file.
- `<connector name>.query.pq`: Calling the function in the <connector name>.pq file. Combination of these two files generates the custom connector's script. This is a test file.
- *.png: Icon files.
- resources.resx: Resource file.

Coding Language: M

Coding language for the custom connector is M: Power Query Formula Language. If you like to learn about the basics of M, read my post here. Good news is that M has an intellisense here in Visual Studio.

```
[DataSource.Kind="PQExtension1", Publish="PQExtension1.Publish"]
shared PQExtension1.Contents = (value as number) =>
    let
        mylist = List.Numbers(1,value),
        out= Table.FromList(mylist, Splitter.SplitByNothing(), null, null, ExtraValues.Err
        y=Table.|
    in
        ou  ⊕ Table.ExpandListColumn          ▲  Table.ColumnCount = (table as table) as number => ...
            ⊕ Table.ExpandTableColumn            Returns the number of columns in the table.
// Data So ⊕ Table.TransformRows
PQExtensio ⊕ Table.Transpose
    Authen ⊕ Table.DemoteHeaders
        // ⊕ Table.ToRows
        // ⊕ Table.ToColumns
//         ⊕ Table.Contains
        Im ⊕ Table.ContainsAll
    ],
```

For an M script geek like me, this is one of the best news I could get!

Structure of Query Files

The main query file is <connector name>.pq. This file includes all the code and M script to connect to the data source and fetch the data out in the desired format. The first time you create the project, this file will come with some default sections.

```
1  // This file contains your Data Connector logic
2  section PQExtension2;
3
4  [DataSource.Kind="PQExtension2", Publish="PQExtension2.Publish"]
5  shared PQExtension2.Contents = (optional message as text) =>
6      let
7          _message = if (message <> null) then message else "(no message)",
8          a = "Hello from PQExtension2: " & _message
9      in
10         a;
11
12 // Data Source Kind description
13 PQExtension2 = [
14     Authentication = [
15         // Key = [],
16         // UsernamePassword = [],
```

```
17 18 19 20 21 22 23   // Data Source UI
publishing description                 24
PQExtension2.Publish = [
    Label = Extension.LoadString("DataSourceLabel"),
```

```
25    Beta = true,
26    Category = "Other",
27    ButtonText = { Extension.LoadString("ButtonTitle"),
28 Extension.LoadString("ButtonHelp") },
29  30 31 32 33 "https://powerbi.microsoft.com/",
PQExtension2.Icons = PQExtension2.Icons,
    SourceTypeImage = PQExtension2.Icons
```

```
35    Icon16 = { Extension.Contents("PQExtension216.png"),
36    Extension.Contents("PQExtension220.png"),
Extension.Contents("PQExtension224.png"),
Extension.Contents("PQExtension232.png") },
    Icon32 = { Extension.Contents("PQExtension232.png"),
    Extension.Contents("PQExtension240.png"),
    Extension.Contents("PQExtension248.png"),
    Extension.Contents("PQExtension264.png") }
];
```

Explaining all functions and code above might be a bit out of scope for this introduction post. I will explain these in details in future posts. For now just a very brief explanation;
• Code above contains a function called <connector name>.Contents. This function will return the result set that will be the input for Power BI when connecting to this connector.

- The credentials configuration for this data source will be configured in an Authentication section.
- <connector name>.Publish is for configuring the location and configuration of showing this connector in getting Data section of Power BI.
- <connector name>.Icons are a list of Icons for the connector.

In the <connector name>.query.pq, then you will see only a function call to the same function which is defined above.

```
1 let
2    result = PQExtension2.Contents()
3 in
4    result
```

This file is mainly to perform testing here in Visual Studio.

If you run this project, you would be able to see the result (after setting the authentication of course)

Write a Sample Function

To make the first connector; I'm not going to explain how to use OData and pass authentication to get data from a web service. That will make things complicated. The very first example I want to show is a simple function that you pass the number to it, and it will give you a table with one single column with values starting from 1, adding one at a time and finishing at that number. It is just a list of numbers. I found it is the easiest way to understand how things work.

In PQExtension1.pq file, change the Contents function as below;

```
1 [DataSource.Kind="PQExtension1", Publish="PQExtension1.Publish"]
2 shared PQExtension1.Contents = (value as number) =>
3    let
4        mylist = List.Numbers(1,value),
5        out= Table.FromList(mylist, Splitter.SplitByNothing(), null, null,
6 ExtraValues.Error)
7    in
```

    out;

In this function, I have used List.Numbers to generate a list of numbers from 1. Adding one number at a time, to the specified number.
After writing the code above, you can call it from the query.pq file with this test line;

```
1 let
2     result = PQExtension1.Contents(12)
3 in
4     result
```

Testing the Result

You can test the query in Visual Studio. just run the project, and you will see the result for 12 rows

Publishing Custom Connector

To publish the custom connector, you have to build it first. This will create a *.mez file in the debug folder of the project. To find that folder, right click on the project in visual studio and click on Open Folder in File Explorer.

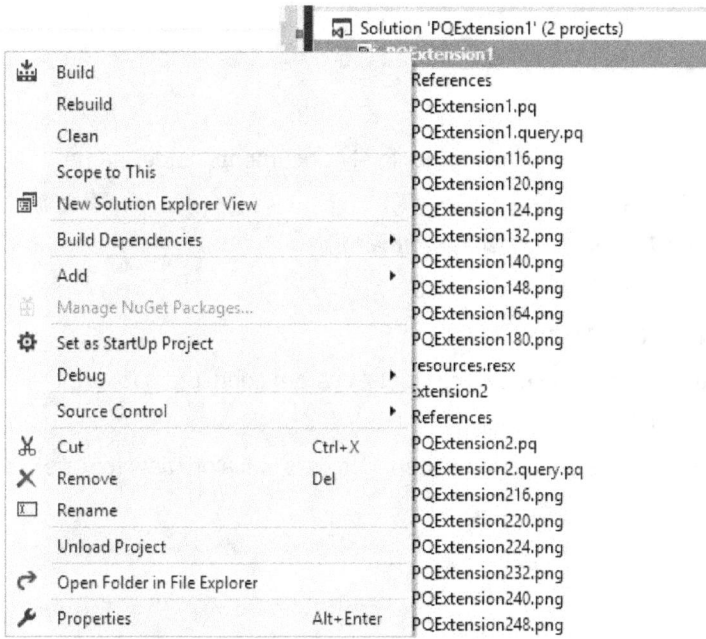

In the project, folder go to Bin Folder, and then Debug, find PQExtension1.mez there.

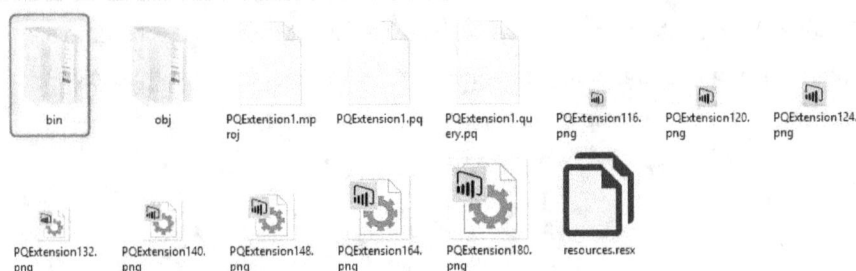

Copy the *.mez file from here into a folder in My Documents. folder name should be exactly this:

Microsoft Power BI Desktop\Custom Connectors

Create the folder above if it doesn't exist.

Using the Connector

After copying the *.mez file in the documents' custom connectors folder, then open Power BI Desktop.

At the time of writing this post, custom connectors is still a preview feature. To enable this feature; Go to File, Options

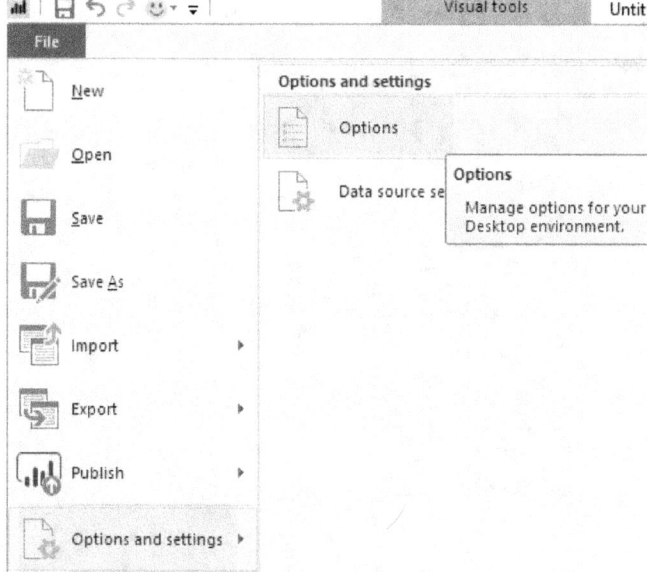

select custom connector preview options. You will need to close Power BI Desktop after this action and re-open it.

After re-opening Power BI Desktop you should see your new connector under Other section (or by searching it);

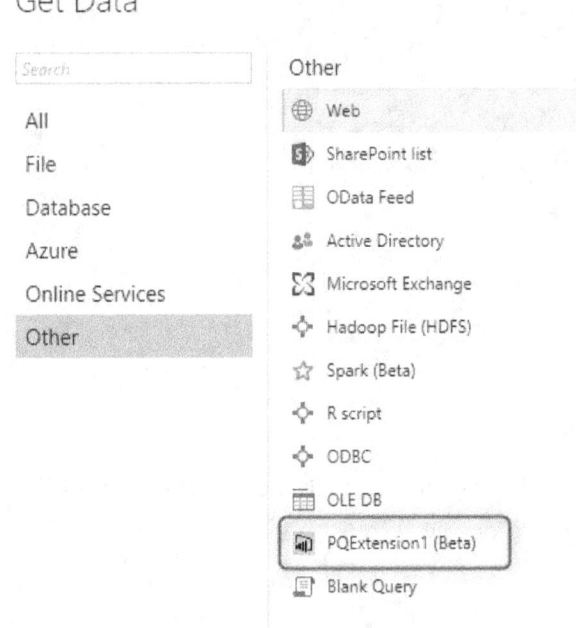

With selecting this connector, you will be asked for an input value (remember, this is the numerical value input for the function that generates the list);

Don't worry about "From PQExtension1.Contents" now. In future posts, I'll explain how we can customize all of this stuff. After entering a value, you will see the result immediately;

Summary

The custom connector that we have created in this post doesn't connect to OData and authenticate through a process to bring some interesting data for you. However, this example was very basic one to show you the main components of a Custom Connector. In the next blog posts in this series, I will write about how to custom each part, and we will have much more complex examples of that. If you are interested in learning more about this the documentation of Power BI team in GitHub is already a great resource for it. In my opinion after the custom visuals which was a great milestone for Power BI visualization; Custom Connector is a big milestone for Power Query. You can now write your connector and connect to the world of data, anywhere, anything. Are you excited about this feature; please let me know your opinion in the comments section below.

Part VII: Performance Tuning

Power BI from Rookie to Rock Star – Book 3: Power Query and Data Transformation in Power BI

Not Folding; the Black Hole of Power Query Performance

Posted by Reza Rad on Nov 15, 2016

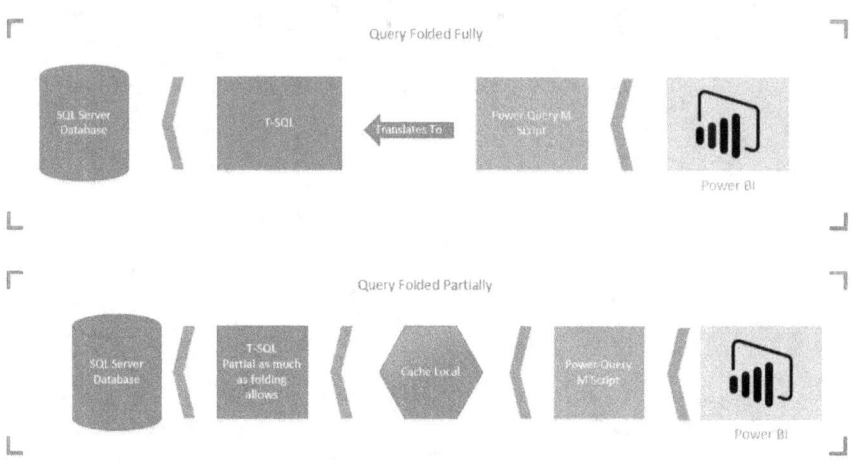

Have you ever thought does your Power Query Transformations happens in the data source side (server side), or on the local memory (client side)? When you use a relational data source, a query can be run on the data source, but it depends on transformations. Some transformations can be translated to query language of the data source, some not. As an example; recently (I believe from last few releases) Power BI Desktop added a feature called Merge Columns. Merge Columns concatenate columns to each other to either create a new column or replace them with the new concatenated result. Previously you could do the concatenation with adding concatenation simply with **&** character, what you've done was adding a new custom column, and writing M expression to concatenate columns. Now with the new Merge Column, this is much easier, you select columns and apply Merge Columns. This easiness does come with a price, a high price I'd say, the price of reducing the performance of Power Query and as a result Power BI! Merge Columns doesn't support query folding, and it means it will affect performance badly. In this post, I'll show you how this cause the performance issue, and how it can be solved. Note that Merge Columns is an example here, this situation might happen with some other transformations as well. If you like to learn more about Power BI; read the Power BI online book from Rookie to Rock Star.

Query Folding

I can't start talking about the issue without explaining what Query Folding is, so let's start with that. Query Folding means translating Power Query (M) transformations into native query language of the data source (for example T-SQL). In other words; when you run Power Query script on top of a SQL Server database, query folding will translate the M script into T-SQL statements, and fetch the final results.

Here is an example of M Script:

```
1  let
2      Source = Sql.Databases("."),
3      AdventureWorks2012 = Source{[Name="AdventureWorks2012"]}[Data],
       Sales_SalesOrderHeader =
4      AdventureWorks2012{[Schema="Sales",Item="SalesOrderHeader"]}[Data],
5      #"Added Conditional Column" =
6      Table.AddColumn(Sales_SalesOrderHeader, "Custom", each if [SubTotal] >= 100 then "0" else "1" )
7  in
       #"Added Conditional Column"
```

And here is the folded version of that translated to native T-SQL query:

```
1  select [_].[SalesOrderID] as [SalesOrderID],
2      [_].[RevisionNumber] as [RevisionNumber],
3      [_].[OrderDate] as [OrderDate],
4      [_].[DueDate] as [DueDate],
5      [_].[ShipDate] as [ShipDate],
```

```
6     [_].[Status] as [Status],
7     [_].[OnlineOrderFlag] as [OnlineOrderFlag],
8     [_].[SalesOrderNumber] as [SalesOrderNumber],
9     [_].[PurchaseOrderNumber] as [PurchaseOrderNumber],
10    [_].[AccountNumber] as [AccountNumber],
11    [_].[CustomerID] as [CustomerID],
12    [_].[SalesPersonID] as [SalesPersonID],
13    [_].[TerritoryID] as [TerritoryID],
14    [_].[BillToAddressID] as [BillToAddressID],
15    [_].[ShipToAddressID] as [ShipToAddressID],
16    [_].[ShipMethodID] as [ShipMethodID],
17    [_].[CreditCardID] as [CreditCardID],
18    [_].[CreditCardApprovalCode] as [CreditCardApprovalCode],
19    [_].[CurrencyRateID] as [CurrencyRateID],
20    [_].[SubTotal] as [SubTotal],
21    [_].[TaxAmt] as [TaxAmt],
22    [_].[Freight] as [Freight],
23    [_].[TotalDue] as [TotalDue],
24    [_].[Comment] as [Comment],
25    [_].[rowguid] as [rowguid],
26    [_].[ModifiedDate] as [ModifiedDate],
27    case
28
29       when [_].[SubTotal] >= 100
30       then '0'
31       else '1'
      end as [Custom]
32 from
33 (  34
35    select [$Table].[SalesOrderID] as [SalesOrderID],
37       [$Table].[RevisionNumber] as [RevisionNumber],
39       [$Table].[OrderDate] as [OrderDate],
         [$Table].[DueDate] as [DueDate],
         [$Table].[ShipDate] as [ShipDate],
         [$Table].[Status] as [Status],
```

```
40      [$Table].[OnlineOrderFlag] as [OnlineOrderFlag],
41      [$Table].[SalesOrderNumber] as [SalesOrderNumber],
42      [$Table].[PurchaseOrderNumber] as [PurchaseOrderNumber],
43      [$Table].[AccountNumber] as [AccountNumber],
44      [$Table].[CustomerID] as [CustomerID],
45      [$Table].[SalesPersonID] as [SalesPersonID],
46      [$Table].[TerritoryID] as [TerritoryID],
47      [$Table].[BillToAddressID] as [BillToAddressID],
48      [$Table].[ShipToAddressID] as [ShipToAddressID],
49      [$Table].[ShipMethodID] as [ShipMethodID],
50      [$Table].[CreditCardID] as [CreditCardID],
51      [$Table].[CreditCardApprovalCode] as [CreditCardApprovalCode],
52      [$Table].[CurrencyRateID] as [CurrencyRateID],
53      [$Table].[SubTotal] as [SubTotal],
54      [$Table].[TaxAmt] as [TaxAmt],
55      [$Table].[Freight] as [Freight],
56      [$Table].[TotalDue] as [TotalDue],
57      [$Table].[Comment] as [Comment],
58      convert(nvarchar(max), [$Table].[rowguid]) as [rowguid],
59      [$Table].[ModifiedDate] as [ModifiedDate]
60     from [Sales].[SalesOrderHeader] as [$Table]
61 ) as []
```

You can see as an example how the conditional column script in M translated to Case statement in T-SQL.

Is Query Folding Good or Bad?

Good obviously. Why? Because performance is much higher to run transformations on billions of records in the data source, rather than bringing millions of records into the cache and applying some transformations on it.

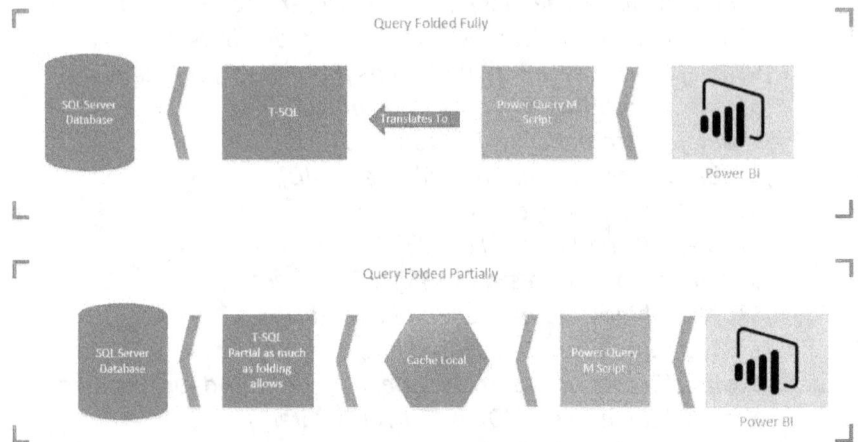

The first diagram shows an M script fully folded (translated to T-SQL). This is the best situation. Server-side operation applies all transformations on the data set and returns only desired result set.

The second diagram shows Query Folding partially supported (only up to specific step). In this case, T-SQL brings the data before that step. And data will be loaded in the local cache, and rest of transformations happens on M engine side. You have to avoid this option as much as possible.

Can I see the Native Query?

The question that might come into your mind right now is that; Can I see the Native Query that M script translates to it? The answer is Yes. If Query Folding is supported on a step, you can right-click on that step and click on View Native Query.

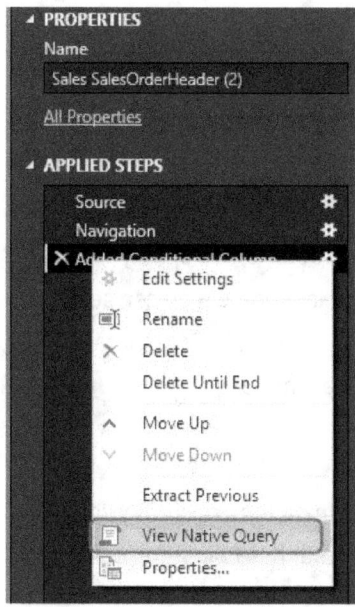

So Why Not Query Folding?

Query Folding is enabled by default. However, in some cases, it is not supported. For example, if you are doing some transformations on a SQL Server table in Power Query and then join it with a web query, the query folding stops from the time you bring the external data source. That means transformations will happen on the data of the SQL Server table. Then before joining to web query, it will be fetched into the cache, and then the rest of steps happens by M engine. You would need to bring data from different data sources in Power BI, and this is the ability that Power Query gives to you. So sometimes you have to step beyond query folding, and there might be no better way of doing that.

There are also some Transformations in Power Query that Query Folding doesn't support them. Example? Merge Columns! Fortunately, there are workarounds for this situation. Let's dig into this more in details.

Example: Merge Columns

Merge Columns concatenates columns to each other in the order of selection of columns. You can also specify the delimiter character(s). So simply if you want to create a full name from the first name and last name, you can select them in the right order, and from either Transform tab or Add Column tab choose Merge Columns. Let's see this through an example;

Prerequisite for running the example

You need to have AdvanetureWorksDW database installed on SQL Server. Or alternatively, you can use any table in SQL Server that has two string columns which can be concatenated.

Merge Column Transformation

Create a new Power BI file in Power BI Desktop, and Get Data from SQL Server with Import Data Mode. Get Data from DimCustomer table only, and click on Edit. When in Query Editor. Select First Name, Middle Name, and Last Name in the correct order, and then from Add Column Select Merge Columns.

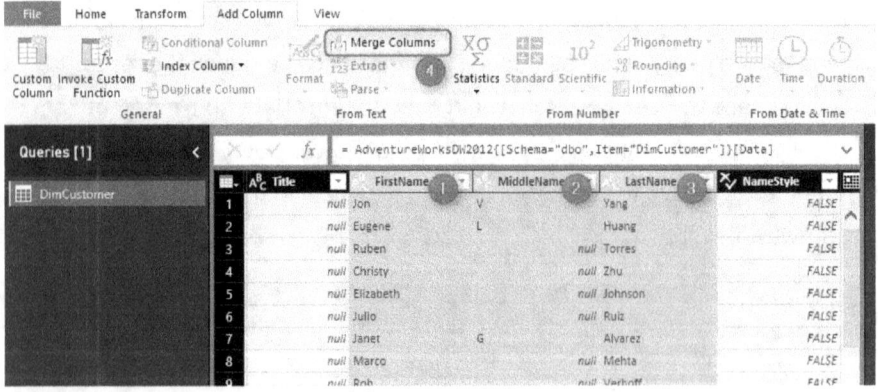

In the Merge Columns Specify the Separator to be space, and name the new column to be Full Name.

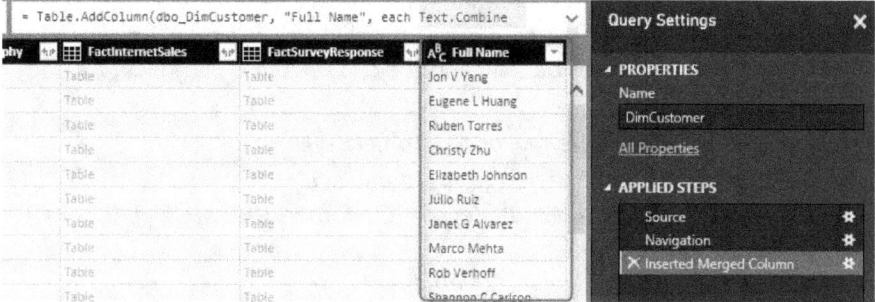

You will see the new column generates simply and adds to the end of all columns. You also may notice that Merge Columns uses Text.Combine Power Query function to concatenate columns to each other.

Now to see the problem with Query Folding, right click on Inserted Merge Column step in Applied Steps section. You will see that View Native Query is disabled.

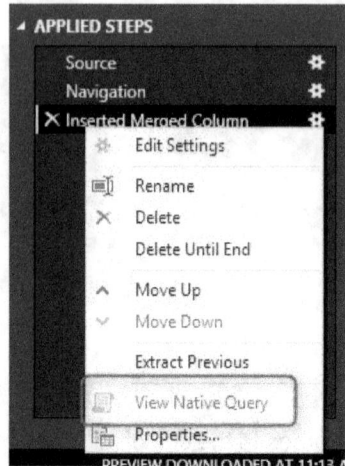

Rule of thumb is that: When View Native Query is not enabled, that step won't be folded! that means the data will be loaded into cache up the step before this step. and then rest of the operation will happen locally. To understand how it works, right click on the step before which was Navigation. You will see the View Native Query. Click on that, and you can see the T-SQL query for that which is as below;

1 select [$Table].[CustomerKey] as [CustomerKey],
2   [$Table].[GeographyKey] as [GeographyKey],
3   [$Table].[CustomerAlternateKey] as [CustomerAlternateKey],
4   [$Table].[Title] as [Title],
5   [$Table].[FirstName] as [FirstName],
6   [$Table].[MiddleName] as [MiddleName],
7   [$Table].[LastName] as [LastName],
8   [$Table].[NameStyle] as [NameStyle],
9   [$Table].[BirthDate] as [BirthDate],
10   [$Table].[MaritalStatus] as [MaritalStatus],
11   [$Table].[Suffix] as [Suffix],
12   [$Table].[Gender] as [Gender],
13   [$Table].[EmailAddress] as [EmailAddress],
14   [$Table].[YearlyIncome] as [YearlyIncome],
15   [$Table].[TotalChildren] as [TotalChildren],

16 [$Table].[NumberChildrenAtHome] as [NumberChildrenAtHome],
17 [$Table].[EnglishEducation] as [EnglishEducation], [$Table].
18 [SpanishEducation] as [SpanishEducation], [$Table].
19 [FrenchEducation] as [FrenchEducation], [$Table].
20 [EnglishOccupation] as [EnglishOccupation], [$Table].
21 [SpanishOccupation] as [SpanishOccupation], [$Table].
22 [FrenchOccupation] as [FrenchOccupation], [$Table].
23 [HouseOwnerFlag] as [HouseOwnerFlag], [$Table].
24 [NumberCarsOwned] as [NumberCarsOwned], [$Table].
25 [AddressLine1] as [AddressLine1], [$Table].[AddressLine2] as
26 [AddressLine2], [$Table].[Phone] as [Phone], [$Table].
27 [DateFirstPurchase] as [DateFirstPurchase], [$Table].
28 [CommuteDistance] as [CommuteDistance], [$Table].[FullName] as
29 [FullName]
30

31 from [dbo].[DimCustomer] as [$Table]

You can see that this is a simple query from DimCustomer Table. What will happen here in this scenario is that Power Query cannot translate Text.Combine to T-SQL Query. So data up to step before will be loaded into the cache. It means the query for a step before (which is above query) will run on the database server, the result will come to the cache, and then Text.Combine will happen on the local memory in the cache. Here is a diagram of how it works;

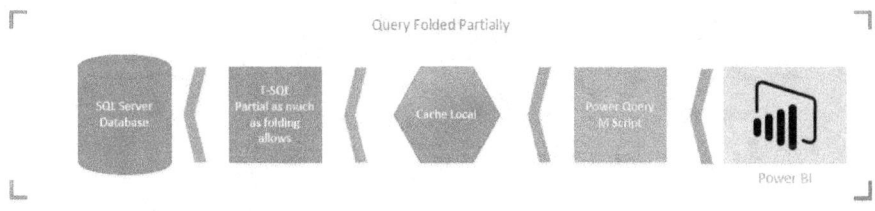

In this example, the data set is so small, but if data set is big, then not folding cause performance issues. It is taking much longer to load the whole data set into the cache and then apply transformations, rather than doing transformations in the data source, and just loading the result into Power BI. Solution: Simple Concatenate with Add Column

Now remove the step for Inserted Merged Column, and go to Add Column Tab, and select Custom Column

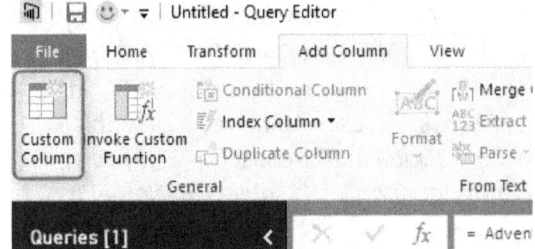

In the Add Custom Column write below expression to generate Full Name;
```
1 =
2 [FirstName]
3 &
4 " "
5 &
6 (if [MiddleName]=null then "" else [MiddleName])
7 &
8 " "
9 &[LastName]
```

Add Custom Column

New column name

Full Name

Custom column formula:

```
=
[FirstName]
&
" "
&
(if [MiddleName]=null then "" else [MiddleName])
&
" "
&[LastName]
```

This expression used the concatenation character which is **&**. and also checked if Middle Name is null or not. Result in Power Query side is the same, and it generates the Full Name column like the previous example;

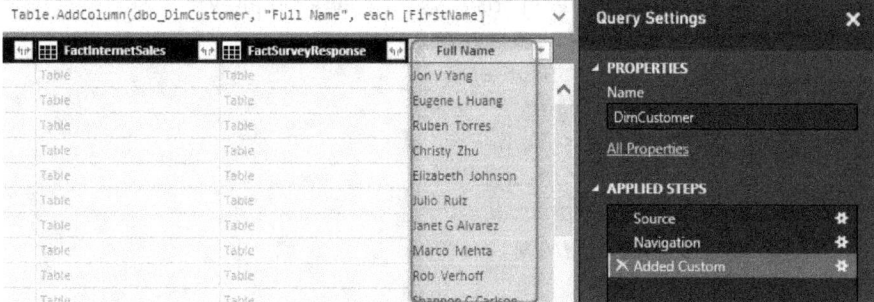

However it is different for Query Folding. Right Click on the Added Custom step, and you will see the Native Query this time.

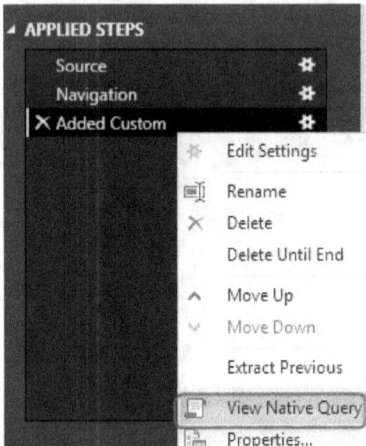

Query is simply the same with a new concatenated column added.

```
1 select [_].[CustomerKey] as [CustomerKey],
2    [_].[GeographyKey] as [GeographyKey],
3    [_].[CustomerAlternateKey] as [CustomerAlternateKey],
4    [_].[Title] as [Title],
5    [_].[FirstName] as [FirstName],
6    [_].[MiddleName] as [MiddleName],
7    [_].[LastName] as [LastName],
8    [_].[NameStyle] as [NameStyle],
9    [_].[BirthDate] as [BirthDate],
10   [_].[MaritalStatus] as [MaritalStatus],
11   [_].[Suffix] as [Suffix],
12   [_].[Gender] as [Gender],
13   [_].[EmailAddress] as [EmailAddress],
14   [_].[YearlyIncome] as [YearlyIncome],
15   [_].[TotalChildren] as [TotalChildren],
16   [_].[NumberChildrenAtHome] as [NumberChildrenAtHome],
17   [_].[EnglishEducation] as [EnglishEducation],
18   [_].[SpanishEducation] as [SpanishEducation],
19   [_].[FrenchEducation] as [FrenchEducation],
20   [_].[EnglishOccupation] as [EnglishOccupation],
```

```
21      [_].[SpanishOccupation] as [SpanishOccupation],
22      [_].[FrenchOccupation] as [FrenchOccupation], [_].
23      [HouseOwnerFlag] as [HouseOwnerFlag], [_].
24      [NumberCarsOwned] as [NumberCarsOwned], [_].
25      [AddressLine1] as [AddressLine1], [_].
26      [AddressLine2] as [AddressLine2], [_].[Phone] as
27      [Phone],         [_].[DateFirstPurchase]         as
28      [DateFirstPurchase], [_].[CommuteDistance] as
29      [CommuteDistance], [_].[FullName] as [FullName],
30      ((([_].[FirstName] + ' ') + (case
31
32        when [_].[MiddleName] is null
33        then ''
34        else [_].[MiddleName]
35      end)) + ' ') + [_].[LastName] as [Full Name]
36 from [dbo].[DimCustomer] as [_]
```

This time there won't be an intermediate cache. Transformation happens in the data source with the T-SQL query, and the result will be loaded into Power BI.

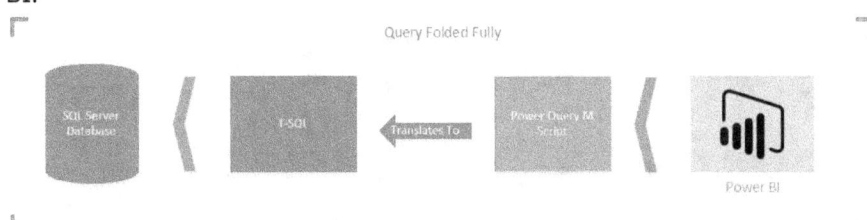

How Do I know Which Transformations Folds?

It is a great question. It is important to understand which step/transformation folds and which doesn't. To understand that simply right click on every step and see if the View Native Query is enabled or not. If it is enabled, Query Folding is supported for that step, otherwise not. Also Note that Query Folding is not supported for data sources such as web query, or CSV or things like that. Query Folding at the moment is only supported for data stores that support a native query language. For Web, Folder, CSV... there is no native query language, so you don't need to worry about Query Folding.

*Important Note: At the time of writing this post Merge Columns doesn't support Query Folding. I have reported this to Power Query Team, and they are working on it, to solve the issue. The Merge Columns is very likely to support query folding very soon as the result of bug fix. However, there are always some other transformations that don't support query folding. This post is written to give you an understanding of what kind of issue might happen, and how to resolve it.

Mine advise to you as a performance best practice is that when working with a relational data source (such as SQL Server). Always check the query folding. Sometimes it is not supported. So use another approach for the transformation. Don't fall into the black hole of not folding. Otherwise your query might take ages to run.

Performance Tip for Power BI; Enable Load Sucks Memory Up

Posted by Reza Rad on Nov 14, 2016

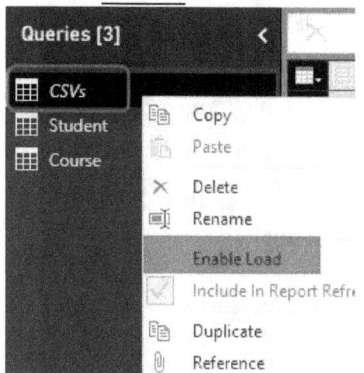

In the area of performance tuning a Power BI model, many things have to be considered, most of them around the consumption of the CPU and RAM. One of the most basic but important consideration is minimizinging the usage of memory. By default, all queries from Query Editor will be loaded into the memory of Power BI Model. In this post, I'll show you an example to disable the load for some queries, especially queries that used as the intermediate transformation to produce the final query for the model. This is a very basic tip but very important when your model grows big. If you want to learn more about Power BI, read the Power BI online book from Rookie to Rock Star.

Prerequisite

For running examples of this book, you need to download the ZIP file here;

Download ZIP file for CSVs

Load Mechanism for Power Query

By Default, all queries in Power Query will be loaded into the Power BI model. This behavior might be the desired behavior if you are connecting to a proper star schema modeled data warehouse because normally you don't need to make many changes in the structure of queries. However this brings some issues if you are connected to a transactional data store, some files, web source, and many other non-star schema modeled data sources. Normally when you get data from a data source, you apply transformations for rows and columns, and merge queries or append them, and you might end up to have five tables out of 10 queries as final queries. By default when you close and apply your query editor window, all queries will be loaded into the model no matter if you want to use them in your final model or not.

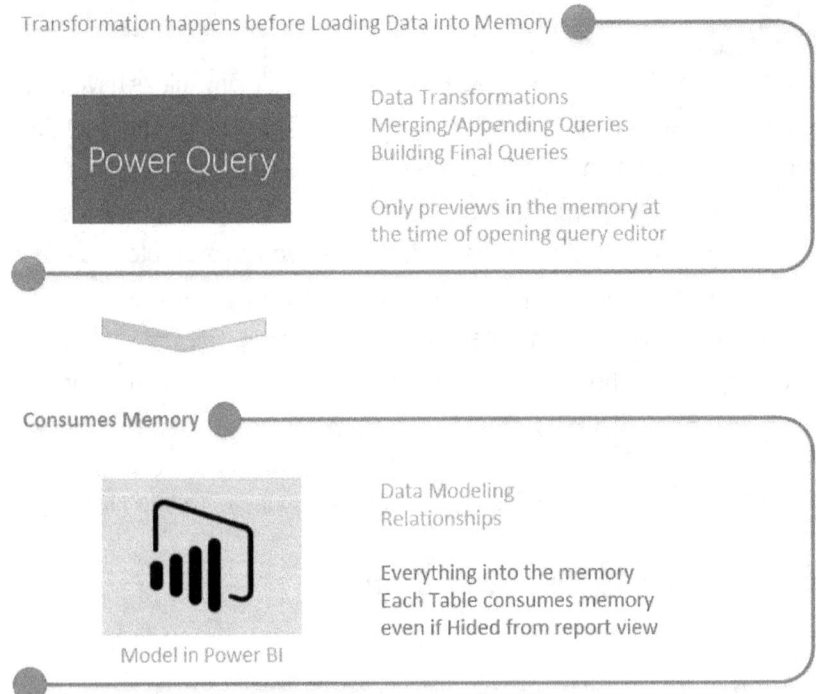

For every query that loads into model, memory will be consumed. And Memory is our asset in the Model; less memory consumption leads to better performance in most of the cases. I have seen lots of models that people Hide the unwanted query from the model; This approach doesn't help to the performance because a hidden query will still consume the memory. The best approach is to disable loading before closing the query editor. Disabling Load doesn't mean the query won't be refreshed, it only means the query won't be loaded into the memory. When you click on Refresh model in Power BI, or when a scheduled refresh happens even queries marked as Disable Load will be refreshed, but their data will be used as an intermediate source for other queries instead of loading directly into the model. This is a very basic performance tuning tip, but very important when your Power BI model grows bigger and bigger. Let's look at this through an example.

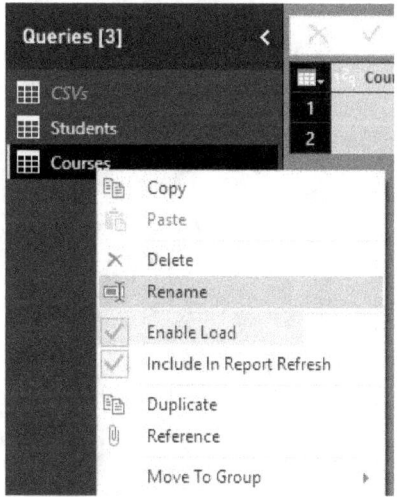

Example Scenario

In this example Scenario, I want to get a list of all files from a directory. There are two types of CSV files in the directory, some Students files, and some course files, both are CSV files, but different structured. Also, there might be some other files in the directory, such as Word files or HTML files which I don't want to process.

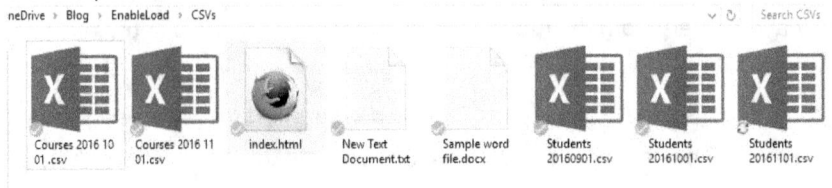

The aim is to load data rows of all students and courses as two separate tables into the model. Instead of fetching files from the folder twice, we use one query to fetch the files and then use it as a reference for other queries. The referenced query itself doesn't need to be loaded into the model. Let's build the solution and see how it works in action.

Build the Transformations
Get Data from Folder

Open a new Power BI file, and stat by Getting Data from Folder

Enter the path of the folder that contains all files (Files in this folder can be downloaded from ZIP file up in the prerequisite section of this post)

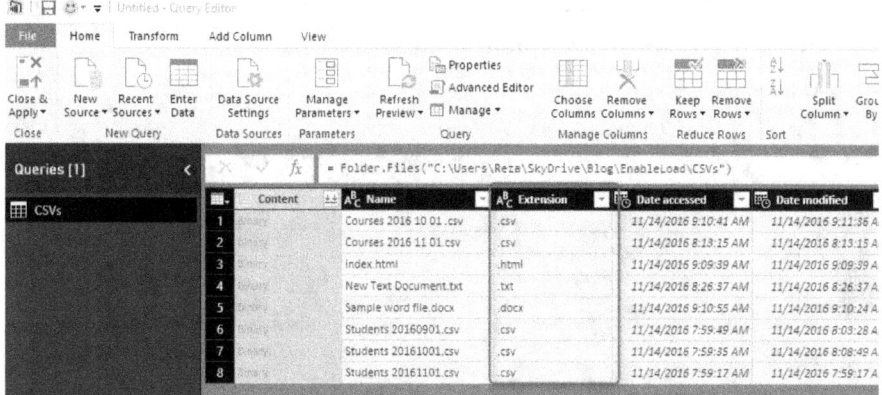

Click on Edit in the preview showed in the navigator window to open the folder content in Query Editor. As you see, there are a number of different files in the folder.

Filter the Extension to only .csv. Note that both Course and Student files are ".CSV" files which are what we need.

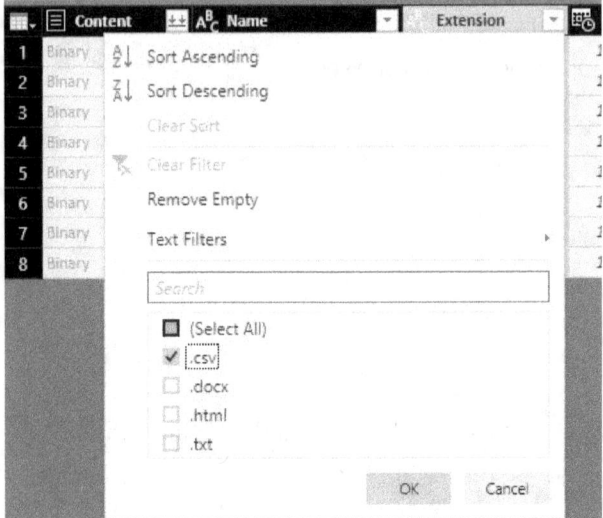

Now the subset includes Course files and Students files which are different in the structure. We have to apply transformations on each set individually.

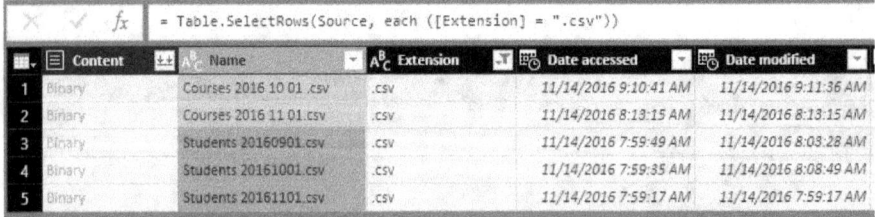

Students Query

Because I don't want to repeat the process of getting all files from a folder, and I want to split the data into two data sets; one for Students and another one for Courses. I'll generate a REFERENCE from the main query. Right click on the query (which called CSVs in my example), and select Reference.

This will generate a new query named as CSVs (2). This new query is NOT A COPY of the first query. This is only a reference from the first query. Which means if the first query changes, the source for this query will also change. Rename this new query to be Student. Filter the Name column to everything starting (or begins with) "Student".

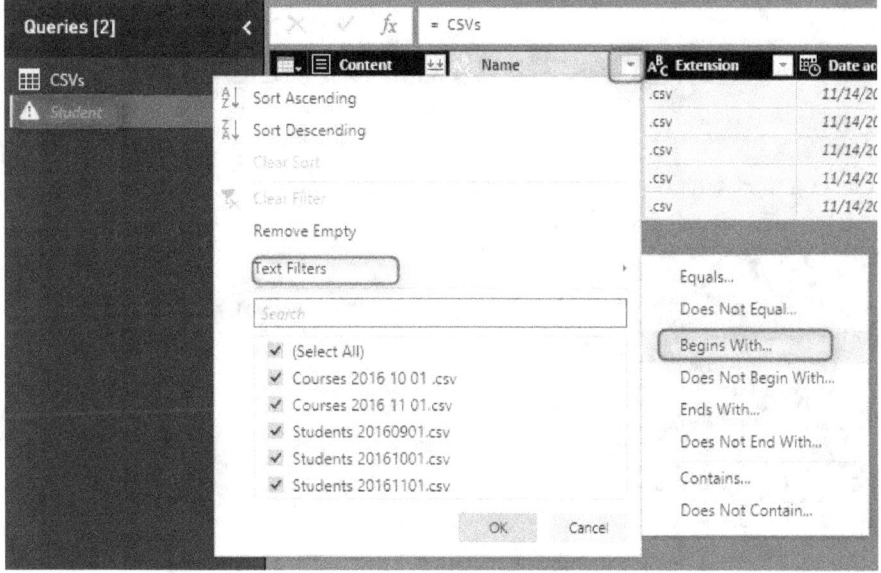

The reason that I don't type it in the search box and use Text Filters specifically is that the search box will filter the data statistically based on values that exist in the current data set. If in the future new values (file names) comes in the folder this won't consider that. However, the Text Filter will apply on any data set because it will be filtered dynamically. (I'll write a post later to explain that in details). In the Filter Rows window type in Student as a filter for begins with.

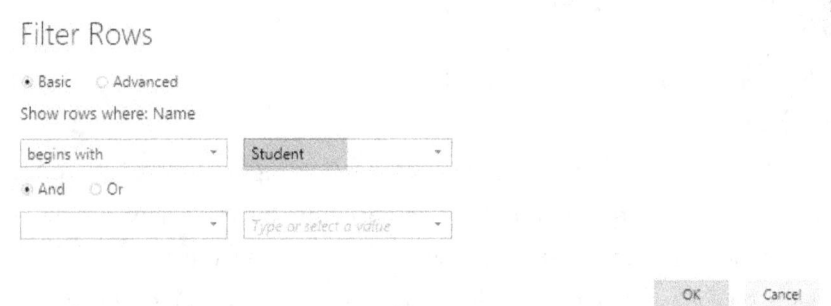

Now you will see only Students files.

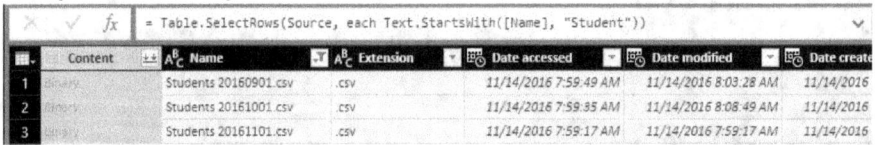

Click on the Combine Binaries icon on the header of the Content column to combine all CSV files into one.

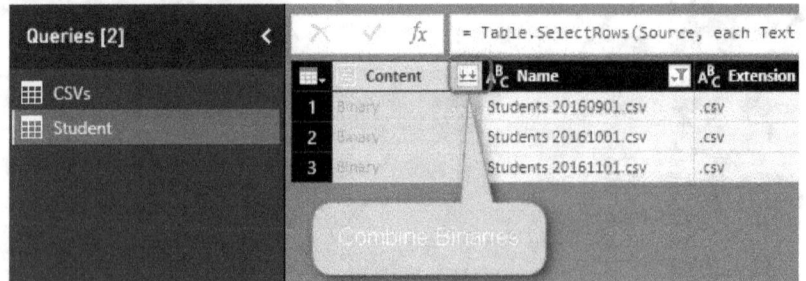

After combining binaries, Power Query will also import the CSV into the table and do automatic data type conversion. You can see all three steps in the Query Editor.

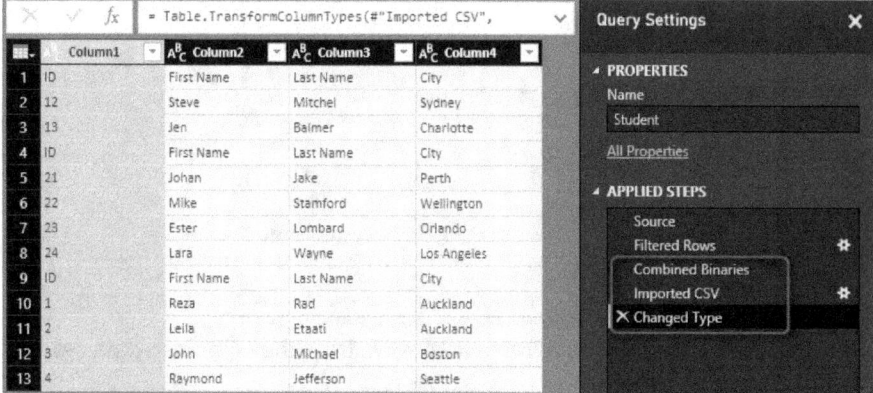

The data table needs a couple of changes before being ready. First; set the column names. The first row has column names. So use the menu option of "Use First Row As Headers" to promote the first row to be column headers.

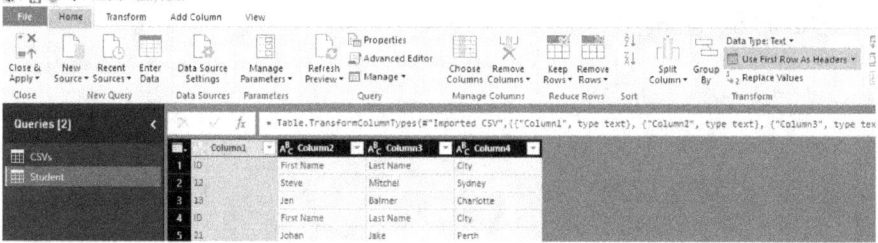

This brings column headers;

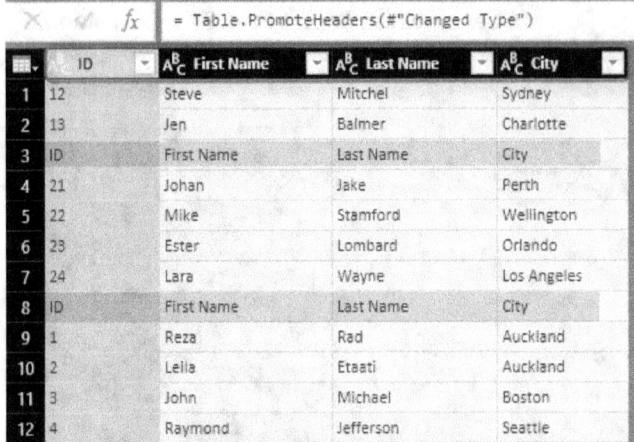

Also, you need to remove all extra header rows from the combined data set. There are some rows with "ID, First Name, Last Name, and City" as their values which should be removed from the data set. You can remove them with a Text Filter of Does Not Equal to on the ID column. Values should not be equal to "ID" because every row with "ID" in the first column's value is a header row and should be removed.

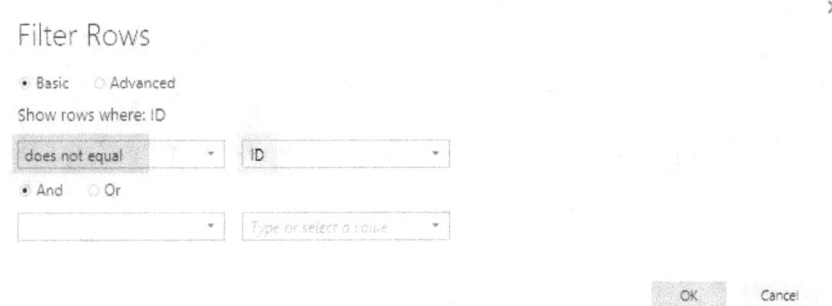

Now you have your cleaned data set for Students. Note that I have also applied a data type conversion for column ID to type the whole number;

	ID	First Name	Last Name	City
1	12	Steve	Mitchel	Sydney
2	13	Jen	Balmer	Charlotte
3	21	Johan	Jake	Perth
4	22	Mike	Stamford	Wellington
5	23	Ester	Lombard	Orlando
6	24	Lara	Wayne	Los Angeles
7	1	Reza	Rad	Auckland
8	2	Leila	Etaati	Auckland
9	3	John	Michael	Boston
10	4	Raymond	Jefferson	Seattle

Courses Query

The other entity is Course which we need to create as a reference from the CSVs query. Create another reference from CSVs, and name it

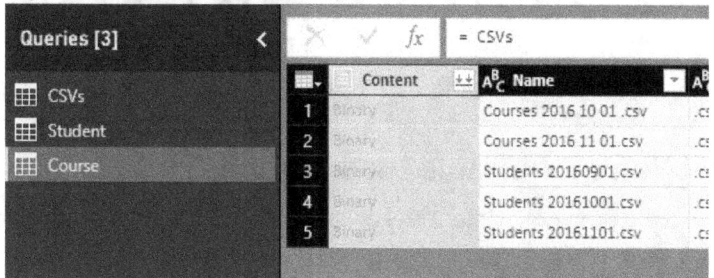

Course.

Create a Text Filter for Begins with on the Name Column with the value of: "Course"

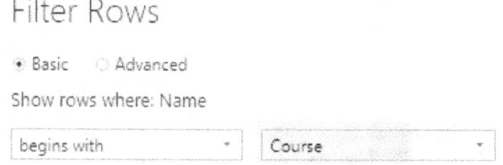

And then you'll have only Course files. Combine Binaries on that.

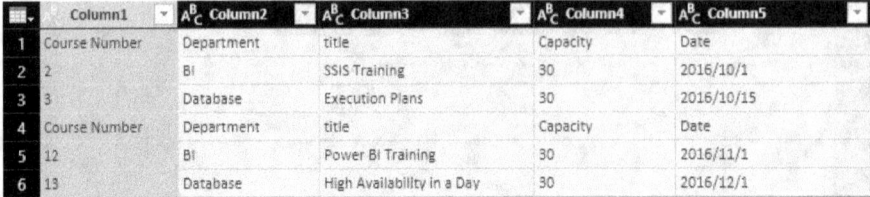

Same as Student query, apply transformations in this order;
• Promote headers with "Use First Row As Headers"
• Create a Text Filter on the Course Number Column that values does not equal to "Course Number".
• Apply data type conversion on Course Number and Capacity to Whole Number and Date to Date.

Here is the final data set for course;

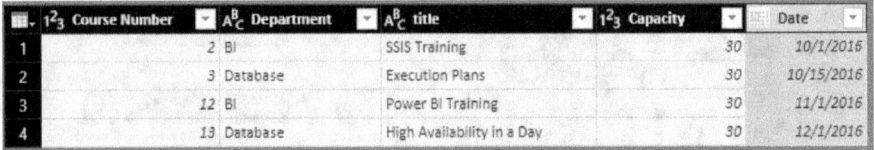

Default Behavior: Enable Load

Now to see the problem, without any changes in the default load behavior,
Close the Query Editor and Apply changes.

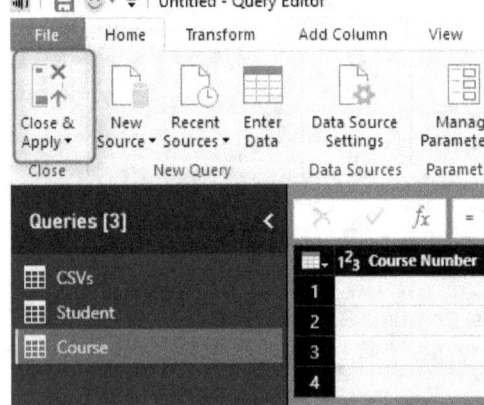

You will see that after the refresh, three queries loads in the model; Student, Course, and CSVs.

Apply Query Changes

- CSVs
  Creating connection in model...
- Student
  Creating connection in model...
- Course
  Creating connection in model...

Student and Course are expected tables in the model. However, CSVs is not useful. We already fetched everything we wanted from the query, and this is used as an intermediate query for loading Student and Course. Having CSVs as a separate table in our model has two problems;

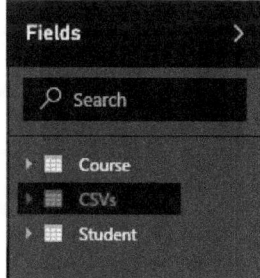

- one extra table; confusion for users
- extra memory consumption

The main issue is the memory consumption for this extra table. and normally memory consumption will reduce the performance and brings a heavier load to the model. In this example, CSVs table only has a few rows. But this is just a sample data, in real-world examples, you might have intermediate tables with millions of rows. You need to remove every unused table from the Power BI model to enhance the memory consumption.

What about Hiding from Report?

The first issue "Confusion for users" can be solved by hiding the table from report view. You can do that in the Relationship tab of the model, right click on the CSVs table, and click on Hide from the report view. This method HIDEs the table from the report view. However the table still exists, and it consumes memory! It is just hidden. Hiding a table from the report view is good for tables that you need for the modeling. For example, a relationship table (that creates many to many relationships) should be kept in the model but be hidden. Because it creates a relationship, but it is not useful for the report viewer. Any other tables that are not used for a relationship and is not used for reporting should be removed before loading into the model.

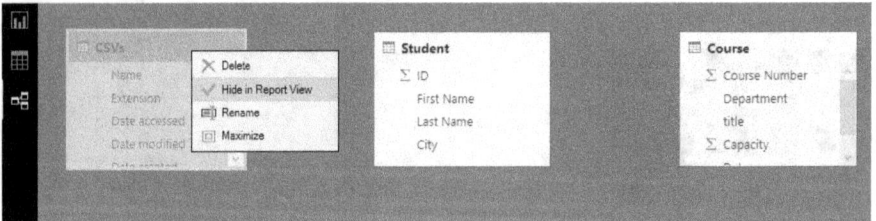

Disable Load to Save Memory

Go back to Query Editor, and right click on CSVs query. You will see that by default every query is checked as Enable Load.

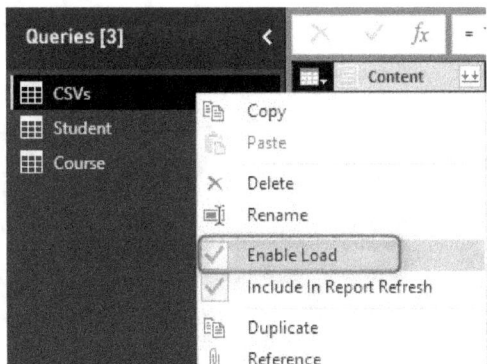

Click on the Enable Load to disable it. You will see a message saying that any visuals attached to this query will not work after this change. Which is fine, because this query is not used (and won't be) for any visualization. The message is: "Disabling load will remove the table from the report, and any visuals that use its columns will be broken."

Click on Continue, and you will see the load is disabled for the query now. The query name will be also in *Italic* font illustrating that it won't be loaded into the model. Note that query will be refreshed and if new files come to the directory it will pass it on to Course and Student Queries. It just won't be loaded into the model itself.

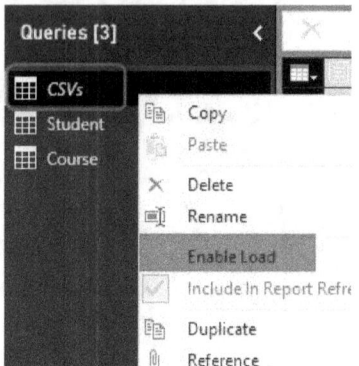

You can also see in the View tab of Query Editor, on the Query Dependencies that this query is the source of the other two queries. And in that view, it also shows which query is load disabled.

Query Dependencies

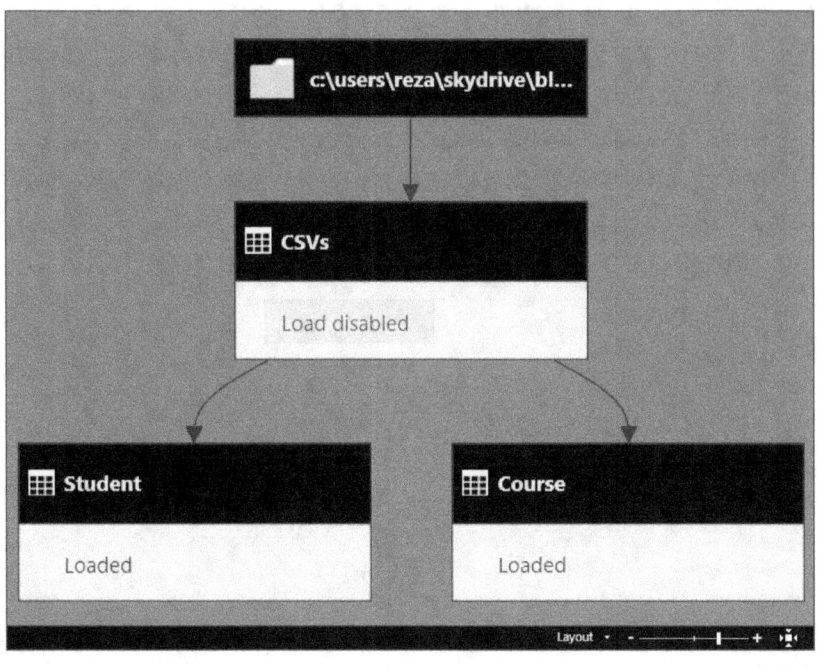

Now close and apply the Query Editor. This time you see that CSVs query won't be loaded into the model. Your relationship tab and the report tab only contains two tables; Course, and Student.

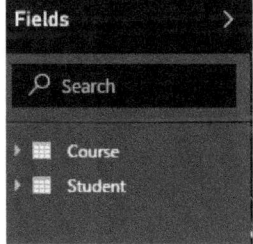

Summary

In summary, you've seen how an easy tip can save the memory and enhance the performance of the Power BI model. Always remember that Query Editor is your ETL (Extract, Transform, Load) engine. It will apply all transformations before loading the data into the model, but once it finished the transformation all queries will be loaded into the model, and they take memory. By default, all queries are Enabled to Load into the model. Simply change that for queries that are not required in the model.

www.ingramcontent.com/pod-product-compliance
Lightning Source LLC
Chambersburg PA
CBHW071909210526
45479CB00002B/347